# Contributions To Phenomenology

In Cooperation with The Center
for Advanced Research in Phenomenology

Volume 98

**Scope**

The purpose of the series is to serve as a vehicle for the pursuit of phenomenological research across a broad spectrum, including cross-over developments with other fields of inquiry such as the social sciences and cognitive science. Since its establishment in 1987, *Contributions to Phenomenology* has published more than 80 titles on diverse themes of phenomenological philosophy. In addition to welcoming monographs and collections of papers in established areas of scholarship, the series encourages original work in phenomenology. The breadth and depth of the Series reflects the rich and varied significance of phenomenological thinking for seminal questions of human inquiry as well as the increasingly international reach of phenomenological research.

The series is published in cooperation with The Center for Advanced Research in Phenomenology.

More information about this series at http://www.springer.com/series/5811

Gustav Shpet

Thomas Nemeth
Editor/Translator

# Hermeneutics and Its Problems

## With Selected Essays in Phenomenology

 Springer

Gustav Shpet (deceased)

Thomas Nemeth
Manchester, NJ, USA

Translated by Thomas Nemeth

ISSN 0923-9545 ISSN 2215-1915 (electronic)
Contributions To Phenomenology
ISBN 978-3-319-98940-2 ISBN 978-3-319-98941-9 (eBook)
https://doi.org/10.1007/978-3-319-98941-9

Library of Congress Control Number: 2018959850

This Springer imprint is published by the registered company Springer Nature Switzerland AG.
The registered company address is: Gewerbestrasse 11, 6330 Cham, Switzerland

# Editor's Introduction to *Hermeneutics and Its Problems*

## Shpet's Early Years

Gustav Shpet (1879–1937), a name once little known in either the West or the Soviet Union, has now become increasingly recognized among scholars of various disciplines both in the West and in Russia. His contributions to phenomenological philosophy include a non-egological conception of consciousness that *in nuce* predates those of Sartre and Aron Gurwitsch by decades,[1] and his rigorous studies of the history of Russian philosophy, though less known in the West, also predate the better known works of V. V. Zenkovsky and N. O. Lossky by many years. Shpet, to his demise, chose to stay in the Soviet Union in the early 1920s even though two distinct opportunities to emigrate appear to have presented themselves, one of which, according to family testimony, was officially encouraged![2] During those years of ever-increasing repression, he persevered after the loss of his professorship as best he could, working in philosophical aesthetics and then writing a pioneering study of Wilhelm von Humboldt's philosophy of language under the auspices of the State Academy for the Study of the Arts (GAKhN). Finally, during the following decade of the 1930s, deprived of all academic avenues to earn a living for himself and his

---

[1] For Shpet's non-egological conception of consciousness, see Appendix 1.

[2] Soon after being appointed the Lithuanian ambassador to Russia in 1920, Jurgis Baltrušaitis, an old friend, offered Shpet Lithuanian citizenship and a passport to his entire family. The second opportunity, allegedly, was to board the "philosophers' steamship" in 1922 bound for a one-way trip to Germany upon Lenin's express "invitation." Shpet successfully appealed presumably to the Soviet Commissar of Education Anatoly Lunacharsky, whom he knew from his student days in Kiev. In her amazing work on the "philosophers' steamship," Chamberlain lists Shpet among those "reprieved." Chamberlain 2006: 312. Although Shpet's name does not appear on any of the surviving lists of those to be deported, those lists may not be complete. The editorial in the 31 August 1922 issue of *Pravda* announced the impending expulsion of "dissident intellectuals," but no names were given. We still today do not have an accurate list or even the number of those to be expelled. Glavackij 2002: 3–4, 6. Galin Tihanov has voiced cautious support for the claim that Shpet was among those to be expelled based on an unsubstantiated report in a Berlin émigré paper that Shpet had been arrested on the night of 16 August 1922. See Tihanov 2009a: 46, 58.

family, Shpet produced a veritable torrent of translations including works by Berkeley, Dickens, and Hegel, among others. Sadly, Stalin's consolidation of power had as one consequence the starkest suppression not only of all but the most simplistic Marxist thought, but of virtually all individuals perceived in any way as opposed to the Soviet regime. Shpet, remaining true to his convictions to the end, was first exiled to Siberia in 1935 and relatively soon afterward summarily shot.[3]

Among Shpet's interests, in addition to those mentioned above, was the theoretical grounding of the "human sciences," or, to use the German terminology, *Geisteswissenschaften*. In fact, it was arguably his earliest philosophical concern. Shpet had selected a historical survey of philosophies of the human sciences as the topic for his *magister*'s thesis while already studying at the University of Moscow.[4] It was in pursuit of original source material that Shpet undertook an extended journey to Western Europe that included Berlin, Paris, and Edinburgh, but, most importantly, Göttingen, where he stayed from September 1912 to July 1913 writing that thesis and where he met Husserl, who was then teaching there.[5]

Returning to Moscow, Shpet went on to defend what had become an enormous thesis in 1916, his *Istorija kak problema logiki* [*History as a Problem of Logic*]. Regrettably but understandably given its topic, his thesis reveals little of the deep influence Husserl had on Shpet's formulations and positions by the time the work was published. He did, however, provide in it a brief sketch of his disengagement with his youthful Marxism and, more specifically, his disillusion with the philosophy of history it offered.

> Already in my student days, I was fascinated by the topic that I am only now beginning to carry out. We entered the university enchanted by the radicalism and the simple solution to the problem that historical materialism temptingly promised us at the time. A deeper study of history – an acquaintance with the original historical sources and with the methods of handling those sources – destroyed many schemas. But most importantly it clearly demonstrated the poverty and the limitations that this apparent "simplicity" had introduced into the discipline.[6]

---

[3] Shpet's increasing intellectual isolation after the loss of his university position surely affected his mental health. Tihanov, gathering an impressive amount of material, concludes that Shpet's "health was distinctly fragile throughout the 1920s." Tihanov 2008: 280.

[4] The expression "*magister*'s thesis" is purposely used here to avert any possible association in the reader's mind with the "master's thesis" of today either in scope or length. Shpet's thesis, as published was approximately 500 pages!

[5] Judging from surviving letters, Shpet quite possibly first met Husserl between October and November 1912. In a letter to his future wife from 8 October of that year, Shpet made no mention of Husserl, but in a letter from 15 November to a friend, Elena Metner, he specifically mentions having met Husserl. See Shchedrina 2005a: 323. Still the question remains what led Shpet to seek out Husserl. Shpet, after all, had come to Göttingen already in late April. Could Lev Shestov, an "existential philosopher" have been an instigator? In a brief letter dated 5 August 1912 Shestov wrote to Shpet that he would be interested in reading his work – presumably Shpet's future thesis. Shestov then adds, "More interesting would be your impression from a personal acquaintance with Husserl. Judging from the card you sent me, he is a very important person." Shchedrina 2005a: 324. Unfortunately, we do not know what Shpet wrote to Shestov.

[6] Shpet 2002: 35.

Thus, taking Shpet at his word in 1916, he entered his university studies infatuated with Marxism taken primarily as a philosophy of history.[7]

The "spell" of Marxism, however, could not have lasted long. Based on his publications, he switched his allegiance to Heinrich Rickert of the so-called Baden School of neo-Kantianism, at least with regard to the philosophy of the human sciences.[8] Importantly for all his future studies and his future orientation, this early neo-Kantianism did not entail an uncritical acceptance of Kant's "Critical Philosophy" even at this early date. Through Rickert's eyes, Shpet believed that Kant had understood science too narrowly. In a 1904 review of an anthology of essays commemorating the one-hundredth anniversary of Kant's death, Shpet wrote that Kant's limited vision of science was understandable and forgivable given the state of, for example, chemistry and psychology at the time. However, since then both have been acknowledged as sciences just as much as physics was a century earlier. Indeed, Shpet writes, "we are now proceeding further, opening up a new sphere of scientific knowledge, viz., the *historical sciences*. The elaboration of their methodology is today's task."[9] Whereas in Kant's day the writing of history was tantamount to the writing of *belle-lettres*, the change in attitude toward the former was largely the result of an infusion of the spirit of Critical Philosophy into scholarship. Nevertheless, natural science, as Shpet saw it at this time, was interested in viewing phenomena in terms of constant and general concepts leading to laws as forms of reason. History, on the other hand, while concerned unlike natural science with separate and individual phenomena, selected the phenomena for study based on their value for us.[10]

---

[7] The difficulty in assigning a year to Shpet's commencing his university studies arises from the fact that he first enrolled in the department of physics and mathematics at Kiev University in 1898 and then was expelled for political activities. He was unable to resume work at the University until 1901, at which time he switched enrollment to the historico-philological department. That his interest in Marxism during this interregnum was not limited to its philosophy of history appears clear from his intention addressed to Petr Struve to translate Engels' *Anti-Dühring*. In a letter from November 1900, Struve replied to Shpet that although the intention was excellent, Engels' book had already been adequately translated. See Shchedrina 2012: 101. Actually, *Anti-Dühring* in its entirety had not yet been translated into Russian and would not be until 1907. A censored translation of the work appeared in 1904 in St. Petersburg, but at the time of Struve's letter to Shpet, only selected sections and pages had yet appeared in print.

[8] Haardt, albeit with less specificity, writes that Shpet during his university studies from 1898 to 1905 began as an adherent of historical materialism followed by an indefinite phase bearing a "Rickertian stamp." Haardt 1993: 72. Tihanov, perhaps with a different interest, sees Shpet's intellectual career as falling into four periods, the first of which begins only in 1903 and ends in 1912/13 with his "turn" to phenomenology. See Tihanov 2009a: 44. During his "Rickertian" phase, Shpet published a translation in 1904 of Rickert's *Der Gegenstand der Erkenntnis*. See Rickert 1904.

[9] Shpet 2010: 53.

[10] Shpet's dissatisfaction with Rickert came about shortly after setting out to write his thesis. In its "Preface," explicitly dated February 1916, he wrote about this earlier period. "I was still under the hypnosis of the Kantian delusion. I still 'believed' in Rickert's assurance that 'in the pre-Kantian philosophy of the past and the present, nothing has been done decisively to clarify the problems of the logic of historical science'." Shpet 2002: 36–37. More than a decade later, Shpet in reflection

Such basically, at least, was Shpet's attitude when he commenced his study of historical methodologies. Only with imprecision can we determine when Shpet actually initiated writing his thesis. The number of surviving letters from these years is comparatively meager, and they are of little assistance. However, in one from Berlin dated June 1910, he wrote that he was working in a library there, presumably gathering material and writing. A month later, he proceeded to Bonn, Würzburg, and Leipzig. Shpet returned to Berlin in the summer of 1911, again to continue researching and writing. During the following academic year, he returned to Moscow, where he taught psychology, but in April 1912 he was in Göttingen, already embarking on what became the second part of his massive work. In the absence of documentation to the contrary, then, we can conclude Shpet had virtually completed the first part of his thesis, which he would defend and publish in 1916, by the time of his extended stay in Göttingen. The mentioned second part would remain unpublished and largely unknown for almost nine decades. That the body of the first part would show no evidence of a Husserlian influence is understandable, given the probable period of its composition minus its final accompanying "Preface" and "Introduction," both of which reveal a distinctly Husserlian imprint.[11] Husserl's name, however, is mentioned but once in the "Introduction," and in a footnote at that in connection with his 1914 book *Appearance and Sense*.

## Hermeneutics as the Epistemology of History

The second part of his huge *History as a Problem of Logic* included long chapters on Dilthey and Rickert.[12] Quite possibly, it was in conjunction with his work on Dilthey that Shpet conceived the idea of a separate third part to his work that would be a history of hermeneutics. Whatever the case, he later decided to try to publish what he had written on that topic independently, incorporating into it only an insignificant amount of the material he had accumulated for the projected second part of

---

on the Baden School of neo-Kantianism viewed its "indisputable contribution" to be a return "to a recognition of the individuality of the historical subject" and that the Baden philosophers "starting from this characteristic attempted to point out the logical specificity of the historical sciences. However, I think that in proceeding fundamentally from Kantianism, knowing only the epistemology of the 'mathematical natural sciences,' let alone the general defects of Kantian subjectivism, they did not completely overcome naturalism." Shchedrina 2005a: 450. This assessment is from a letter of 1928 to the historian D. M. Petrushevskij (1863–1942).

[11] Given the explicit date of its completion, a Husserlian influence on the "Preface" should hardly be surprising. And whereas the "Introduction" bears no date, a primary concern throughout is to combat any form of reductionism. Additionally, in it, Shpet wrote, "Therefore, philosophy always studies *beginnings*; its object is 'principles' and sources, foundations. Philosophy is by its essence always *first philosophy*." Shpet 2002: 51. Cf. Husserl 2002: 294: "But by its essence, philosophy is the science of the true beginnings, of the origins ..."

[12] In a letter from Göttingen to his wife dated 10 January 1913, Shpet mentions that he had previously decided to be finished with Dilthey on that date "no matter what" and start writing about Rickert the next day. See Shchedrina 2005a: 170.

the *History*.[13] The text for the separate work on the history of hermeneutics was already completed in July 1918 and prepared for publication in 1919, but the widespread chaotic conditions in Russia at the time made such an undertaking quite impossible. Only many decades later in the period 1990–1993 did *Hermeneutics and Its Problems* posthumously appear serialized in the Russian journal *Kontekst* and then later newly edited by Tat'jana Shchedrina in 2005 as part of her edition of Shpet's collected works. It is this edition that served as the basis of the present translation.

Turning to the impetus behind Shpet's work on the history of hermeneutics, we find Shpet already in his quickly composed *Appearance and Sense* – a commentary and meditation on Husserl's recent (1913) *Ideen I* – troubled, as it were, with, among other issues, how the understanding or comprehension of an actual object is possible.[14] Is such a comprehension tantamount to an interpretation? The issue becomes all the more acute when the object of study turns from being a physical thing actually before us to a historical object, something that we obviously cannot directly examine. Nevertheless, the general question of the means of "penetrating" into the real object, into its authentic being to reveal its "inner sense," is the question to which the entire development of phenomenology has led. The historian, unlike the natural scientist, has only documents filled with printed words as the object of investigation.[15]

Shpet, in his *History*, remarked that historical evidence is not an "observation," but always a sign that can be interpreted. Unlike in natural science, where the repetition of events aids to corroborate the veracity of our knowledge-claims, in history such corroboration can only be by way of an appeal to the testimony of witnesses. Even a witness to an event can become aware that he or she is "observing" a historical phenomenon only by means of an appropriate interpretation. Thus, historical cognition is never simply a matter of either the empirical or the rational cognition of experience. No, historical cognition always presupposes interpretation or comprehension. In this way, such cognition requires its own epistemology.[16] Moreover, our issue is more complicated when dealing with historical concepts than with concepts in the natural sciences, for the very meaning of the former appears as a sign requiring a special hermeneutics for the disclosure of its meaning. Documents – indeed all documents – are signs, and, as such, they demand the comprehension of certain actions that, in turn, are signs that shield the movement of historical factors. These factors can be grasped only through comprehension. Thus, Shpet reasons that there

---

[13] Shpet 2005: 416.

[14] Husserl's *Ideen I* appeared in April 1913. By mid-October 1913, Shpet had already finished the bulk of *Appearance and Sense*. Shchedrina 2014: 142.

[15] We should keep in mind here and throughout Shpet's account of historical methodology that in his time historians had to rely on written documents alone. Today, we have access to video recordings and audio files as source material for recent historical events.

[16] Shpet 2002: 287. Since these statements appear in the third chapter of the first part of the *History*, we can conclude, albeit with measured caution, that Shpet set out these thoughts before 1912 and, therefore, before his acquaintance with Husserl.

is only one path – the path of comprehension. History, then, is not like the other sciences; it is not a technical discipline, but a hermeneutical one. We acquire the sense and significance of the historically concrete not by means of instruments, but by means of understanding.

Shpet's intellectual path from an initial interest in the philosophy of the human sciences to philosophy of history and then to hermeneutics becomes understandable in light of what we have just seen. In fact, his estimation of history as a "scientific" discipline grew in these years to the extent that he viewed it as standing alongside mathematics as a scientific model. In the conclusion of the long (approximately 600 pages!) second part of his *History*, Shpet writes, "Just as mathematics is considered the 'model' for the ideal sciences, history can actually be considered the 'model' for any concrete science."[17] However, the application of the historical method alone to the history of, say, the mineral or organic world, does not make that history a "science."

Such reasoning, as above, underlies Shpet's quest to make history, that is, the historical discipline, into a rigorous science. Proceeding from a recognition of history as the basic human science, Shpet recognized that all of the evidence, its source material, is in the form of documents that stand in need of interpretation or comprehension. That is, the study of history, as a discipline, is hermeneutical. Going even further, however, he stated that "surely history is ultimately the reality that surrounds us, and from its analysis philosophy must start."[18] In comparison with history, any other aspect of reality is no more than an abstraction from reality as a whole. Therefore, any particular science ultimately extracts its object from the historical whole. The implication is clear: Whereas the neo-Kantians took mathematical physics as the paradigm model of knowledge, Shpet, in the end, views history, that is, rigorous history, as a science, not simply as the paradigmatic model of "concrete" knowledge, but of all knowledge in general.[19] Since historical science works throughout with signs, and signs need to be understood, the need for a "science" of the comprehension of the sense of signs arises. This science is hermeneutics.

In the "Preface" to his *Hermeneutics*, Shpet wrote that he presented his general position in a separate long article "*Istorija kak predmet logiki*" ["History as an Object of Logic"].[20] For this reason, it is incumbent on us to take a closer look at the ideas presented therein. Experience, he tells us, is always of *something*. There can be no "empty" experience. Likewise, there is no experience without an awareness, a consciousness, of it. Whether we experience an objective event, an objective thing, a (subjective) phantasy, or a subjective fear, the experience, lived experience

---

[17] Shpet 2002: 1073.

[18] Shpet 2002: 61. Shpet's emphasis on most of the words here has been omitted as unnecessary in this context.

[19] In this attempt to discredit neo-Kantianism, Shpet evidently made no attempt to distinguish between the Baden and Marburg Schools, painting, as it were, both with the same broad strokes.

[20] This journal article should not be confused with his 1916 thesis with its slightly different title. The article, though bearing the date 25 February 1917, was finally published only in 1922 in the rather obscure journal *Nauchnye izvestii* [*Scientific News*].

(*perezhivanie, Erlebnis*), is always of something. This correlativity of consciousness to an object is the genuine principle of knowledge and the foundation of a rigorously scientific study.[21] The correlativity of consciousness is ideal and essential. We obtain this determination not through abstraction from empirical, that is, contingent, examples, but through an ideal, or eidetic, study. Such a study yields the ideal forms of consciousness in relation to reality, these forms becoming an object of study. Since these forms are ideal, we must not forget that they represent pure possibilities.

To be realized, the ideal forms need a "material complement" – what Husserl would call "hyletic data." This complement, of course, has its own forms, although these are contingent and not ideal. Nevertheless, they can be "abstracted," one might say, by the empirical sciences to form general laws of reality. In this way, we obtain the respective empirical natural sciences of physics, chemistry, etc. However, if our concern is, above all, with concrete reality, we will see the error in locating the sources of our scientific study in segmented, nonhuman parts of reality. If our concern is not with the technical details of science or with the possible practical benefits to be accrued from the study, but is undertaken from the standpoint of the ideal of the pure cognition of reality, then we must, according to Shpet, accord primacy to the science that offers the most perfect cognition of the integral and limitless concrete. This "science" is history.[22] Countering the reigning paradigm that the philosophy, or logic, of science is the philosophy of physical science, Shpet contends that philosophy should be, above all, the philosophy of historical science. He, in this way in 1917, comes expressly to the same conclusion to which his ruminations on Husserlian phenomenology led him in 1914. He wrote, "Nowhere is the significance and the role of logic in the cognition of reality manifested as clearly as in the science of history."[23]

The study of history, of all human history, in Shpet's day meant the reading and understanding of documents, in short, the comprehension of words. Words are the form through which the historian obtains the content of reality. A broader conclusion with respect to the other sciences can be drawn from this simple fact. The other sciences use observation and other techniques, but all invest their experiences in words. In this respect, the resulting cognition is less immediate. "Since historical science is directly concerned with the 'reading of the word,' this clearly shows its logical primacy among the empirical sciences. Logic, for its part, knows only one true *principium cognoscendi – the word*."[24] Shpet, in the decade following the composition of this article, devoted himself to, among other scholarly pursuits, the role of language in cognition. In this sense, we can see him as among the first advocates of a "linguistic turn" in (phenomenological) philosophy. Already in 1917, he connected his ideas with those of Wilhelm von Humboldt, seeing his own conception of logical forms as analogous to Humboldt's inner form of language. For Shpet, words

---

[21] Shpet 2005: 219.

[22] Shpet 2005: 223.

[23] Shpet 2005: 227.

[24] Shpet 2005: 229.

serve as form and sign. They serve to express historical concepts and content. As signs, they serve the purpose of communication. The historian is to read the words, which were put down to communicate something, and, in turn, to put down his/her own words in an attempt to communicate to the reading public what and how he/she "sees" the original words. Thus, the study of communication lies at the base of historical science. How communication is accomplished is the basis of historical methodology.[25]

If, following Shpet's train of thought, historical science is the fundamental empirical science, then the epistemology of that science is at the same time the basis of all other such sciences. Moreover, as we have also seen, hermeneutics is the epistemology of historical science, and, therefore, of course, the basic epistemology of all empirical sciences. The pressing need for philosophy today is a fundamental analysis of the elementary concepts of hermeneutics, namely, understanding and communication. At the end of his article, Shpet – without a more complete explanation – asserted, "History by its *logical* method is the foundation of all empirical knowledge, just as we can and should consider *philology* as the foundation for history by virtue of its investigative method."[26]

A number of the figures Shpet discusses in the following pages have received only limited attention in English-language literature on the subject. Still, much of Shpet's *Hermeneutics* text is of a historical nature and would require little introduction were it not for his fundamental guiding idea, a central element of which is the gradual elimination of psychologism from the theory of signs and their understanding. It is this guiding idea, the leitmotif, and its realization throughout Shpet's work that is arguably of particular philosophical interest and that distinguishes this work and its relatively early composition within the phenomenological movement. Shpet, in this work reveals, albeit yet tentatively, the vital role of hermeneutics in philosophy and, more specifically, the *understanding* of signs in general and of words in particular as a phenomenological problem. It is this concern with language, while yet adhering to the central Husserlian theory of intentionality, that distinguishes his attempted "linguistic turn" in phenomenology. This focus on intentionality in hermeneutics and the absence of it in the various historical theories examined is the other central element in Shpet's work. We see in this Shpet's debt to Husserl and the *Hermeneutics* as an example of a history of one aspect of philosophy from a phenomenological viewpoint.

---

[25] Shpet 2005: 244–246.

[26] Shpet 2005: 247. Shpet's assertion allows him to contrast history and hermeneutics, as empirical knowledge, to phenomenology (owing to its concern with essences), as ideal knowledge – phenomenology as the fundamental ideal science.

## The Structure of the *Hermeneutics*

As for the text of the *Hermeneutics* itself, Shpet states that with Origen we have the first introduction of European reason, albeit in the form of a distorted Platonism, for the purposes of a Christian hermeneutics. If we contend that the actual writing of some work – in this case the Bible – was divinely inspired, then it is quite plausible to infer that its correct understanding, in turn, requires such inspiration. Origen, though, framed the issue, of course, within a religious context and unsurprisingly finds a religious solution. The correct understanding of the written work, namely, the Bible, requires, in Origen's eyes, divine grace.

St. Augustine too turned to hermeneutics, and he provides us with what amounts to a textbook on the topic. His interest was practical, rather than theoretical. As a result, he presented the results of his investigations bereft of arguments and analyses. Nevertheless, Augustine's advance over Origen lies in recognizing the ambiguity of words as well as in his acknowledgment of the problem of signs in general, namely, that they require understanding from us. What he did not study are, on the one hand, signs as such, as things that have meaning and, on the other hand, the meanings themselves.

The Reformation's religious conflicts entailed conflicting interpretations of the key texts, leading to attempts to expound the principles of hermeneutics. Shpet signals out Flacius as "a monument" to the erudition and the efforts of the time. He, together with Melanchthon, presented a clear solution to the problem of the ambiguity in the sense of a word, and with his work we confront a truly scholarly formulation of the problem of signs. However, although the logic of Flacius' thought led to the recognition of a sign as a concept, he himself did not pursue the development of a theory of signs. The Protestant theologians who turned to issues in hermeneutics eagerly seeking to distance themselves from the Scholastics divorced modern theology from its philosophical foundations. In this way, this entire movement within modernity lost any connections with the problem of meaning, particularly the intentional relation between sign and meaning. When the problem did resurface, it appeared in a psychological guise.

In the wake of the Reformation, the demands confronting the burgeoning concern with hermeneutics led to a changed conception of philosophy. Two directions emerged: one faced the *object* of understanding and interpretation, whereas the other concerned itself with the *processes* involved in such efforts. These directions, transposed into the sphere of hermeneutics, meant a concern with the problem of the sign as an object with meaning, on the one hand, and a concern with the cognitive process of understanding the sign and its correlative meaning, on the other hand. John Locke's empiricism pursued the latter, but his approach and construal of the cognitive process was imbued with psychologism. He misunderstood the problem of the sign–meaning relationship as a problem of the psychological processes involved in the formation of concepts. Rationalism, on the other hand, being directed to the reason of things, saw no need to reflect on the understanding *process* itself. Yet, when we look closer at its assertions, we see that it accorded a role to an immediate rational insight, which Shpet believed could be developed further in pursuit of a solution to our problems.[27]

Among those of a general rationalist direction was Johann Ernesti. Although he provided a solution neither to the problem of the sign nor to that of understanding, he helped maneuver hermeneutics onto the road that when followed would lead to their respective solutions. His disciples, Boeckh and Schleiermacher, took up the challenge. The former revealed the historical nature of words as signs, and Schleiermacher probed the process of understanding and interpretation. However, their respective paths leading, on the one hand, to philology, conceived as a historical endeavor, and psychology, on the other, represent only the empirical foundations for solving hermeneutical problems.

Schleiermacher's understanding of hermeneutical problems remained, in Shpet's eyes, unsurpassed up to Shpet's own time. The former desired to make hermeneutics a rigorous, or scientific, discipline. To be sure, Shpet faults Schleiermacher for his deficiencies and even some mistakes, but his dichotomy between a grammatical and a psychological moment of interpretation was important. Unfortunately, he thought a single understanding grounded both, which thereby deprived the dichotomy of its due importance. Shpet feared, one might say, that Schleiermacher's dichotomy would be undermined by interpreting the object as a representation, which would lead to a nullification of the dichotomy and a subordination of all interpretation to a psychological one. In this way, we retreat back to psychologism. Alternatively, a theoretically ungrounded opposition between grammatical and psychological interpretation can lead to one of them being empirically utilized unilaterally. Shpet concludes his study of Schleiermacher writing that to avoid these possible pitfalls we must undertake a fundamental analysis of understanding and sense, an analysis the latter did not do.

Another of the many figures Shpet discusses is Heymann Steinthal, whom Shpet calls a psychologist of the Herbartian school, rather than a philologist. Indeed, psychology in Steinthal's construction occupies the dominant place among the human sciences with a diminished role allotted to both history and philology. Interpretation in general becomes a matter of the clarification of the sense of the linguistic unit, be it a word, then a sentence, and then the connection between sentences. But in all this, Steinthal never informs us how he understands "sense" or how we obtain it. Nineteenth-century methodologists of history could conceivably have taken up and probed deeper into Schleiermacher's distinction between grammatical and psychological interpretation, asking, for one thing, whether historical interpretation coincides with either. However, none gave more than hints toward illuminating and resolving problems associated with the fundamental problem of understanding.

With Dilthey, we find an acknowledgment of the fundamental significance of hermeneutics in the human sciences. His early writings, however, failed to formulate the general problem involving signs, and his procedure was imbued with psychologism. His approach at the time was subjectivistic without a clear recognition

---

[27] For Shpet, phenomenology develops the rationalists' idea of rational insight together with the empiricists' concern with the process, yielding the theory of eidetic intuition.

of the problems associated with the objectively communicable content involved in signs, broadly speaking, and speech, more specifically.

Eduard Spranger built on the foundations the early Dilthey had established. The former's concern for an analysis of understanding is for a psychological analysis. The principle at work in history is taken to be a matter of psychological relations. Spranger's psychological analysis of understanding extends only so far, and it is this limitation that marks his divergence from the overt psychologism of others, such as Wundt and Sigwart. Whereas the latter believe historical events can be explained in terms of psychological causes, Spranger recognized that the historian understands that each event must be situated in a whole, in a broadly conceived context. Nonetheless, his conception of understanding is, like that of the early Dilthey, based on the understanding of the human individual.

Shpet, next, returns to the late Dilthey, who in his last work, *Aufbau der geschichtlichen Welt in den Geisteswissenschaften*, published just one year before his death, attained the highest point yet achieved in the formulation of hermeneutical problems. Dilthey, there, recognized, as he did not previously, the difficulties encountered with the introduction of psychologism into historical methodology. Nevertheless, Shpet avers that Dilthey still failed to correct his omission of a fundamental analysis of understanding. He should have seen the need for such, since he recognized the objectification of the spirit in the object of understanding. It is this objectification, the autonomy, of the spirit that places Dilthey among the greatest sociologists (!) of the decades just prior to World War I.

Shpet also briefly examines several figures who, in their own way, wrestled with the problem of understanding albeit from the viewpoint of experimental psychology. Philosophers, however, have recognized that these efforts to contribute thereby to the age-old quest for a fundamental science were misguided and illegitimate. Nevertheless, they, in turn, too have come to recognize the importance of the problem and its associated issues along with a recognition of the value of such fields as linguistics and psychology. The turning point in the philosophical treatment of understanding was Husserl's *Logical Investigations*, but the highest point reached in the linguistic treatment of the problem is found in the work of Marty and Gomperz. However, the "static" character of semasiology makes determining its place within philosophy difficult, which in turn accounts for the absence of a comprehensive analysis of understanding. Shpet ends his study without firm conclusions. Presumably, this text was intended to serve as the prelude to his own analysis, an analysis that he never was quite able to set out. Still, essential features of it are clear. Such an analysis would have to remain without the slightest hint of any reductionism, psychologism in particular, and without a grasping of understanding as a solitary process on the part of the human individual. Understanding, whether of a text or signs in general, is a social activity fundamentally dependent on its sociohistorical milieu.

Despite the fact that Shpet set out his ideas on hermeneutics 100 years ago, it may yet be too soon to juxtapose them meaningfully to those of such other hermeneuticists as Gadamer, Ricoeur, and, especially Heidegger. What is clear from the start is that all had a definite and firm background in Husserlian phenomenology, but differ from Shpet in their understanding of what hermeneutics even is, let alone what is involved in its definitive formulation. A striking feature of Gadamer's *Truth and Method*, at least in its early portions, is the emphasis on the distinctive methodology of the human sciences, whereas Shpet's emphasis is on the understanding of a written text, for the most part, and on language. Here, we notice that Shpet throughout sees the text as a sign between the consciousness of the writer in a particular socio-historical setting and that of the text's reader again in a particular setting, which is often different – essentially different – from the former. In this way, Shpet's study is still a reflective phenomenology in that he never loses sight of the intentionality of the process. In keeping with the general tenor of his overall modification of phenomenology, the consciousness that he has in mind should not be understood as that of the individual person, but of the "collective consciousness," argued for and elaborated in his essay "Consciousness and Its Owner." In contrast, Gadamer's concern, rooted more in Heidegger's thought than Husserl's, is with the hermeneutical person – a philosophical anthropology. Gadamer's interest is in a hermeneutic of the human condition, a hermeneutics of being-in-the-world as against Shpet's more focused textual hermeneutics. In this respect, Shpet's outlook can be contrasted more easily with Cassirer's neo-Kantian theory of symbolic forms than with certain other "hermeneutic phenomenologies."[28]

## Shpet's Legacy Today

Shpet stands as one of the great "might-have-beens" of twentieth-century intellectual history. Had the Soviet era not been so drenched in human blood, Shpet, as "the most pronounced and most persistent"[29] Westernizer in Russian thought, conceivably could have nudged – probably no stronger word is suitable – his country's philosophical scene along professional lines not dissimilar to those practiced in Western Europe and America. As already mentioned, his non-egological conception of consciousness long antedated those of Sartre and Gurwitsch. Unfortunately, Shpet's publication appeared in an obscure *Festschrift* in a language unfamiliar to most Western scholars and at a time when the world was engulfed in a mindless conflagration. These factors hampered a greater dissemination of its ideas. And while he strew the seeds of transcendental phenomenology in his homeland, they were irretrievably swept away, again for decades, just as the first buds were emerging. As late as 1989, in the editor's "foreword" to the first anthology of Shpet's

---

[28] It is common in Russian secondary studies of Shpet to refer to his "hermeneutic phenomenology." See, for example, Kuznecov 1991. Likewise, it is common to see in the West various approaches, which display a distinct Heideggerian influence, refer to their respective approach as a "hermeneutic phenomenology." Kockelmans labels his own position that way: "From a methodological point of view the position outlined here follows Heidegger who reinterpreted Husserl's transcendental phenomenology as a hermeneutic phenomenology." Kockelmans 1993: 71.

[29] Tihanov 2008: 278.

writings, Elena V. Pasternak, Shpet's granddaughter, wrote, "Unfortunately, in his native land the level of research into the philosopher's creativity is almost nil."[30]

From a Western perspective, only in the past few decades at most has appreciable attention turned to the early phenomenological movement. Only recently have scholars turned to the circle of students around Husserl in his Göttingen years and to the reception and interpretation they afforded Husserl's *Logische Untersuchungen* and *Ideen I*. As one of those students, albeit somewhat detached from the others owing likely to his somewhat more mature years and family circumstances, Shpet's understanding of phenomenology sheds light today on the philosophical diversity of that movement and on its vivacity. One research topic that surely remains utterly unexplored is an inquiry into Shpet's interpretation of Husserl's thought against that of the others at the time.

Shpet, during a particularly productive decade after his return from Germany, authored a number of studies dealing with the history of Russian philosophy. Owing for the most part to their specialized nature, they have attracted scant attention in the West. In both Soviet and émigré circles – those with an extra-philosophical agenda on the left and on the right – Shpet's detailed historical treatises received a caustic reception for their illumination of the sheer poverty of that history and for his condemnation of the subordination of individual creativity to abstract ideals and extraneous authority. Nevertheless, it is for the very values his studies displayed, namely, on the one hand, the frank admission of the philosophical poverty of the pertinent subject matter all the while exploring what lessons, both positive and negative, it extends to us now, that he stands as a beacon for future historical work on Russian philosophy.

During the 1920s and early 1930s, Shpet's name was much better known than others in Russian literary criticism and psychology that we know today, such as Bakhtin, Vygotsky, and Sergej Rubinshtein.[31] That Shpet was virtually forgotten in Russia until late in the Soviet period and unknown in the West during that same time span, should not obscure what Shpet accomplished under quite trying conditions.[32] Admittedly the significance of his writings was more locally confined than it might have been had the convulsions of the previous century not prevailed. Nevertheless, institutionally Shpet played a key role in establishing along with Chelpanov the Moscow Institute of Psychology in 1912 modeled on Wundt's Institute of Psychology in Leipzig, and in December 1920 he spearheaded the creation of an Office for Ethnic and Social Psychology. Indeed, his theoretical influence in psychology can be traced in the work of Vygotsky, despite the latter's silence regarding any such influence.[33]

---

[30] Pasternak 1989: 8.

[31] Zinchenko 2006: 11.

[32] Even in the third revised edition of his otherwise authoritative history of the phenomenological movement, Spiegelberg mentions Shpet merely as being a student of Husserl's and an early advocate of his thought. Spiegelberg 1994: 666.

[33] For far more detail, see Zinchenko and Wertsch 2009. Zinchenko comments that Vygotsky, "willingly or not, founded a psychological tradition of ignoring Shpet's works." Zinchenko 2006: 14.

Shpet was a member of the Moscow branch of the Free Philosophical Association (*Vol'fila*) after its establishment in 1921, and he served as the founding director of the short-lived Institute of Scientific Philosophy. More importantly, after being removed from teaching at Moscow University, he was a member of the State Academy for the Study of the Arts (GAKhN) during most of the 1920s and for a time its vice president. After it was closed, Shpet was forced to make a living producing translations. Apart from philosophical classics, he translated Dickens, Byron, and Tennyson and worked on an eight-volume edition of Shakespeare, published in 1936–1949.[34] Shpet's involvement in the theater, both writing on theory and as translator and adviser, in Moscow and later in Siberian exile, led him to establish many personal contacts surely not typical of a professional philosopher. The esteem with which Shpet was held in these theatrical circles is perhaps best shown by a letter one of the leading actors of the early Soviet era, Vasilij Kachalov, wrote on Shpet's behalf to Stalin: "We are fully aware of our responsibility in appealing to you, but we are concerned not just about a person close and dear to us. We would consider it to be unworthy cowardice on our part not to point out to you a possible mistake made with respect to a man we consider an honest Soviet citizen and who with his exceptional knowledge can be extremely useful to our homeland. G. G. Shpet is one of our specialists on Shakespeare, knows 19 languages, was a candidate in the Academy of Sciences, and is a great and subtle expert of the theatrical art."[35]

In another seemingly different facet of his interests, Shpet became a member of the Moscow Linguistic Circle in March 1920 after he presented at one of its sessions a paper "Aesthetic Moments in the Structure of the Word," which he later incorporated into his book *Aesthetic Fragments*. In defining philosophical aesthetics as "the theory of aesthetic consciousness, which is correlative to the ontological theory of the aesthetic object,"[36] Shpet attempted both to avoid reducing such experience to psychology as well as to continue with his vision of a phenomenological philosophy that never separates the object of study from intentional consciousness. With such a definition and project, Shpet left a legacy for future followers to help elaborate and execute. However, his most concrete historical influence was, arguably, through the linguists associated with that Moscow circle, which included Roman Jakobson. Shpet's participation in the ongoing disputes was a significant factor leading eventually to its dismemberment, but its continuance, of course, as an independent, non-Marxist discussion group would have been impossible for political reasons. The disputes centered on methodological approaches to linguistics. Those around Jakobson favored an empirical approach, whereas those around Shpet affirmed a holistic approach through concrete historical studies. With Jakobson's emigration, the Circle came under the dominating influence of Shpet and his Husserlian-inspired

---

[34] For additional information, see Tihanov 2009b and for an exhaustive amount of information see Shchedrina 2013.

[35] Kachalov 1995: 284. This letter is dated, apparently by the editors, from 1939 to 1940. Kachalov, clearly, was unaware that Shpet had been shot before the letter was written.

[36] Shpet 2007: 234.

approach. Jakobson wrote on occasion to Shpet in the late 1920s affirming in one letter dated 24 November 1929 some affinity between their respective approaches: "It is becoming all the clearer to me that an analysis of a system of language can be radically emancipated from psychology starting from the productive assumptions that you gave in your *Introduction to Ethnic Psychology.*"[37] Whereas Jakobson in Prague helped found the Prague Linguistic Circle and pursued the approach known as structuralism, Shpet and his group, remaining in Soviet Russia advocated a "historical and hermeneutical investigation of the inner forms of signs."[38] Whereas Jakobson's approach in Prague and then eventually from his position at Harvard became widely known, any advocacy of Shpet's fell victim to the Soviet behemoth. Nevertheless, in long reflection Jakobson would write, "The foundations of a phenomenology of language in the arresting treatment by Husserl's disciple G. G. Špet left a notable imprint on the development of MCL [Moscow Linguistic Circle – TN] in its final period and provoked heated arguments about the place and limits of empiricism and about the role of semantics in the science of language. ... Yet the contribution of the Circle both to Russian and to international linguistics should not be minimized."[39]

## This Translation and Acknowledgments

Gadamer asserted that a perfect translation, one that stands the test of time without requiring revision, is an impossible dream. Even a brief scan of translations of great philosophical works, some done by eminent scholars in their own right, bears this out, witness the numerous English-language translations of, for example, Kant's *Kritik der reinen Vernunft* still available today, several of Husserl's *Ideen I*, and of Hegel's *Phänomenologie des Geistes*. Translating Shpet's writings poses an additional challenge in that his literary style on many occasions borders on the poetic replete often enough with unusual constructions not typically found in the far more succinct and precise essays commonly written by analytically trained scholars today.[40] A potentially additional problem in translating a text that frequently quotes and cites texts from various schools of thought over centuries is that existing English-language translations of those works have rendered those texts using a far from uniform set of terms. Were the present translation to utilize throughout the existing translations of these other works, the result would certainly be to the detriment of understanding Shpet's ideas. For this reason, the translator has decided to

---

[37] Shpet 2005: 506.

[38] Shchedrina 2005b: 25.

[39] Jakobson 1985: 281.

[40] The late noted Russian psychologist Vladimir Zinchenko wrote regarding Shpet's books that "although written in brilliant Russian, they are difficult to understand. ... In addition, we must not forget that Shpet worked with Husserl for a while. ... Shpet was not 'transparent' like Chelpanov." Zinchenko 2006: 15.

render Shpet's Russian terminology into English whenever possible with references to English translations, when they exist, in footnotes. An admittedly small matter but one that the reader will undoubtedly notice concerns the transliteration of Russian words. Although there are few instances where this issue arises in the texts before us, we can see the possibility of confusion already in that Shpet himself rendered his own name in his early writings as "Spett," and when writing to Husserl as "von Spett"! The confusion may be compounded in that whereas in English the name is typically rendered "Shpet," German literature has it as Špet and the French spell his name as "Chpet." Finally, all items in square brackets in both this extended essay and in the accompanying appendices comprising this collection are the editor's/translator's insertions. References for textual quotations preceded by "Cf." indicate that the respective quotation has been taken from an existing English translation but modified, occasionally significantly, so as to conform to Shpet's vocabulary.

The original basis of the present translation is an English-language typewritten manuscript prepared by a co-translator of the German-language version, Erika Freiberger, who came to an interest in Shpet from her own studies on Boris Pasternak, an early student of Shpet's. She regrettably and prematurely passed away a number of years ago before she was able to see her translation through to its finalization and publication. At some time after completing her work but before her death, she gave her manuscript to George L. Kline, then of Bryn Mawr College and a renowned scholar of Russian philosophy and literature, for editing. Professor Kline, in turn, gave his copy of the translation to Peter Steiner at the University of Pennsylvania at the latter's request. Professor Steiner carefully retained for many years this possibly sole surviving copy of Prof. Freiberger's English translation. On my inquiry as to the fate of Professor Freiberger's manuscript, Professor Steiner generously and without the slightest hesitation forwarded it, arranging for its transfer at a mutually convenient rest stop along the ever-peaceful and picturesque New Jersey Turnpike! To what degree Professor Kline edited Professor Freiberger's translation is well-nigh impossible to determine with assurance, for the manuscript is clean with no handwritten remarks that would help determine the intervention of any particular hand. A comparison of the published German translation to that English translation reveals a distinct similarity but also notable differences, possibly the result of the collaboration of the German co-translator Alexander Haardt of the University of Bochum.

In preparing the present English translation, I frequently referred for help and clarification to the Freiberger English-language translation as well as to the German translation prepared by Professors Freiberger and Haardt. No responsible translator could or would forego any such assistance. However, I and I alone am responsible for any errors, inaccuracies, and omissions in the present work. Were it not for those translations, the present one would, most likely, not even have been undertaken. Thus, the present work is dedicated to the memory of Professor Freiberger, who always demonstrated sincere friendship and scholarly integrity. Whereas the German translation utilized an original copy of the manuscript in the hands of Shpet's descendants, the present translation is based on the Russian text as found in Shpet

2005, edited by Professor T. G. Shchedrina, whose indefatigable efforts to promote Shpet scholarship is nothing short of amazing. Professor Shchedrina notes that the basis for her own edition of this text is a typed copy supplied by Elena Pasternak, Shpet's granddaughter. Whether this copy was the same as that employed by Freiberger and Haardt is unclear. In the absence of the respective original Russian manuscripts used by Freiberger and Shchedrina, no conclusions can be drawn as to whether they used the same original copy or whether any differences in the respective editions were introduced by the respective editors. In any case, the present translator/editor has attempted to point out easily discernible differences in footnotes to this edition.

Of the five attached appendices, all but one originally date from the second decade of the last century and help establish Shpet's *own* understanding of Husserlian phenomenology and help *us* understand his place in the burgeoning phenomenological movement. Each appendix has a short introduction. For that reason, we need not prolong this one. The first appendix presents Shpet's view of consciousness, expanding on a position argued for by the late Solov'ëv, bereft of the highly metaphysical shell in which Solov'ëv expounded it. Shpet conceived consciousness not merely as the personal possession of an individual – "my" consciousness, "your" consciousness, etc. – but also meaningfully as a possible possession of a group and even a society, namely, a shared or group consciousness and even a social consciousness.

The second appendix oddly alternates between technical philosophical issues and popular ones, covering numerous different concerns. Sensing what he considered the dangerous influence of both Bergson and Nietzsche, he ends his long essay on a polemical note. Whereas we certainly can recognize the thrust of his presentation from a phenomenological viewpoint, Shpet's delimitation of what he considered the *proper* concerns of philosophy makes him appear to be more like the positivists he chastised than he surely would have cared to admit. Philosophy, in his eyes, is to concern itself with neither moral issues nor, for example, the meaning and purpose of life. Such matters are of interest to *pseudo*-philosophy and are a sign of, what he called, "Eastern" laziness.

The third and fourth appendices demonstrate Shpet's concerns with, on the one hand, combatting skepticism – which would be an ongoing endeavor for him – and, on the other hand, accommodating historical methodology – largely at the expense of mathematical physics – as the paradigm of rigorous science. The fifth appendix, dating from at least a decade later than the other pieces in this collection, provides us with Shpet's last reflections on his general philosophical stand. It, arguably, firmly establishes his own commitment to the Husserlian conception of the intentionality of consciousness and to the phenomenological reduction, albeit idiosyncratically conceived. In summarizing his philosophical path through the 1920s, however, we get a glimpse of how Shpet would develop the "linguistic turn" he adumbrated in the other texts in this collection, including in the main text here on hermeneutics.

A work such as this would not have been possible without the help and input of numerous voices. Although no longer with us, thanks go, above all, to the pioneering work of Professors Erika Freiberger and George Kline. A sincere expression of thanks also goes to the anonymous reviewers of the texts that follow. Their patience and keen observations were of tremendous assistance. Prof. Tat'jana Shchedrina of Moscow State Pedagogical University helped throughout with encouragement and answers to a string of questions. She was also of great assistance in obtaining permission from the Russian publisher of her edition of the *Hermeneutics*. In this regard, thanks also, of course, go to Irina Dmitrievna Kantemirova, the general director of *Rossijskaja politicheskaja enciklopedija* (ROSSPEN), the Russian publishing house, for granting permission for this translation. Much of the work involved in preparing this volume was undertaken while this translator/editor was a "Writer in Residence" at NYU's Jordan Center for the Advanced Study of Russia. For that experience and for availing itself of its tremendous resources, I would like to express my sincere appreciation. A deep expression of thanks also goes to Professor Nicolas de Warren, the series editor of "Contributions to Phenomenology," for considering this set of translations and for much else associated with this publication. Last, but certainly not least, this translator/editor would like to thank Cristina dos Santos and Anita van der Linden-Rachmat of Springer for their help throughout the publishing process.

Manchester, NJ, USA                                                       Thomas Nemeth

# Bibliography

Chamberlain, Lesley. 2006. *Lenin's Private War: the Voyage of the Philosophy Steamer and the Exile of the Intelligentsia*. New York: St. Martin's Press.

Glavackij, Mikhail E. 2002. *«Filosofskij parokhod»: god 1922-j: Istoriograficheskie etjudy*. Ekaterinburg: Izd. Ural'skogo universiteta.

Haardt, Alexander. 1993. *Husserl in Rußland: Phänomenologie der Sprache und Kunst bei Gustav Špet und Alexsej Losev*. Munich: Wilhelm Fink Verlag.

Husserl, Edmund. 2002. Philosophy as Rigorous Science. Trans. Marcus Brainard. In *The New Yearbook for Phenomenology and Phenomenological Philosophy II*, 249–295. Seattle: Noesis Press.

Jakobson, Roman. 1985. Toward the History of the Moscow Linguistic Circle. In *Contributions to Comparative Mythology. Studies in linguistics and philology, 1972–1982*, 279–282. Berlin: de Gruyter & Co.

Kachalov, Vasilij. 1995. Dokumenty. In *Shpet v Sibiri: ssylka i gibel'*. Tomsk: Izd. Vodolej.

Kockelmans, Joseph J. 1993. *Ideas for a Hermeneutic Phenomenology of the Natural Sciences*. Dordrecht: Springer.

Kuznecov, V.G. 1991. Germenevticheskaja fenomenologija v kontekste filosofskikh vozzrenij Gustava Gustavovicha Shpet. *Logos* 2: 199–214.

Pasternak, Elena V. 1989. G. G. Shpet. In Shpet 1989: 3–8.

Rickert, Genrikh. 1904. *Vvedenie v transcendental'nuju filosofiju. Predmet poznanija*. Trans. Gustav Shpett. Kiev: V. A. Prosjanichenko.

Shchedrina, T.G. (ed.). 2005a. *Gustav Shpet: zhizn' v pis'makh. Epistoljarnoe nasledie*. Moscow: ROSSPEN.

Shchedrina, T.G. 2005b. Gustav Shpet i put' filosofa. In Shpet 2005: 7–31.

Shchedrina, T.G. (ed.). 2012. *Gustav Shpet: Filosof v kul'ture. Dokumenty i pis'ma*. Moscow: ROSSPEN.

Shchedrina, T.G. (ed.). 2013. *Gustav Shpet i shekspirovskij krug. Pis'ma, dokumenty, perevody*. Moscow and St. Petersburg: Petroglif.

Shchedrina, T.G. 2014. Fenomenologicheskie studii Gustava Shpeta: *Javlenie i smysl* v kontekste "Archiva epokhi". *Gumanitarnye issledovanija v vostochnoj Siberi i na dal'nem vostoke*. 1: 142–147.

Shpet, Gustav. 1989. *Sochinenija*. Moscow: Izd. Pravda.

Shpet, Gustav. 2002. *Istorija kak problema logiki*, ed. V. S. Mjasnikov. Moscow: Pamjatniki istoricheskoj mysli.

Shpet, Gustav. 2005. *Mysl' i Slovo. Izbrannye trudy*. Moscow: ROSSPEN.

Shpet, Gustav. 2006. *Philosophia Natalis. Izbrannye psikhologo-pedagogicheskie trudy*, ed. T.G. Shchedrina. Moscow: ROSSPEN.

Shpet, Gustav. 2007. *Iskusstvo kak vid znanija. Izbrannye trudy po filosofii kul'tury*, ed. T.G. Shchedrina. Moscow: ROSSPEN.

Shpet, Gustav. 2010. *Filosofskaja kritika: otzyvy, recenzii, obzory*, ed. T. G. Shchedrina. Moscow: ROSSPEN.

Shpet, Gustav. 2015. Consciousness and Its Owner. *Kronos: Philosophical Journal* 4: 10–52.

Spiegelberg, Herbert. 1994. *The Phenomenological Movement. A Historical Introduction*. Dordrecht: Kluwer Academic Publishers.

Tihanov, Galin. 2008. Multifariousness under Duress: Gustav Shpet's Scattered Lives. *Russian Literature* LXIII(II/III/IV): 259–292.

Tihanov, Galin. 2009a. Innovation and regression: Gustav Shpet's theoretical concerns in the 1920s. In *Critical Theory in Russia and the West*, 44–62, ed. Alastair Renfrew and Galin Tihanov, New York: Routledge.

Tihanov, Galin. 2009b. Gustav Shpet's Literary and Theater Affiliations. In Tihanov 2009c: 56–80.

Tihanov, Galin (ed.). 2009c. *Gustav Shpet's Contribution to Philosophy and Cultural Theory*. West Lafayette: Purdue University Press.

Zinchenko, Vladimir P. 2006. Zhizn' v mysli i slove. In Shpet 2006: 7–20.

Zinchenko, Vladimir P. and James V. Wertsch. 2009. Gustav Shpet's Influence on Psychology. In Tihanov 2009: 45–55.

# Preface

While working on the methodology of history, I amassed a significant amount of material that I did not want to introduce directly into the texts of the respective investigations in the hope of avoiding to make them unnecessarily unwieldy and discordant. I felt it would be useful to publish the part of this material dealing with the history of hermeneutics as a scientific discipline in the form of a separate monograph. On the one hand, I had in mind to lean on this material in preparing a projected third volume of my investigations on historical methodology. On the other hand, I nurtured the hope that the proposed book could prove to be of interest and of some use to historians, philologists, and historians of literature.

I did not intend to provide a systematic history of the issue. I repeat that this work consists of remnants of material that was prepared for other reasons, where an excursus into the sphere of hermeneutics was intended to serve only an auxiliary role. The interest of my pursuit is not so much history as it is a clarification of the consistent emergence and development of the fundamental problems in hermeneutics, ranging from their empirical-practical formulation to their fundamental and philosophical grounding. To illuminate the philosophical and methodological significance of the techniques in hermeneutics and their role in the development of the sciences of the word[1] is to show the prospects opened up for philosophy upon a fundamental deepening of this subject. At the same time, such an illumination retains the possibility of revealing the consequences that ensue from this in a third volume of my investigations, which will be devoted to the principles of historical knowledge. My task consisted simply in allocating the material that I had to a separate work.

---

[1] We must keep in mind throughout Shpet's discussion that, as Alexander Haardt has correctly pointed out, Shpet's frequent usage of "word" – however awkward in English – is to be understood "in the broad sense of the Russian expression for 'word,' namely, *slovo*. *Slovo* can refer not only to words but also to clauses and complex sentences, even to literary texts and the totality of a natural language." Haardt 2009: 172.

The article "History as an Object of Logic," which serves as an "introduction," presents my general position in this matter and has to do with showing how the following exposition should be understood.[2]

Moscow, Russia                                                                        Gustav Shpet

---

[2] Shpet had in mind here his article "Istorija kak predmet logiki" ["History as an Object of Logic"], which, although written in February 1917, was first published only in 1922. Its contents are summarized in the editor's "Introduction" above.

# Contents

# [Origin of the Idea and of the Methods of Hermeneutics]

## 1 [Introduction of Biblical Hermeneutics]

If we were to trace, as it were, the basic features and only the chief moments in the discovery and realization of the idea of hermeneutics, we would accomplish two goals: (1) From the development of the subject matter of hermeneutics, we would recognize the problems that we can analyze; (2) By indicating the position that these problems occupy in contemporary philosophical consciousness, we would see how and why the solution to these problems must lead to a radical reconsideration of the tasks of logic and to a new elucidation of positive philosophy as a whole.[1]

The very essence of hermeneutical questions, clearly, shows that these questions must have appeared where there was a desire to provide a conscious account of the role of the *word* as a communicative sign. The first formulation of these questions as well as attempts at their particular, practical solution arose in close connection with, on the one hand, questions of rhetoric, grammar, and logic, and with, on the other hand, the practical demands of pedagogy, morality, and even politics. Thus, Homer, above all and in particular, became an object of interpretation in the schools – apparently not only of grammatical, but also of moral interpretation. Naturally, Homer remained during a Greek's entire lifetime – as Plato, incidentally, attests[2] – the source of one's moral and political principles, the application of which required not just a recitation of verses, but also their interpretation. Apparently already very early, from the end of the sixth century B.C.,[3] a special "scholarly" exegesis of the national epic poems began, an exegesis that sought to find a certain hidden allegorical, moral and physical sense (τας ὑπονοιας) in Homer's myths and

---

[1] [Shpet here appeals to a conception of "positive philosophy" that can be traced in the Russian tradition back at least to the nineteenth-century philosopher/theologian Pamfil Jurkevich and that is concerned with being rather than the Kantian project.]

[2] Plato 1969: 832 (Republic X, 606e).

[3] See Blass 1892: 151.

© Springer Nature Switzerland AG 2019                                      1
G. Shpet, T. Nemeth, *Hermeneutics and Its Problems*, Contributions
To Phenomenology 98, https://doi.org/10.1007/978-3-319-98941-9_1

images. Thus, the Sophists, who emerged as teachers of higher education, particularly of the art of oratory,[4] and, in general, the rhetoricians continued and extended the work of these first "exegetes." On the other hand, however, the Sophists were perhaps the first to connect questions of interpretation for practical purposes with theoretical questions in linguistics and, in particular, with the problem of the correct use of language.[5]

The question whether words are conventional, νομωι, or natural, φύσει, was not a matter of their *origin*. Whether words are νομωι or φύσει is not a question of whether language arose either "by agreement" or "naturally." Rather, the issue is whether a word *signifies* this or that object "legitimately" (νομωι) or "contingently" (φύσει). In this way, both the Sophists and Plato (*Cratylus*) connect the question of the meanings of words and their interpretation to problems of knowledge and logic. For Plato – as we clearly see particularly in the *Sophist* – the question about words, thoughts, and things (λεγόμενα, νοήματα όντα) was one coherent question, and Aristotle treated it in that same way.[6] In particular, his *Περι ερμηνείας*[7] is closely related to Plato's thoughts.[8] We can quite properly see his work as a part of logic, since for Aristotle the issue concerned the forms of the expression of thought. That is, Aristotle treated the logical forms of judgment with respect to their veracity or falsity, and not with respect to interpretation or understanding nor with respect to the techniques of achieving one or the other.[9] Finally, although apparently the Stoics did not concern themselves with the "art of interpretation," they closely linked questions of logic and grammar.[10] Nevertheless, they established the beginning (with Crates of Mallus) of a tendency (the Anomalists) that later played such a large role in the interpretation of texts.

Life, in turn, brought new demands, both practical and theoretical. Acquaintance with the East and relations with it demanded an ability to *translate*. On the other hand, the language of Homer, who continued to be the national teacher, became all the more difficult to understand immediately. It is also impossible to overlook the fact that even the simplest "pedagogical" interpretation of Homer was connected not only with a grammatical analysis of the form of his poems, but also with a certain kind of moralistic interpretation of their content. It is precisely here, under the

---

[4] See Gomperz 1912: 41ff.

[5] See Steinthal 1863: 75 f.: "It was tacitly assumed that words must be created, must be given. The question was only whether they are correct or not."

[6] Steinthal 1863: 210, 182ff, etc. Cf. Maier 1896: 106. Regarding the fact that, on the basis of his works in logic, Aristotle was regarded as the founder of grammar already in antiquity, see von Prantl 1855: 353.

[7] [The Greek title of Aristotle's work *On Interpretation*. It forms the second text in his *Organon* and is better known in the scholarly world by its Latin title *De Interpretatione*.]

[8] Besides Steinthal, see also Michelis 1886: 16 – "We see how Aristotle was born, so to speak, from Plato."

[9] [See Aristotle 1984: 2–3 (*De Interpretatione*, §2); Plato 1969: 1007–1011 (*Sophist*, 259e–264b).]

[10] Steinthal 1863: 274ff; von Prantl 1855: 414ff.

influence of rationalistic, philosophical, and historical criticism (already by Hecataeus), that we find an interest in a theoretical discipline that combines with a practical interest in interpreting the traditional religious worldview and the mythology of Homer and Hesiod. Here again, relations with the East created a broad field for criticism and interpretation. In any case, we see already in the third century B.C. the outlines of three definite tendencies in the interpretation of myths: a moralistic-psychological interpretation, an allegorical interpretation (with the Stoics), and a historical interpretation (with Euhemerus and his followers).[11]

Hellenistic culture, with its distinctly expressed "philological" character, had two chief centers – Alexandria and Pergamon – and offered two different directions in hermeneutics, one presented by the Analogists and another by the Anomalists.[12] If we do not credit these two directions with establishing a special science of interpretation, then, in any case, they were seeking at least the general and fundamental foundations to justify their own respective positions. As Dilthey remarks, this was an "opposition of hermeneutic tendencies that had world-historical significance."[13]

Along with the Hellenization of the East, there was an "orientalization" of the Hellenic World. Thus, Alexandria emerged as the center from which the wisdom of the East was imported into Europe. The translation of the Old Testament into the Greek language posed new questions about the technique employed in such work and about the art of interpretation. Apparently, however, we have no evidence that Alexandrian scholars conceived the idea of a special discipline of hermeneutics before[14] the need arose to interpret and explain the new Christian teaching – not only that of the New Testament but, perhaps, even in particular, that of the Old Testament.[15] For a long time, Christianity distracted scholarly minds from the investigation of the literature and science of antiquity and directed all of their efforts to the study of the Bible and theology. Thus, hermeneutics, as an independent theory, was construed, above all, as an auxiliary discipline to theology.

---

[11] [Euhemerus – late fourth century BC Greek mythographer, to whom is traditionally attributed the position that mythological personages and events refer to actual persons and events that have over time become exaggerated and altered.]

[12] The Anomalists of the Pergamene School are connected with the Stoics through Crates. The most prominent representative of the Alexandrian Analogists is Aristarchus. Apparently, Aristarchus and Crates initiated the unending dispute between the Analogists and the Anomalists. On this dispute, see Steinthal 1863: 347–63, 435–524. See also Immisch 1909: 33ff.

[13] Dilthey 1996: 240.

[14] However, according to Philo, there are "canons" and "laws" of allegorical interpretation of the Old Testament. Hillel, with his seven rules of hermeneutics, has no connection with these philosophical directions.

[15] For a short historical survey, or, rather, a chronological listing of the chief authors and the basic works of Biblical exegesis in both Christian and Jewish literature, see Szlagowski 1908: 250–78. A very detailed survey of the tendencies in hermeneutics, particularly with regard to the New Testament, is found in the textbook of the Utrecht University professor Doedes. (I use the English translation: Doedes 1867.)

Different directions in hermeneutics became apparent already in the first schools of theology. The Alexandrian school of theology, which unfolded in the first and second centuries A.D., showed a decisive inclination toward the so-called *allegorical*[16] interpretation of Holy Scripture.[17] In contrast, the School of Antioch, which arose toward the end of the third century A.D., promoted a "literal" – *grammatical and historical* – interpretation (the most prominent representative of this school being John Chrysostom, died 407). We can see the difference between these two directions running right up to our own time. However, along with the development of history as a discipline,[18] the second of the two directions has had a decisive preponderance at least in *systematic* theology from the second half of the eighteenth century.[19]

The essence of the so-called allegorical interpretation is usually seen in the fact that the words being interpreted have, along with a direct sense accessible to all, another sense that is not accessible to all, or not always – a deeper (ὑπόνια) and predominantly mystical sense. However, if we turn to representatives of this direction, we see that, for the most part, they actually admit, in addition to a direct sense, *not just one* deeper sense, but two, three, or even more. Thus, Origen, for example, distinguished all three of the senses that St. Jerome distinguished: the historical, the tropological, and the spiritual. In St. Gregory, we find the same number (the historical, the typical, and the moral); in St. Augustine – *secundum historiam, allogoriam, analogiam, aetiologiam* (interpretation "according to history (i.e., content), allegorical, analogical, and aetiological").[20]

The Scholastics usually distinguished four senses (the historical, the allegorical, the tropological, and the analogical). For example, St. Bonaventure listed one literal sense and three "spiritual" senses: the analogical, the allegorical, and the tropological

---

[16]Of the philosophical schools mentioned above, the Pergamene, apparently, used not only allegorical interpretation widely, but even abused it. Crates, for example, wanted to find all of Stoic philosophy in Homer. See the sketch of the history of philology in Immisch 1909: 29.

[17]Dionysius of Alexandria (died 264 or 265 A.D.), a pupil of Origen, apparently was an exception to this general direction of Alexandrian theology.

[18]See part 1 of [Shpet's] investigation *History as a Problem of Logic* [Shpet 1916].

[19]For a general survey, see Doedes 1867: 13–15, 19–50. Doedes distinguishes three periods in the history of New Testament hermeneutics: (1) the period of preparation (before the start of the Reformation); (2) the period of the first attempts (from the start of the Reformation); (3) the period of the rise of scientific interpretation (from the second half of the eighteenth century). In all three periods, he distinguishes three directions in the schools of exegesis (Doedes 1867: 17–18): (1) the *unrestrained arbitrary* interpretation (the allegorical ones of Origen, Augustine, Pope Gregory the Great, Bonaventure, et al.), but also the common-sense (*sana ratio*) interpretations of the Socinians, as well as the "philosophical" interpretations of Spinoza, Kant, et al.; (2) the *slavishly bound* interpretation (for example, that of Alcuin, Albert the Great, St. Thomas, et al.); and (3) the legally free interpretation (Erasmus, Semler, Ernesti, Schleiermacher, et al.). The last direction, being scientific, in Doedes' opinion, is now on top. The inadequacy of Doedes' division lies in the fact that it is guided not so much by fundamental principles as by his own evaluations.

[20]See Augustine 2002: 116.

(moral), the foundation of which he sees in the fact that God is one but in three persons (the first refers to the Father, the second to the Son, the third to the Holy Spirit). St. Thomas made precisely the same distinction. There is the *literal* or *historical* sense, which consists in the denotation of the words themselves, and the three spiritual senses, constituting the significance of the very objects that the words indicate. These are the *allegorical* sense, the *moral* sense, which follows from the allegorical and which indicates how we should behave, and the *anagogical* sense, which refers to "objects of eternal glory."[21] However, St. Bonaventure counts seven senses (corresponding to the Seven Seals of the Apocalypse).[22] To those already mentioned, he adds: the symbolic, the synecdochal, and the hyperbolic.[23] The Kabbalah provides the best example of the kind of logical monstrosities that can arise in pursuit of hidden meanings.

Taking all this into account, I think we should replace the expedient traditional designation "*allegorical* direction in hermeneutics" by a characterization stressing an admission that words and expressions have *several* meanings as against the direction that assumes a single *definite* meaning. Setting them against each other is, as we will see, of fundamental importance. In addition, we, therefore, encounter here the first problem raised by an examination of hermeneutics in its historical context. The fact is that various hidden presuppositions underlie the distinction between the directions already examined. That is, the very concept of *meaning* is assumed to be either something that is objective or something that is psychological and subjective. In the first case, a word as a sign, which we can interpret, refers to some "thing," some object, together with the objective relations between things that are disclosed by means of interpretation. These objective relations themselves obviously bind those who communicate about them. In the second case, a word indicates only the intentions, wishes, and ideas of a communicator, and the interpretation is as free and even as arbitrary as is the communicator's wish freely to invest any meaning or set of meanings into one's words, insofar as that corresponds to the person's intentions. The *criterion* for veracity in communications of the first kind is

---

[21] See Aquinas 1911–1925: 1.10 co.; Aquinas 2.102.2. Following Thomas, Dante in *The Convivio*, Treatise 1, chapter 1, distinguishes the same four senses in *poetic* works: (1) the *literal* (*litterale*); (2) the *allegorical* (*allegorico*), which hides itself under the cover of a tale and is the truth hidden under a lovely lie, (Dante notes that theologians take this sense differently than do the poets); (3) the *moral*, which the reader should trace in order to derive for oneself usefulness and moral instruction; (4) the *anagogical* or 'above the sense,' which rises to things of eternal glory. The literal sense forms, as it were, the subject matter and material (*suggetto e materia*) of the others, particularly of the allegorical sense. Without the literal sense, it is impossible to enter into a knowledge of them. In turn, the moral and the anagogical senses are derived from the allegorical. See Dante 1889. Fraticelli quotes Buti's brief formulation: "*Litera gesta refert, quid credas allegoria, moralis quid agas, quid speres anagogia.*" ["The literal reports facts; the allegorical what you are to believe; the moral what you are to do; the anagogical what you are to hope for."] See Dante 1889: 53 f. In a letter to Can Grande, Dante also refers to the allegorical sense as "mystical" (*mysticus sensus*) and considers this designation to be common to all three senses, which are opposed to the literal or historical sense. See Dante 1920: 199.

[22] [See Revelation, Chapters 5–8.]

[23] See the examples in Doedes 1867.

by itself clear. Properly speaking, there is no criterion with a presupposition of the second type, or we must necessarily assume it consists of certain peculiarities of subjectively psychological experience itself. Thus, for example, the criterion is assumed to lie in a special kind of experience, such as intuition, inspiration, divine inspiration, etc. In other words, one can say that, given the mentioned presupposition, we have to see the objective validity of what is communicated as having an *involuntary* and *unconscious* character, or as a subordination of the will and consciousness of the communicator to something higher, something that cannot be doubted or criticized.

Of course, objective interpretation does not exclude the possibility that, in communicating something about an object and its relations, a word can, depending on the circumstances, point out this or that particular content of the object and its various moments, including also those relations (be they psychological or other) in which the communicator stands to what is being communicated. However, all of these factors are only "parts" of some objective totality and do not represent a multitude of senses and meanings. To a certain extent – and contrary to its own claims – the subjective-psychological direction must recognize this, since it itself seeks justification in the existence of the *associative transitions* that lie at the foundation of figurative speech, such as, images, tropes, allegories, etc. In other words, it itself recognizes, as it were, that there are no objective grounds for designating different meanings by a single sign and, consequently, that this occurred is only a contingent result of the history and psychology of language. The fundamental problem connected with all this lies in the following. If we can distinguish many of the senses, in terms of a large number of associative connections, their groupings and transfers, and thereby come ultimately to an arbitrary construal of the senses and meanings, how are we to understand not just the bifurcation, but even the fragmentation of the very act or "faculty" of *understanding* these various senses? Alternatively, if there are not several "faculties" of understanding but only one, then how do we explain the fact that when confronted with various aspects of an object, we, nevertheless, come to an understanding of a single object through its different contents?

## 2   Origen

Although an unambiguous interpretation would seem at first to be simple and natural, it would conceal behind that simplicity an actual complex of hermeneutical problems. Likewise, the complexity of an ambiguous interpretation requires, from the very start, justification and grounding. It is not surprising, then, that we encounter the first attempts at a theoretical justification of hermeneutic techniques among representatives professing the ambiguity of interpretation.

Apparently, the fourth book in Origen's work *Concerning First Principles* contains the first attempt at a Christian hermeneutics.[24] The foundation of Origen's

---

[24]There are references to objections against Origen from the side of Theodore of Mopsuestia, a representative of the School of Antioch, but his work *"De allegoria et historia contra Origenem"*

ideas lies in his conviction that words signify real things and relations. However, just as there is a fundamental difference between the things themselves, so there is also a difference between what the words mean. It turns out, therefore, that a word can have multiple senses. It is not difficult to detect in Origen's conception of things the echo of a peculiarly refracted and distorted Platonism. On the one hand, he distinguishes bodies and on the other substance, "which any one names as he pleases; for the Greeks call such ἀσώματον, i.e., incorporeal, while Holy Scripture declares it to be invisible."[25] Furthermore, since the Scriptures say that Christ created all things, visible and invisible (Colossians 1:16), this means that "among created things, certain 'substances' are, according to their peculiar nature, invisible. But although these are not themselves corporeal, they, nevertheless, make use of bodies, while they themselves are better than any bodily substances."[26]

Despite the crude spiritualism of this representation, it still does not predetermine an ambiguous interpretation of the words that depict such a reality. Nor does the special faculty that Origen assumes to be responsible for apprehending pure intellectuality (*intellectualia*) predetermine such an interpretation.[27] However, does the state of things really become confused, particularly in a subjective-psychological sense, when we attempt to account for how these two sorts of reality are to be reconciled? Here we must recognize one of them to be "invisible," to be "incomprehensible," etc. Such is the logic of this type of dualism. And we must recognize a faculty of a special kind for apprehending each of the realities in which we live. Thus, Origen is only being consistent when he affirms that there is also a *special* faculty for understanding the verbal expression of pure intellectualities. It is with this special "divine sense," in his words, that we "are to hear what we say and weigh what we write."[28] Since, naturally, the invisible is invisible and the unknowable is unknowable, it "cannot be expressed in general by any words (*sermonibus*) of human language."[29] Here, we acquire complete freedom for a subjective interpretation: "under this rule must be brought also the understanding of Holy Scripture, in order that its statements may be judged not according to the worthlessness of the letter, but according to the divinity of the Holy Spirit, by whose inspiration they were caused to be written."[30]

---

has been lost. Among the Alexandrians, St. Dionysius the Great, a disciple of Origen, is mentioned as an opponent of the Allegorists. (Szlagowski 1908: 261.) On the basis of the preserved excerpts, however, this can hardly be categorically affirmed (cf., for example, fragment III of his "*De promissionibus*"), although in general (as can be seen from these same fragments and from his interpretations of *Ecclesiastes* and *Job*) his exegesis is distinguished by great sobriety and restraint. (See Dilthey 1996: 242.)

[25] Origen 1895: 341–42.

[26] Cf. Origen 1895: 341–42.

[27] Origen 1895: 354–56.

[28] Cf. Origen 1895: 356.

[29] Cf. Origen 1895: 342.

[30] Cf. Origen 1895: 342. See Origen 1895: 285–291.

If some piece of writing requires divine inspiration, then it would be strange not to recognize that such inspiration is also required for reading and interpreting what was written. Origin said, "if there be no want of a desire, at least, nor of an instructor, and if divine knowledge be sought after, as it ought to be, in a religious and holy spirit, and in the hope that many points will be opened up by the revelation of God – since to human sense they are exceedingly difficult and obscure – then, perhaps, he who seeks in such a manner will find what it is lawful to discover."[31] That there is "also an inner, namely a divine sense," is revealed "by that grace alone."[32] After all this, how Origen, in fact, realizes his principles of interpretation already seems unimportant for the essence of our question. It is interesting, however, to notice the inconsistency in the following *ambiguous* interpretation. Origen distinguishes three kinds of senses in Holy Scripture – the ordinary and historical sense (*communem et historialem intellectum*), the soul of Scripture, and the spirit (*anima et spiritus*) of Scripture: "just as a person, it is said, consists of a body (corpus – σῶμα), a soul (ψυχή), and a spirit (πνεῦμα), so too Holy Scripture is given by the Divine bounty for human *salvation*."[33] However, it turns out that these three senses are not hidden behind every word in the way that, we must think, a tripartite structure is inherent in each human being. This, certainly, opens up even greater scope for arbitrariness in interpretation. On the other hand, this recognition reveals a certain feeling that, nonetheless, a word *should* have a single sense. Thus, on the one hand, "in Holy Scripture, we do not always find what we call body, i.e., a historical consistency of sense. But there are also passages in which we must understand only what we call soul or spirit."[34] On the other hand, "we clearly establish that in the majority of cases it is possible and necessary to have recourse to the truth of history. ... There is much more that conforms to history than what has merely a spiritual sense."[35]

## 3   Augustine

St. Augustine in his *De doctrina Christiana* [*On Christian Doctrine*] already gives us something like a textbook of Biblical hermeneutics, organized along the lines of a textbook on rhetoric.[36] As befitting a textbook, there are, properly speaking, neither

---

[31] Cf. Origen 1895: 297.

[32] Origen 1895: 297.

[33] Origen 1895: 301.

[34] Cf. Origen 1895: 303. Such an argument by Origen is very indicative. If the historical order were observed everywhere in Holy Scripture, we would not guess that something even deeper and more inward is contained in it. "For this reason, divine wisdom took care that in the historical sense there are certain omissions and interruptions, thereby introducing into them something impossible and incongruous." Cf. Origen 1895: 312–13.

[35] Cf. Origen 1895: 323–24.

[36] P. I – Inventio, P. II – Elocutio: "There are two things on which all interpretation of Scripture depends: the mode of ascertaining the proper meaning, and the mode of making known the meaning when it is ascertained." Augustine 1873: 7; 120–21. Books I-III in Augustine's work are

analyses nor substantiations, but only, so to speak, results. Nevertheless, from Augustine's divisions and definitions, it is clear that he saw and thought through a significant number of questions connected with the problems of sign, meaning, sense, and their understanding and interpretations. However, the same interest in the practical role of interpretation, which hindered the Alexandrians, also prevented Augustine from clarifying the purely scientific, theoretical significance of these questions.

Augustine begins his presentation in *De doctrina christiana* with a division which, in my opinion, should be placed at the base of any classification of the sciences. Up to now, neither philosophy nor, in particular, logic has thought through this division in terms of all of its fundamental significance. Every doctrine, he asserts, refers either to *things* or to *signs*. However, things are studied by means of signs. He calls that which is not used to signify something else a "thing" in the proper sense, whereas signs (for example, words) signify something. However, other things, clearly, can serve as signs, so that even one and the same thing can appear to us at one time as a thing in the proper sense and also at another time as a sign.[37] Thus, a *sign* is a thing that not only conveys its appearance to the senses, but also introduces something into thought along with itself.[38]

Augustine divides signs into *proper* ones (*propria*, which are interpreted *proprie, historice*) and *figurative* ones (*translata*, which are interpreted *figurate, prophetice*).[39] Proper signs are used to signify the things for which they were devised; figurative signs are "when the things themselves which we indicate by the proper names are used to signify something else."[40] It is impossible to deny that there is clarity and even a certain subtlety in this definition. However, it requires conclusions in the

---

devoted to the first part, the "mode of ascertaining." Book I is devoted to "things," Books II and III to "signs," and Book IV is devoted to the second part. Augustine himself speaks of the relation to rhetoric in the first chapters of Book IV. *De doctrina Christiana*, apparently, served to a certain extent as a prototype for later hermeneutics (since they serve not so much the aims of knowledge as of apologetics), remaining, by the way, free from the tedious and minute rules that are illustrated by Augustine's own example: when walking, do not lift one foot until you have put the other foot down. Augustine 1873: 72. On the connection in Roman literature between hermeneutics and rhetoric, see Immisch 1909: 34. On the anti-historical role of rhetoric in this connection, see Immisch 1909: 35.

[37] "All instruction is either about things or about signs; but things are learnt by means of signs. I now use the word 'thing' in a strict sense, to signify that which is never employed as a sign of anything else: for example, wood, stone, cattle, and other things of that kind. ... There are signs of another kind, those which are never employed except as signs: for example, words. ... and hence may be understood what I call signs: those things, to wit, which are used to indicate something else. Accordingly, every sign is also a thing; for what is not a thing is nothing at all. Every thing, however, is not also a sign." Augustine 1873: 8–9.

[38] "For a sign is a thing which, over and above the impression it makes on the senses, causes something else to come into the mind as a consequence of itself." Augustine 1873: 34.

[39] "And everything of this nature that is there narrated we are to take not only in its historical and literal, but also in its figurative and prophetical sense...." Augustine 1873: 93.

[40] Augustine 1873: 43.

pursuit of which Augustine already does not demonstrate the necessary commitment.

In the first place, given such a definition of figurative signs it is clear that in order to understand them it is necessary to know and to study the real relations themselves. Augustine does draw such a conclusion, stressing that in order to understand Holy Scripture one must have some knowledge of history, geography, physics, astronomy, etc.,[41] as well as of dialectic (which, although it does not teach us the veracity of meanings, does give us the rules for connecting truths),[42] and logic (*scientia definiendi, dividendi atque partiendi*),[43] and arithmetic.[44] However, despite the fact that even in dialectic and logic Augustine understands relations *objectively – in rerum ratione* – he seeks the *spiritual* sense[45] and *the will of God* (*voluntas Dei*[46]) in figurative signs. Furthermore, as we would expect, the fact that the will of God also turns out to be the will of the Church stamped in its dogmas[47] is not of fundamental significance. As with Origen, the problem of understanding is, therefore, eliminated without even having been properly formulated. On the one hand, we attain understanding through an acceptance of Church dogmatics.[48] On the other hand – and only with respect to the first – the divine inspiration of Scripture demands also divine inspiration from the reader.[49]

In the second place, Augustine's definition obliges us to recognize the *unique nature* of the sense behind a sign, since the apparent multitude of senses, by this definition, arises simply from the fact that the very *meaning* of a sign can function, in turn, as a sign.[50] However, it does not follow from this that the reverse, that a

---

[41] Augustine 1873: 64–67.

[42] Augustine 1873: 68–69.

[43] Augustine 1873: 71 ["Again, the science of definition, of division, and of partition…."].

[44] Augustine 1873: 73.

[45] Augustine 1873: 87.

[46] Augustine 1873: 37, 80.

[47] Augustine 1873: 41, 80ff, because of 78–79. "For whatever man may have learnt from other sources, if it is hurtful, it is there condemned; if it is useful, it is therein contained." Augustine 1873: 78.

[48] Characteristically, the criterion that Augustine offers to distinguish in Holy Scripture between figurative and literal language is the inappropriateness of the former. (We saw above that Origen saw in this a special forethought of Divine inspiration.) "Whatever there is in the word of God that cannot, when taken literally, be referred either to purity of life or soundness of doctrine, you may set down as figurative." Augustine 1873: 90. (See also Augustine 1873: 95–6.) In regard to this "hermeneutic rule," Doedes notes that it "necessarily opened the floodgates to the most unlimited caprice" (Doedes 1867: 20). However, Augustine himself accepts great freedom in the transition from literal (historical) interpretation to allegorical (spiritual) interpretation, as is apparent, as it were, from the examples of his attitude toward the interpretation of the building of the Ark, on the one hand, in which he *overly* defends the historical interpretation (Augustine 2003: 645–48), and the interpretation of the sayings of the prophets concerning Jerusalem, where he asks: "But who refuses to attach a spiritual understanding to them, if one could, or say that they should not be so interpreted by anyone who can?" Cf. Augustine 2003: 715.

[49] Augustine 1873: 117–119.

[50] It is certainly a matter of the essential connection between a sign and its sense or meaning (of the individualized context); the contingent coincidence – ambiguity – is not a rare phenomenon.

single meaning (sense), like a single content, cannot be expressed by different signs. This multitude of modes of expression (figures of speech, tropes, images, etc.) is not infrequently taken for a multitude of meanings. The multitude of expressions is a question of syntax, poetics, rhetoric, and logic. Hermeneutics, however, should start from the thesis that every sign *given* to hermeneutics has a single meaning. The basic falsehood of Biblical hermeneutics consists in the fact that it allows, as a premise, the duality of sense – human and divinely inspired – in an expression. The foundation is already then supplied by this premise: It fundamentally affirms that a sign can have several meanings.

As long as it is a matter of the "second" meaning, the one that is divinely inspired, no matter how *scientifically* the thesis of the ambiguity of a sign may be justified, all of this remains simply *extra-scientific*. However, the stubbornly consistent pursuit of this view also touches on science when this thesis rests upon a new foundation that demands recognition, viz., at least the possibility that every sign has several *literal* meanings or senses. However, such a recognition is consistent only from the standpoint of someone who recognizes the first division, as St. Augustine did, admitting that, however many senses may be found in Scripture, we must recognize them, as long as they "do not contradict the truth" and "as long as all this was intended by the divinely inspired writer, through whom God adapted his holy writings to the various degrees of understanding of the many, so that they should comprehend in these writings one and the same truth in its various forms."[51]

The whole theory of the understanding and interpretation of the words of others rests on this "intended" (*vidisse*). Is it a matter of *objective* relations, about which the author reports, or is it a matter of his *subjective* ideas of these relations? We can understand divine inspiration itself differently with this. In the first case, it may refer to the especially subtle faculty of "seeing" what is objective. In the second, it can refer to the faculty to phantasize about what is objective. Augustine, contradicting his own definition, chooses the second way of explaining the role and meaning of signs, i.e., the *psychological* way. According to such a theory, the meaning of signs and words is the idea of the communicator. It is understandable, then, that there is such ambiguity here, and how it is possible. Here is the schema of understanding in an extremely simplified form: $A$ – the thought (idea) – a sign (the pronounced or written word) – $B$ – a sign (as heard or seen) – the thought (idea).[52]

Since it requires an understanding of objective relations, it may seem that such a theory, although incorrect in general, can be correct in a particular case, when it is a matter of understanding the very person who is communicating something about

---

Nevertheless, however, homonyms essentially have not only different meanings, but they *are* also different signs. It does not matter how identical the combinations of sounds may be in words derived from various roots. For example, in Russian the word "*tri*" (the number "three") and the word "*tri*" (the imperative mood of the verb "*teret*"), or, in German, the words "*acht*" (the number "eight"), "*Acht*" ("care"), and "*Acht*" ("disgrace"), etc.

[51] Cf. Augustine 2006: 285. [The translation has been considerably adapted to fit Shpet's Russian rendering of the passage.]

[52] See Popov 1917: 282. See also the schema in St. Dionysius the Great. Dionysius 1999: 97.

objective relations. However, we must distinguish here two cases: either we understand another person through his/her words (acting as signs) about him/herself – and such a case is not different in principle from any other understanding of objective relations; or else we understand the other person through *other* signs that accompany the other's speech (mimicry, tone of voice, emotional expressions, etc.), for which we also demand an unambiguity of their meaning. The rare case is also possible where, as it were, we take *one* sign both as an objective indication and as an indication of mental excitement. Without doubt, we need a more thorough analysis, one that will reveal that what we take to be one sign with two meanings in fact consists for us of two different signs. Augustine does not make this distinction, because his psychological theory blinds him to the fact that at the foundation of understanding – in any case the understanding of a person – there is no "anamnesis," as he thought, of something known earlier, no "association," but, to use the newer terminology, a certain *originary* act that is irreducible to something else.[53]

The theory of "anamnesis," being a natural consequence of a general psychological theory of understanding, involves yet a new complication. The problem of the *veracity* of what is understood does not cease with a correct understanding, and that veracity can be established only through a verification of the objective relations in what is understood. Thus, it is natural that someone who considers what is understood to be a subjective idea about what is communicated gets into the greatest difficulty and will be unable to find *any* criterion for establishing the objectivity of the content that is communicated. Augustine did not skip over this difficulty and drew the corresponding *skeptical* conclusion.[54] But he did not provide a satisfactory resolution to this skepticism. He appeals to *mystical* experience, to "the inner truth present within our mind," to "Christ who dwells in the inner man."[55] However, this means a return in principle to one's own experience and to the experiencing process in general, i.e., a return to the start of the theory of "anamnesis" – which means running in a circle.

Moreover, when Augustine is not explaining, but presenting, he persistently stresses the correct idea that one who asks a question is to be answered only *from the point of view of the objects* that are designated by words, that we should accept or reject what is said *from the point of view of the object signified.*[56] Augustine himself suggests a way by which we should eliminate the apparent ambivalence of the meanings of a single sign when, for example, we understand the word "*homo*" both as a living being (the real interpretation) and as a noun (the grammatical interpretation).[57] However, Augustine does not know what these two ways of

---

[53] Augustine's theory of the understanding of signs is presented in his work *Concerning the Teacher* (*De magistro*), which he wrote 8 years before *On Christian Doctrine*. See especially Augustine 1938: 39–46.

[54] Augustine 1938: 51–54.

[55] Cf. Augustine 1938: 47, 48.

[56] Augustine 1938: 29–35.

[57] Augustine 1938. Cf. also the classification of the objects indicated for study. We indicate either the objects themselves without using a sign or by the use of signs – either signs or something else that is not itself a sign. (Augustine 1938: 26–29.)

studying signs mean and what role they play. He knows neither the study of signs as signs, i.e., of what *has* a meaning, nor the study of meanings as such, i.e., what a meaning *is*. Nor does he know whether these two ways exhaust the study of signs. In any case, as compared to Origen Augustine expands the subject matter of hermeneutics, adding to the problem of the ambiguity or unambiguity of a word the additional problem of *signs in general* as well as the problem of *understanding* as a transition from sign to meaning.

# Flacius [and Biblical Hermeneutics in the Renaissance]

The fundamental inadequacy of ambiguous theories of interpretation is that the presupposition of ambiguity leaves the door wide open for *arbitrary* interpretations of a text. With this presupposition, we can naturally see the absence of any method for establishing a single generally-accepted understanding. A new phase in the development of hermeneutics begins when the need for such an unambiguous interpretation is fully revealed. The Renaissance of the arts and sciences was supposed to revive an interest in hermeneutics from philologists, but apparently they were more content with the practical work of editing, criticizing, and interpreting texts than with theoretical reflection on the problem of interpretation.[1] However, the question of hermeneutics turned out to be even more vital for theology than for philology during the Reformation era. Protestant interpretation was to conflict decisively with Catholic interpretation, and this conflict could not help but lead to attempts to provide an account of the very principles of hermeneutics.

The 1567 work *The Key to Sacred Scripture or the Language of Sacred Books* [*Clavis scripturae S. seu de sermone sacrarum literarum*][2] by Matthias Flacius Illiricus Albonensis is truly a monument to the erudition and industry of the time, a work evoked by the need for a critique of Catholic Church tradition and Protestant apologetics.[3] Over the centuries, the results of the "allegorical" interpretation had their impact. Alas, its supreme criterion, viz., Church dogmatics, was forced to conform both to the tastes of the time as well as much else. The obscurity and unclarity of Sacred Scripture itself only increased the number of interpretations,

---

[1] Blass 1892: 162ff.

[2] Citing from the Basel edition of 1617. [See Flacius 1617.]

[3] On the significance of Flacius and his *Clavis*, see Dilthey 1914a: 113ff. Dilthey testifies to the great scholarship of Flacius with the following words: "Thus, this book, in fact, is a summing up of all preceding exegesis." Dilthey 1914a: 120. Dilthey here (Dilthey 1914a: 127) examines and evaluates other representatives of Protestant hermeneutics, in particular those who comprise together with Flacius the "hermeneutic triumvirate," namely Frantze and Glasius. See Frantze 1619 and Glasius 1623. A *general* examination of Flacius' intellectual development is sufficient for our purposes.

© Springer Nature Switzerland AG 2019
G. Shpet, T. Nemeth, *Hermeneutics and Its Problems*, Contributions
To Phenomenology 98, https://doi.org/10.1007/978-3-319-98941-9_2

which frequently contradicted each other. This not only happened with the new "Papists," but also with the Church Fathers themselves.[4]

Nevertheless, it was necessary to return to the text itself and to find the means to eliminate its difficulties as well as the rules for understanding it. Already in the preface, Flacius complains that no one studies the text with the proper diligence. Moreover, if they do study it, they ignore the context, the whole, and the general purpose of the work.[5] A demand arises from this to return to the study of the text and to interpret it according to the principle that Flacius now prioritizes in his hermeneutics, namely, to understand each particular element in the context of the whole and in terms of its purpose, coordinating each part with the rest in strict correspondence and interrelation.[6] He never tires of returning to this demand, since only with its fulfillment can one overcome all the difficulties and misunderstandings that have been generated by the arbitrary interpretation of Sacred Scripture by the "Papists and the Sophists": "It is all the more necessary, then, to show pious diligence in looking for the sense of the separate passages in terms of both the intention of the passage itself and the entire context."[7]

Flacius intended his *Clavis* to be a kind of encyclopedia from which Protestants could draw material and learn techniques both for the struggle with the Papists and for the creation of their own exegesis. The first part of his *Clavis* contains a meticulous and detailed dictionary[8] of Biblical terms. One must seek hermeneutical rules and advice in the varied content of the second part, the aim of which he character-

---

[4] Flacius also recognizes the obscurity of Holy Scripture and diligently enumerates the reasons (51 of them) for this. See Flacius 1617: vol. 2, 1–6.

[5] Flacius 1617: vol. 1, preface: "…not one of them has interpreted the text itself and the words of the Scriptures with utmost care. Even when, it would seem, that they wish to interpret some sacred book, they often digress in explaining the content, followed then by allegory and exercises in eloquence. Citing examples from Scripture in their true sense, they are more likely to pay attention to elegant and well-chosen phrases than to the integrity of the narrative's fabric. Is this not unlike a person, who, plucking little flowers from a field to suit one's fancy, would fashion wreaths and garlands; or like one who, expressing his own thought in the words of another, would stitch together a kind of patchwork quilt."

[6] Flacius 1617: vol. 1, preface: "It follows from this that the true sense of Scripture could never be grasped when the text was separated into parts like the straws of untied brooms. The fact is that the true sense of the Holy Scriptures, as well as of all other writings, surely depends in the majority of cases on the context, the aim of what was written, and the correlation and congruence of its parts and, so to speak, of its members. As is the case everywhere else too, the individual parts of some whole are best understood by taking into account the undivided whole as well as the other parts and the harmony of the whole."

[7] Flacius 1617: vol. 2, 26.

[8] Likewise, Flacius distinguishes 17 meanings of the word "*Spiritus*" in Holy Scripture and gives an ingenious classification of the nine meanings of the word "*Gratia*," a classification of the meanings of the word "*benedicere*," and a very original classification of the word "*peccatum*" ("sin"), etc. See Flacius 1617: vol. 2, 1159–1166; Flacius 1617: vol. 2, 377; Flacius 1617: vol. 2, 859.

izes as *synthetic*.[9] He emphasizes here his own innovation: "In fact, I found few whom I could follow as guides or, as it were, assist in their effort, having turned to them for help and advice."[10] However, in reality he found assistance, full of advice, in *rhetoric*, which, since antiquity, had been closely connected with hermeneutical considerations. Flacius connects his hermeneutics with the rhetoric of Melanchthon, who, in turn, understood the central tasks of rhetoric in the spirit of the tasks of hermeneutics – it "helps in the reading of good authors."[11]

Since in his *Clavis* Flacius pursues exclusively practical goals, we cannot expect him to meet our theoretical demands with respect to hermeneutics. Nevertheless, several aspects of his argument deserve to be noted, insofar as we can extract from them material for determining the problems that are part and parcel of hermeneutics. Above all, his attitude toward allegorical interpretation, i.e., toward the question of ambiguous and unambiguous interpretation, deserves attention. He refers quite negatively toward Origen's interpretations, precisely owing to their allegorical nature.[12] Flacius then traces the *fourfold* meaning of Holy Scripture (the literal sense, the moral or tropological sense, the allegorical sense, and the anagogical sense)[13] proceeding from Origen and that became traditional among Catholic writers after Augustine. Flacius, "in order to facilitate my work," mentions the opinions of other authors in this regard. Incidentally, while giving a consistent account of the history of ambiguous exegesis in Hyperius's[14] words, Flacius shares Melanchthon's opinion, which to him is well-founded (*sane probatur*) ("unconditionally satisfies him") and which offers a harsh critique of the "four-part" (*quadrivariam*) interpretation, "since the general sense becomes uncertain when broken up into so many

---

[9] Flacius 1617: vol. 1, preface: "Here is why, having discussed in the first part the meaning of individual terms, particularly difficult ones, and of expressions arising from them, I have now in this new part, following a synthetic order, discussed various Hebraisms, paying attention to various rules and even whole treatises arranged according to parts of speech, tropes, and figures, and finally according to whole sentences." Of the seven treatises of the second part, two of them (IV and V) are concerned with rhetoric and one with grammar, while the first two deal directly with hermeneutics. The content of the second of these treatises is adequately expressed by its title: *Sententiae ac regulae patrum de ratione discendi Sacras Literas*. (By the way, it also contains a treatise on hermeneutics by the African Bishop Junilius, pp. 201ff.) Consequently, it is the *first* treatise – *De ratione cognoscendi Sacras Literas* – that attracts our greatest attention. [The editor has been unable to confirm Shpet's remark concerning Junilius. However, see another work: Flacius 1624: 651–657.]

[10] [Flacius 1617: vol. 2, 1.]

[11] Dilthey 1914a: 119.

[12] "As one distinguished Church Father wrote, Origen replaced Divine mysteries with a game of his mind." Flacius 1617: vol. 2, 64. [The Russian text incorrectly gives the reference as vol. 1.]

[13] Cf. Augustine 2002: 116.

[14] [Rendered in comformity with the German translation. The Russian text gives the name as "Hinerius." Andreas Gerhard Hyperius (1511–1564), real name Andreas Gheeraerdts, was a Flemish Protestant theologian. Flacius mentions him in his text.]

meanings."[15] Nevertheless, Melanchthon admits that there are also statements in Holy Scripture that must be interpreted allegorically. Flacius follows him, trying to set such an interpretation within a framework of conformity to law and suggesting in his "observations" certain conditions and rules, the observance of which must guard against the abuses of allegorical interpretation.

Thus, there is, as it were, a certain wavering: on the one hand, Melanchthon recognized unambiguity as a principle of interpretation, and Flacius finds this well-founded (*sane probatur*) ("unconditionally satisfies"). On the other hand, he recognized "observations" as the principle of allegorical interpretation.[16] We are presently concerned with a transitional phase in the development of hermeneutics and as such this should not be considered strange: the new and correct principle had been noted, but (1) no theoretical rationale had yet been found for it; (2) it was impossible to deny the *fact* that there is allegory in speech. However, as long as the principle is unjustified, there is doubt as to whether it is compatible with this fact, and if it is, just how it is. The most difficult thing of all is precisely to answer both questions affirmatively at the same time, i.e., to recognize that unambiguity does *not* exclude allegory, and that one need not regard allegory as only a *second sense* where one is already present.

Additionally, there is the unconditional instability of the very concepts of "sense" and "meaning," for we must not forget that it was precisely attempts like those of Flacius that led, and lead, to *a theory of sense* and not vice versa. Otherwise, theory would have preceded, and we would only have to define the extent to which it was consistently put into practice or "sustained."[17] If we keep in mind the *historical*

---

[15] [Flacius 1617: vol. 2, 65.] Cf. "However, we will remember that a single, precise, and simple sense ultimately should be sought everywhere according to the teachings of grammar, dialectic, and rhetoric. For speech that does not have an unambiguous, simple sense conveys nothing definite. If figures of speech are encountered in the narrative, they must not generate ambiguities, but, on the contrary, in conformity with the usual principles of speech, give a single sense that conforms with everything that is being presented. Here, however, someone may ask whether there is nowhere a place for other senses. To this I answer that if we begin arbitrarily to ascribe various shades of sense to everything, there would be nothing definite in Scripture. Thus, Origen is surely refuted, since he transforms everything, however simply it was said, into allegory." Flacius 1617: vol. 2, 66–67.

[16] This wavering was the basis of Dilthey's evaluation of Flacius' views as less than they are worth. Further on I will offer grounds for my own higher estimation. Dilthey 1914a: 124.

[17] The question concerning what constitutes the meaning of a word or concept is until now still not properly resolved. The fluctuation in the concept of "sense" arises not only from this status of the question, but also from the substitution of such a solution by the vulgar opinion that the "meaning" of a word is a "representation." However, in the most elementary formulation of the question it also arises simply from the unfulfilled requirement of at least a *conditional* distinction between "meaning" and "sense." In order to make it easier for the reader to follow the development of my ideas, I propose, in a preliminary way, prior to a more precise analysis, that the following distinction be kept in mind. *The meaning of a word or a concept* – for a *concept is a word* viewed in its logical function – is that part of the corresponding object's content that we connect with the word as long as we consider the word independently of the context in which we use it. Thus, for example, we find the meaning of foreign words in dictionaries of the appropriate languages. When we examine words or concepts in the context in which they are concretely given, which of course is always unique, we are looking for their *sense*.

point of view on the matter, we will have to recognize that in reality Melanchthon and Flacius approached the clearest solution to the problem of ambiguity, which can be formulated as follows: if we speak about the ambiguity of the *senses* of a single word or expression, this arises solely from the fact that *one and the same* word is found in *many passages* (contexts). "In itself," or absolutely, a word has no sense. However, a word has only *one sense* in *each given passage*. It follows from this that the central problem of hermeneutics turns out to be the same task that Flacius clearly formulated as the fundamental hermeneutic demand, viz., the relation of a part to the whole, of an interpreted expression to the context.[18]

Just how close Melanchthon and Flacius were to the given formulation is clear from the following excerpt: "I thought it necessary to say at this point the following concerning the four senses. Let everyone be reminded that a single, simple, and precise sense should be sought in each individual passage, a meaning that is *compatible with the general context of the narrative and with the facts of the matter*. One must not look everywhere for allegories or rashly invent some other sense from the grammatical meaning. On the contrary, *one must see what is appropriate in each passage* without inventing anything that contradicts the articles of faith."[19]

It seems to me that this excerpt not only anticipates the resolution of the task that Flacius had set for himself, but also designates in advance the method that one should employ to solve every particular task of interpretation. This method can be called the method of *specification and individualization*, since it leads from a general sign to a special meaning, from the concept's general scope to its specific sense, from the common parts to a single whole, from the means to its end and intention. Applying this method is by no means just a simple juxtaposition of "parallels,"[20] but is something considerably more complex, as Flacius reveals with considerable conscientiousness and an understanding of the matter.

Flacius clearly distinguishes two "kinds" of interpretation, which Augustine had already outlined, viz., the grammatical and the real. Moreover, he establishes their inner consistency and the inner transitions from the very first to the culminating phase in the entire process of interpretation. To be precise, he recognizes the following four steps in the process of understanding (*quadruplex intelligentia*)[21]:

1. The initial understanding is that by which the reader understands individual words and sounds (*qua Lectores voces singulas intelligant*); it requires knowledge of the appropriate language;
2. The second understanding is that by which the sense of what is being said is understood, where what is being said consists of words in individual periods (*qua sensum orationis, quem verba in singulis periodis constituunt, intelligant*).

---

[18] See above. Dilthey himself stresses the sense of this formulation of the question, calling it "Schleiermacherian" and even (possibly to the detriment of Melanchthon's claim to priority) calls this formulation Flacius' "discovery" (Dilthey 1914a: 122).

[19] Flacius 1617: vol. 2, 69. [Shpet added the emphasis here to the Latin text.]

[20] Dilthey once again simplifies Flacius' point of view. See Dilthey 1914a: 121, 123.

[21] Flacius 1617: vol. 2, 82.

Here one must not only understand the individual words, but also correctly connect what must be connected and separate what must be separated;

3. The third understanding is that by which the mind of the speaker is understood,
where it is a matter of understanding not only the fact, but also the cause and aim
of what is said ("by which listeners understand the spirit of the speaker, whether
it be God, a prophet, an apostle, or an evangelist. By 'mind,' I mean the reason,
the thought, the intention, the idea of the speaker. In this way, one understands
not only what is said, but also why and the purpose behind it.")[22];

4. The fourth understanding is that by which the particular use of every passage in
Holy Scripture is understood (*qua uniuscujusque Scripturarum loci usus aliquis
intelligatur*). He is motivated by the words of the Apostle: "All scripture is given
by inspiration of God, and is profitable for doctrine, for reproof, for correction,
for instruction in righteousness: That the man of God may be perfect, thoroughly
furnished unto all good works" (2 Timothy 3: 16–17).

The first two moments of his "four-fold understanding" refer to *grammar.* ("You can
refer these two understandings of a text to grammar. Grammar, therefore, is its own
sort of interpretation.") The next two are *theological* understandings. ("They can be
embraced under the general title of a theological interpretation of Scripture."[23]).

This schema may not satisfy us in many respects. Above all, it is precisely a
*schema.* Behind it, there is nothing that justifies its analysis and no indication of its
principles. We saw in Augustine, unlike in Flacius, a premonition of the need for an
ontological analysis of the *sign.* There is also no analysis of the act of understanding
as a transition from a sign to what it signifies. On the contrary, the same psychologistic conviction that we saw in Augustine leads Flacius away from a strictly objective interpretation of Holy Scripture and toward the subjective "spirit," toward the
thoughts and intentions of the author of the interpreted expression. Perhaps the
absence of a theory of signs in particular favored this deviation. Overall, however,
we undoubtedly stand on the threshold of a genuinely scholarly formulation of the
problem, and in this regard it is worthwhile to pause longer on certain aspects of
Flacius' *Clavis.*

We saw that the presupposition of the ambiguity of Holy Scripture was alone
already sufficient to generate great arbitrariness in Biblical hermeneutics. The criterion and the supreme sanction to which one was supposed to turn in cases of difficulty and unclarity were based on the dogmas and decrees of the Church. The
Church's abuse of this power is just as natural as the disgusting forms these abuses
assumed. Melanchthon's and Flacius' assertion of the principle of unambiguity was
already a definite protest against these abuses and arbitrariness in Biblical interpretation on the part of the "Papists and Sophists." However, what new criterion did
they nominate to take the place of Church dogmatics?

This question is more difficult to answer, because Flacius did not deny the divine
inspiration of Holy Scripture. So long as it is not a matter of the formal requirements

---

[22] [Flacius 1617: vol. 2, 82.]
[23] [Flacius 1617: vol. 2, 83.]

(of grammar and dialectic) but of *real* interpretation, Melanchthon nominated *theology*, as a discipline, to be this decisive authority. That is, one must appeal to the principles and definitions of this discipline as they are formulated in the so-called "*Loci communes.*"[24] The latter, according to Melanchthon, play the role of *loci* (*topoi*), which are known in rhetoric as the ultimate grounds on which the principal dispute should rest. This designation is then in general extended to the fundamental, universally-recognized firm foundations of every discipline, and hence of theology in particular.[25] This is, certainly, a new step forward and is quite indicative of the era of Humanism and the Reformation, but the fundamental grounds for replacing Church *dogmas* with the *dogmas* of theology are not clear. Ultimately – and history confirms this – the new criterion permitted the same arbitrariness that had prevailed earlier. Protestant theology followed the path that had already been laid out by the Catholic Church, and the Catholic Church itself readily turned to its own theology for support.

Flacius is also interesting by virtue of the fact that he illuminates, if not the fundamental grounds by which preference should be given to the new authority, then at least the psychological grounds for such preference. They are specified quite clearly in the first volume of his *Clavis* in the essay "Interpretari." Within the Church, he says, there is a dispute as to who has the authority to interpret Holy Scripture. In his opinion, *every conscientious* and *prudent* person has this right on the condition that he or she agree with Scripture as a whole and consider the entire context and possess a fear of God. It is unacceptable that the Pope should usurp this authority and arbitrarily invest Holy Scripture with a sense from which no one then dare deviate. One may simply not deviate from what in the clear words of God is obvious and reliable.[26]

There can be no doubt as to the inner sense of all this. Flacius appeals to *common sense* as an authority. True, together with this there still remain "faith" and the "obviousness of the word of God." However, it is clear that they can now be checked with the help of common sense. This checking is organized in the "science" of theology. Here, the transition from common sense to "science" is direct and immediate,

---

[24] Flacius 1617: vol. 2, 66.

[25] See Melanchthon 2007: 66 – As a rule … in every art there are topics or places where the very essence of each art is concentrated. These topics or places are for us the goal to which we direct all of our efforts. Cf. Melanchthon 1900: 33 f.

[26] Flacius 1617: vol. 1, 464–65: "In the Church, there is a dispute about the interpretation of Scripture: Who has this power? The true answer is that *every* devout person, especially a rational person or one endowed with such a gift, has the right to interpret Scripture, but certainly after comparing Scriptural passages, considering the context and subject matter, and praying reverently to God that the entire interpretation may be compatible with faith. Above all, however, it should be known that by no means must the Church admit that kind of juridical and bureaucratic interpretation which the Pontiff and his Councils now usurp so as, at their own pleasure, to attribute some specific meaning to Scriptural passages on the basis of their authority or even of their plenary power, a sense from which no one, no matter how much better his own perceptions, can or should presume to, depart. Indeed, the following rule should always be unwaveringly observed. No one – not even an angel – can change the meaning of Holy Scripture, since the word of God must be seen in no other way than that proven with obvious clarity."

since the techniques in both are unified here *by one and the same logic* and since the word "science" *here* is only a more refined designation for "common sense."

A considerable amount of time will be required before theology will proceed to constitute itself as a *science* (no longer in quotation marks), and will pass from the abstract logic of common sense to the concrete logic of historical facts (as in Christian Baur).[27] Incidentally, this takes place under the influence of the development of hermeneutics itself, which from then on embarks on a new path. In any case, the simultaneous recognition of the two authorities mentioned above is clearly from the historical point of view a temporary and transitional phase but one that is hardly sustainable, since the specific essences of their different tendencies will begin to show. This simultaneous recognition can be explained quite clearly from a psychological point of view as the position of the new hermeneutics, a position that hermeneutics assumed in Protestantism under the influence of a *protest*. We still have no idea here of a *pure* theory of hermeneutics, a theory free from the influence of both practical demands as well as psychological presuppositions.

In accordance with these two criteria, Flacius also provides two sets of rules for interpreting Holy Scripture.[28] It seems rather interesting to me to mention one aspect that conclusively determines the essence of this new phase in the development of hermeneutics. It is neither a matter of the practicality of the practical guidelines he gives for a correct interpretation nor of the truly scholastic refinements with which he surrounds its method, but of a certain illumination that radiates from them toward his fundamental principle, viz., that one must understand the part from the whole and the text from the context. Both sets of rules are directed toward a single goal: to show how one should in fact use this principle. The first set of rules goes with two (Old and New Testament, "the Law and the Gospels") basic presuppositions of theology: What God says is true ("Everything God says is true. This is in no need of proof, since such is the first principle of all *theology*, deservedly revered by every creature."),[29] and the Prophets' description of the Messiah is quite correct ("Everything that the Old Testament or the prophets foretold about the Messiah and about everything else is true. In other words, the prophets gave a true description of the Messiah.").[30] Every separately interpreted passage consistent with all the *parallel passages*, must, in the final analysis, be connected to these fundamental principles, and we can, thus, count on creating from Holy Scripture a certain internally consistent *theological system* – a *corpus theologiae*. The creation of such a system,

---

[27] [See the work Baur 1824–25. Ferdinand Christian Baur (1792–1860), who taught at Tübingen University, was a pioneer in historical theology. His methodology was strongly influenced by Hegelian philosophy of history.]

[28] On the one hand, "The Rules for Understanding Holy Scripture *drawn from Scripture itself*" (Flacius 1617: vol. 2, 7) are based, that is to say, on certain information in Holy Scripture itself and on a rigorous theological elaboration of it. On the other hand, "The Precepts for a Proper Reading of Holy Scripture *collected or thought by our own judgment*" (Flacius 1617: vol. 2, 21), i.e., what I characterize as "common sense."

[29] [Flacius 1617: vol. 2, 9.]

[30] [Flacius 1617: vol. 2, 9.]

with the appropriate allocation of all commonplaces (*locorum communium*),[31] is, therefore, the culmination of all knowledge (*cognoscendi*) of Holy Scripture, for which, by the way, hermeneutics serves as a means.[32]

The second set of rules establishes the following sequence in the search for sense. First, one must define the *aim* of the work as a whole ("in the first place, you must know the aim or intention of the entire given work – its, so to speak, head or face").[33] Second, one must include the entire argument on the whole ("so that you can include the entire argument, its basic thrust, and an abbreviated presentation of its main point. On the one hand, I call the 'argument' a succinct indication of the aim and, on the other hand, a brief outline of the entire work.").[34] Third, drawing up a general arrangement or allocation for the entire work is recommended so that all the parts can be seen in their mutual relationship to the whole, in particular to the goal ("that before your eyes you have a depiction of the arrangement or division of the entire book or work; that you must observe with special care where, so to speak, to find the head, breast, legs, etc. You should consider with accuracy in mind, then, what kind of body it is, how it embraces all those members, in what way all these members or parts fit together to create this single body; what is the nature of the connection, correlation, and proportion of the individual members, between themselves, whether in relation to the whole and in particular to the head itself.").[35] Fourth, Flacius considers it useful to draw up a synoptic table that would make it possible conceptually to survey, quickly and easily, all of the parts of the whole being studied, and to fix them in one's memory ("It would also be useful to make a chart breaking down this single body into so many different parts. In this way, you will be able to have a clearer understanding of this work in your mind and to fix it more firmly in your memory. You will, then, have everything together before your eyes, everything in a synopsis, as though it could be grasped in a single glance.").[36]

However, what really happens if we carry out this complete program? We will have a certain abstract schema, all the parts of which, let us assume, we can easily see in their mutual relationships. Let us also assume that this is *what* is called *understanding*, or the disclosure of sense. However, from what does Flacius accurately derive the certainty that this *abstract* schema precisely conveys the *living* content of what is understood, something that, by his own comparison, must be an *organism*? We *dissect* this organism, but in so doing do we not lose sight precisely of its spirit, life, and movement? In Flacius, there is, obviously, an additional presupposition – again, in the spirit of his time – of a pseudo correspondence between abstract-logical constructions and the vital life of thought.

---

[31] See the table [*Declaratio Tabulae*] on Flacius 1617: vol. 2, 53.

[32] [We should recall here that Philipp Melanchthon's chief work was entitled *Loci communes rerum theologicarum seu hypotyposes theologicae*.]

[33] Flacius 1617: vol. 2, 22. Praecepta 9.

[34] [Flacius 1617: vol. 2, 22. Praecepta 10.]

[35] [Flacius 1617: vol. 2, 22, Praecepta 11.]

[36] [Flacius 1617: vol. 2, 22, Praecepta 12.]

If we now compare Flacius' schema with his "fourfold understanding," we find a great discrepancy between them. The issue here concerns the relations between *things* that are rigorously interconnected with each other and, according to his rules, are revealed nothing short of automatically. Flacius promised us to penetrate into an author's thoughts, ideas, and intentions. However, where is true understanding; to what should it lead? This is a serious deficiency – the *absence of any analysis of the very act of understanding*, the absence of a disclosure of the sign's meaning. The correction of this deficiency is obviously an urgent problem, which hermeneutics vitally needs to solve, just as there is a deficiency in Flacius' theory of signs. Therefore, even though indirectly, i.e., by a negative route, we do come to these problems, as problems, without which hermeneutics cannot be constructed. For their solution should form the *ready-made* presuppositions without which there can be no hermeneutics and which hermeneutics cannot provide *by its own means*. Along with the positive route to which Flacius' work led, we face here a large number of quite varied tasks.

Unambiguity – in place of ambiguity – is the most important of Flacius' positive directions. His abstract schematism turned out to be the reverse side of this direction, since it is not clear how, from it, we come to a sense and what understanding is. However, when we emphasize the logical and ontological moments we obtain something new. We saw that, starting from the simple substitution of scientific dogmatics for Church dogmatics, it is difficult to guess Flacius' next step forward. But if we keep in mind that the substitution of the authority of logic for the authority of the Church is a transition from the *practical* stage in the development of hermeneutics to the stage of its *theoretical* consideration, then its *novelty* becomes noticeable. This theoretical consideration is still not *pure*, and owing to its abstractness it clearly is insufficient. However, another new question then arises, although again by a negative path. Namely, how do we find a *purely* theoretical approach to hermeneutics and, above all, indicate its genuinely scientific orientation, and not the quasi-scientific one that the theology of the time represented? With this new scientific orientation, we can hope that hermeneutics will find a clearer formulation of the problem of the *relation of meaning to sense* and *of the actual process of understanding* and interpretation. We hope to find also the fundamental grounding for all the problems that *go beyond grammar and rhetoric*, disciplines to which the fate of hermeneutics in Flacius' work was still entirely bound. Along with this, the hope rises that by seeking a correct scientific orientation for hermeneutics we will get closer to the *locus* of those fundamental problems, the resolution of which would give scientific foundations and presuppositions to hermeneutics.

# General Remarks on the Relation of the Sciences [to Hermeneutics] as a Transition to Ernesti

Hermeneutics is not an independent science, but only an auxiliary discipline in scientific work. To reveal its place in the system of knowledge means, above all, to specify the cycle of scientific questions in relation to which hermeneutics plays an auxiliary role. Up until now, *practical* interests have stood in the foreground among those writers who have thought about the problems of hermeneutics. They wondered little about the problem of the scientific nature of the subject matter that led them to their concerns with interpretation. It was necessary to become aware of the *theoretical* value of this subject matter in order to pose the problem regarding the place of hermeneutics fully and with the appropriate clarity.

A determination of the scientific subject matter, a study of which demands hermeneutical techniques, reveals also that aspect in the *logic* on which these techniques rest. In this respect, the development of hermeneutics up until now has also proceeded blindly. Logic as a science was not involved in the grounding of its methodological techniques. It is true, Flacius was led, it seems, in precisely this direction. However, what essentially was the *purpose* behind his need of logic? He sought a criterion to replace the rejected authority of the Catholic Church. However, there was also a practical interest, particularly in the formulation that we find in Flacius. He had no need of logic as a theoretical foundation of hermeneutics, but of logic as *volgo dicta*, i.e., common sense systematized according to a certain abstract schema.

Nevertheless, hermeneutics sooner or later had to turn toward logic. That is, it had to see a *sign* not only as an object, but also as a *concept*. Its fate was foreordained for this. Already from its first steps, its fate was connected with the sermocinales disciplines (*scientiae sermocinales* – to use medieval terminology): grammar, rhetoric, and logic. It seemed that the break with grammar and *rhetoric*,[1] the

---

[1] [The editors of the German translation point out that the typed manuscript they used as their basic text reads at this point "grammar and *logic*." They go on, however, to point out that the manuscript copy in the Lenin Library reads "grammar and rhetoric." See Špet 1993: 84f. Apparently, the editor of the latest Russian edition of this work, T. G. Shchedrina, agrees with the reasoning of the German editors, for the text simply follows the latter reading.]

© Springer Nature Switzerland AG 2019
G. Shpet, T. Nemeth, *Hermeneutics and Its Problems*, Contributions
To Phenomenology 98, https://doi.org/10.1007/978-3-319-98941-9_3

beginning of which we observed in Flacius, led hermeneutics to logic. However, Flacius' disregard of a *theory of signs*, which I have noted, perhaps played a role. It seems Augustine already had viewed such a theory only either from the grammatical side (*De Magistro*) or the ontological side (*De doctrina Christiana*), but not from its logical side. On the other hand, medieval logic with its valuable dispute about universals, particularly by the Nominalists and in a sharper and more comprehensive form by William of Ockham, succeeded in providing precisely a deep and many-sided analysis of the logical theory of signs. Luther knew and respected Ockham and quoted Gabriel Biel by heart. However, it was certainly not owing to their logic that they were interesting to him.[2] Protestantism, following behind Humanism, had an excessive admiration for what was *its own*. Not only in its own time, but for a very long time afterward, it slandered all of Scholasticism. The history of European thought has had to pay for this and is still paying for it to this day. Protestantism's peculiar *skepticism* in relation to traditional philosophy, which for so long had been exploited by Catholicism, placed all of this philosophy under suspicion. This included – and perhaps especially – logic. A decisive turning point was needed, one with palpable fruits for philosophy itself, to change this attitude toward it. Only as a consequence of all this could one expect essential changes in the formulation and solution to the hermeneutical problems that interest us.

Therefore, in order to satisfy all the demands that we have presented to hermeneutics up to now, one *general condition,* above all, had to emerge: a change in the general conception of philosophy and, in particular, in the conception of what such a pure science itself is. All the problems concerning the grounding of hermeneutics that we have noted up to now should take on a new look in this new light. One may divide them broadly into two groups: on the one hand, questions arose concerning the object of understanding and interpretation; on the other hand, questions arose concerning the very processes of understanding and interpretation.

The century that followed the Reformation era brought with it a new conception of philosophy, which was to shed new light on the sense and subject matter of both of these groups of questions. The more *rationalism* delved into ontology, the more deeply *empiricism* penetrated into its investigation of the processes of consciousness. Thus, the needed new horizons were opened up and expanded. It was in the eighteenth century that the constructive rationalism of an earlier time was replaced, with increasing energy, by a rationalism with a rational foundation, a *rational rationalism*, and the results and fruits of the new philosophy already became clear. This century was also to introduce something *new* and decisive for the questions that interest us. The problem of *historical knowledge*, in both its ontological and its logical formulation, raised by rationalism in the most *generalized* form, was to prove

---

[2] To what extent Luther himself, with his understanding of a word, its meanings and its means of interpretation, could and did promote the movement of hermeneutical thought would require a special investigation. Theophilos's work in some respects is interesting, but it has an excessively apologetic tone, and it modernizes Luther to such an extent that it is difficult to rely on it as an investigation. See, in particular, Theophilos 1870: 59ff.

especially fruitful for these questions.[3] However, the second group of questions was also placed on a new foundation, although not yet one of principle, but still a theoretical, scientific foundation, to the extent that *psychology* was organized as a science at that time.

The semi-reform of logic that was initiated by Ramus in the middle of the sixteenth century could not facilitate the correct formulation of the problem of hermeneutics. Instead, it further complicated the situation to the extent that the logic of Ramus and his followers, as an *ars bene disserendi*,[4] was more closely connected with rhetoric. However, apparently the pressing need for a serious reform of logic was strongly felt in the sixteenth century in connection with both philosophical and non-philosophical interests. Is this not the reason for the renewed interest in Llull's *Ars Magna*? Although not a logic,[5] it stood to logic up to then in some not yet properly determined relationship.[6] Llull's work was published together with treatises about him by some of the most famous men of the sixteenth century – one who opened the century, and another who brought it to a close – namely, Agrippa von Nettesheim and Giordano Bruno.[7]

Llull's *Ars Magna* still continued to attract attention in the seventeenth century. It was improved upon (by Kircher), and in the second half of the century it was detached from cabalistic and ignorant hopes and elaborated into an original conception of a theory of signs as a universal "philosophical language."[8] Leibniz conceived such a *Lingua characteristica universalis* as a kind of *Ars inveniendi et judicandi*. It is not difficult for us to see in this very combination, or division, of its tasks the influence of rhetoric with its basic division into two parts. Nevertheless, as the idea of an *Ars signorum*, it points to the felt need to fill in a gap in the discussion of philosophical principles. The form in which Leibniz expressed his idea – as an *Ars characteristica combinatoria* – did not meet with special sympathy on the part of Wolff.[9] Or perhaps, as some[10] think, Wolff simply did not fully understand Leibniz's true intentions. (Wolff was not acquainted with Leibniz's most important ideas concerning this problem and which were published by Raspe only in 1765.[11]) In any case, Wolff and the Wolffians did not elaborate this idea further. In this respect, the only successors of Leibniz in the eighteenth century were Ploucquet and Lambert with the latter's *Semiotik*.

---

[3] See Shpet 1916.

[4] [Latin: art of speaking well.]

[5] See Shpet 1916: 84f.

[6] Couturat's zeal testifies to this, but it is obvious even apart from this zeal.

[7] Lullii 1651.

[8] Dalgarno 2001. Wilkins 2002. Concerning the history of this question, see Couturat 1901: in particular chapters 3, 4 and the notes on page 541ff.

[9] See Wolfio 1732: §297ff. [page 210ff].

[10] See, for example, Semler 1822: 8. The first edition dates from 1811.

[11] [See Leibnitz 1765. As the German translation notes, Shpet's reference here is surely to Rudolf Eric Raspe, who edited for the first time Leibniz's work *New Essays on Human Understanding*. Shpet's Russian text gives Raspe's name as Raske. See Shpet 2005: 278.]

Therefore, although it was connected to logic, the theory of signs was at one time ousted from strictly logical treatises, and at another time, it was included in them. In any case, however, it, becoming a theory of the "logical calculus," lost the qualities that could make it interesting for hermeneutics. A "sign," in this new formulation of the problem, was understood to be not correlative to *meaning*, but to be a token or "characteristic." Already as early as the seventeenth century, even in the logic texts that paid some attention to the issue of the *signum*, signs were conceived predominantly as "indicators" or "tokens."[12] Thus, the disclosure of the nature of signs held little promise for hermeneutics. All of this, by the way, already concerned the "reformed" logicians. The "peripatetic" logicians, or, more precisely, those who followed Peter of Spain and his *Summulae logicales*[13] – which, however, was updated on occasion by Duns Scotus and William of Ockham – continued to reproduce the old scholastic materials in the section *de terminorum proprietatibus*. They at one time compressed and then at another time expanded this material. In their theory of the *signum*, they sometimes went all the way back to Augustine's own definitions.[14]

However may we regard the value of the results obtained by science and philosophy, even if the idea of an *Ars Magna* were finally realized, we would still have to recognize that this very idea decisively diverted attention away from the problems that arose for philosophy in connection with the hermeneutical requirements of knowledge. We have already noted two groups of such questions above:

1. the problem of the sign *together* with its correlative meaning, and
2. the cognitive process as an act of transition from sign to meaning.

As long as meaning has a place in hermeneutics – and without it there would be no hermeneutics – and however we may solve the problem of the sign taken in its peculiar correlation to meaning, we will not lose sight of the problem itself. The search for an "authority" that sanctions our transition from a sign to its true meaning also guarantees the very existence of the problem. As we saw, after the work of Melanchthon and Flacius the problem of the theoretical *principles* of such a sanction was clearly raised. Having repudiated – at least unjustifiably – the earlier work

---

[12] See, for example, the popular logic textbooks by [Franco] Burgersdijck, [Adrianus] Heereboort, [Johannes] Scharfius, et al. (The fourth edition of Heereboort's logic is significant owing to its very valuable notes.) [Shpet's reference is to a 1690 edition, which this editor has been unable to locate. However, see Heereboort 1680.] Scharfius's work was also republished with commentary by Stübelius. See Scharfii 1694. The Port-Royal logic devotes only one very small chapter (chapter IV) to "signs."

[13] [Reading with Špet 1993: 89 instead of *Summula*, as in Shpet 2005: 279.]

[14] For example, I encountered this in a seventeenth century Jesuit textbook. See Casilio 1629: 23. [Shpet refers here not to this edition, but to one from 1635, which this editor was unable to locate.] Speaking of the "Peripatetics," I have in mind the texts *only* of the conservative Catholic logicians, excluding therefore *all* the opponents of Ramus. There were a number of these among the representatives of Lutheran Protestantism, beginning with Melanchthon himself. These were the so-called *Philippists* (the mixed or Philippo-Ramists – the semi-Ramists, pseudo-Ramists – formed a special group), who also could be characterized as "Peripatetics." Cf. Waddington 1855: 394.

of the Scholastics, in particular that of William of Ockham, modern theology remained without philosophical foundations. It was necessary to wait until philosophy itself came to formulate the problems that were essential to theology and until the demands that philosophy had to satisfy in the interests of theology would be presented to it by another science with analogous interests. In the eighteenth century, as I have noted, both of these happened: philosophy became aware of the historical problem, and philology, above all, made demands, analogous to theology. In order to understand this new turn of ideas in scientific philosophy, we had to take into account the just presented twist in its general course in the direction of the *Ars Magna*, as well as some new circumstances to which we now turn.

The fact is that an essential feature of this *Great Art* [*Ars Magna*] was simply its loss of the *correlative* nature of the concept of a "*sign.*" In regard to this concept, the advocates of the *Ars Magna* spoke only of a "*characteristica*," or, as Leibniz more appropriately expressed it "a *characterica.*"[15] In this way, this entire movement lost its connection with hermeneutics. Having turned away from its Scholastic heritage, it failed to raise anew the problem of *meaning*. We saw that the logicians of the sixteenth and seventeenth centuries at least, once they had emancipated themselves from Scholasticism, in this respect came up empty-handed. In fact, the peripatetic logicians did not advance further. If the followers of Ramus allied themselves with rhetoric, the Port Royal reform of logic strongly pulled toward grammar. The problem of *meaning* as such slipped away from logic, but it would be incorrect to think that this problem was not posed *at all*. It was disconnected from the problem of the sign, but already in the eighteenth century it again popped up in connection with the problem of the *transition* from sign to meaning. From a logical problem, it became a purely psychological one. We noted the psychologism in the solution, and even in the formulation, of this problem already at the very early start of its development. Now it bore fruit. We see an advantage in the fact that the new psychological treatment of the issue comes in connection with the organization of psychology into a *science*. Toward the end of the eighteenth century one had to harmonize in one way or another the psychological and logical aspects of the problem and to restore it to us in the form needed by hermeneutics.

Hobbes, who was no stranger to philosophical and even poetic interests and who was likely still under the influence of Scholastic nominalism, devoted a certain amount of attention to the role of signs and, in particular, of words. For him, there was no doubt that *names*, insofar as they serve the goal of communication, i.e., insofar as they are precisely signs (and not notes), are signs of ideas. However, these ideas are necessarily ideas of individual things. Generality is a property neither of things nor of ideas, but only of words. Therefore, sentences receive their universality only from names. Consequently, truth or falsehood is a peculiarity not of things, but of speech: "For *True* and *False* are attributes of Speech, not of Things."[16]

---

[15] [We follow here the German translation. See Špet 1993: 90. The Russian text (Shpet 2005: 280) reads simply: "In this regard, it was only a matter of a 'characteristic' or, as Leibniz better expressed it, a 'characterica'."]

[16] Hobbes 1996: 27.

However, Hobbes, as it were, did not notice the difficulties that arise from such claims. Locke tried to eliminate them. He originated all contemporary theories of knowledge. Although he departs from Hobbes on a very important, if not the most important, point, allowing the existence of general ideas, he, nevertheless, accepts the problem in Hobbes' formulation[17] to a significant degree. He placed it, however, on an explanatory *psychological* foundation. Locke, by his own admission, became convinced of the close connection between words and ideas only in the course of his investigation.[18] However, perhaps just for this reason he examined the problem at great length, devoting an entire book of his [*An*] *Essay* [*Concerning Human Understanding*] to it.

Unfortunately, Locke did not connect this expansion with either a subtle analysis or an understanding of the essential problem that one finds in the Scholastic thinkers. In any case, it is strange to read in Locke – after all the work the Scholastics did – the assertion, which sounds in him as though it were a *discovery*, that knowledge "has greater connexion with words than perhaps is expected," so that apart from a consideration of words, "there could be very little said clearly and pertinently concerning knowledge, which being conversant about truth, had constantly to do with propositions" and that words "seemed scarce separable from our general knowledge."[19] Although he grasped the importance of words, Locke, nevertheless, did not capture the essence of the problem and replaced the problem of the essence of a sign and of the comprehension of its sense with the problem of the origin and the explanation of the psychological processes of the formation of general concepts. He transfers the old medieval dispute to psychological ground and boldly renews it in a psychological illumination that received the designation "*conceptualism.*" Therefore, the assertion that the meaning of a word is a representation – "ideas in the mind of the speaker"[20] – needs only to find a psychological explanation. Hypotheses concerning the "origin" of language should serve as this explanation – and again a vain and lengthy dispute begins concerning this. On the other hand, since, after all, we study things and their relations in words, a new problem arises in place of the unresolved one of the relation between a sign and its meaning. This new problem leads to a series of quite serious complications, viz., the problem of whether and how our ideas or representations correspond to things.

It is to Locke's credit that, having raised the problem of words and having presented it in a new light, he aroused interest in it anew. His simplified and straightforward solution was the culmination of an earlier vague psychologism, and in this culmination revealed its weak aspects so that they were completely visible. Moreover, it is impossible to refrain from imputing to Locke not only negative, but also *positive* credit for his new formulation of the problem. As I have mentioned, the connection of this problem with a psychological explanation of meaning advanced it to play a new *scientific* role. This, in turn, by virtue of the classificatory and sys-

---

[17] See Grimm 1890: 265.
[18] Locke 1997: 360; Locke 1997: 435.
[19] Locke 1997: 363; Locke 1997: 435.
[20] Locke 1997: 366; Locke 1997: 364.

tematic requirements of science, demanded a precise determination, at least, of the place of those *principles* upon which one could build, as it were, such a psychological theory. Locke asserts categorically that one person addresses another in speech in order to be *understood* by the latter, i.e., in order that the hearer should know the speaker's ideas by means of sounds functioning as signs.[21] However, such an assertion points directly to the fact that the nature of understanding, i.e., of the transition from sign to meaning, is *social*, however we may define meaning and however we may explain the mentioned transition.

Actually, Locke himself recognizes that *communication* is what constitutes the condition for the flourishing of society itself.[22] This is a new theme, which demands for its elaboration appropriate principles, but which, up to now, has not yet even been understood as it should be. The problem of *society* after Locke, and in the course of the entire eighteenth century, was perhaps the most popular problem. However, precisely the issue of *communication*, as a psychological and fundamental problem, it seems, was not posed. Only at the very end of the century, did Thomas Reid *raise* it, after which it was again either ignored or "resolved" in terms of individual psychology – on the basis of a theory of association – in a most naïve and superficial way.

Thus, although Locke liberated the problem of sign-meaning from its rhetorical setting,[23] he, on the other hand, wrested it equally from the fundamental logical connection in which the problem was posed in Scholasticism. And, of course, Condillac, who was enthused with phantasies on the theme of the origin of language – where usually the little expressions "once upon a time" (*un jour*) and "bit by bit" (*peu à peu*) played a magical role in clearing up all mysteries – did not happen to probe deeper into the problem, although he too displayed interest both in the theory of signs (*la langue des Calculs*) in general as well as in language and the role of the word in the cognitive process in particular.[24]

As for eighteenth-century English philosophy, to the extent that it moved within the set of problems that Locke had raised and *despite* its nominalistic tendencies, it proceeded along a path which deviated from the essence of the nominalistic problem, a path on which Locke himself had placed it, as we indicated above, and concerned itself more with the problem of an idea as an "expression" or "reflection" of reality than with the problem of understanding a *word*. It follows from this that the *new* nominalism – this applies particularly to Berkeley[25] – could also more accurately

---

[21] Locke 1997: 364.

[22] Locke 1997: 363; Locke 1997: 449; Locke 1997: 388; Locke 1997: 425.

[23] This certainly did not prevent the rhetoricians from continuing to elaborate this question, but for their own special purposes, and sometimes quite cleverly and subtly as, for example in the remarkable book Campbell 2008. [Shpet remarks that he used a "new" edition of this 1776 work from 1850.]

[24] Condillac 2012: 78–91; Condillac 2012: 113–195.

[25] In my opinion, Meinong has shown that the usual designation of Berkeley as a nominalist in the history of philosophy is incorrect. Meinong presents other reasons than those that I indicated in the text. Cf. Meinong 1877. Reprinted in Meinong 1914.

be called "conceptualism," since in its extreme and consistent form it states: words are merely *substitutes* for meanings in the mind. In other words, this formula expresses the idea that *words have no meanings at all* that would have to be *understood*, the whole point being that a word *as an idea* substitutes for a set of other ideas. A word, therefore, is detached from its correlative meaning and plays the role only of a *token*. With such presuppositions, we must consider it quite natural that the entire problem of understanding is *replaced* by that of the binding of ideas or representations. This problem is resolved in a most elementary fashion through an absolutely empty and naïve explanation of the transition from sign (a word) to meaning, according to the laws of *associative* connection, an explanation we still find today. Indeed, we still encounter such an explanation among defenders of the "nominalist" point of view of Campbell in his philosophy of rhetoric. Campbell only articulated clearly what Locke had already suggested in referring to *habit*. Campbell himself based his position in this on Berkeley and Hume, who rejected Locke's *abstract* general ideas but accepted habit as an explanation of understanding, i.e., of the immediate transition from the idea of a sound (of a word) to the corresponding idea of a thing.[26]

Campbell, in raising the problem concerning how we understand or fail to understand another person's words, expresses his surprise that up to now there have been no attempts to explain this fact. He proposes his own explanation, which relies entirely on Hume's theory of association.[27] Campbell distinguishes three kinds of connections: those between things, those between words and things, and those between words. Connections of the first kind are explained in terms of Hume's theory of association. They are natural and are based on experience. Connections of the second kind are artificial and arbitrary. They depend on convention, but have the same effect on the human mind as those of the first kind. "For having often had occasion to observe particular words used as signs of particular things, we hence contract a habit of associating the sign with the thing signified, insomuch that either, being presented to the mind, frequently introduces or occasions the apprehension of the other. Custom, in this instance, operates precisely in the same manner as in the formation of experience formerly explained."[28]

As for the third kind of connections, those between words as signs correspond to the connections or relations between things. For, just as there is an axiom in geometry that things equal to one and the same thing are equal to each other, so also

---

[26] Cf. Berkeley 2012: 74 [Introduction, §12]: "...an idea, which considered in itself is particular, becomes general by being made to represent or stand for all other particular ideas of the same sort." For references to *custom*, see Berkeley 2012: 80 [§20]. See also Hume 2003: 12–18 (Book 1, Part 1, §7). Berkeley, in §20 of his mentioned work, notes the one-sided nature of the usual view, according to which speech serves only for the *communication* of ideas, since it also has other purposes: it incites action; it incites this or that feeling, etc. However, Berkeley's remark bears the character of merely a formal amendment to the usual, widespread opinion and contains not the slightest suspicion concerning the fundamental significance of this fact.

[27] Campbell 2008: 256, 258ff.

[28] [Campbell 2008: 258.]

in psychology we must admit that "ideas associated by the same idea will associate with one another."[29]

In this way, the problem of *understanding* was simply resolved within the psychological train of thought that started with Locke, resolved, by the way, by one of the best representatives of that train of thought. He undoubtedly felt the influence – a direct and critical one[30] – from another current of eighteenth-century British thought, a more scientific and profound current, coming from Thomas Reid. It must be recognized that Reid actually understood better where to look for the fundamental ground to resolve the psychological problem concerning the process of understanding. Unfortunately, the ideas that he expressed remained undeveloped.

Reid, incidentally, subdivides the operations of the mind into *solitary* and *social* ones.[31] The latter does not usually garner attention in speculative philosophy. Moreover, these social operations present certain original peculiarities. Such acts as, for example, communicating, ordering, testifying, promising, and agreeing, etc., are neither reducible to simple acts of judgment, perception, or inference, nor are they composed only of such acts: "social operations appear to be as simple in their nature as the solitary."[32] They presuppose the mind and the will but also something more, namely, society as an interaction with other intelligent beings. The very existence of the acts mentioned presupposes mutual understanding. We perform social acts that involve our intellects before we are able to make judgments. Consequently, such acts presuppose a conviction in the existence of other intelligent beings. Language equally expresses both social as well as solitary operations of the mind, but the primary and direct purpose of language is to express the former. This is the case to such a degree that *we must recognize expression as essential for social operations*. They cannot be performed without being expressed *in words and signs*, on the one hand, and not being known, on the other.

It is impossible not to be astonished by Reid's insights. He not only noticed a very important omission on the part of philosophy and psychology, both of which had ignored the specific peculiarities of psychic life insofar as such life is a result of human interaction, but he also noticed the *originariness* of the corresponding processes. That is, he saw that they could not be reduced to purely individual psychic acts. This made it possible for Reid, first, to come close to the *fundamental* formulation of the problem of the social itself, *as an object* toward which the corresponding experiences are directed. It turned out to be possible then to establish a very promising[33] thesis for a *theory of the social object*. We clearly see from this thesis that a

---

[29] [Campbell 2008: 259.]

[30] Campbell was one of the active members of the Philosophical Society founded by Reid in Aberdeen. Beginning in 1750, he gave a series of lectures that were incorporated into his *Philosophy of Rhetoric*.

[31] Reid 1872: 244–245; 663ff.

[32] [Reid 1872: 664.]

[33] The fruitfulness of Reid's thesis that expression is essential for a social act of the mind can be easily understood if we compare it with the understanding, stemming from Hegel, of the social and *historical* as objectifications of (subjective) spirit.

theory of signs from its material side is nothing but a theory of the social object. Second, the correct formulation of one problem involves the correct formulation of another problem, viz., that concerning the place and the essence of *understanding* as a transition from sign to meaning. Since social operations of the mind are originary acts, which appear *as such* prior to any individual inferences, they cannot be explained, moreover, from the point of view of such "solitary" processes of the mind as *association*. It is quite correct to recognize the act of understanding, in its foundation as *original* and to formulate it in a way that corresponds to the ontological problem of the social object as a problem that is, above all, a fundamental one and then, of course, also a psychological problem. "No man," says Reid, "can perceive any necessary connection between the signs of such operations, and the things signified by them. But we are so formed by the Author of our nature, that the operations themselves become visible, as it were, by their natural signs: This knowledge resembles reminiscence, in this respect, that it is immediate. We form the conclusion with great assurance, without knowing any premises from which it may be drawn by reasoning."[34] Therefore, Reid sketched the correct direction for solving our problems, but the problems themselves neither excited him nor apparently did they interest his followers. Or perhaps the time had not yet come for drawing the necessary general and special conclusions from Reid's ideas. In any case, they were nipped in the bud.

Meanwhile, we have already stated the increased interest in social and historical matters in the eighteenth century as well as the intense search for answers to the question of the nature of *language*. It is remarkable that, having dedicated investigations into the latter sphere despite the fact that they had to exercise their ingenuity in vain trying to solve the problem of the *origin* of language, and despite their hostility to Locke's conceptualism in the problem of the meanings of words, they also failed to appreciate Reid's ideas. Instead, they reproduced ancient Platonic-Aristotelian realism with increased perseverance. In England, this applies particularly to the philosophizing philologist James Harris and his extravagant friend Lord Monboddo (J. Burnet), who combined an enthusiasm for ancient philosophy with an enthusiasm for problems of language.[35] Lord Monboddo responded very sharply and decisively to the works of Locke and Berkeley. He made an effort, above all, to restore the correct meaning to the term "idea," relying upon his knowledge of ancient philosophy. He could not, by his own admission,[36] give a philosophical account of the origin of language without an understanding of the origin of ideas. For this reason, he believes that, contrary to Locke and Berkeley, the principles

---

[34] Reid 1872: 665. In order to understand Reid's reference to reminiscence, one must keep in mind that memory, according to Reid, is an immediate perception of the past. (Cf. Reid 1872: 339ff. On the relation of memory to reminiscence, see Reid 1872: 359.) As is well known, Hamilton fervently opposed such a definition.

[35] Harris 1751 [Shpet refers specifically to a 1750 edition, which the editor has been unable to locate.]; Monboddo 1773–1792. See the very interesting correspondence of these friends in Knight's edition: Knight 1900.

[36] Knight 1900: 72.

involved in investigating this problem must lie within the sphere of "first philoso-phy," i.e., ontology, since precisely such philosophy clarifies the "principles of human knowledge."[37] The basic error of Lockean psychology consists in the fact that Locke failed to distinguish between *feeling* and *intellect* with their equally dif-ferent objects: a feeling is passive, the intellect is active. There are no ideas of indi-vidual things obtained by means of sense perception. No, "the mind is only passive, receiving as it were like wax the impression of the object. And this," he writes, "I call Sensation, and the object so perceived the object of Sense: but if the mind goes farther, and pronounces that the object perceived by the Sense is a man, or a horse, or a new species never seen before, then, and no sooner, it becomes an Idea and an object of the Intellect."[38] It goes without saying that, with such presuppositions, understanding as a function of the active intellect cannot be explained by mechani-cal association, and the *meaning* of words or signs cannot be recognized to be merely *ideas* alone, as conceptualism asserts.

Lord Monboddo explicitly acknowledges the influence that Harris' book exerted on him and repeatedly expresses his enthusiastic attitude toward it. However, one has only to acquaint oneself with this interesting, fresh, and lucid book to under-stand Lord Monboddo's enthusiasm. Harris was very well informed about ancient literature and philosophy, as is clear from his numerous notes, which truly adorn his book. He takes the position of Platonic-Aristotelian realism and, in particular, uses Aristotle's philosophy very successfully for his own purposes. He completely rejects the opinion that words, as "symbols" *of something*, denote *things*, i.e., the individual and singular beings that surround us.[39] If that were the case, all words would be proper names, there would be infinitely many of them, and they would be incomprehensible. They would be transitory, and every generation would have its own special language, etc. If meanings are not things, then they must be *ideas*. But what kind of ideas would they be? Against sensory ideas, one could repeat the same arguments used against things. "If then words are neither the Symbols of external Particulars, nor yet of particular ideas, they can be symbols of nothing else except of General Ideas, because nothing else, except these, remains."[40] But, furthermore, since we understand by general ideas that which is common to many individuals, not only those now existing but those that have existed and those that will exist, regardless of the *indeterminacy*, and even the *transitory nature* of every individual, language remains *determinate* and *stable*, insofar as it expresses *what is truly and essentially common* to many individuals.[41] Therefore, "words are the symbols of ideas both general and particular; yet of the general, primarily, essentially, and immediately; of the particular, only secondarily, accidentally, and mediately."[42]

---

[37] Knight 1900: 54.

[38] Knight 1900: 52–53.

[39] Harris 1751: 337ff.

[40] Harris 1751: 341.

[41] Harris 1751: 341–342.

[42] Harris 1751: 347–348.

Such a definition of meaning, naturally, not only contradicts theories that language "originates" from an "imitation" of the sounds of things,[43] but, more importantly for us, it cannot be reconciled with primitive explanations of understanding in terms of the association of ideas. In place of this psychological explanation, it is necessary to pose the question: how do we come to general ideas, and what exactly are they? Harris sharply rejects both the vulgar opinion and the opinion of the philosophers who do not see further than what he calls "*experimental Amusements*" concerning sensibility as the only source of ideas. Along with the senses, he singles out the independent and specific activity of the *imagination*, which keeps the fluid forms of things, when the things themselves pass away and all sensation has ceased. But the imagination, of course, cannot act without the preliminary activity of the senses and the equally independent activity of *reason* and the *intellect*, which, however, in turn rests upon the imagination. The intellect's specific function lies precisely in seeing *the one in the many*, or *what is similar or the same in what is different.*[44] This one, this "the same" in things, is what words as symbols mean, namely, *ideas*. What sorts of things are they, or what kind of beings are they?[45] When we learn that Harris solves this problem in a neo-Platonic spirit,[46] admitting to the existence of ideas in the mind of the Creator, we will hardly be critically satisfied. But historically, for an eighteenth-century writer, this is a sufficient answer, and independently of his interpretation, it is worth remembering his bold reversal (*conversio*): *Nil est in sensu, quod non prius fuit in intellectu.*[47]

In any case we are dealing here with the assertion that ideas have a certain *sui generis* being, different from the being of things and of sensible representation, a being, consequently, that is stable and abiding in the full (i.e., in both the subjective and the objective) sense of something *supra-individual*. In this way, the extraordinary difficulties that have defeated every psychological explanation of *understanding* are resolved. Words mean *ideas*, in the sense that Harris has revealed. The communication of one person with another, which presupposes their mutual understanding, consists above all in hearing and in speaking, i.e., in the speaker's passing from ideas to words and from words to ideas in the listener.[48] The congeniality or similarity of minds that mutually understand each other rests ultimately on the permanence of the very meaning of words as ideas. However great may be the individual difference in the understandings and the individual variety in what is understood, the source of the corresponding knowledge is firmly established. In this way, Harris easily attains what for a long time could not be attained by continental

---

[43] Harris rejects such a theory on other grounds. See Harris 1751: 332ff; Harris 1751: 336.

[44] Harris 1751: 362.

[45] Harris 1751: 374.

[46] In his assertion of the existence of ideas in the form of three orders (*ante multa, in multis, post multa*), Harris refers to the Aristotle commentaries of *Simplicius, Ammonius* (Hermiae), and *Nicephoros Blemmydas*. Harris 1751: 381f, 383f.

[47] [Latin: "There is nothing in the senses that was not already in the mind."] Harris 1751: 391.

[48] Harris 1751: 398.

rationalism, despite the fact that the latter claimed to be – and in fact was – a development of the same principles of positive philosophy in antiquity.

I believe one of the chief reasons for Harris' greater success and greater clarity both in terms of his procedure and in his results is that he approached the problem of the relation between sign and meaning not in the general and abstract form of a problem in formal ontology, but in a form specifically applicable to a *word*. In this concrete and special form, the mutual relationship between sign and meaning was immediately clear to him, and not for a minute did he lose sight of it. "To Language," he asserts, "a Meaning or Signification is essential."[49] In essence, the simple application of the more general correlation of *matter* and *form* predetermined Harris' conclusions as expounded above: "From hence it becomes evident, that Language, taken in the most comprehensive view, *implies certain sounds, having certain meanings*; and that of these two Principles, the Sound is as the Matter, common (like other Matter) to many different things; the Meaning as that peculiar and characteristic Form, by which the Nature or Essence of Language becomes complete."[50]

In relation to things, this form also appears as an idea, i.e., an *inner form* corresponding to the *outer form*, with the difference that the inner form is free from matter, and the outer form is connected with it.[51] As already indicated, the specific being of ideas functions as an inner form. However, the clear and simple path Harris took also has its own quite understandable deficiency. That is, he failed to resolve the question in its general form. Along with this, he has an individual weakness. Namely, his attempt to resolve the problem of *how we grasp* a meaning, which is limited to a simple reference to the specific nature of the intellect's activity, is quite inadequate and reminiscent of a vicious circle (*circulus vitiosus*) – not to mention his appeal, concerning which we remarked above, to the Creative mind just when the related problem of the being of ideas arises. Nevertheless, on the whole, Harris and, following him, Monboddo, with their realistic presuppositions, present a very instructive contrast to Lockean psychologism.

The position that Leibniz took with respect to Locke also was determined by the same presupposition of realism. Locke, as we saw, reduced the problem of the meaning of words to the problem of the habitual replacement of general ideas by words, i.e., by a single sensible (auditory) impression. This is why he has a further interest in the problem of how general ideas *arise*, on the one hand, and the problem of *their* name, on the other. From the "genetic" point of view – beginning with Locke and to our own time – the matter is clear: from sense impressions – "gradually" – to general ideas (according to Locke, by means of abstraction) and from proper names – also "gradually" – to common nouns. Leibniz, on the contrary, does not doubt that common nouns are original.[52] Along with this, Leibniz explains the very concept of "origin," which at once reveals the difference between a *fundamental* and a *psychological* investigation of the problem. If we investigate the origin of

---

[49] Harris 1751: 314.

[50] Harris 1751: 315.

[51] Harris 1751: 375.

[52] Leibniz 1996: 276 (Book III, Chapter i, §3).

language in the sense of *the history of our discoveries* (*l'histoire de nos décou-vertes*), we will revolve in the sphere of contingencies to which the human species, in general, is prone. On the contrary, if we investigate *the origin of concepts* (*l'origine des notions*), we abstract from our "interests" and deal with what is com-mon to "angels and men and to intelligences in general."[53] Moreover, Leibniz is ready to follow Locke's psychologistic path. However, as soon as the issue of the *meaning* of words and terms comes up, the advantages of Leibniz's realism are revealed. He does not recognize the view, according to which we can, as it were, pass from the individual to the universal by means of abstraction.[54] On the contrary, commonality is directly revealed in the *similarity* of single things and is a *reality* – in which one must seek the essence of species and genera.[55] This makes it clear as a bell that it is quite impossible to regard the *meanings* of words as ideas and have them, therefore, depend on our subjectivity. The meanings of general terms are not *things* in the reality surrounding us, but they are also not our *ideas*. Rather, being *essences* (*l'essence*) they are nothing other than *possibilities*.[56] "If people differ in naming," Leibniz asks rhetorically, "does that change the things or their resem-blances? If one person applies the name 'covetousness' to one resemblance, but another person applies it to another resemblance, these will be *two different species designated by the same name*."[57] Leibniz pointedly stressed the *objectivity* of mean-ings and their independence from our representations. We cannot always infer from external similarities to internal ones. But, he asks, do the latter become less real as a result of this, *est-ce qu'elles en sont moins dans la nature?*[58] Here, finally, is a clear declaration of the antipsychologism that should serve as a principle of a theory of meanings: "In any case, whether people combine these or those ideas or not, or even whether they connect them in the reality (*actuellement*) of nature or not, plays no role in essences, genera and species, since it is a matter only of possibilities, which are independent of our thinking."[59]

As a whole, the *New Essays* were able to exert an influence on philosophy only in the second half of the eighteenth century. But Leibniz's thoughts as presented here are so general and at the same time so fundamental for his philosophy that it would have been impossible for Leibniz's successor not to recognize them. In the corresponding parts of his system, Wolff starts with them, and, although he adds little that is new to the essence of this matter, he, nevertheless, puts them into a cer-tain order and system. The *Ars characteristica* was supposed to be a study of signs as features in isolation from their meaning. However, Wolff's idea was for it to form a special practical discipline with a purely conventional task, a discipline with a

---

[53] [Leibniz 1996: 276 (Book III, Chapter i, §5).]

[54] Leibniz 1996: 289ff (Book III, Chapter iii, §6). Leibniz quite correctly notes that this path pro-vides a transition only from species to genera.

[55] Leibniz 1996: 292 (Book III, Chapter iii, §§11, 13).

[56] See Leibniz 1996: 294 (Book III, Chapter iii, §15).

[57] Cf. Leibniz 1996: 292 (Book III, Chapter iii, §14). [Shpet's emphasis.]

[58] [Reading with Špet 1993: 108 (*est-ce qu'elles*) instead of Shpet 2005: 291 (*est-ce qu'elle*).]

[59] Cf. Leibniz 1996: 293 (Book III, Chapter iii, §14).

distinctive semi-mathematical and semi-grammatical character.[60] Apparently, this discipline could not address purely theoretical questions concerning the nature of the sign or its objective essence. Naturally, therefore, it, together with the psychological theory of signs, as it was formulated, for instance, by Locke, required some fundamental grounding. In one way or another, *ontology*, as *first philosophy*, should have paid attention to the fundamental objective aspect of a sign.[61]

As did Augustine before him, Wolff now undertook a formal-ontological examination of signs as *things*, for "S*ignum dicitur ens, ex quo alterius praesentia, vel adventus, vel praeteritio colligitur*" ["*A sign is a thing from which the presence or the emergence or the passing of a thing is deduced*."].[62] However, this was by no means of much use for the purposes of hermeneutics. Nevertheless, a sign is seen here, if not entirely as a feature, then primarily as a term of a relation (e.g., of cause or effect), which portends something about another term of the relation. Moreover, Wolff was far from combining his theory of signs with its scientific role in the historical sciences. He was also far from approaching his theory not just from the formal point of view, but also, like Reid, from a material-ontological point of view and endowing this theory with a *universal* logical, methodological, and, in general, cognitive significance.

However fruitless Wolff's ontological theory of signs may appear to us, it attracted the attention of his successors and was not only repeated but also somewhat improved upon. One even comes upon attempts to advance the question of a generalization in the sense just mentioned. However timid and even naïve these attempts were, they were nevertheless revealing: (1) in the sense that we are dealing here with a quite overdue problem, and (2) in the sense that the general philosophical foundations of that time were favorable to a maturation of the problem.[63] Especially symptomatic in this regard is the position the Wolffian *Georg Friedrich Meier* took.[64] He showed, more clearly than Wolff, the connection by which the theory of signs is introduced into ontology, (1) defining a sign as one of the sources of our knowledge of the reality of the things signified, and (2) indicating more precisely where in ontology the theory of "signs and things signified" should be referred. To be precise, "every sign is related to the knowledge of its meaning as the means to an end, and since all means are connected to their ends (according to §271) … there is also a connection between every sign and its meaning, a connection that we call the *signifying connection*."[65]

Further on, Meier gives a more detailed classification of signs. Finally, he places the idea of a *characteristica* or *science of signs* in a somewhat new light, which also provides some basis for us to say that he is moving in the direction of the

---

[60] See Wolfio 1732: 208, 210–211 (§§294, 297).

[61] Cf. Wolfio 1736: 695–696 (§§965, 966).

[62] Wolfio 1736: 688 (§952). Cf. Wolff 1751: 160ff (§292ff).

[63] Since the issue concerns the same conditions that in the eighteenth century favored the formulation of the problem of history as a science, I must refer to my work Shpet 1916.

[64] Shpet 1916: 175f; cf. Shpet 1916: 251–252.

[65] Meier 1755: 441–442 (§273).

generalization indicated above. This science, in his opinion, "not only embraces all of philology and all of linguistics (*alle Sprachkünste*) but also contains the foundation of all the arts and sciences that have to do with signs of any kind."[66] Meier divides this science – perhaps by analogy with the rhetoric and logic of the corresponding direction – into two parts: (1) an inquiry (*die erfindende Charakteristik oder die Bezeichnungskunst*), which answers the question: How should a thing be signified? And (2) an interpretation (*die Auslegungskunst*) with its question: How can we learn the meaning from the sign? The latter, the art of interpretation, is obviously nothing other than *hermeneutics*.[67] Meier expresses the idea of a *general* hermeneutics (*eine allgemeine Auslegungskunst*), which would examine only the rules that must be followed in interpreting all or the majority of signs and which, consequently, must have a quite universal significance.[68] However, we should pay attention especially to the fact that finally the necessary word has been said. Hermeneutics has finally been placed on a broader and more solid foundation. As I have already noted, Biblical hermeneutics certainly not only pursues above all *practical* ends; it now embraces the entire aggregate of the *sciences of the word*.[69] Actually, it is only in this *philological* context that hermeneutics – as we will see below – will play its scientific role and offer real assistance to the historical and in general literary disciplines.

Therefore, in comparison with Wolff, Meier actually made a significant step forward in the sense of realizing the place and the role of the questions that arose in connection with the problems of sign and meaning. His realization and formulation of the tasks of hermeneutics as an independent discipline is to me particularly fruitful, precisely because it was carried out on a fundamental (ontological) basis. In doing so, this procedure immediately revealed the relation of hermeneutics to his principles and its fundamental relation to contiguous spheres of knowledge.[70] A result of this was the indication, which we have been seeking, of *philology*, as the scientific subject matter by which hermeneutics must be oriented in order that its fundamental bases can be clarified in terms of their concrete content. I do not think

---

[66] Meier 1755: 444–446 (§276). In order not to complicate this presentation further, I will not pause to disclose the meaning of this idea, but I cannot help, at least, to stress here that it already contains certain anticipations of contemporary *semasiology* with its fundamental role, on the one hand, with respect to logic and, on the other hand, to linguistics.

[67] The first part, the "inquiry," under which we must understand the inquiry into the designations that correspond to knowledge, i.e., ultimately the mode of expression and presentation of knowledge, naturally refers to logic. Cf. Meier 1762: 651ff. (§484ff).

[68] Meier even made an attempt to carry out his idea in the form of a work, *Versuch einer allgemeinen Auslegungskunst*. Unfortunately, I could not find this book in any of the libraries in which I was able to work. [However, see Meier 1757.]

[69] Cf. also Meier 1755: 446–448 (§276).

[70] Nevertheless, after Meier several eclectic logicians of the so-called school of *popular* philosophy introduced a presentation of hermeneutic rules, although in such a general form as to be trivial. See Feder 1794: 175 (§131). (By the way, it is interesting to note in order to characterize the eighteenth century's increasing awareness of the connection of all relevant problems in a single large *problem of history*, that Feder raised the question of hermeneutics immediately after raising the question of a critique of the "testimony of eyewitnesses" in historical knowledge. See Feder 1794: 170–174 (§§127–129).

that the ontological determinations from which Meier came to his results by themselves predetermined them to such a degree. On the contrary, one can see from Wolff's same example that the mere recognition of an ontological problem in the problem of signs is inadequate. At least in his hermeneutics,[71] Wolff himself does not display a conscious application of philosophical principles to the practical pieces of advice and rules that he offers the reader. He seldom rises beyond commonplaces and everyday psychology.

I think, however, that the dialectical approach to solving the problem took precisely the route indicated. The fault here is not with the route, but with Wolff himself if he failed to notice it. Conversely, it is not so much to Meier's credit that he himself apparently turned out to be luckier than Wolff. Rather, it was, perhaps, a result of the fact that *historical* development here coincided to a certain extent with the dialectical route. The eighteenth century occupied itself very zealously with the *problem of language* and placed its highest hopes on the success of the respective sciences. The eighteenth century was populated with more than a large number of outstanding philologists. The scientific foundations of *comparative linguistics* were also laid in this century, along with new methodological demands and an organic connection with purely philosophical problems of language. (Besides the already mentioned Harris and Monboddo, there were William Jones, then Desbrosses, Court de Gebelin, Tiedemann, Tetens, Herder, et al.) True, primary attention in the study of language during this *evolutionary*-minded[72] century was turned toward the question of the origin of language – a question that perhaps is empty in itself, providing only ample fodder for the constructive activity of phantasy. Nevertheless, this is a question that cannot help but lead to deeper and more serious problems of language when approached with any degree of scientificity.

Therefore, in order to evaluate Wolff's legacy correctly with respect to fundamental problems, which may have essential significance for hermeneutics, one must keep in mind not his own hermeneutics, but the general course that he laid out for eighteenth-century German philosophy. Wolff apparently did not sense the importance and the acuteness of the problems whose resolution hermeneutics demands as its foundations. In situating hermeneutics in the "practical part" of his logic and

---

[71] Wolfio 1740: 641–706 (§§902–981). [Shpet does not mention which edition of Wolff's work he used.]

[72] In popular scientific literature up to now, one encounters the assertion that the idea of evolution is a specifically nineteenth-century idea. Such an opinion does not even have to be refuted, but simply corrected, as factually imprecise. Beginning with Leibniz, this idea firmly penetrated not only into the minds of philosophers, but also naturalists and psychologists. See Shpet 1916: 465. Connected with the idea of evolution, the idea of progress also blossomed in the eighteenth century. In popular opinion, however, the theory of the origin of the human being from the ape is considered a characteristic of the "evolutionary worldview," but even this is an eighteenth-century idea. See the letter of Monboddo to Pringle in Knight 1900: 84. Hypotheses that explain the fact of evolution are another matter. Not all of them, certainly, stemmed from the eighteenth century. Darwin, for example, lived and wrote in the nineteenth century.

referring it to an *ars inveniendi* (§902),[73] he merely satisfies his own requirement that every presentation be systematically complete. He fills its content with practical rules and pieces of advice, and only in passing does he make remarks, whose development would have comprised a permanent philosophical contribution. He comments that the understanding of an author's thoughts is not a reproduction of his "ideas," but is knowledge of truth itself.[74]

In the same way and quite consistently in the spirit of rationalism, he sees that such an understanding can be achieved only by someone who has in mind a certain system of truths, which undoubtedly should also serve as the supreme sanction of understanding. The reader has a right, after this, to expect solutions to the problem of understanding in the spirit of the truths of rationalism. But this reader will be immediately disappointed upon learning that the entire problem amounts to a very narrow demand, namely, to connect the author's individual words to precisely the same concepts that the reader connects to them (§903).[75] What remains is to offer appropriate instructions, but hermeneutics, as it turns out, is then placed on an extremely narrow foundation, namely, on a theory of the logic of *terms*, and the entire matter is reduced simply to an analysis of *definitions* (§§904, 905).[76] In other words, definition should be the task of logical presentation, something which became fashionable in the seventeenth century,[77] or even a *usus loquendi* (linguistic usage) (§906) with respect to "dogmatic" works or even in "historical" works – the same dogmatic definitions (of geography, chronology, genealogy), or *sermo communis* (common language) (§912),[78] or finally, experience (*ipso uso*) (§934).[79]

All of this is poor in content and even poorer in philosophical reflection. Wolff's philosophy on the whole, as a consistent and strict *rationalism*, is another matter. Here, *ratio* turns the most essential side of its meaning toward us: *reason* appears before us here in its objective aspect, as *sense*. Consequently, the correlative problem of its *comprehension* arises in its full scope not only as a psychological problem, but also as a fundamental problem, insofar as reason, functioning as comprehending the reason (the sense) of things, is considered in its essential and transcendental nature. Rationalism, in essence, contains every philosophical hermeneutics and presupposes all the possibilities of being concretely realized in the form of methods of real acts of understanding and interpretation. The Leibnizian principle of sufficient reason is the basis of this type of rationalism. However, it was none

---

[73] [Wolfio 1740: 641.]

[74] This remark on Wolff's part implies the assertion, which later became popular, that a reader can understand an author better than the author himself (see §929). [Wolfio 1740: 660.]

[75] [Wolfio 1740: 641–642.]

[76] [Wolfio 1740: 642–643.]

[77] See Spektorskij 1910: 275–276.

[78] [Wolfio 1740: 648.]

[79] [Wolfio 1740: 663.] Correspondingly, also in the interpretation of Holy Scripture (§968ff) [Wolfio 1740: 692.] it is not a matter of a special grace of understanding, but of the "force of the word" (§970) [Wolfio 1740: 693–694]. The definition is replaced *ipso opere* ("by the work itself"). Therefore, the interpretation bears a real-historical character (see §973) [Wolfio 1740: 697–698].

other than Wolff himself who taught the eighteenth century how to apply this principle, above all for the purposes of understanding.[80] Nevertheless, Wolff saw the problem entirely from one side, viz., the ontological, and failed to consider its philosophical meaning with respect to an analysis of rational *consciousness*. This is why Wolff also failed to see that rationalistic philosophy is, in essence, hermeneutical philosophy. Moreover, in this respect, i.e., as the problem of understanding, rationalism remains up to the present obscure.

Wolff made the concept of a sign an object of an ontological investigation, but he did not recognize that a *word*, as a peculiar type of sign, includes its own specific problems, the solution of which must have a universal philosophical significance, despite the apparently particular character of the question concerning it. This lack of recognition is the usual mistake of rationalism. Hegel had already rebuked it for this, viz., for not seeing that the resolution of the general problem is also a resolution of all of its particular forms. It is impossible to be satisfied with the simple transference to the concept of a *word* what can be said about a sign in general. After all, rationalism is unthinkable without the recognition that a word should not only have meaning as a sign, but must also contain the *ratio* itself as its sense. What is the relation of meaning to sense? Is *meaning* really a type of sense? When, and under what conditions, is this so? What are the specific problems? Where does the mechanism of recollection of what has been learned earlier end and the creative activity of understanding begin? Furthermore, *ratio*, as sense, lies in the *essentia* of things. What is the meaning of the demand that follows from this for an interpretation of *reality* itself? If, as every Platonist knows, the meaning of a word is neither a thing nor a representation, then what is a sense in general and in particular the sense of reality? *Does not the solution to the problem of the word appear to be a guiding thread for solving* this basic philosophical problem – and in a way that is decisively different from all of its pseudo-philosophical formulations and solutions? But there is still more.

Rationalism, being oriented toward the *ratio* of things themselves, and not to the psychological organization of the understanding subject, contains in itself what provides the supreme sanction for every act of understanding and interpretation. This is not a solution to the problem, but only an indication of its place. However, this very indication already sweeps aside, as is obvious, an entire series of inappropriate problems and their solutions – problems that have already been expressed or are only possible.

Finally, how do we get to sense and understanding? The simple answer of rationalism, with its appeal to the criterion of clarity and distinctness in an idea seems at first glance to be an absence of reflection on the corresponding process, and, consequently, the absence of a right to, and even a denial of, the need for such an answer. However, upon closer examination, when we see behind this simple criterion an assertion of the role of an immediate rational insight, a direction is revealed to us that we can follow to reach a solution to these problems as well. In any case, one thing becomes clear a priori from this, viz., that this fable of the purely mechanical

---

[80] I gave the corresponding elucidation of Wolff's rationalism in Shpet 1916: 163–244.

nature of understanding – whether it be on the basis of an associative process or some other automatic one – does not even remotely relate to the serious essence of the problem. For it is clear that something original and originary underlies the corresponding acts – something that is neither derivative from nor reducible to anything else.

All of these questions, hints, and conclusions, however, as we remarked above, arise only when we pass from general theses to their particular and specific forms, though not by way of a simple subsumption of a particular under the general, but by way of a conscious reflection on the specificity of the new species-content. Kant already attempted to eliminate this aporia of modern rationalism. Schelling, having become convinced of the impossibility of descending from heaven to the Earth, proposed that we raise ourselves up from the Earth to heaven. In this way, he opened up a new era of rationalism.[81] Hegel, however, accused Schelling of formalism and sought in the *dialectic* a path to connect the universal with the concrete, and an answer to the question about the "something" in the bosom of the absolute.[82]

As I remarked, the development of scientific interest in the historical corresponded to the dialectical effort of philosophy toward the *concrete* and its comprehension. Therefore, both at the level of principles and at the level of scientific investigation itself, we approach at the end of the eighteenth century a definite answer to the question of that real sphere of knowledge around which the mentioned questions concerning hermeneutical principles are to be oriented. As Meier had already wanted, *philology* becomes such a science – a science, moreover, in the sense of a *historical science*, as it was again constituted toward the end of the eighteenth century.[83] The role of theology, which hitherto had been connected with hermeneutics, ended. Theology itself became more philological and also, little by little, was reconstructed on the model of a historical investigation. Of great interest is that important moment in the history of hermeneutics when theology itself became aware of the need for a philological orientation. We find this moment impressed in the hermeneutics of *Ernesti*, Boeckh's direct teacher, a philologist of the purely real-historical direction.

---

[81] See Shpet 1916: 456–473 (.Chapter V, §§10–12).

[82] [See Hegel 1977: 9.]

[83] It is very interesting to follow this transformative phase of eighteenth-century "humanistic philology into historical philology" in Immisch, i.e., of a philology that, above all, strives for value judgments (*Werturteile*), for a scientific philology. (In my view, the term "humanistic" is not precise here. In the eighteenth century, the term "humanist" applied most directly to Herder, and Immisch himself regarded Herder as a "major element," who played a role in the formation of *historical* philology.) Of great value are certain remarks made by Immisch about the role of *rationalism* in the progress of eighteenth-century philology (already from the time of Bentley (1662–1742) with his principle: "To us, reason and the thing itself are more powerful than a hundred manuscripts."). It would be interesting to trace this connection further and, on the other hand, the position of Boeckh's *Kantian* antagonist Gottfried Hermann. See Immisch 1909: 18–118.

# Ernesti [and Ast: The Reorientation of Hermeneutics from Theology Toward Philology]

## 1   Johann August Ernesti

In his philosophical views, Ernesti (1707–1781) adhered to the general Leibnizian-Wolffian direction.[1] He was by no means an original thinker; his fame rests on his interpretation of the New Testament.[2] Ernesti's hermeneutics is a vivid expression of a new era in the interpretation of Holy Scripture. Rationalism here bore fruit: the interpretation of Holy Scripture is freed not just from the pressure of the supreme sanction of Church dogma, but also from the instability of common sense. Historical philological criticism and interpretation acquired their legitimate rights. In hermeneutics itself, the center of gravity was transferred to philology; hermeneutics broke its earlier connection with the comparatively limited sphere of Biblical investigations and became freer in its techniques and more scientific in its content. In fact, Ernesti proved to be just as much a predecessor of Schleiermacher as was Boeckh.[3]

The old question of the ambiguity of language, which presented difficulties for hermeneutics already with its first steps, finally found a positive solution in Ernesti. It is interesting that the solution to this problem turned out to be directly connected to the correct understanding of the relation that must be established between hermeneutics and rhetoric. It goes without saying that Ernesti's solution to the problem is only *formal*. He entered neither into an examination of the essence of the relationship between sign and meaning nor into an examination of the corresponding acts of consciousness. However, he understood that the problem posed by the numerous *meanings* of a word is that of its numerous *denotations*, i.e., the problem of the *application* of words, or, even more precisely, of the use of one and the same sound-complex for the expression and transmission of a number of meanings. Therefore,

---

[1] See his *Initia doctrinae solidioris* with an appendix "Initia Rhetorica." The book was reissued many times. I have used the fifth edition, Ernesti 1776.

[2] Ernesti 1792. I have used the fourth edition with notes by Christopher Friedrich Ammon.

[3] For an evaluation of Ernesti's role in the development of philology, see Boeckh 1877: 304. Johann August Ernesti should not be confused with the philologist Johann Heinrich Martin Ernesti.

© Springer Nature Switzerland AG 2019
G. Shpet, T. Nemeth, *Hermeneutics and Its Problems*, Contributions
To Phenomenology 98, https://doi.org/10.1007/978-3-319-98941-9_4

the problem concerning the multiplicity of meanings is a strictly "practical" and psychological problem. It is psychological insofar as, in examining the appropriate example, we are interested not so much in understanding a word as in understanding the *intention* of the person who uses it. It is "practical" insofar as we examine the word here as the *means* for achieving a goal, viz., in the given case, as a means through which we can reach different goals. In this last direction, a word is studied in such disciplines as stylistics, poetics, and rhetoric.

From this point of view, the imagery of a word – and imagery is the main source of ambiguity – is the means of applying a word to express the required meaning. Since it is obvious that in each separate case of using a word, the speaker is pursuing a definite goal, the meaning of a word in each instance of its application is singular. A word appears to be ambiguous only so long as it is not used to convey one meaning or as long as we do not yet know, upon encountering it, which meaning it is then intended to convey. One may think, however, that sometimes the author intends to employ one and the same word to achieve two or more significative goals.[4] However, the disclosure of these goals is an analysis obviously not of meaning, but of the author's intentions, which can have their own rhetorical form (allegory, personification, parable, etc.). The interpretation of the meanings of words, taken as the task of interpretation, therefore, should be concerned not only with the meaning as such, but should take into account also the various *forms* of a word's usage, as well as the psychology of the user of the word. Nevertheless, the *proper* work of interpretation should be understood as the work of pure disclosure and an analysis of the meanings themselves, meanings that emerge after they have been freed from these external forms and that are also external and extraneous to the meaning as such. Therefore, the theory of meanings should be detached from hermeneutics itself and cannot be its foundation. On the contrary, the foundation – a fundamental theory of meaning – must still be found. Such a theory can play only a certain auxiliary role in hermeneutics. The latter can turn for help to it in case of need.

In my view, it is within the direction developed here that we must evaluate Ernesti's ideas concerning the unambiguity of words and concerning the reduction of the problem of their ambiguity to problems of rhetoric, as long as rhetoric deals with the kinds of words and their varied usage (*de verborum generibus et vario usu*).[5] Nevertheless, analogous to rhetoric Ernesti poses two tasks for hermeneutics: understanding and explication (*tum intelligendi, tum explicandi*), i.e., the discovery and the explanation of sense,[6] both in the form of simple translation and in that of paraphrase, annotation, and commentary. Clearly, hermeneutics as such has no need of this second part. Ernesti restricts himself in this part to a few practical suggestions, formulated briefly and concisely. He appar-

---

[4] There may indeed be goals that are not just significative but also produce a certain impression – aesthetic, intimidating, encouraging, etc. However, we do not call this πάρεργον a *meaning*.

[5] Ernesti 1792: 31–46.

[6] Ernesti 1792: 11. See Ernesti 1792: 130ff.

ently ascribes no fundamental significance to this part. In fact, the theory of explication, as the second part of hermeneutics, is extremely narrowed, losing its fundamental sense, as a result of which its aid to hermeneutics is diminished. The problem of explication must be posed in its full scope, for then we will be convinced that this is a problem not only of stylistics, but also of logic. It is precisely in logic that it becomes a fundamental problem. However, logic is not just an auxiliary science in relation to hermeneutics; a correct elucidation of the relation between them reveals logic's guiding and decisive role. Hermeneutics itself then appears in a new light and acquires a fundamental significance in its full philosophical scope.

It is possible that Ernesti's excessive expansion of the tasks of hermeneutics arose from his excessive contraction of the tasks of interpretation, which, by his definition, is the "ability to *teach*" (which is the meaning of a speech) or "to act" (so that the other person thinks the same thought as the writer).[7] Therefore, if it is not a contradiction, it is, in any case, somewhat surprising when Ernesti goes on to assert that a good interpreter should show not only subtlety of explication (*subtilitas explicandi*) but also subtlety of understanding (*subtilitas intelligendi*).[8] The latter is defined by two things: (1) by an insight into what one understands and does not understand, and also by the difficulties of understanding and the reasons for them, which depend on perspicacity (ευφυΐα), attention, and the habit of distinguishing the ideas of things from the ideas of sounds; and (2) by a thorough examination of the sense of what it is that presents difficulties. This depends on a thorough knowledge of the languages and of the corresponding science, then on the science that gives the rules of interpretation ("knowledge of the instructions regarding interpretation")[9] and, finally, on practice. Therefore, despite all the obscurity in distinguishing the methods of "investigation" from those of "presentation" it, nevertheless, follows that interpretation, above all, should be the concern of the former. A sad consequence of this confusion was that Ernesti, who primarily had the interests of "presentation" in mind, was completely indifferent to the first and fundamental problem, with which he himself had begun, namely: what is understanding itself, how do we attain a sense, what is the nature of that ευφυΐα, with the help of which interpretation, as an *investigation*, is called upon in difficult cases, before we can *teach* others.

Bypassing the problem of understanding as the basis of interpretation, Ernesti limits himself, as usual in such cases, to a reference to the habitual connection

---

[7] Ernesti 1792: 7 (Proleg. §3).

[8] Ernesti 1792: 7–10 (§§4–7). In his Dialectic, Ernesti contrasts *understanding*, as the faculty that connects the same ideas and thoughts with the words of another, even more sharply to *interpretation*, which *teaches* what meanings, ideas, and thoughts are connected with words. Ernesti 1785: 263 (*Initiorum Philosophiae Pars altera*, Cap. II, §25). With such a contrast, it would seem that interpretation should be entirely related to explication. The reasons for this vacillating stance toward interpretation are clear from its essence.

[9] [Ernesti 1792: 8 – "scientia praeceptorum de modo interpretandi."]

between the original arbitrary conjunction of a word with its sense, understood as the idea and conception of a thing.[10] Apparently, more important to him was the ancient problem of the ambiguity or unambiguity of words. His position in this matter leaves nothing to be desired in terms of clarity and categoriality. For him, an allegorical or typical sense is not, strictly speaking, even a sense. In any case, contrary to Augustine, he does not allow for several literal senses. As noted above, allegorical and similar techniques of *using* words are considered, along with other tropes and figures of speech, as problems more of style than of sense. However, an analysis of the use of words itself is doubtless inconceivable without a preliminary literal or grammatical interpretation.[11] The apparent multiplicity of senses of a word, being the multiple ways in which a word is used in speech (*usus loquendi*), depends on the variety of relations that establish the connection of a word and an idea and on the variety of habits supporting this connection. Understanding and interpretation, therefore, require a determination of the specific circumstances in which the word being understood was used by the writer, i.e., his time, religion, party, and theory, the conditions of social life and the structure of the state.[12]

It is clear from this that interpretation must obtain its sanction not from the Holy Spirit and not in the logic of common sense, which interprets things rather than the given word to be understood, but from knowledge of the word itself. This scientific discipline of the word will appear as the foundation of a hermeneutics that will reveal to us the life of the word itself in all of the listed circumstances of its use and development. However, *philology*, in our conception – and moreover in its definite *historical* direction – is just such a science. The greatest and the preeminent part of the grammarian's art, in Ernesti's words, consists in "carefully investigating what each word expresses at each time in each writer and, finally, in each theory and form of speech."[13] It follows from this that the literal sense is nothing other than the *grammatical* sense. The very word "literal" (*literalis*), Ernesti explains, is the Latin rendering of "grammatical" (*est latine interpretatio "grammatici"*). It is equally correct to call it *historical*, since, like everything else that is "in fact," it depends upon testimony and authority.[14]

With this, Biblical hermeneutics as such is supposed to end. It remains only as a particular issue to be handled by the methods of philology and history. Dogma and revelation are no longer to be considered as sanctions and sources or, in any case, they assume their specific place only *after* philological interpretation. Theology itself, after this, should be concerned with their scientific or other sort of rigor. "Scripture cannot be understood theologically," Ernesti sympathetically quotes

---

[10] Ernesti 1792: 14, 15–18 (P. I, S. 1, c. 1, §§1, 3–5).

[11] Ernesti 1792: 15, 18–22 (§§2, 6–11).

[12] Ernesti 1792: 22–23 (§§12–13).

[13] [Ernesti 1792: 23.]

[14] Ernesti 1792: 23–25 (§§14–17).

Melanchthon, "unless it has first been understood grammatically."[15] Scientific hermeneutics and interpretation has found *its* ground, indeed a scientific ground.[16]

Ernesti gave us an answer neither to the question of the sign nor to the question of its understanding. Nevertheless, he played a pivotal historical role in the history of our problems by guiding hermeneutics onto the correct path, connecting it with philology as its foundation. Both Boeckh and Schleiermacher, Ernesti's followers, drew everything that follows from this conclusion. Boeckh fully discloses the *historical* nature of the *word, as a sign*, insofar as it is an object of philology, particularly in its role as the foundation of hermeneutics. Schleiermacher, limiting his concern to Biblical hermeneutics, penetrated more deeply into the very *process of understanding* and interpretation. However, philology, and behind it history, on the one hand, and psychology, on the other, are only the empirical foundations for the solution of hermeneutical problems. As an ideal, there still remains the problem of their *fundamental* foundations. However, it is quite understandable if philology itself is not always aware of the need for this new and even greater deepening, and it is quite understandable that, in place of this, philology sought the closest possible connection with history, leaving the latter to take care of its own philosophical foundations. However, it would be incomprehensible and unnatural if, in this search for a philosophical illumination of the question, the very problem of understanding were avoided. Indeed, we experience great satisfaction when we observe that such evasion did not occur. However fruitless the efforts in this regard may seem to us here, the sheer fact of striving in this direction is of particular interest to us. Strictly speaking, the philosophical – in the good sense – eighteenth century provided definite directives. As we saw, not only the more subtle minds, such as Harris and Monboddo, but also the less subtle ones, such as Meier, were able to sense the fundamental nature of the newly-emerging problems, precisely thanks to retaining the connection with the specific philosophical presuppositions of the positive tradition. The same philosophical character of the problems of the *word* also inspired such admirers as Herder and Hamann.

It seemed that for the needed deepening of Ernesti's ideas one only had to adhere to the philosophical foundations that were already achieved and formulated and follow, as it were, in the tradition of Leibniz.[17] However, at the end of the century philosophy itself, in its development, suddenly reached Kant's notorious "revolution."[18] Before turning again to Leibniz and positive philosophy, we meet an

---

[15] Ernesti 1792: 26 – "Non potest Scriptura intelligi theologice ... nisi ante intellecta sit grammatice."

[16] Dilthey believes that the basis for Ernesti's hermeneutics was prepared by the critique of Semler and Mechaelis, the predecessors "of the great Christian Baur," who had already reduced all of Biblical interpretation to two elements: interpretation based on "linguistic usage" and on "historical circumstances." He affirmed, "With this, the liberation of exegesis from dogma was complete; the Grammatico-Historical school was founded. The sensitive and careful mind of Ernesti then created the classic text for this new hermeneutics with his *Institutio interpretis*." Cf. Dilthey 1996: 245.

[17] We will see below that certain ideas of Leibniz's proved fruitful in his nineteenth-century follower Bolzano.

[18] [A reference, of course, to Kant's celebrated "Copernican revolution."]

attempt to show the fundamental place of hermeneutics in the light of "idealist" philosophy. This applies to Schleiermacher himself as well as to Ast, with whom Schleiermacher polemicizes.


# 2    Friedrich Ast

Strictly speaking, the shift of philosophical interest shown by Kant himself and his closest followers toward the "mathematical science of nature" prompted his immediate followers simply to ignore our problem. The anthropological interpretation of Kant's transcendental philosophy, typified by Fries and his followers, did not differ in its concentrated attention on natural science from straightforward Kantianism. Fichte's subjectivistic and abstractly theological tendencies, with a moral foundation in his understanding of history, on the one hand, and Schelling's tendency toward a philosophy of nature, on the other, also failed to touch on our problems. Hegel was fascinated more with the ontological side of the problem of historical knowledge than with our linguistic-logical one. Only the Romantics, who were in many respects still connected through Herder with the earlier "pre-revolutionary" philosophy, valued and understood the role of *the word*, although not as it touches on its role as a hermeneutical object. The new understanding of *history* in Schelling, the Romantics, and Hegel gave no ground for them to pay the necessary attention to this object. It became the primary asset of the philologists. Only philological or, more narrowly, Biblical studies – but on an also new philological basis – were forced to attend carefully to the problem of whether there was anything in the "new" philosophy that could contribute to a fundamental elucidation of the problems of hermeneutics. This was precisely the situation of Schleiermacher,[19] who started with Ast's grammar, with the Bible, and with classical translations (of Plato).

Ast demands that the philologist not be a simple *Sprachmeister* – a master of language – or an antiquarian, but also a philosopher and an aesthetician. For this reason, the philologist should not limit oneself to an investigation merely of the letter and form of language, but should also disclose the spirit that permeates them as their higher meaning. Only its philosophical spirit can raise philology above craftsmanship and mere technique to the level of genuine scientificity, since the spirit and the idea of science are its supreme and ultimate principle.[20] Ast's demand alone obviously leads beyond the bounds of what had satisfied Ernesti. Philology itself, as the scientific basis of hermeneutics, presupposes a wider foundation and, of chief importance, a fundamental foundation. We have a right to desire that the new philo-

---

[19] Unfortunately, I cannot refer to the still unpublished second part of my investigations to justify my general considerations expressed here. In this sense, I will limit myself merely to a promise. [Presumably, Shpet is referring here to the second part of his large treatise *History as a Problem of Logic*, which finally first saw the light of day only comparatively recently. See Shpet 2002: 546–1165.]

[20] Ast 1808: iii–viii (Vorrede).

sophical deepening of the hermeneutical problem permeate all directions of the problem that we have noted in its history. We stand before a new, quite important, and – insofar as it concerns the formulation of problems – final step in the development of hermeneutics, for it is a philosophical step. Therefore, it will be useful now to formulate briefly the directions indicated.

Hermeneutics seeks the means to disclose the meanings and the sense of signs, in particular, of the words of human speech. Consequently, in the final analysis it takes as a basic presupposition a philosophical answer to the question what is a *sense* and, in connection with this, whether each given sign has one sense or many. The problem of sense is the problem of the correlation of sign and meaning.

As a problem in formal ontology, the problem of the sign was detached from its inclusion in this necessary correlation and, as we saw, was forgotten. If it did not disappear altogether, this was only out of a hope of transferring the problem to some new, still unknown but anticipated science. On the other hand, in its more particular form as the problem of the *word*, this problem found shelter in the empirical-historical theory of words and, at least in this direction, an empirical foundation for hermeneutics was ensured. True, this conclusion led to a new aporia and, consequently, created a new problem, which we have not yet touched upon but which we will encounter below. However, as we shall see at that point, this problem was not a problem of hermeneutics itself, but of another science, viz., that of history, which methodologically guided philology as the empirical foundation of hermeneutics.

The problem of the relation of sign to meaning as the ideal foundation of philology itself was posed in a genuinely philosophical way significantly later. The absence of such a foundation also makes itself felt in the fact that the correct relation of hermeneutics to logic and, in general, the role of logic in the study of the relation of a word to a sense remained undisclosed. We will encounter additional misunderstandings in this regard. The problem of sense is not limited to this chain of problems, and hermeneutics has also suggested another direction from which to attack this problem. The correlation of sign to meaning, in turn, corresponds to a penetration into the meaning of a sign, into sense or *understanding*. Ernesti did not move us forward in this regard, and I cannot see any reason why philology itself, as a support for hermeneutics, with its naturally ontological aspirations, might have moved us in this direction. However, it is all the more natural to expect that this problem will arise with all of its importance in the face of the new philosophical deepening of all the problems that lie at the base of hermeneutics. Indeed, this is actually what we encounter, above all, in both Ast and Schleiermacher. However, in this connection we also find a philosophical formulation of a rather new question.

Previously, we saw that the problem of the ambiguity of meanings arose from the correlation of sign to meaning. Likewise now the problem of the uniformity or complexity of an act of understanding directed toward this correlation, as its object, arises. This problem is due to the consequent understanding of this correlation, and, consequently then, the problem arises of the uniformity or diversity of what is understood as the object and content. A certain aporia, connected with the irreducibility of this act to other acts of consciousness and of cognition, arose in close correspondence with the above-mentioned aporia, and could perhaps here be

called the *aporia of historical knowledge*. The present investigation aims to eliminate this aporia, but both Ast and Schleiermacher had also already encountered it.

Corresponding to the new turn in philosophy which was evident already from the
time of Schelling's first works and which was also reflected in the determination of
the tasks and the methodology of history, Ast transferred this new understanding of
philosophy to philology and, consequently, also to hermeneutics. For this philosophy, *spirit* is the ultimate reality, the final principle, and the *sense* of all reality. In its
work, philology, which should now not only be an abstract and resonating grammar,
but also cannot be satisfied with merely empirical foundations, is directed toward
this same spirit. The philologist takes *humanity* to be the concrete form of this spirit.[21] The *ratio* of eighteenth-century philosophy of history (Herder)[22] now becomes
its spirit. However, the penetration into spirit, as *ratio*, is nothing other than *understanding* or comprehension. Therefore, the problem of understanding falls, by itself,
into its proper philosophical place.

However, along with establishing this coordination of spirit, as the object of
understanding, with understanding itself, the above-mentioned aporias arise. (1) In
order to recognize this coordination, one must admit that understanding is, in some
sense, a source of knowledge, even if it is not an independent source. However, the
question, then, immediately arises: How do we acquire knowledge of what is singular and contingent, that with which history (in the given case – philology) deals, if
spirit as a philosophical reality must, in essence, be a locus of the non-contingent
and atemporal? It was precisely this aporia that compelled Schelling[23] to assert in
his time that *philosophy of history* is impossible. Incidentally, Ast sees a "cleansing
of the spirit of what is temporal, contingent, and subjective" to be the ultimate philosophical goal of a *"philological* education."[24] Moreover, Ast was evidently convinced that only a recognition of spirit as the ultimate goal of knowledge resolves
the problem of historical knowledge. "Therefore," he writes, "everything sprang
from a Single Spirit and moves back toward a Single Spirit. Without a knowledge of
this original Unity, which departs from itself (dividing itself in time), and again
seeks itself, we are not only incapable of understanding Antiquity but incapable in
general of knowing anything about history and human culture."[25]

Thus, on the one hand, spirit comprises a certain "one, true and original life,
which is neither ideal nor real, since both arise from it as temporal oppositions," an
idea which is itself the "fullness of all reality," as it manifests a "higher history (not
the history that merely assembles facts)."[26] However, on the other hand, hermeneutics deals with the factually given of history and language, with the entire variety of
content and form not only of the sciences and the arts, but – at the same time, and

---

[21] Ast 1808: 169.

[22] See Shpet 1916.

[23] See Shpet 1916.

[24] Ast 1808: 169.

[25] Ast 1808: 171.

[26] Ast 1808: 169–170.

even especially – with the individuality of the writer.[27] However, it is not clear that Ast is aware of the aporia that springs from this opposition. In any case, he did not try to eliminate it and even seemed not to have noticed it.

(2) The second aporia, which is included in Ast's formulation of the problem, is connected with the question: What function does understanding perform in apprehending the spirit? If it refers to the passive side of perception, spirit is disclosed to it in a direct sense intuition as something given, and the difficulty lies only in establishing this givenness and, so to speak, how it, as a species, differs. However, if – as we usually think – understanding refers to the functions of the active intellect, then the matter is more complicated. In that case, spirit is not given to us immediately but, on the contrary, is actively revealed *behind* what is given to the senses, which faces us like something that is, at least, *alien* to our own spirit. The aporia is not a matter of how we penetrate into this alien something – that is indeed a problem – but if this penetration, being active, also has a creative character, are we not inventing a history of spirit where, perhaps, there is none at all, or where it has an entirely different character than what we claim or assume it to have? However, Ast also does not sense this aporia. All of life, he asserts, is spirit; apart from spirit there is no life, no being, not even a sensuous world: "For Spirit, there is absolutely nothing that is alien *an sich*, because It is the higher infinite unity, the center of all life, limited by no periphery."[28] Without this, it would be impossible to penetrate into those views, feelings, and ideas that are so alien, to the point of being completely unknown to us. "Understanding or conceptualizing (*Auffassen*) not only an alien world, but in general any other world, is absolutely impossible without there being an original unity and equality of everything spiritual and without the original unity of all things in spirit."[29] If Ast is correct, then one must agree that he proves much more than is necessary. Schleiermacher[30] already noted that, with Ast's assumptions, understanding would be given together with reading or listening and would be a gift of divination. Consequently, we would understand entirely on our own. We could say, in other words, that in such a case, not only would we not need hermeneutics, but, moreover, we would not be able to explain something else, namely, how, under such conditions, a *misunderstanding* or an error in understanding is possible. Ast himself probably sensed this, stressing the *an sich* that qualifies the word "alien," but even with this restriction the question remains in full force. Ast approached understanding as the central problem and foundation of hermeneutics, but he failed to recognize the unique nature of this problem.

Moreover, if one reflects more deeply on the sense of both of the mentioned aporias and takes into account that they arose after we realized the scientific orientation of hermeneutics toward philology, conceived not as an abstractly dog-

---

[27] Cf. Ast 1808: 173, 176, 192ff.

[28] Ast 1808: 166.

[29] Ast 1808: 167–168.

[30] Schleiermacher 1835: 349–350. I quote below from the "Lectures," i.e., the lectures that Schleiermacher presented to the Prussian Academy of Sciences on 13 August and 22 October 1829 under the above-cited title.

matic but precisely as a historical conception, then naturally the question arises whether both aporias are not connected with the one basic problem of *concrete historical knowledge*. Does not the solution of this problem involve an elimination or overcoming of both of our aporias? Furthermore, it is not hard to see that, properly speaking, hermeneutics already included the *formula* of this problem in the practical rule that it recommended with its very first steps, namely, that *one should proceed from the parts to the whole and from the whole pass to the parts*. This surely meant taking the path of understanding and interpretation. However, this is the path of all concrete and, consequently, historical knowledge. *Therefore, understanding would turn out to be nothing other than historical knowledge, and historical knowledge nothing other than understanding.*[31] In any case, though, this formula remains the formula of understanding for hermeneutics itself. What did Ast do for its discovery or development?

As indicated above, this *canon* of hermeneutics was established, one might say, from the very start, and, as a practical basis of interpretation, it seems self-evident. As Schleiermacher characterizes it, this fundamental principle of hermeneutics is "of such scope (*Umfang*) for this art and so indisputable that even the first operations cannot be carried out without applying it, so that a large number of hermeneutical rules are based on it to a greater or lesser degree."[32] But however important this thesis may be in practical terms, for us it is precisely its theoretical elucidation that is essential (especially keeping in mind the consideration mentioned earlier that it contains a characterization of all historical knowledge, an indirect confirmation of which is Schleiermacher's assessment of it). With respect to theory, the first and most important task should be to provide an answer to the question: From what features of the object that is intended by the understanding and that is indicated in the formula of the hermeneutical canon, albeit only formally, does this canon arise? We also equally have the related question: From what features of the very act of understanding does this canon arise? Instead of posing this question, Ast analyzes the formula itself and, although he lends it a more refined shape than it had previously thanks to his philosophical approach, he, nevertheless, achieves little, since he concentrates on the *supposed* difficulty that he discovers and that he easily eliminates. As we already saw, he overlooks the real aporias.

Ast himself formulates the hermeneutical canon in the following way: "The fundamental principle of all understanding and cognition is to find the spirit of the whole in the individual part and to grasp the individual part through the whole. The former is the analytic, the latter the synthetic method of knowing. Both of them are established only with and through the other, just as the whole cannot be conceived without the individual part, as its member, and the individual part cannot be conceived without the whole, as the sphere in which it lives. Consequently, neither is prior to the other, since each of them reciprocally conditions the other. In them-

---

[31] This is not the place to discuss how historical science itself came to this conclusion. The question is also taken up in the second part of my investigations.

[32] Schleiermacher 1835: 366ff. Schleiermacher analyzes this fundamental principle in some detail, but with respect to practical hermeneutics, which is for us of little importance.

selves, they comprise a single harmonious life."[33] All this is quite clear in itself, although the juxtaposition of methods contributes nothing at all to its clarity. Nevertheless, Ast is afraid of the "circle" here that arises from the fact that both acts – the comprehension of the whole and the comprehension of the individual part – follow upon one another and are not accomplished simultaneously. "The circle," he writes, "that I can know $a$, $b$, $c$, etc., only through $A$, but this $A$ itself, in turn, only through $a$, $b$, $c$, etc., is insoluble if we conceive $A$ and $a$, $b$, $c$ as opposites that reciprocally condition and presuppose each other. We would fail to recognize their unity, fail to recognize that $A$ does not first arise from $a$, $b$, $c$, etc., and is not formed by them, but itself precedes them and permeates all of them equally. Consequently, $a$, $b$, $c$ are nothing other than individual representations (*Darstellungen*) of the one $A$. Already originarily present in $A$ are $a$, $b$, $c$. These members are themselves individual manifestations of the single $A$. Consequently, $A$ is already present in a particular way in each of them, and there is no need first to run through an infinite series of individual cases to find their unity."[34] Ast develops this idea further, translating it into the terminology of "spirit" and illustrating it with concrete historical examples but, astonishingly, avoiding the problems connected with it and whose solution could have had a reforming significance for all of philosophy.

*Ontologically*, we are dealing here with the quite peculiar relation of "part" and "whole," which can by no means be resolved into the schemata of spatio-physical relations as is usually done in an analysis of this problem. Accordingly, we stand here before an original *methodological* problem, which is separated in a peculiar way from the logic of the mathematical sciences. But the most essential point is that Ast does not epistemologically (understood either psychologically or fundamentally) illuminate the obvious peculiarity of the knowledge that he characterizes as relations between the individual part and the whole, between manifestations of spirit and the spirit itself. This peculiarity, however, also forms the central problem for everyone who confronts the epistemological problem as one of *understanding*.

Therefore, as a result, Ast's well-formulated problem is *in no way* resolved, and it happens that his position lacks the means for answering the question that hermeneutics itself requires, namely, the question of interpretation and that necessarily presupposes an answer to the question: What is understanding? All of this, in Ast's treatment, comes down to understanding the answer to certain purely *factual* questions, and it turns out that understanding, together with this answer, should proceed "by itself," actually by means of divination. Ast cites Pindar as an example. In Ast's opinion, an understanding of Pindar requires establishing the *general relation* of Pindar's poetry to the spirit of antiquity as a whole, or locating that spirit as it is revealed in Pindar, on the one hand, and knowledge of his individual spirit in its unity with the spirit of the time, on the other. The latter is an answer to the questions: In what epoch did Pindar live, what was the nature of his genius, how was he educated, and in what circumstances did he live? All of this should give a "true and living picture of the spirit and character of Pindar's poetry," and "this is what it

---

[33] Ast 1808: 178–179.

[34] Ast 1808: 180.

means to understand an ancient author."[35] One may agree that as a result of this work we will really understand Pindar, but it is quite obvious that how we come to our understanding and what this understanding is, still remains a mystery to us. Similarly, this cannot reveal to us the process of interpretation from either its epistemological or its methodological side.

It, certainly, cannot help matters to depict what has been presented in a disjointed schema, since its meaning in the absence of philosophical reflection remains at most only a practical one. However, since certain interesting details, which are useful upon a fundamental formulation of the problem, are clarified with the establishment of such a schema, we should still pause on certain aspects of it. Hermeneutics (or exegetics, also known as "historics") in Ast's definition presupposes understanding, and on it both *interpretation*[36] and *explanation* are based. According to Ast, it is necessary for understanding to capture both the external as well as the internal elements – the form as well as the content – of the work being interpreted. Both are originally a single spirit, a single form-giving life, as the original unity of all being, constituting the highest point from which any forming begins and to which all that has been formed must be reduced. This understanding, accordingly, turns out to be threefold. There is: (1) *historical understanding*, in relation to the content of the work; (2) *grammatical understanding*, in relation to form or language; and (3) *spiritual understanding*, in relation to the spirit of the individual writer and all of antiquity.[37] "Historical understanding knows *what* shapes the spirit; grammatical understanding knows *how* the spirit shapes this; and spiritual understanding reduces the *what* and the *how*, the content and the form, to their original harmonious life in the spirit."[38] Since explanation (*Erklärung*) presupposes understanding and rests on it – "*to explain* means to develop (*entwickeln*) and present understanding"[39] – everything that we already know about understanding transfers directly to explanation, i.e., the same apparent circle in determining the mutual relations of parts and whole, and the same three "kinds" of meaning. A consideration of the latter, therefore, comprises the proper content of hermeneutics as a theory of interpretation.

What is individual or particular, taken by itself, in its external empirical life, is the *letter*. In its inner essence, in its meaning, and its relation to the spirit of the whole that is individualized in it, the particular is the *sense*. The perfect conceptualization of the letter and the sense in their harmonious unity is the *spirit*. The letter is the body of the spirit. The sense is its herald; the spirit itself is the true life. In every explanation, we first ask *what* the letter says; then *how* it expresses this, what sense the expression has, what is its meaning, and finally, what the idea of the whole – or

---

[35] Ast 1808: 184.

[36] Ast 1808: 172. Ast contrasts understanding, *Verständnis*, to explanation, *Erklärung*. This term is now used primarily in the sense of *explicatio*, but in Ast it has, *apparently*, both meanings – both as *interpretatio* and *explicatio*.

[37] Having in mind the orientation of hermeneutics toward philology, Ast speaks the whole time of classical antiquity.

[38] Ast 1808: 177.

[39] Ast 1808: 184.

the spirit as a unity – is from which the letter resulted and to which, through the sense, it again seeks to return. Such are the three elements of explanation. The hermeneutics of a letter is an explanation of individual words and events (*Wort- und Sacherklärung*), which presupposes grammatical and historical knowledge. The hermeneutics of sense is an explanation of their meaning[40] in connection with a given place and is based on a penetration into the genius and tendency of antiquity in general and of a given writer. The hermeneutics of spirit is an explanation of their higher relation to the idea of the whole, where separate elements are dissolved into the unity of the whole. The idea is not present in all writers; sometimes only its elements are present: intuitions in historical writers, concepts in logico-philosophical writers. Only in truly artistic and philosophical writers does everything arise from the idea and strive to return to it. There happens to be, in turn, a dual explanation of spirit. There is an internal, or subjective, explanation insofar as it holds within the given sphere of the idea being investigated, and there is an external, or objective, explanation when it goes beyond the limits of the given sphere and connects the idea with kindred ones, establishing their relation to the fundamental idea (*Grundidee*).[41] On the whole, however, according to Ast, *both* tasks of hermeneutics fulfill one goal: "the understanding and explanation of some work is a true reproduction or imitation of something that has already been formed."[42]

It is impossible to deny what I said above about Ast: his philosophical formulation of the problem provides a wealth of material for reflection and deepens the aims of hermeneutics in comparison with its empirically philological or historical orientation. However, it is also indubitable that the results, to which Ast himself came, with all their meagerness, generate a large number of misunderstandings. Although it rests on his schema of "understanding," his schema of "explanation," upon closer examination, nevertheless fails to correspond to it fully. The understanding of *form* and *content* is, as it were, reduced in the "explanation" to a single moment – to the "hermeneutics of the letter." On the other hand, the "hermeneutics of sense" enters as a new element. However, Ast leaves us helpless in both cases if we wish to give an account of the objective or epistemological side of the corresponding act of understanding or explanation. Ast's schema is constructed and undertaken completely in the spirit of German idealism. It is intriguing and gives rise to many problems. However, it leaves us entirely on our own if we want to find a solution to at least one of these problems, or even if we want to undertake a more sober analysis of some concept introduced into his idealistic ballet of concepts by this skillful stage-manager.

---

[40] [That is, the meaning of individual words and events.]

[41] Ast 1808: 191–192, 193, 194, 197–198, 201–203.

[42] Ast 1808: 187 – "Therefore, understanding and clarification of a work is a true act of reproducing or recreating of something already formed." If we compare this formulation with Ast's assertion that the "historical or antiquarian writer reproduces in oneself what has already been produced," then, it seems to me, it is unquestionably the source of Boeckh's formula, which later became so popular and which defines philology as the knowledge of what has been known (*die Erkenntnis des Erkannten, also eine Wiedererkenntnis eines gegebenen Erkennens*).

Least of all can we be satisfied by the simple transfer to interpretation of what belongs to understanding. Ast does not distinguish between interpretation, so to speak, *for itself*, i.e., interpretation as a cognitive act or process, and interpretation as a process that is carried out for *another*, for communication, as Ast himself correctly states,[43] i.e., interpretation as a method of logical presentation. Apart from that, how can one ignore the fact that interpretation, although it directs us toward understanding, emerges precisely when we do *not understand* something immediately. Certainly, it is a means that leads to understanding. One can unravel its nature only having revealed the nature of the process of understanding. Moreover, it is indubitable that, corresponding to the different aspects of understanding, there will be special techniques of interpretation as techniques of investigation. However, there will also likewise be special techniques of interpretation as techniques of presentation. It does not follow from this, though, that having related these techniques – *without relying in the least on an analysis of understanding* – we have thereby also solved the problem of understanding. Moreover, it is precisely in this *treatment* that Ast's self-deception apparently consists. He is confident that he has shown how we attain the final and highest goal of understanding, namely, *spirit*. Ast is not moved by, or interested in, the old dispute about ambiguity and unambiguity. His schema overcomes this ultimately pseudo-problem of hermeneutics. The moments of understanding and explanation in his schema are not the search for the various senses, but are the stages or the ascent of a single understanding to a single ultimate sense in the various moments or stages of its depth.

The immediately above view of the matter is not, strictly speaking, Ast's personal contribution. One might say that it is the almost automatic result of his *philosophical* formulation of the problem. However, it is already a great failure of his not to notice that if the moments of *understanding* are also moments of a single deepening and ascent, the moments of interpretation that correspond to them have their respective self-contained meanings in addition to an aspiration for a philosophical end. They have specific epistemological and methodological features. Each indicates its own set of scientific problems, and each is capable of an independent development. Without providing a philosophical justification or illumination of all these features of the separate moments of interpretation, Ast has thereby left them as before at the mercy of the respective empirical sciences and left each of them to resolve the associated epistemological and methodological difficulties in its own way and not in the light of a fundamental analysis. Moreover, he, therefore, gives reason to think that perhaps *his* philosophy is not suitable even for resolving these difficulties. His remarks about "empirical historical writers" and the "logico-philosophical" ones may be seen precisely as a rebuke. However, what did Ast do to satisfy the legitimate demands of an understanding that consciously and methodologically limits its tasks in advance? This understanding rightfully refuses to follow the "higher life" of the spirit that Ast postulates in such a contradictory way.

One can understand, i.e., penetrate into, the spirit under only one condition. One must recognize "the original unity and equality of all that is spiritual ... and the

---

[43] Ast 1808: 184.

original unity of all things in the spirit."[44] However, one can recognize this only through understanding, i.e., through a penetration into the spirit. But if this is not a statement of a simple correlation or mutual relationship, then it is a *petitio principii*. One would have to find a way here to break out of the circle, and not to celebrate the resolution of the imagined circle on which Ast dwells. On the other hand, stressing the unity of spirit too categorically can lead, as we saw, to a negation of what is "alien" to us, which in turn, threatens the existence of hermeneutics. As I noted, Schleiermacher already indicated the inadequacy of such a presupposition for hermeneutics.

Thus, the results of Ast's philosophical grounding of hermeneutics are really meager. He provides too little to philosophy. For even if we simply recognize in the mentioned *petitio principii* a statement of a correlation, then, not having offered an analysis of the act of understanding, Ast made no advance in comparison with the rationalist theory of the correlation of reason (*ratio*) and rational foundation (*ratio*). Moreover, in some respects – insofar as he substituted metaphysical concepts for fundamental and ontological concepts – he even moved backward, replacing reason with "spirit." However, Ast contributed just as little to empirical hermeneutics, the orientation of which toward philology and history we recognized as a large step forward in the development of hermeneutics. Ast neither disclosed nor utilized the significance of this orientation, although he seemingly proceeded from the interests of philology. On the contrary, transferring the center of gravity of his reflections to the understanding and explanation of spirit, he went directly beyond the bounds of what is necessary for empirical philology and history.

Finally, we can also extract less than we would like from Ast's schema of the moments of understanding and explanation. On the one hand, he contrasts understanding and explanation, but, on the other, he does not provide a complete correspondence between the two moments. Ast unites the first two moments of understanding – the historical (content) and the grammatical (form) – in the single moment of explanation (*Wort- und Sacherklärung*), which requires grammatical and historical knowledge. However, the second moment of explanation – an explanation of the sense – particularly stresses the significance of an understanding of the *author himself and his spirit*,[45] which was concealed in the third moment of understanding, namely, the spiritual, "in relation to the spirit of the individual writer and antiquity as a whole." If we limit ourselves to empirical hermeneutics and take into account the fact that linguistic knowledge is also historical knowledge (of a language, an epoch, a nation, an individual), does not another distinction thrust itself upon us? This distinction, as we shall see, is really of paramount importance, and it was Schleiermacher's great merit to have illuminated it, namely, the difference between the understanding of an event, a historical fact, and an individual, the person of the writer. These are not just "moments" of understanding, but different directions and types of understanding.

---

[44] Ast 1808: 168. [Shpet omits the ellipsis in this quotation.]

[45] Ast 1808: 195.

Can they be reduced to one, are they made up of identical moments, do they constitute *two* meanings in a single unit subject to understanding, do they belong to the same hermeneutics, are they subordinated to a single set of interpretive rules, and do they rest on the same fundamental foundations? All of these are questions that arise from this division. However, in seeking to illuminate them – though not yet to solve them – we must turn to Schleiermacher.[46]

---

[46] From his own point of view, Schleiermacher also criticizes Ast's distinction of the three phases in understanding and interpretation. However, he considers the chief source of Ast's misunderstanding to be Ast's distinction between understanding and exegesis as a development (*Entwicklung*) of understanding. Whereas, according to Schleiermacher the entire issue amounts to a distinction between inner speech and audible speech, the development here is nothing other than a reflection of the genesis of understanding, communicating how we come to understanding. It, consequently, introduces nothing into understanding except how to apply the rules of eloquence. (Schleiermacher 1835: 382–383.) On this point, I hold a different opinion. I believe that Ast's fundamental error lies in the fact that he inadequately distinguished understanding and interpretation, and this in a two-fold sense: as a technique of investigation and as a technique of presentation. The latter is distinguished not only by the application of the rules of eloquence, but also – and this is of the highest importance – of the rules of *logic*. On this condition, the distinction must be rigorous and must be implemented even through the fundamental foundations of the knowing process itself – epistemologically, on the one hand, and methodologically on the other.

# [Friedrich] Schleiermacher

In terms of its depth of understanding of the tasks of hermeneutics as well as the subtlety and elegance of the analysis of its content, Schleiermacher's work in this direction stands on a level that to this day remains unsurpassed.[1] He distinguishes three stages in human activity – including the activity of interpretation: (1) a non-intellectual, mechanical stage; (2) a stage based on empirical observation; and (3) an orderly, planned stage. He believes the third stage must be guided by a special art (*Kunstlehre*), and he sees the chief task of his research to be the search for the appropriate form for the content of this art as well as the clarification of the foundations of its scientific techniques.[2]

We must limit ourselves, however, only to what is necessary for our purposes – a consideration of the problems associated with the fundamental principles of hermeneutics. Therefore, regardless of how interesting certain ideas of Schleiermacher's may be in their details, we cannot dwell on them. Such a limitation forces us, unwittingly, to approach Schleiermacher from an angle that is most unfavorable to him, when the mere absence of something must be seen as a deficiency. The source of both his strength and of his weakness is precisely his desire to make hermeneutics into a genuine scientific discipline. Schleiermacher is interested in ends and pays little attention to beginnings. His hermeneutics is not only sensible, it is also wise and free from the truisms and commonplaces that are typical in such practical disciplines. However, Schleiermacher's analysis of the foundations of his distinctions and "canons" usually stop at just that point where greater depth and more details are wanted. Therefore, it is only from their application that we can judge the breadth of Schleiermacher's fundamental presuppositions.

Dilthey asserts that although hermeneutics, drawing on the philological virtuosity of the centuries, had arrived at an awareness of the rules to which the functions exhibited in interpretation should be subordinated, Schleiermacher went further. Going beyond these rules, he turned to an analysis of understanding and from it

---

[1] Besides the already mentioned "Lectures" [Schleiermacher 1835], see Schleiermacher 1998.

[2] Schleiermacher 1835: 344–345.

© Springer Nature Switzerland AG 2019
G. Shpet, T. Nemeth, *Hermeneutics and Its Problems*, Contributions
To Phenomenology 98, https://doi.org/10.1007/978-3-319-98941-9_5

derived the possibility of a universally valid interpretation, its auxiliary means, limits, and rules.[3] Still, I think that this is an exaggeration. True, Schleiermacher indicated the starting points for such an analysis, but he did not give an analysis of understanding as such. Moreover, he obscured the problem in its very formulation by insufficiently distinguishing between understanding, properly speaking, and interpretation. He himself, in other words, made the same mistake that Ast did, although he felt the consequences in a different way than did Ast. Schleiermacher wanted to separate strictly heuristic tasks from logical ones, or, more precisely, from what he considers "rhetorical" tasks. However, failing to draw a sharp line between interpretation and understanding, on the other hand, he transferred to understanding what belongs to interpretation, and in so doing conceals from himself, what above all, in the analysis of understanding, should be revealed as something essential, something that is present in it originarily.

Schleiermacher sees Ast's mistake in the fact that the latter, in distinguishing understanding from interpretation, gives non-congruent schemas of understanding, on the one hand, and of hermeneutics itself, on the other. It turns out that the hermeneutics of sense and of spirit correspond to only one moment of understanding – spiritual understanding. Strictly speaking, in Schleiermacher's opinion, this is the way it should be, since he does not consider the "explanation of words and things" to be an interpretation, but only the *elements* of an interpretation. Hermeneutics begins only with the determination of its sense,[4] although it is by means of these elements. Along with this, he thinks that the hermeneutics of spirit – insofar as it is not reduced to the hermeneutics of sense – also goes beyond the bounds of the hermeneutical sphere.[5] Therefore, there remains only the hermeneutics of sense *alone*, and obviously we need only a *single* principle of understanding for its construction, since interpretation is distinguished from understanding only in a purely external way, just as audible, externally expressed speech is distinguished from internal speech. This principle is the principle of the correlation of part and whole, the seeing of sense in a certain connection. Since, of course, the object of hermeneutics is not internal speech but expressed speech, the problem of understanding is thereby subsumed under the problem of interpretation. Understanding is, as it were, a form of interpretation, and it begins to appear that the solution to the latter problem also resolves the former. At the same time, Schleiermacher, as it were, simply identifies these concepts. They do not even stand in a relation of genus to species. The solution of one problem is also a solution of the other: "I include," he writes, "under this expression (i.e., interpretation, *Auslegen*) every understanding of another's speech."[6]

Therefore, Schleiermacher too ignores the fact that interpretation begins precisely at the point where understanding ends, where immediate understanding is

---

[3] Dilthey 1996: 246.

[4] [The German editors note that the typed manuscript they used reads here "subject" instead of "sense" as found in a hand-written copy and which they prefer. See Špet 1993: 147f. The 2005 Russian edition also reads "sense" (*smysl*).]

[5] Schleiermacher 1835: 383–384.

[6] Schleiermacher 1835: 344.

lacking and insufficient, in other words, where the source of interpretation is precisely a non-understanding. Evidently, it seems to Schleiermacher that once the analysis of interpretation, with which the *art* of hermeneutics is concerned, gives "more" than could be found in an artless immediate understanding, then the problem of the latter is thereby also resolved. He sees the entire difference between an interpretation that conforms to art and one that is artless to lie not in the fact that, on the one hand, the encounter is with something "alien" and, on the other, with something "of one's own," nor in the difference between written and oral speech. Rather, the difference lies exclusively in the fact that *one wants to understand some things precisely*, but another does not.[7]

It turns out that the entire difference between understanding and interpretation is in the degree of precision. However, even from the point of view of this difference one can raise the question: Are there not also certain *qualitative* foundations in this difference? Without entering into an examination of this question, let us simply turn our attention to something that is connected to the same identification of understanding and interpretation, but from the other side of this identification. In an interpretation even *for oneself* (and *to* oneself) one must have recourse to some verbal fixation of understanding. That is, it is necessary to introduce into an interpretation the *logical* moment that is not felt directly in immediate understanding. Consequently, this general problem has, among other things, the following particular and definite meaning: Does the difference between the precise and the imprecise not lie in the fact that a certain *logical* activity is joined to the former?

Finally, after all this, can one maintain that the elimination of certain – particularly logical – moments will give a simple immediate understanding? By gaining precision, do we not lose something specific in understanding, which perhaps also determines in a quite peculiar way the cognitive role of understanding and which evades analysis as soon as it assumes the general logical form of knowledge? True, it is precisely the logical "plus" in interpretation in comparison with the understanding that Schleiermacher fails to notice. He thinks that the only addition here is an "application of the general rules of eloquence" (*Wohlredenheit*).[8] However, this is only another new oversight on his part, which is a simple consequence of the identification mentioned above. We must recognize that Schleiermacher did not remove the consequences of this confusion by separating the tasks of *explanation* and *presentation* from the tasks of interpretation, since, in excluding *presentation* from among the tasks of hermeneutics in accordance with his definitions,[9] he excluded only its stylistic and entire rhetorical forms, but not its logical forms. However, all of the problem's difficulty arises from the fact that logic too enters into the investigation itself – as we have already said – insofar as one has to "express" what is being investigated "to oneself." The problem should be posed clearly, its limits should be determined from both sides. It must be shown that interpretation preserves certain traits – and which ones they are – even when motives of explanation are eliminated

---

[7] Schleiermacher 1998: 20.

[8] Schleiermacher 1835: 383.

[9] Presentation (*Darlegung*), in his opinion, is only "a special part of the art of speaking and writing, which could depend only on the general principles." Schleiermacher 1998: 5.

from interpretation. These are traits that distinguish interpretation from understanding but also distinguish it from logical "presentation."

In any case, there is, in fact, in Schleiermacher no analysis of understanding itself
as such – or of sense as such. What he places in the foreground is, with respect to the
external aspect of interpretation, the thing being interpreted and, with respect to its
internal aspect, the bearer of the interpretation. All of Schleiermacher's efforts are
concentrated on revealing the *species* of what is interpreted and of its bearers. Here,
his work, as we will see, turned out to be very productive and determined in advance
all further investigations in this sphere. However, his general formulation of the
problem of the thing being interpreted as something that is always alien to the interpreter is not devoid of originality. Consequently – I will repeat again – what is being
interpreted is taken as something that is not understood or not fully understood. On
the other hand, an immediate understanding, as an immediate apprehension of the
sense, should have sooner been placed before what is *one's own* and what is one
with it. In general, of course, the problem here is both uncomplicated and clear by
itself. What is being interpreted should not be entirely alien to us, nor should it be
entirely "our own." However, given Schleiermacher's approach, the problem of the
"other" must appear, of course, to be almost the fundamental problem along with the
problem of pure interpretation. Given his presuppositions, his attacks on Ast in this
matter, then, are understandable. Also understandable is his conviction that, however much we admit is common between the speaker and the person who is understanding, the problem of hermeneutics as theory arises only when we realize
something to be other.[10] As a result, immediate understanding is pushed back still
further. It appears to be cut off even from the sphere of theory and turns out to be
something *divinatory*, as though such an exclusion could eliminate the problem.

However, with respect to content, Schleiermacher attempts to expand as much as
possible the sphere of application of interpretation as a methodological technique.
He considers the limitation of its tasks with respect to classical philology alone to
be too narrow. Other kinds of philology (e.g., Romance philology)[11] as well as
theology should be added to it on an equal basis.[12] Its foundations should be as
broad as possible; it should take every word into account, both written and oral
speech, and not only in its scientific, but also in its everyday application.[13] With this,
Schleiermacher did not violate Ernesti's requirement that an interpretation should
be *methodologically* a homogeneous and unified philological-historical interpretation. It is only a question of the *material* that hermeneutics has a right to include in

---

[10] Schleiermacher 1835: 350 – "wherever there is an expression of ideas in speech with something
intentional, there is a problem that we can solve only with the help of our theory." Cf. Schleiermacher
1998: 9.

[11] [The editors of the German translation point out that Shpet erred here. Schleiermacher was not
concerned in the pages Shpet references with the language and literature of the peoples speaking
the Romance languages (=Romance philology), but with the philology of Romantic literature. See
Špet 1993: 150f.]

[12] Schleiermacher 1835: 347, 348.

[13] Schleiermacher 1835: 351f.

its examination. Nevertheless, this, of course, provided the occasion for certain generalizations that, on their part, led to a deeper evaluation of the principles that already compelled Ernesti to orient hermeneutics precisely toward philology. This new orientation formed a very important moment in the history of hermeneutics. It was freed from the vagueness and arbitrariness that revelation and common sense had introduced into it. However, philology as an empirical science, essentially, could not give a fundamental grounding to hermeneutics. It needed one itself. An awareness of this guides Schleiermacher as well. Thanks to history, philology, in his words, is becoming something positive. This is why it can provide hermeneutics only with an aggregate of observations. On the other hand, Schleiermacher also considers as incorrect the connection that is sometimes established between logic and hermeneutics, when hermeneutics (as we see, for example, in Wolff) is considered a supplement to logic. Schleiermacher remarks quite correctly that such a connection disappears when everything applied is eliminated in general from logic. In fact, according to Schleiermacher, hermeneutics should be connected with thinking as the inner aspect of speech and, consequently, should be *philosophical*.[14]

That is a good wish, but how can it be fulfilled? Did not Schleiermacher himself deprive us of an escape in this direction when he so strangely turned away from an examination of the problem of understanding? Unfortunately, the way Schleiermacher formulates his determination of the place of hermeneutics is too general and to us is unsatisfactory. Contrasting the art of speech with understanding and stating the philosophical character of hermeneutics, Schleiermacher notes a certain parallelism between hermeneutics and "composition," in the sense that hermeneutics (*die Auslegungskunst*) "depends on the composition and presupposes it."[15] Are we not returning again to logic, but only in a new way, not in order to make a "supplement" out of it, but in order to find in "composition" a light that would also illuminate interpretation? No, since by "*composition*" Schleiermacher understands again only a purely verbal art. However, one can see a major gain for the correct understanding of hermeneutics in the fact that finally the problem of the relation of hermeneutics to rhetoric has been clearly resolved. Hermeneutics was freed from rhetoric long ago, but it did not establish its relation to the latter. For Schleiermacher, the relation is clear: rhetoric[16] and hermeneutics are *parallel* just as speech and understanding

---

[14] Schleiermacher 1998: 7.

[15] Schleiermacher 1998: 7.

[16] Instead of "rhetoric," Schleiermacher also uses the word "grammar." In his opinion, a rhetorical "composition" forms, as it were, one of the particular tasks of grammar. Schleiermacher 1838: 10f. [The English translation omits this particular note judging it to be "misleading." See Schleiermacher 1998: 7f.] Schleiermacher's own definition of the relation of hermeneutics and grammar to logic (and to dialectic, which, according to Schleiermacher, is not a formal, but a metaphysical or transcendental discipline – cf. Schleiermacher 1839: 7) is so confused that I dare not discuss it: "The dependence of both (hermeneutics and rhetoric) on the dialectic consists in the fact that the entire development of knowledge depends on both (speech and understanding)." Schleiermacher 1839: 10. Some of the clarifications of this, produced by the editor on the basis of Schleiermacher's lecture notes (Schleiermacher 1839: 10–11, cf. Schleiermacher 1839: 260), in reality, explain nothing, already to say nothing of their inauthenticity.

are parallel – "every act of understanding is the inversion of a speech-act."[17] Therefore, the fundamental problem now of the relation of hermeneutics to philosophy and of its philosophical and, in particular, its logical foundations remains unclear. Since I do not anticipate an occasion for returning to this matter, I will make a few clarifications here in connection with Schleiermacher's formulation of the question. The fact is that the parallelism to which Schleiermacher refers creates a certain kind of circle, which is more difficult to resolve than the circle that Ast confronted. For Ast, the problem focused, so to speak, on the "material" conditions of understanding and interpretation, while clarifying the interdependence of hermeneutics and grammar (with rhetoric and stylistics), on the one hand, and with logic on the other. Thus, we are talking about *formal* conditions. These are the same difficulties we discussed in the first chapter.

It is impossible, of course, to interpret without a knowledge of grammar and logic, since the formal structure of a language communicated by them must be clearly presented to the interpreter. On the other hand, an immediate understanding precedes any grammatical or logical formulation on the part of the person who hears the speech. Moreover, the speaker himself clothes his speech in grammatical and logical form, *because* he already understands what he intends to say and, what is more, he clothes it in this or that form, depending on *how* he understands it. The "circle" that is, thereby, created must be displayed in a preliminary fundamental analysis of understanding, since this circle is nothing other than an expression of the *two-sidedness* of the very act of understanding, which requires for its realization the presence of the speaker who composes, on the one hand, and the hearer who understands, on the other. Consequently, there is a fundamental problem here. However, in the way of an anticipatory classification, one can note here several important factors. Hermeneutics, precisely by virtue of the primacy of understanding, a primacy that underlies every systematic – *kunstmässig*, as Schleiermacher would say – interpretation is not a simple sounding board for logic and grammar, the more so since they in general refer only to the *formal* side of interpretation and must, to a certain extent, determine their tasks independently. In this way, even a logical and grammatical analysis can be hermeneutically useful. This independence is, of course, relative, but reference to it means that hermeneutics is in some sense closer to its principles, i.e., is not mediated by logic. Moreover, this closeness makes itself felt precisely in its fundamental interest in relation to understanding, which, in its essence, foresees its own special and independent tasks. This, in turn, sets new problems for logic, problems that allow it now to look at itself from the viewpoint of the goals of hermeneutics – a special aspect, which gives us the right to speak of a special *hermeneutic logic*.

Let us turn some attention at least to the *canons* of hermeneutics that Schleiermacher establishes: "(1) Everything that still requires a more precise definition in a given utterance can be determined only from the language of the author and his original circle of readers. (2) The sense of every word in a given passage must

---

[17] Schleiermacher 1998: 7.

be determined by its connection with the sense of the context."[18] These ideas are, in essence, already very familiar, but the question now is: What is their *fundamental grounding*? Neither logic nor grammar supplies it, nor does history or philology as such, although these propositions can be formulated as a result of the work of the latter disciplines, as a certain empirical observation or generalization. Whether the canons are correct or not, it is clear that only an analysis of understanding, and, respectively, of the sense that is correlative to it, can find their ultimate philosophical ground. And if these canons are in some way interesting to logic, this is not because they follow from logical rules, but rather, on the contrary, because they indicate the problems to which logic itself must turn its attention in order to satisfy the demands of those who are beginning to look to logic for the elucidation of the nature of those sciences that have a need for hermeneutics. Thus, it is clear that, in the sequential order here, there is a second set of problems. These problems go beyond a presentation of the principles of understanding as such. Likewise, in a fundamental sequential order, logic comprises a second set, which goes beyond observation and experiment, guided by hypothesis, and beyond mathematical insight with its method of analytical investigation. These problems are of fundamental significance. Only on this condition does logic itself become the foundation for the mathematical or natural sciences – as a logic of analysis and prediction – and for the philological and historical sciences – as a *logic of interpretation*, or *hermeneutic logic*.[19]

Thus, we have a circle: in order to understand one must be able to detect in the reading (or in the hearing) the logical (as well as the grammatical and, in general, the formal) structure, but in order to present logically one must be able to understand. This circle can be resolved in a schema where a simple succession of questions eliminates the circle itself. If we approach that which is understood and that which is presented not only from the side of form, but also from that of their content, we will see that it is not a matter of two different contents, but of *one and the same*. It is also not difficult to convince ourselves that this content has *its own* forms, namely, the *ontological* forms that are inherent in every content and are also general – from the side of understanding as well as from that of presentation. Only when this *whole* appears to us in *relation* to its expression (language), either as the "theme" or as the sense, can we speak, on the one hand, of the theme of the presentation and, on the other, of the sense for understanding. Here we are dealing with a certain still novel content, which is given in the corresponding acts of understanding or of "composition," with their specific forms. However, whereas the forms of a presentation turn out to be, in essence, the forms of an *external* impression, the forms of understanding also remain essentially *internal*. This means that the latter are constructed and are directed to the sense itself, while the former seek their guiding principle in something that lies outside of this principle, for example, the goals

---

[18] Cf. Schleiermacher 1998: 30, 44.

[19] The juxtaposition I have made of the principles and logic of the natural sciences, on the one hand, and the historical sciences, on the other, clearly indicates that the corresponding situation of hermeneutics itself is parallel to the methodologies of the natural sciences.

that are pursued in an aesthetic, rhetorical, etc. presentation. Forms of presentation as well as of understanding can be determined by certain contingent or individual goals, and we then come to an empirical (psychological) analysis of them. But if we remain on the ground of a fundamental analysis, we will be able to note only one modification in the direction of external forms: namely, when choosing a goal for them, we can turn again to the sense itself and, in constructing our forms of presentation on the basis of the principle involved, we can convert them into inner forms, i.e., once again into forms of understanding. Thus, it turns out that, thanks to this technique, understanding itself also requires an examination of the logical forms of what is understood, and we begin to speak of the circle or, more precisely, the parallelism, of understanding and presentation.

In transferring this sequence to the classificatory allocation of the sciences, we are dealing, above all, with a *fundamental* analysis of the content, to which we turn in the case of both understanding and presentation. We will never have a need for presentation so long as we ourselves do not understand. But once we understand something, we need – at least *for ourselves*, but even more in order to communicate and transmit what is understood – some formulation of what is understood (its sense) to serve as the theme of the presentation. In short, we need some formulation for the development of this theme. A fundamental analysis examines understanding on the first level as an immediate understanding – in psychological terminology, an "instinctive" or "automatic" understanding – and the very possibility of proceeding from it to interpretation already presupposes the presence of certain inner logical forms and formations of form.

Abstractly, one can nevertheless assume, following immediate understanding, a certain kind of "primitive," "natural" presentation, which, not only in its empirical (historical) forms but also in its ideal (grammatical) external forms, falls under the special jurisdiction of *linguistics* (both empirical and philosophical). An examination of these forms as *methodological* forms – insofar as this methodology is defined by the *goal*, namely, "to give understanding" – leads us to the division between external (e.g., aesthetic) and internal (logical) forms of a purely ideal order in the sphere of presentation. These are distinguished from the forms previously examined by their immediate correlativity with the special ontological forms peculiar to them (forms of "the thing in general") as *pure* aesthetics and *pure* logic.

Finally, when we proceed to extract from what is understood the methodological forms themselves of what is understood and to interpret, the goal being "to understand what is given for understanding," we are already dealing with the philosophical foundations of *hermeneutics*. Its special tasks are determined only in connection with the corresponding empirical material: philological, historical, theological, etc. Accordingly, we can speak of various kinds of interpretation, the problem concerning which, incidentally, must still be posed separately and more precisely. In any case, one can see a priori that all of them share a correlativity with their forms of presentation, i.e., a parallelism of the logical and the hermeneutic, which is revealed in its foundations by the entire schema presented here.

The issue concerning the "kinds" of interpretation, as we know, has been connected up until now with that of the "number" of meanings that a sign has, or with that of the direction of the interpretation corresponding to the given material. In other words, the issue of the "kinds" of interpretation is connected with that of the "number" of applications a sign has. Only the first could be important in a fundamental examination. Thus, when we assert the unique nature of the sense or meaning of what is understood or interpreted, we assert something that is essential to these acts. However, a complete analysis requires an illumination of the alleged problems that result from the deficiencies of the usual analysis. Such illumination is considered to have been achieved when the actual sources and the actual significance of these alleged problems have been indicated.

Schleiermacher considers the view "as if there were several kinds of interpretation" to be "strange."[20] Whatever kinds we might distinguish, however, the source of this view, as we saw, is the conviction that, along with the "dogmatic" interpretation, an *allegorical* one is also possible, i.e., the conviction that along with the proper sense of a given passage there is also another sense, one that is not proper. Concerning this, Schleiermacher quite correctly remarks that if a certain passage carries an allegorical sense, then this is its unique and simple sense – regardless of whether what underlies a parable is truth or fiction. For example, a supplementary historical interpretation would simply not be true. It would add a sense to the passage being interpreted, a sense that the passage does not have.[21] Nevertheless, Schleiermacher admits the possibility of a "second sense," as long as it is not a special kind of interpretation, but only as a simple understanding of the *hints* that can be found in the text being interpreted. They can be – and in essence only appear to be – insignificant and isolated, but they naturally arise from the parallelism that establishes a connection between the actual sense and the easily graspable ideas accompanying it, for example, by virtue of the parallelism of phenomena – physical and ethical, musical and visually picturesque, etc.[22] But obviously such an "admission" of a "second" or *background* sense has no fundamental significance, and the grammatical or historical method remains the sole legitimate method of interpretation. If, however, we recognize the possibility of such a "second" sense, we must admit that the usual view about the subjectively psychological nature of sense, which is *inserted* into a presentation by the very author according to his/her wish or, in general, deliberately, has a foundation. Additionally, although it is impossible to solve the problem of the reciprocal role and the mutual relation between the "first" and the "second" senses, so long as we do not know what sense is, properly speaking, or what its "bearers" are, we, nevertheless, can see at once that the problem is more complicated than one might think from reading Schleiermacher's reference to a simple parallelism. Although in no clear connection with the explanations that he offers, Schleiermacher himself raises this problem with all of its philosophical significance. Here lies his greatest contribution from the perspective of the history of hermeneutics.

---

[20] Schleiermacher 1998: 15.

[21] Schleiermacher 1998: 15; Schleiermacher 1835: 385.

[22] Schleiermacher 1998: 16.

We saw that Schleiermacher was dissatisfied with the schema Ast proposed, since he admitted only one goal for hermeneutics, namely, the disclosure of sense. However, scrutinizing the "whole," to which every individual passage is to be referred in the interpretation, we can note that this "whole" can be, so to speak, of two different orders: we can relate the given passage to language as a whole or to the entire thought and the entire person of the author. It is a clear fact that the very object, as the bearer of sense, will turn out to be quite different, depending on from which direction we approach the whole: whether from language or from the individual person. Whatever other mistakes Schleiermacher allowed, his great contribution remains not so much his formulation of this contrast by itself as his indication of their mutual *independence*. For him, these are not *stages*, but moments of understanding and interpretation, neither one being either subordinate or reducible to the other.[23]

In his omission of a fundamental analysis of understanding, Schleiermacher's division of the moments or components of interpretation strikes us as quite dogmatic. Moreover, separating one from the other, he could not show the true nature of each of these moments – again thanks to his omission of such an analysis. This is why he did not prevent new confusions from entering into this sphere. In part, he even provided the ground for these confusions in the writers who followed him. In this respect, we must consider the most dangerous thing to be perhaps his excessively straightforward effort to equalize both moments in terms of their rights and significance, since it seemed to him that a complete interpretation is impossible without disclosing both moments. Such a disclosure seemed to him in both cases to be an *understanding*. Schleiermacher himself came upon the difficulties that arise from this "equalizing." However, it must be recognized that he overcame them in a quite superficial manner, mainly because he saw before himself only one side of the question – the *art* of hermeneutics in *interpretation*.

Generally speaking, Schleiermacher sees two methods of interpretation, which are associated with the two moments of interpretation mentioned above. These are the methods of the reconstruction of the form: the historical and the *divinatory* (prophetic) method, both *objectively* and subjectively.[24] The *objectively* historical method examines a given speech within the entire language as a whole and what is included within it as a product of language. The *objectively* divinatory method anticipates how the given speech will become a point from which the development of language will proceed. On the contrary, the *subjectively* historical method shows speech as a given fact in the soul. The *subjectively* divinatory method anticipates how the thought contained in a given speech will develop further in the speaker.[25] The division here, apparently, is clear: The objective side refers to the interpretation of language; the subjective side to the interpretation of the author as a person.[26]

---

[23] Schleiermacher 1998: 8ff. "Both are completely equal, and it would be wrong to call grammatical interpretation the lower and psychological interpretation the higher." Schleiermacher 1998: 11. Cf. Schleiermacher 1835: 373ff.

[24] Schleiermacher 1998: 23. Cf. Schleiermacher 1835: 355.

[25] Schleiermacher 1998: 23.

[26] Schleiermacher 1998: 24.

However, even with such a dogmatic division, a doubt prevails: Is not the subjectively historical method really *divinatory*? In general, would it not be more correct to connect the interpretation of language to history alone, leaving an understanding of the author as an individual person to divination? Without an analysis of understanding both in general and in its two kinds, however, it is difficult to answer this question.

Nevertheless, such a problem did arise in Schleiermacher's own mind,[27] but his attempt to confer equal rights on both moments of interpretation still had a hold over him and he allowed for a psychological interpretation of both methods – the divinatory and the comparative.[28] This admission, however, generates new difficulties that, once again, he himself formulated. As he saw the situation, the *divinatory* method, interpreted psychologically, turns the interpreter, as it were, into the author himself with the goal of *immediately* apprehending what is individual ("*das Individuelle unmittelbar aufzufassen sucht*").[29] On the other hand, the *comparative* method begins by establishing that what is subject to understanding is something universal and only then does it identify what is peculiar (*das Eigentumliche*) by comparing it to the other particulars that are subsumed under that same universal something. Both of these methods are really inseparable from each other: "The universal and the particular must penetrate each other and this always only happens thanks to divination."[30] Nevertheless, it turns out, then, that the entire theory of interpretation as an art hangs in the air, as long as we know nothing about this *immediate* divinatory understanding without which it is impossible even to proceed to a "*comparison.*"

Finally, the question becomes completely confused when, on the one hand, we encounter Schleiermacher's division of psychological interpretation into an interpretation in the strict sense, i.e., a purely psychological interpretation, and a technical interpretation (an understanding of the author's style). With the latter, it is not only not clear why the style should be ascribed to the psychological side of understanding, whereas grammar is ascribed to the objective side. However, it is also not clear how, in general, a "technical" interpretation can be a kind of psychological interpretation.[31] On the other hand, we come upon Schleiermacher's attempt to unite both moments – the grammatical and the psychological – into one. In addi-

---

[27] Contrasting the divinatory and comparative methods and comparing them with the two mentioned moments of interpretation, he himself asks: "So, I ask you, first of all, whether both of the mentioned methods are also valid for both of the mentioned aspects, or is each method appropriate for only one aspect?" (Schleiermacher 1835: 361). Cf. Schleiermacher 1835: 379 – "This much, however, is also already quite clear, that we cannot avoid the preponderance of the divinatory moment in the face of the psychological issue."

[28] Schleiermacher 1998: 92–93. Cf. Schleiermacher 1835: 379–380.

[29] [Schleiermacher 1998: 92.]

[30] Cf. Schleiermacher 1998: 93.

[31] I cannot enter into an analysis of Schleiermacher's corresponding opinions (see particularly Schleiermacher 1838: 148ff), since unfortunately they have come down to us only as notes by the audience. Of course, such material is utterly unreliable (cf. the editor's preface to Schleiermacher 1838: x).

tion, while the latter attempt is wholly erroneous, as we shall see, the former, on the contrary, is based on new and very interesting peculiarities of interpretation.

Anticipating my subsequent analysis, I will dwell a little on some of these peculiarities in order to untie somewhat the knot formed by Schleiermacher's not altogether clear explanations. By separating the *grammatical* from the *psychological* moment of interpretation and ascribing an independent role to each of them, he made a very important distinction. However, considering that a *single* understanding underlies both, i.e., a single *type* of lived experience, he deprived his division of much of its significance. Meanwhile, if he had not refused from the very start to analyze understanding as such, or sense as such, he would have seen that their independence is conditioned precisely by their *heterogeneity* and by the fact that if one of these moments is called *understanding*, the other cannot also be called by that name. Consequently, the term "*interpretation*" is applied to these two moments *in two different senses*. The relation between them is quite complicated, and only a careful and detailed analysis can prevent the confusion that can very easily arise here.

It is comparatively simple to imagine a schema of *understanding* when one is dealing with *grammatical* interpretation. We attempt to penetrate from the given *external forms* of a sign or word to its *sense*, and we call such penetration "understanding." We call the *relations* of these given external forms to the sense the "*inner logical forms*." They are transformed external forms in a stricter sense (see above). These forms rest immediately on so-called *pure* (ontological) forms. Schematically, our concern is limited to this if we do not try to penetrate further by means of *comprehension* into the rational bases (*ratio*) of the content that is given with a sense. The problem of what the content itself is, what its sense is, what kind of thing its bearer-object is – we will leave unexamined for now.

When we turn to a *psychological* interpretation, we easily see that the analogous schema is established there with great difficulty, and the attempt to carry it through reveals its full heterogeneity in comparison with a grammatical interpretation. Proceeding to this interpretation, we must assume a certain new, *second* order of the meanings of words and of speech, the order of sense.[32] It will always accompany the first order and will always be to a certain extent *correlative to the sense*. However, in the first place, this will always be a certain empirical and contingent series of lived experiences, rather than sense as such in its objective stability. Second, we cannot, properly speaking, say that we pass to it from any definite external (grammatical) forms. There are no such forms for it, and we come to it, rather, by means of conjecture or intuition, on the basis of certain indirect indications, e.g., the tone of voice, etc., and most frequently on the basis of the gestures, expressive movements, mimicry, etc., which accompany speech. When we further examine the *relations* of these lived experiences to sense, we can also – and with every right – speak of *internal forms*. However, the latter, being individual and personal representations

---

[32] With the exception of the instance where a given expression directly communicates something about the psychic experiences of its author, but such cases obviously belong entirely to the grammatical type of interpretation.

(*predstavlenija*) or emotions, necessarily remain purely *psychological* forms, which rest not on ontological relations but on the character of those very psychic experiences that are directed toward the sense. A very careful and detailed analysis is necessary in order to find among these experiences also acts of representation and determination (judgment), which one could isolate in their essence (*an sich*), insofar as they are directed toward the sense in its logical forms (logical experiences). These logical forms are correlative to the logical forms built on ontological (*purely* logical) relations. As for the rest, our concern, consequently, is with *psychology*, and in trying to extract it, we should expand the framework of our investigations as much as possible. That is, we should investigate not only the experience of representing and judging, but also that of desire, attitude, feeling, etc., etc., which moves us even further away from the proper (grammatical-historical) interpretation of a given passage. Such an investigation is, by no means, a part of the latter's task.

It must be obvious here that in speaking of a "psychological interpretation" and meaning that the object of the disclosed sense is a *soul*, a *person*, a people, or any other collective group, we are imprecisely expressing ourselves. We are not interpreting them, and, consequently, we do *not understand* them. Rather, we penetrate into them, feel them, sympathize with them, and understand them "sympathetically" (not intellectually). And however we may still express it, it is not a matter of understanding in the strict sense of the term, which designates a certain act of *revealing* a sense. We also understand and interpret them (in the strict sense of the word) just as little as we understand and interpret, in the same strict sense of the term, nature or any natural phenomenon. Insofar as it is a matter of the methodological tasks of the corresponding sciences, we *explain* their appearance, but we do not interpret.

Psychological explanation stands in a single objective order with all the explanations of another kind. One must understand this not only in the sense of a methodological possibility, but also in the sense of the factual situation of things. For example, in explaining the course of the Gallic Wars, which we have learned about through an interpretation of Caesar's memoirs, we come, through an interpretation of his own behavior, to a recognition of that behavior along with the other explanatory reasons for the events of that war. Only by virtue of an equivocation of the term "*exegesis*" or "*interpretation*" do we take an explanation – the method of logical presentation – for an interpretation. In addition, by virtue of the "circle" to which we are led by juxtaposing the techniques of investigation and the methods of presentation, we identify the two as homogeneous methods.

The picture changes, however, only when we begin to view the activities and deeds of the respective persons (the authors) not as the effects of causes, but as *signs* that conceal a certain sense (motivation?), i.e., when they are placed into the context of the general motives that predetermine the place and situation of the given deed. One can again speak here of understanding, but then in the interpretation that follows from this there is again no fundamental difference with a "grammatical" one. This interpretation, however, is not an interpretation of a person, but an interpretation of that person's actions. In any case, the analogy is restored. The interpretation consists here in adducing general motives taken as a whole, i.e., as arising from the individual or the collective, and an explanation of the given individual deed based on these motives: the "text" in relation to the "context" of the individual person. Further revealing the motives (the "grounds"[33] of the interpretation) of the deed or behavior, we also go deep into the comprehension of an individual person (finding the *ratio*). This, therefore, again stands on the same level with the comprehended object of the grammatical interpretation and, consequently, enters into a single real chain with it that, for its part, serves us also as a heuristic device that leads to an explanation as a method of a logical presentation.[34]

Therefore, however different the tasks of "grammatical" and "psychological" interpretation may be, there is a certain relation between them, and although it is not a relation of *species* subsumed under a single genus, but only a *correlation* in a very limited and subtle sense, the idea, nevertheless, seems natural to conceive the unification of both moments as the ultimate goal of hermeneutics. Schleiermacher thinks[35] that each of these moments demands its own type of interpreter. That is, the issue, as it were, amounts to the difference between the inclinations and talents of the interpreters. Nevertheless, for a "complete understanding" he demands a certain unification of both moments. The interpreter, in his opinion, should not neglect either of these sides to the detriment of the other.

Saying nothing of the fact that in making such an appeal to "talent," Schleiermacher abandons his goal of creating hermeneutics as an art. In admitting a contradiction between this goal and the contingent means ("talent") for its realization, he raises a serious doubt: How is such a unification or unity possible? It is a matter of a *mutual relationship*, and, apparently, the entire issue lies in passing from its "abstract" aspects in themselves to the "concrete" whole. However, if we remember that, with the exception of the very narrow location of this correlation, we face in all other respects a heterogeneous difference. We have to recognize that this "unification" represents a rather difficult task. The main point is that if it is understood in too primitive a fashion, it leads to a fatal error for hermeneutics, namely, to *psychologism*. We have to "unite" the two objective bearers of sense: *things* and *persons*.

If these are really two orders of meaning or sense, i.e., two orders of *ideas*, then, thereby, by being ideas, they are unified. However, if they are two directions of empirical interpretation, then the more deeply they are understood, the deeper will be the divergence between them. We can return to their unity only from the viewpoint of a hypothetico-metaphysical interpretation. However, such an interpretation – in Schleiermacher's own words – would carry us beyond the bounds of hermeneutics as an empirical discipline. Moreover, if our concern here is with two directions of empirical interpretation, which obviously depend on two types of reality itself, then we have every reason to suppose that the number of directions of

---

[33] Interpretation requires an indication of the grounds; a concept, as opposed to this is immediate – "without grounds." Hence, we see the special *logical* character of interpretation.

[34] There is a parallel here. The heuristic principle in the natural sciences posits a quasi-goal *(als ob)* and a ground by means of hypothesis, even though mechanical "force" is substituted for it. In this or that form, it is, nevertheless, a *personification*.

[35] Schleiermacher 1835: 375f.

interpretation can be further multiplied, insofar as one can note the differences in reality itself. This is actually another new problem, to which we should turn. It is very important to disclose both the difference and the uniformity, at least of the different types of such interpretive directions.

One can anticipate, however, that, regardless of how far we go with such distinctions, the fundamental oppositions between *thing* and *person* will always play at least an initial role in the definitions of different kinds of interpretation. It would then be enough simply to recognize that the *thing* itself is comprehended in the text being interpreted as a *representation* in order to destroy the independence of grammatical and psychological interpretations that Schleiermacher discovered and to arrive at a new way of "unifying" them, namely, by subordinating all of interpretation to *psychological* interpretation. It is all the same, then, whether meaning (sense) itself will be reduced to a representation and a psychological image, or psychological interpretation appears as the ultimate deepening and completion of interpretation, or the psychological "factor" will be put forward as the ultimate *ratio* of reality itself or some such thing. The penetration into the life of the individual – and the very individual – is, as a rule, made to be the final goal of understanding and interpretation, and we will go backward compared with Schleiermacher – to *psychologism*. We can escape from this only by doing what Schleiermacher himself did not do, a *fundamental* analysis of understanding and sense itself.

# [Hermeneutics After Schleiermacher]

## 1 [August] Boeckh and Philology

Studying the attempts at a theoretical grounding of hermeneutics and its problems after Schleiermacher, we are convinced that the distinctions made in Scheiermacher's hermeneutics fundamentally predetermined its path. The inconsistency of the distinctions he drew made itself felt not only among his immediate followers. The absence of a fundamental basis did not allow for a deepening or development of Schleiermacher's ideas that were in need of development. The opposition of grammatical and psychological interpretation goes either in the direction of a one-sided empirical application of one of them or in the direction of subordinating the grammatical to a psychological interpretation.

In the second case, the problem, on the whole, is sometimes distorted to an extreme degree, when psychological interpretation, which is proclaimed to be the ultimate goal of hermeneutics, prompts one to seek the fundamental foundation of hermeneutics in nothing other than psychology. On the other hand, one can notice that there are some who, although consistently holding onto the object of their science, be it philology or history, and seeking in hermeneutics a methodological foundation, recognize a psychological interpretation as the final goal. They not only do not know how to approach a psychological interpretation, but also, in essence, do not want this, since they have no need of it. On the contrary, the authors of a "logical" grounding of hermeneutical methodology, starting from psychological principles, see in the entire process of interpretation a method for disclosing the purely psychological explanatory principles of the same empirical sciences. By the way, it is only very recently that we encounter the idea, or rather the feeling, that hermeneutics has a self-sufficient methodological significance. In this connection, the need arises to find independent fundamental foundations for hermeneutics. Understandably, however, these foundations are not free at first from those same psychological prejudices.

© Springer Nature Switzerland AG 2019

G. Shpet, T. Nemeth, *Hermeneutics and Its Problems*, Contributions
To Phenomenology 98, https://doi.org/10.1007/978-3-319-98941-9_6

Empirical hermeneutics is now connected with philology – primarily with classical philology – and with history. The connection between theology and hermeneutics turns out to be only indirect – through the mediation of philology and history. We saw in the example of Ernesti how the consciousness of such an indirect connection penetrated into theology, insofar as the latter needed a firm scientific ground. Only the extra-scientific paths of theology are now paved apart from, and sometimes in direct violation to, the demands of philology and history.

The views of August Boeckh turned out to have a decisive influence on the evaluation of hermeneutics and its role in philological knowledge.[1] His formulation of the problem and his definitions still remain our guide up to the present, despite the limitations, amplifications, and corrections that his expressions have undergone. The absence of a fundamental analysis of the foundations of hermeneutics – of understanding – and of a logico-methodological analysis of interpretation in a representative of positive knowledge should be recognized as quite natural, as natural, it seems to me, as the aspiration of philology to free itself entirely from a fundamental discussion of these problems, limiting itself to gathering empirical material, which we observe in contemporary philology.[2] However natural the tendency of positive science to evade a fundamental discussion of the philosophical foundations of its science may seem to us, the consequences entailed are by no means favorable to science. Science cannot at all do without these foundations, since being quite unaware of it, and perhaps not even wishing it, science repeats, in the form of its own empirical generalizations, the old general views and opinions that, in philosophy, are antiquated and have lost their significance.

Science, therefore, deprives itself of revitalizing nourishment from new philosophical sources, which are purer and deeper than those upon which empirical investigation itself unconsciously depends. On the other hand, without turning to philosophy for a review of its foundations, this special science provides no occasion for philosophy to address its current perplexities. Thereby, it once again condemns itself to unnecessary hardships, which are occasionally harmful to it. Owing to this, we will limit ourselves in our further presentation – to the extent that it is a matter of the tasks of hermeneutics that have arisen in connection with the needs of philology and of history – to an examination of only those new problems that have emerged for hermeneutics by virtue of its union with philological knowledge. These problems, then, give us a chance, upon a deeper formulation of the problem, to notice some essential features of the fundamental and principled problem of hermeneutics. As we will see, the main problem here will be that of the sorts and types of interpretation. This now occupies a position in some respects analogous to the one occupied by the problem of the ambiguity of words and expressions.

---

[1] Boeckh 1877. Concerning the special tasks of a theological hermeneutics, as distinct from those of philology, Boeckh writes: "The distinction between them … becomes understandable." Boeckh 1877: 80.

[2] Quite indicative of the sense of this self-limitation is Birt's hermeneutics in the new (3rd) edition of Iwan Müller's handbook. See Birt 1913.

Turning to Boeckh, although we should recognize that he himself did not lay such rigorous demands on his *Encyclopedia* as those that we encounter in contemporary philology, he did not entirely reject attempts to introduce certain general considerations in order to ground his views. Nevertheless, if they suffer from considerable vagueness and inconsistency, then, perhaps, this arises from Boeckh's conviction that Schleiermacher gave or already outlined the appropriate philosophical foundations. A disciple of Ernesti and Schleiermacher, Boeckh calls Schleiermacher's *Hermeneutics* "a complete system, sketched by a masterly hand." Emphasizing his dependence on Schleiermacher's ideas, Boeckh states that in his own presentation he is "not in a position to distinguish between what is his own and what is another's."[3]

Actually, one can trace Schleiermacher's influence in many of Boeckh's very important and responsible assertions, although he seldom mentions his teacher by name. This influence reveals itself above all in Boeckh's understanding of the relation of philology to philosophy and to other disciplines, and additionally in his entire division of the types of interpretation. All of science, as a whole, is philosophy in the form of a science of ideas. Additionally, depending on whether we examine everything from its material or ideal side, i.e., as nature or as spirit, as necessity or as freedom, we obtain two different spheres of scientific knowledge with respect to content: *physics and ethics*.[4] Where does philology belong? If we simply refer it to ethics, as it seems obvious at first sight, we would gain a considerable advantage in comparison to the widespread division of the sciences into sciences of nature and human sciences (which are based on psychology) and which includes philology and history among the latter. However, Boeckh, in fact, goes further and deeper than this, so that from the fundamental point of view his positions become even more interesting. He determines the position of philology – in a clear parallel to the position of the dialectic in Schleiermacher – as the science of conducting a conversation (*Gesprächführung*). Philology, it turns out, according to Boeckh, embraces to a certain extent both of the mentioned spheres of knowledge, and yet is neither the one nor the other. In order to understand the significance and place of philology in the general system of knowledge, one should compare it not with the special types and parts of philosophical knowledge, but with *philosophy itself on the whole*.[5]

---

[3] Boeckh 1877: 75.

[4] Boeckh 1877: 270. Cf. Boeckh 1877: 18, 57. Cf. Schleiermacher 1998: 8 – "The science of history, though, is ethics. Since language also has a natural aspect, the differences of the human spirit are also determined by the nature of the human being and by that of the planet. Therefore, hermeneutics is rooted not only in ethics, but also in physics. Ethics and physics lead, however, back again to the dialectic, as the science of the unity of knowledge." See also Schleiermacher 1839: 8, 370ff, 480ff, 568ff. Cf. Weissenborn 1847: 9ff.

[5] [The German editors note that the typed manuscript they used reads here "philological knowledge, but with philology itself on the whole" whereas the hand-written copy has the text reading as above. See Špet 1993: 173f. The 2005 Russian edition serving as the fundamental text in this translation follows the decision of the German editors to read "philosophical ... *philosophy itself on the whole*."]

I believe it necessary to pause on Boeckh's development of this position, since I find here the first hint of that idea, the disclosure of which is the fundamental idea of my entire investigation. It is my conviction that a consistent development of this idea will significantly change our views not only of the nature of verbal and histori-cal knowledge and, in connection with this, not only of the nature and character of all scientific methodology, but also of the very essence of all philosophical knowl-edge on the whole.

As philologists, Boeckh argues, we need not philosophize like Plato, but we must, nevertheless, understand Plato's works, not only with respect to their artistic form, but also with respect to their content. For an essential philological explanation refers chiefly to the understanding of the content. The philologist should understand a work on the philosophy of nature, such as Plato's *Timaeus*, exactly in the same way as Aesop's fables or a Greek tragedy. It is not the philologist's task to *contribute* to the field of the philosophy of nature, but he should know and understand what others have contributed in this science, since we should work on the *history* of the philosophy of nature philologically. The same applies to all of ethics, the historical development of which we similarly investigate in a philological manner. Likewise, philology elaborates the individual branches of both physics and ethics, for exam-ple, natural history and politics. The speculations and experiments of physics simi-larly are not among the tasks of philology just as logical and political investigations are not. However, the works of Pliny [the Elder], Dioscorides, and Buffon are objects for philology. Starting from such an understanding of the role of philology, Boeckh formulates its task in the following way: "... the proper task of philology is to be the *knowledge of what has been produced* by the human spirit, i.e., of what is *known*."[6]

As I have tried to show above (in my "Introduction"[7]), in determining the role of the *word* and, consequently, of philological techniques of investigation, our philo-sophical and, in general, scientific knowledge can and must go significantly further and deeper. Only a fundamental deepening of the problem in the appropriate case will reveal the actual role and philosophical value of philological methodology in all of its importance. However, even from Boeckh's brief indications – or rather hints – one can see the direction in which one should carry out the indicated deepening. In any case, it is clear from them that the mutual correlations of philology and philoso-phy are more interesting and more fraught with consequences than they may seem from the point of view of the hitherto widespread, but very elementary, inclusion of philology among the human sciences. Even more important, however, and even more helpful for a correct formulation of the problem are Boeckh's explanations regarding the proper definitions of philology and its method. A knowledge of the known, i.e., the task of philology, according to these explanations, is nothing other than understanding.[8] He writes, "According to the concept we have found, philology

---

[6] Boeckh 1877: 10.

[7] [The editors of the German-language translation understandably take this to be a reference to Chapter 1. See Špet 1993: 174.]

[8] Boeckh 1877: 52. Cf. Boeckh 1877: 15, 75.

is *knowledge of the known*, consequently, a secondary knowledge (*Wiedererkennen*) of given knowledge. However, to know again what is known means to *understand*. Just as philosophy examines the very act of knowledge and the moments of cognitive activity in *logic*, *dialectic* or – as the Epicureans called it – the 'canonic,' so philology too should investigate scientifically the act of *understanding* (*den Akt des Verstehens*) and the moments of comprehension (*die Momente des Verständnisses*)."[9]

Certainly, it is impossible to think that, with this, philology sets for itself the task of a fundamental investigation of the act of understanding. Since this is the task of philosophy, philology would go beyond the bounds of its competency if it would take it upon itself to accomplish this task. We need to understand Boeckh's explanation only in the sense that the methodological part of philology should presuppose a theory of understanding, and should, consequently, isolate that corresponding part for an examination of the problems connected with this presupposition. Analogous to the position of logic within philosophy, philology has its formal, methodological discipline, namely, *hermeneutics*. The question of the place and the tasks of such a formal discipline, however, depends to a significant degree on how the tasks of philology are determined with respect to the content of the latter. Nevertheless, it is impossible to say that Boeckh indicated the place of philology in this respect with sufficient clarity.

Boeckh explains that insofar as philology is knowledge of the known, it presupposes the existence of certain already given knowledge at some time. Every history of science is, in this sense, philological. "But this," he asserts, "does not exhaust the concept of philology. Rather, it coincides with the concept of history in the broadest sense."[10] Ultimately, history is also precisely *a knowledge of what has been known*.[11] Moreover, the historical character of philology is due not to its subordinate place with respect to philosophy, but to its coordinated place. All the sciences are rooted in philosophy and philology, precisely because, on the one hand, they are seen as offshoots of philosophy and, on the other hand, "they have their object in their own history." The goal of philology itself turns out to be *purely historical*.[12] Through history, philosophy and philology uniquely interact: philology constructs historically, not from concepts. Nevertheless, however, its final goal is to reveal the concept in the historical. Consequently, this task is resolved in philosophy, because the concept in general cannot be known in the historical, if the direction to it is not indicated beforehand.[13]

The concept of philology, therefore, merges indistinguishably with the concept of history. The coordination of philosophy and philology is equivalent to a coordination of philosophy and history. As indicated above, Boeckh's definitions have

---

[9] [Boeckh 1877: 53.]

[10] Boeckh 1877: 10.

[11] Boeckh 1877: 11.

[12] Boeckh 1877: 18.

[13] Boeckh 1877: 17. Cf. Boeckh 1877: 11 – "History, therefore, differs from philology only in terms of appearance, namely, with respect to its scope, since it usually is limited chiefly to the political sphere and examines the rest of cultural life only in connection with the life of the state."

exerted an influence on the determinations of the tasks of philology up to the present, although for example, Blass, the author of the section on hermeneutics in Iwan Müller's *Handbuch*, does not consider Boeckh's identification of philology and history to be entirely precise. Nevertheless, thinking that he himself *expands* Boeckh's definition Blass outlines the tasks of philology in a formula that can freely be transferred to *history*. Philology, in his opinion, has to do with the products (*mit den Erzeugnissen*) of the human spirit.[14] Consequently, this is the same as Boeckh's "production." He asserts, "That which is historically produced is something spiritual, which has passed into action (*in That*)."[15]

I do not see anything fundamentally new and different in comparison with Boeckh and in the definition offered by Birt, who authored the section on hermeneutics in the new, third edition of the same *Handbuch*. In it, the task of philology is thought to be the appropriation of everything that "once was (*einmal gewesen ist*) in the sphere of human culture; philology is the *reconstruction of past human cultures*."[16] More interesting to me is Birt's attempt to demarcate the spheres of philology and history while retaining this definition. We are again dealing only with a hint, but it is not difficult for a logician to draw certain methodologically important conclusions here. "The philologist," he says, "elaborates what has been (*das Gewesene*), the historian, what has happened (*das Geschehene*). As long as I establish and investigate what is past (*vergangen*) and distinguish among separate phenomena in sufficient detail, I am a philologist. I become a historian only when I begin to place separate facts in a causal connection and only when a course of events (*ein Hergang*) arises. *The historian combines what has been (das Gewesene) with what has happened (zum Geschehenen)*, observing its movement, formation, and development, and inquiring into the motives for the changes."[17]

*Logically*, Birt's conclusions emphasize once again the unity of the subject matter and content of philology and history, transferring the difference between the two sciences to the sphere of their methodological peculiarities. If we follow Birt's thought in this direction to the end, the difference between philology and history – given their material unity – appears as the difference between *description* and *explanation*. Philology then turns out to be descriptive history, and history – explanatory philology. Insofar as such a formulation of the problem can be subjected to a logical critique, it is impossible not to recognize some veracity behind it, but it is not

[14] Blass 1892: 165. Cf. in this volume the comments of Ludwig von Urlichs: "It (philology) is therefore essentially a recognition and assimilation." Philology, in his opinion, adjoins closely to history and is distinguished from it by the fact that it has to do not with changes (*Veränderungen*), but with states (*die Zuständlichkeit*), not with the political characters (!) of politicians, but with culture in general. Urlichs 1892: 5. Cf. moreover the opinion of Steinthal, who noting his agreement with Boeckh, thinks that philology in its broadest sense must be understood as the history of the human spirit. Steinthal 1878a: 27. Even clearer is Steinthal's statement: "… in short, philology is history. With any other presupposition, philology is either understood one-sidedly, or it entirely loses the status of a science and becomes only an auxiliary discipline." Steinthal 1864: 28–29.

[15] Boeckh 1877: 11.

[16] Birt 1913: 4.

[17] Birt 1913: 4.

difficult to convince oneself that it, nevertheless, does not solve the essential problem. The veracity of this opposition lies in the fact that philology – insofar as it limits its methodological techniques to critique and hermeneutics – is, actually, not an explanatory science but only a descriptive one. Likewise, it is also true that history, as a science, cannot be limited merely to the goals of description, but is essentially an explanatory science.

Doubts arise, however, from another side: does philology genuinely not have *its own* explanatory tasks, and does history genuinely not have *its own* kind of description? These questions can be answered independently of an examination and the allocation of the content of philology and history, i.e., independently of how we solve the problems about the place and the role, for example, of grammar, the history of literature, and poetics, on the one hand, and of explanatory hypotheses drawn from sociology, political economy, etc., on the other. Independently of this, the doubts mentioned seem so well grounded that, however tempting the conclusions resulting from Birt's division may appear by themselves, this division can hardly be considered as resolving the problem satisfactorily. Actually, if Birt were correct, that fact would eliminate the *raison d'être* of one of the sciences that he opposed to the other. In any case, it would eliminate one of the *names* of these sciences, and, in all probability, that would be *philology*. This would even coincide with a fairly widespread view of philology, one which has supporters among philologists themselves, and which draws sustenance from the directions in philology that stem – if not from Friedrich August Wolff himself, then, in any case, from Gottfried Hermann. The sense of this view is that philology is not so much an independent science as a certain encyclopedic "multiplicity."

However, we need only attribute to this "multiplicity," which lacks any original subject matter, a certain, as it were, methodological uniformity in order to restore the independent logical significance of philology. Birt himself suggests the appropriate intellectual direction: Philology is not a science, but an aspiration to it, a desire (*ein Verlangen*) to be one. It is an investigation (*Forschung*).[18] Since this assertion is not a simple play on the word φίλος but actually a serious intention, philology claims a place of honor in the system of knowledge, despite the absence in it of a definite and independent subject matter. Boeckh's formulation, which contrasts philology with philosophy, makes sense, again revealing the fundamental position of philology. It seems that Usener revealed this sense most vividly and with the greatest methodological depth already in his lecture, "Philology and the Science of History." In Usener's opinion, "philology is not a historical *science*."[19] It could appear to be such when historical science in the modern sense did not yet exist, and so it appeared for the first time only before the eyes of the classical philologist. Its real significance lies in the fact that, through its grammatical ability, it establishes and explains the written word as the ground of every historical science. It is the ultimate presupposition of any historical investigation (*"die letzte Voraussetzung*

---

[18] Birt 1913: 3.

[19] Usener 1882: 19 – "So it is: philology is not a historical *science*."

*alter geschichtlichen Forschung*").[20] "Philology is, therefore, a method of historical science and, moreover, the fundamental, guiding (*massgebende*) method."[21] Perhaps, philology is not an exclusively historical method, but it is *one* of the methods of historical science and, moreover, its fundamental method. The relation of philology to history turns out to be analogous to the relation of mathematics to natural science. All historical disciplines require a philologically secure foundation and the intro-duction of the philological method.[22] Usener says, "I could call philological meth-odology and encyclopedia '*historics*' for short. In fact, the same elementary operations that the philologist practices, i.e., *recensio* (review) and *interpretatio* (interpretation), the establishing of facts passed down by tradition, and spiritual penetration into them and their understanding (*begreifen*) are repeated at the most varied stages of historical investigation, but applied to the different material in stages."[23] It is precisely in this sense that Usener sums up his lecture with the short but vivid aphorism: "The philologist is the pioneer of historical science."[24]

It seems to me that Usener's ideas nicely complete the ideas originating from Boeckh. However, they are only the *beginning*, the starting point, of a fundamen-tally deep formulation of the problem that I intend to reveal through the following investigation. In contrast, I will express here one more consideration that is critical for the transition to the following problem that is fundamental to nineteenth-century hermeneutics, namely, the problem of multiple types of interpretation. Let us take into account Usener's assertion that the philologist is the pioneer of history. We can, then, logically reconcile ourselves with the fact that, contrary to Birt's prohibition, the philologist sometimes passes beyond the bounds of description and interpreta-tion into explanation – provided that we do not follow the path taken by Gottfried Hermann of restricting philology to the tasks of grammar and pure exegesis. However, it seems to me that it would be arbitrary to limit historical description only to philological interpretation. The foundations for such a restriction are not clear in Birt's distinction, and what Usener says apparently pushes us toward the opposite conclusion. He says that the philologist practices the same operations *repeatedly* at the most varied stages of historical investigation. Obviously, it is impossible to understand the word "repeatedly" here in the sense of complete identity. For we encounter new – *qualitatively* new – material in the new stages of a purely historical investigation, material upon which the mentioned operations are applied. Does this not also change the logical character of the corresponding description and corre-sponding interpretation? Does the historian not find his own tasks here, tasks that perhaps are similar to those of a philological interpretation but that are not identical to them and that have *their own* methodological peculiarities? Should *history itself* – again before it starts explaining – interpret *in its own way* what will subsequently be subject to explanation? And is this not some living and vivid interpretation of which

---

[20] Usener 1882: 29.

[21] Usener 1882: 30.

[22] Usener 1882: 35.

[23] Usener 1882: 34.

[24] Usener 1882: 39.

philology does not yet know, particularly insofar as it exceeds the bounds of a grammatical interpretation even in the broadest sense? Should it not frequently recognize a means of proceeding beyond its own bounds? Obviously, these questions are already themselves hermeneutical questions, since answers to them presuppose an examination of the possible kinds and types of interpretation with the goal being the determination of the place of *historical* interpretation in them.

As we saw, Schleiermacher distinguished grammatical interpretation from psychological interpretation. Now a question arises about a new distinction: Does historical interpretation coincide with one of these kinds, or does it occupy a subordinate position with respect to one of them, and, if so, then to which one? Since the solution to the problem of the relation of philology to history is unclear, the answer to these questions must also appear so, at least to the mentioned philologists. We must turn for help to the historians themselves. In any case, it should be clear from our presentation that the question of the kinds of interpretation now becomes of topical importance, and we have a right to expect to find new material in the history of this question that will prepare us for a fundamental formulation of the entire problem.

## 2  Boeckh and Others: Hermeneutics and Its Problems

I consider the ideas developed by Usener to be only an inference drawn from Boeckh's fundamental definitions. If philology acquires significant importance within the system of knowledge thanks to the quality of its methodology, i.e., thanks to the application of the methods of interpretation and critique to the material being studied, then, obviously, philology, in its concern for self-definition, should turn its attention most carefully to this side. Boeckh, actually, starts from the fact that the *subject matter* (*der Stoff*) of philology has much in common, as we saw, with philosophy,[25] on the one hand, and with history, on the other. However, philology is distinguished among the sciences by its *form*, "which consists in the mode of treatment or in the activity that is directed to the given subject matter."[26]

In this sense, as we have noted, the position of philology for Boeckh with respect to philosophy is compared to that of logic. The "philological organon," certainly presupposes, in Boeckh's opinion, a general logic, but it is a "particular, independent branch of it."[27] Nevertheless, there is in Boeckh a hint that provides an occasion for going even further into determining the logical significance of philological methodology. One can attribute a broader and more general significance to logic, precisely in its "philological" aspect, than merely that of a "branch." One can attri-

---

[25] [The German editors note that the typed copy of Shpet's work – clearly in error – reads here "philology" instead of "philosophy."]

[26] Boeckh 1877: 4; cf. Boeckh 1877: 45, 52ff, 75ff. Cf. Conrad Hermann contrasts *"wie"* [the "how"] and *"was"* [the "what"]. Hermann 1875: 237. On the contrary, Urlichs distributes *"wie"* and *"was"* between hermeneutics and critique. Urlichs 1892: 9.

[27] Boeckh 1877: 52.

bute to it a quite universal significance.[28] This is so insofar as one can look on philological methodology – in Boeckh's words – as a *"theory of the knowing of knowing,
i.e., as a theory of understanding in general."*[29]

Understanding, therefore, is the criterion by means of which one distinguishes
what in philology belongs to its formal part.[30] The problem of understanding, therefore, is a task of the formal part of philology, to which Boeckh assigns hermeneutics
and critique. Under such conditions, hermeneutics cannot be a simple collection of
practical rules and suggestions. It "must contain a scientific development of the *laws*
of understanding."[31] An absolutely fundamental task is assigned to hermeneutics so
conceived – regardless of whether it will be carried out by hermeneutics itself using
its own means and powers, or borrow the solution from philosophy conceived as the
general source of all the fundamental principles of science. In any case, it is obvious
that the analysis of the act of understanding is the next, urgent problem. Moreover,
as is clear from everything that has been said, it is above all a *philosophical* problem. For Boeckh, this problem was a problem of hermeneutics itself as a science of
forms, since, as we saw, Boeckh understands form, in a Kantian spirit, as nothing
other than *activity*. On the other hand, Boeckh considered what he found in
Schleiermacher to be philosophically sufficient. In any case, after Boeckh the situation in philology did not get better in this respect. The philologists either themselves lost their sense of the urgency and fundamental importance of the problem of
understanding, moving all the more toward a "practical" discussion of the problems
of hermeneutics, or they turned to popular psychological theories, being content
with an extremely loose and popular resolution of the problem. Certainly, it is even
more astonishing that in philosophy itself there was for a long time no awareness of
the original aspect of the problem, or – and this is of chief importance – of the originary and unique character of understanding as an act of consciousness.

Boeckh leaves the problem concerning the correlative *object* of the understanding, philosophically speaking, in the same unclear state. But in this connection too,
one can find remarks in Boeckh that cannot be overlooked and that must be thought
through more deeply than has been done up to now. "Philology, or – what amounts
to the same thing – history, is knowledge of the known."[32] Knowledge of the known,
as we saw, is understanding. The unique nature of this definition lies in the valuable
idea, which I will develop in the following presentation, that *understanding is a sui
generis kind of knowledge*. Consequently, "the known," toward which the act of
understanding is directed as its own knowable object, also presupposes an object
that is *sui generis*. What is this object; what are its features? One becomes annoyed

---

[28] See the Introduction.

[29] Boeckh 1877: 33. "Philology attains its *third* auxiliary goal thanks to its methodology, which is
the theory of knowing the act of knowing, i.e., of *understanding* in general."

[30] Thus, for example, Boeckh refers grammar to the formal part of philology only insofar as it is a
matter of grammatical *understanding*. Conversely, as the *object* of language, grammar, in its history, is a part of the content of philology. Cf. Boeckh 1877: 53–54.

[31] Boeckh 1877: 76.

[32] Boeckh 1877: 11.

by the short answer that satisfies Boeckh, even more since, up to now, the significance of the new problems contained in Boeckh's answer has remained unnoticed. Of course, in order to find these problems, we have to subject Boeckh's own words to interpretation. The legitimacy of that interpretation, however, was recognized by both Boeckh himself and all the philologists who came after him. With their interpretation, they claimed to understand the author better than the author himself did.

Boeckh continues the just adduced definition, writing "by 'the known' we understand *also*[33] all representations (*Vorstellungen*).[34] For often, we recognize only representations, e.g., those in poetry, in art, in political history, where the concepts are only partially laid out, as in science, and the rest are representations that the philologist must recognize."[35] This means: (1) that *"the known" as an object is nothing other than a "concept."* Consequently, it still must be accepted as the meaning that results from understanding and interpretation. It also means: (2) that *the "representation" is not their direct object, but appears – "also" – with the concept* as the direct object of understanding. Consequently, as the goal of understanding and interpretation, a representation appears in a specific role, which follows by itself from the distinction between the two types of interpretation. The direction of these types was anticipated in the opposition between *concept and representation* that they themselves set.

Furthermore, for an analysis of understanding or of what is understood, it is absolutely necessary to show the *data* without which one obviously cannot speak about the content of what is understood. Boeckh continues, "Since in philology some given knowledge is everywhere presupposed, it cannot exist without communication. The human spirit communicates through all kinds of signs and symbols, but language is the most adequate expression of knowledge."[36] With this, Boeckh provides us with more than just an indication of the data we need in the form of signs in general and of language in particular, which to a certain degree is a fact that we take for granted. However, it also indicates that there is one more – a third – fundamental problem of hermeneutics, namely, that of the necessary conditions or sphere of consciousness in which we must carry out the entire fundamental analysis of understanding, namely the problem of *communication*. Additionally, it is precisely this indication that alone thoroughly makes sense of the right of philology, emphasized above, to its fundamental place alongside philosophy, and particularly of hermeneutics alongside logic: "… without communication the concerns of science in general and even of life would be in a rather bad state, so that philology is, actually, one of the first conditions of life, an element (*ein Element*) that happens to be something original in our deepest nature and in the cultural chain. It rests on a

---

[33] [Shpet adds here that the emphasis is his addition.]

[34] [Boeckh apparently understands *Vorstellung* and *Idee* as virtually, if not in fact, synonomous: *"es ist in allem eine Vorstellung oder Idee ausgeprägt."* Boeckh 1877: 56.]

[35] [Boeckh 1877: 11.]

[36] [Boeckh 1877: 11.]

fundamental drive of civilized peoples; an uncivilized people can do philosophy (φιλοσοφεῖν), but not philology (φιλολογεῖν)."[37]

Communication is that element of consciousness in which understanding lives and moves. That which is communicated is the sphere of hermeneutics. The data that lead to the object of understanding and on which all of its content is organized are words as signs. We have known this for a long time. However, here too Boeckh drops a hint, which we cannot help but value as an indication of yet another new – a fourth – fundamental problem of hermeneutics. We all too commonly subsume under the concept "sign" everything with which understanding and interpretation begin, and this is why we are not clear about whether a sign actually serves on this occasion *as a sign* or whether there are not along with the sign also any "data" that would lead to the same path of understanding. In other words, does a sign, as a sign, guide our understanding and that, consequently, everything directed to the same goal must be characterized thereby as a sign? Or must we still find the essential element in a sign that endows it with such qualities and that, consequently, may not be confined to the sign alone as such? The following remark of Boeckh, despite all of its indeterminacy, points to these questions. "What is communicated in all of its variety is, in any case, either a *sign* of what is known, i.e., is different in form from the latter, as is any linguistic communication, a letter, musical notation, etc., or else it is an image (*ein Gebilde*), which, in its form, *agrees* with what is expressed by it, such as, for example, works of art and technology, the vital arrangements given immediately in intuition, etc."[38] However vague this distinction may be, I attribute great importance to it, not only because it raises the problems formulated above, but also because it directly outlines in advance the distinction that I already drew above between a "grammatical" interpretation and a new type of interpretation, which in the strict and proper sense should be called *historical*. Clearly, this new distinction should be drawn on a different level than the division of interpretation into a grammatical one, in a broad sense, and a psychological one, a division that Schleiermacher had already indicated. The distinction could have been connected with Boeckh's own opposition between "concepts" and "representations," insofar as they embrace "the known." For Boeckh himself, however, neither this opposition between kinds of "meanings" nor the just indicated opposition between kinds of "signs" serves as the basis of his distinction between kinds of interpretation.[39]

---

[37] Boeckh 1877: 11–12. It seems to me that this final conclusion is unexpected. In my view, just the reverse follows from what was just said. Precisely because φιλολογεῖν is the beginning of civilization, it is also the beginning of φιλοσοψεῖν.

[38] Boeckh 1877: 77–78.

[39] Boeckh's opposition loses its fundamental significance if we understand it not in the sense of a generic opposition, but only in the sense of a difference between species or, even worse, in the sense of a relation between genus ("sign") and species ("image"). Apparently, Blass imagines the case to be this way when he defines the object of hermeneutics not only as the written or spoken word, but also as other signs "or any product in general of the human spirit." Blass 1892: 167.

# 3   Kinds of Interpretation

This is why Boeckh is only being consistent when he, in general, denies a specific difference within hermeneutics that depends on a difference in the objects being interpreted. "The functions of understanding," he claims, "are everywhere one and the same."[40] From this point of view, it is impermissible, for example, to distinguish between *hermeneutica sacra* and *profana*.[41] Clearly, this assertion also solves in advance the old problem of the distinction between literal, allegorical, and other types of interpretation. Boeckh provides a formula that easily eliminates the problem of allegorical interpretation as a special device for discovering a special meaning and that would be difficult to find only as long as hermeneutics was tightly linked to rhetoric. The simple elimination of this source of misunderstanding lies in pointing out that *allegory* itself is nothing but a kind of *presentation*.[42] Consequently, its understanding does not require a special kind of interpretation. An allegorical interpretation consists precisely in the same hermeneutical activity as the interpretation of any other type of literary work. Although all of this is correct, does it follow from Boeckh's assertion? Since an allegory is a kind of literary work, it is naturally subject to the same rules of interpretation as other literary works. There is precisely no difference between the objects here. As for the division of hermeneutics into *sacra* and *profana*, the entire history of hermeneutics and the very reduction of Biblical hermeneutics ultimately to philological hermeneutics clearly shows the untenability of this opposition.

A more careful check of Boeckh's assertions can, in fact, reveal several essential deficiencies. Even if it were correct that all the functions of understanding are generically one and the same, it would not follow from this that we should not distinguish between the *kinds* of understanding – and do this precisely in close connection with the "objects" toward which understanding is directed. For the generic unity, or identity of understanding, presupposes the identity of the objects of the various kinds of understanding. Only where there is a completely artificial and forced distinction between the act of understanding and the object toward which it is directed, the two being correlatively connected, could one speak of an empty act of understanding directed toward an object. A consequence of such formalism in the analysis of understanding would be that the distinction between the kinds of understanding, while still possible, would have to be derived from the purely *subjective* conditions of the one who is understanding. As we will now see, however, this would already be contrary to Boeckh's desire, although the general place that he designated for hermeneutics in the general system of philology inclines him, properly speaking, to formalism. Whatever the case, we can foresee difficulties from two

---

[40] Boeckh 1877: 80.

[41] [hermeneutics pertaining to the Scriptures and secular hermeneutics.]

[42] Boeckh 1877: 92.

sides[43] that are of interest to us, and Boeckh's formalism must lead to these difficulties.

1. If we ignore the difference between the objects, it is difficult to differentiate a psychological interpretation, as Schleiermacher understood it, from a historical interpretation in the sense indicated above.[44]
2. It is also difficult to differentiate a psychological interpretation – that is, insofar as it is immediately a matter of the understanding of a given *person*, from an interpretation that has to do not directly with a person, but with the objective circumstances that are merely reflected in the person of the author being interpreted.
3. Finally, it is also difficult to differentiate between hermeneutics and historical interpretation.

Moreover, Boeckh's position turns out to be quite vague when he first attempts to find a different principle for distinguishing the kinds of interpretation instead of the difference between the objects. When he asserts that the "real specific differences in interpretation can be derived only from the essence of hermeneutical activity,"[45] one cannot but recognize this truly philosophical statement as quite correct. However, at the same time this specification should clearly also be a specification of the sense and, consequently, also of the object as the bearer of this sense, for the disclosure of the sense of what is communicated belongs, in any case, to the "essence of herme-neutical activity." Meanwhile, Boeckh continues, "Interpretation, which is essential for understanding and its expression, is the *consciousness* of that by which the sense and the meaning of what is communicated or transmitted is *conditioned* and *determined.*"[46] Outwardly, it seems that what is essential for understanding is not a consciousness of the sense, but of its conditions. That is, one must think of the con-ditions for its realization, for the sense is always an *idea*. However, the issue, in fact, is how to separate one from the other. Sense, apart from these conditions, is actually *only* an idea, and, it can be said, we see it but still not understand it. We understand an idea only in its realization, i.e., only when we take it as already the sense, as the *ratio*, of what has been realized. It follows from this that Boeckh's assertion is not in fact as absurd, as it might appear at first sight. Nevertheless, however, the intel-ligibility of his words is purchased at the cost of consistency. With his principle of distinguishing the types of interpretation, he indirectly introduces a distinction in the object that he had previously rejected. For whatever may be the "conditions" of the sense of what is communicated, they fundamentally have the same character as

---

[43] [Shpet mentions here "difficulties from two sides" but then presents three. This anomaly is not mentioned in the Russian text (Shpet 2005: 348), but the German translation remarks that the third difficulty that follows was inserted only in a typed version of the original Russian work and is not found in the handwritten copy. See Špet 1993: 189f. Presumably, then, Shpet overlooked correct-ing the text when he inserted the third difficulty.]

[44] See Boeckh 1877: 103.

[45] Boeckh 1877: 81.

[46] [Boeckh 1877: 81–82.]

does that sense. That is, they refer to objects of a single order.[47] This is why we have a right, a priori, to expect that Boeckh will further on either implicitly also introduce a distinction between the objects or will talk about just one object and one kind of interpretation.

However, if we find in Boeckh neither the one nor the other, this is merely a consequence of the other false presuppositions of his investigation, namely, of his subjectivism, or, if you will, his psychologism, by virtue of which sense and meaning are for him not ideas, but representations. This is why the conditions that he discusses are not so much the conditions of a realizable sense as they are the conditions of *communication* itself, as such. "Communication" (*Mitteilung*) and "what is communicated" (*das Mitgeteilte*) are terms that Boeckh uses promiscuously. Thus, they are not objective relations that would exist even if in reality no one thought of them or *communicated* them. They are, rather, precisely the products of a communicator's subjective activity. Only as such can they be examined both with respect to their "objective" conditions, i.e., those that are "external" to the communicating subject, as well as with respect to their "subjective" conditions, i.e., those that are "internal" to the subject. This is precisely the sense of Boeckh's distinction between hermeneutics as (1) "understanding based on the *objective* conditions of what is communicated," and as (2) "understanding based on the *subjective* conditions of what is communicated."[48]

Since both of these types of interpretation are directed toward one object, and since this object is determined in advance, it is clear from what we are cut off by this distinction. If this interpretation has to do with the object of a given communication, the very author of this communication, his/her *person*, as a possible special, and quite independent, object of interpretation, will always remain inaccessible to us. Either the person is not in general the *sui generis* object of interpretation or else the person is subject to interpretation only when he/she forms the object and the content of what is communicated. Since this last restriction is unacceptable, the first horn of this dilemma remains – as a serious reproach to Boeckh – if we wish to preserve the fundamental formulation of the problem to which Boeckh so aspired in his basic definitions. Moreover, it is revealing that constricting the tasks of philology to the limited bounds of an ordinary empirical science leads to the fact that, in general, *psychological* interpretation – for in this case we are dealing with a peculiar type of psychological interpretation in the genuine sense – has no place in the division of the kinds of interpretation. That is, the place it has in Boeckh's conception – as another type – in "an understanding, based on the *subjective conditions* of what is communicated," is taken away from it.[49]

---

[47] If this statement is understood and thought through in all of its details, it will be clear that it resolves in advance a series of issues that sometimes evoke futile disputes. One thing, in particular, is important: Psychological interpretation cannot rise to objective conditions (such an interpretation is only a reflex), and, conversely, historical interpretation cannot rise to psychological conditions. Concerning all this, see below. This is not the place.

[48] Boeckh 1877: 83.

[49] From the viewpoint of the interests of the objective *content* of what is communicated, I consider this correct, but in a *general* analysis of the types of interpretation we cannot ignore one of its independent types, even if it is not the direct object of the given special study.

Thus, for example, Blass[50] does not understand, as he should, the distinction that Steinthal had made between a "psychological" and an "individual" interpretation and brackets the two together, dispersing them between three kinds of interpretation, which he himself distinguishes as grammatical, historical, and technical. Deprived of an independent place and dispersed between the other kinds of interpretation, psychological interpretation now begins to paint the other kinds in its color. The result is the reverse of what one could have expected. All types of interpretation are imbued with an unnecessary *psychologism* that is also detrimental to the issue. Ignoring the difference between acts of understanding with different objects, Boeckh himself provided the basis for this, and his own distinction – as we already indicated – suffers from a covert psychologism.

Schleiermacher contrasted grammatical interpretation and psychological interpretation, subordinating the former to the latter. He understood psychological interpretation to be primarily the interpretation of the person of the very author. Historical interpretation as the understanding of a real social process remained an unresolved problem. To outward appearance, Boeckh reproduced Schleiermacher's distinction, but, in fact, he lost sight of the author as a person, seeing the author only as a "subjective condition," thereby liberating the real, historical condition from subordination to the individual person. However, he here infected this condition with subjectivism. An unfortunate consequence of this was that Boeckh too failed to notice that historical interpretation in the strict sense is concerned with an object *sui generis,* which in his psychologized grammatical interpretation – "based on the *objective* conditions of what is communicated" – drowns.

(I) Understanding based on objective conditions is an understanding that is (a) based on the sense of the words *in themselves,* i.e., a *grammatical* interpretation, and (b) based on the sense of the words *in connection with real relationships,* i.e., a *historical* interpretation. Grammatical interpretation must understand each element of the language – the word itself, its grammatical and syntactical forms: (1) in its basic meaning, and (2) in the special conditions of the time and the sphere of its application, and, finally, the sense of the given word in its *connections,* in its "linguistic setting," with respect to both content and form.[51]

A simple knowledge of lexicon and etymology is insufficient to fulfill these tasks. Every communication is conditioned by *real relationships.* In other words, it also takes place in a definite *"real setting."* Grammatical interpretation naturally passes over into historical interpretation, becoming intimately merged and intertwined with the latter.[52] It is easy to see how intimate and essential this connection is if we bear in mind that grammar and lexicon are themselves givens, conditioned, above all, by real historical conditions. Therefore, regardless of the fact that Boeckh distinguishes *by definition* these two kinds of interpretation, proceeding to a

---

[50] Blass 1892: 175.

[51] Boeckh 1877: 82, 93–111.

[52] Boeckh 1877: 82, 111–112.

disclosure of their content, he too is concerned with only one type, just as Schleiermacher did. True, he indicates the criterion by which one can determine where historical interpretation, properly speaking, begins, namely, where a grammatical understanding turns out to be inadequate for disclosing the objective sense of a word.

It is difficult to imagine, in the work of an interpreter, an abstractly philological self-limitation such that the interpreter would have no need for clarification of the real historical setting from the very start of one's enterprise. Nevertheless, if this criterion makes sense for such "pure" philology, then clearly, on the other hand, it subordinates history itself to *its own* goals. We learn nothing from Boeckh regarding what, properly speaking, historical interpretation, as such, i.e., an interpretation that is of value above all *for the historian* – should be. By virtue of this natural consequence of failing to distinguish between the kinds of understanding with respect to the objects of the latter, Boeckh's hermeneutics does not entirely fulfill the hopes that were entrusted to it. Philology itself, brought together through hermeneutics with history, profits from this, but it is still not clear in what way history benefits from such a close union with philology.

Another even more notable deficiency of Boeckh's distinction that, it seems to me, arises from ignoring the objective basis of understanding, is the absence in his work of a fundamental analysis of the kinds of interpretation, or understanding, that he distinguishes. This deficiency is even more striking in that it results from a direct failure to fulfill the promises that were given by Boeckh's general determinations of the tasks of philology and hermeneutics. Boeckh, even at this point, does not approach the issue of what, strictly speaking, is the peculiar characteristic of understanding, as a specific kind of knowledge. It is not hard to convince oneself – and the history of this issue confirms this – that the solution to this riddle is the most difficult thing of all as long as we, in our search for an answer to it, do not go beyond the point where this riddle begins: the understanding of the word as such. Appealing for help only to real historical conditions, however, shows that, if we remain at this starting point, we will never find an answer. The attempt to subordinate this very appeal to the forms of a purely verbal "understanding" deprives us of the possibility of expanding the horizon of understanding. New moments of understanding, including perhaps those that would solve the riddle, are not enlisted in the analysis. The most essential element of understanding is overlooked and only the shell, in the form of an indeterminate type of "preliminary knowledge" or "acquaintance," remains in the hands of the investigator. We obtain certain formulas noted more for their edification than for their content: in order to understand, one must *know* the words, forms, constructions, etc., and as an aid to this be familiar with the historical setting, etc.

However, where is understanding itself, and what is its role? It is not surprising that the authors who worked on hermeneutics subsequent to Boeckh – Blass and Birt – are exclusively preoccupied with the formally-practical tasks of teaching others how to "comment" on texts. They demand no more than just "familiarity" with dictionaries, grammars, realia, etc. Apparently, it is enough to study all these things in order for the mechanism of understanding to set itself in motion. Perhaps this is so, but then the role of hermeneutics is not to clarify the principles of this apparatus, but only, so to speak, to lubricate its moving wheels and gears. This clearly contradicts the purpose of hermeneutics, which, following Schleiermacher, Boeckh himself correctly saw.

If one does not want to get a clear picture of the presuppositions and foundations of any cognitive process, then one is, in fact, guided by current opinions, which have not been critically validated but which are taken as such foundations. We saw how the problem of understanding eluded investigators in the eighteenth century thanks to the vulgar identification of understanding with a clear representation. An understandable sign was supposed to evoke a definite representation, and it was considered to have been understood. The mere thought alone that meaning is not a representation, but an idea, contributed more to the clarification of this problem than any theory of representations. Nevertheless, Boeckh again falls back into the same rut of psychologism that has flooded philology with its waters up to the present. From this point of view, a new defect in Boeckh's distinctions is revealed: wherever, for him, historical interpretation comes to help grammatical interpretation, it turns out, in fact, to be subjectively psychological. "A literary work (*ein Schriftwerk*), for example," he himself declares, "receives its true meaning only in connection with the current conceptions (*mit den gangbaren Vorstellungen*) of the time in which it appeared. We call this explanation in terms of the real setting an 'historical interpretation'."[53] It is as though what is historically important is not what was the case at a given time, but what people thought was the case at that time. It is as though historical psychology could replace history as a real objective fact or could be identified with the latter. This is the way, consequently, that psychologism – of which we already spoke earlier – penetrated and took the place of a *sui generis* objective historical interpretation and occupied this place so solidly that when Bliss later eliminated the very term "psychological interpretation," it, nevertheless, was "distributed" between his three remaining kinds of interpretation. However, Boeckh's own *external* schema apparently transferred psychological interpretation into "the understanding based on the *subjective* conditions of what was communicated."[54] That is, he continued to assign it an independent place.

(II) This side or part of hermeneutics – understanding based on the subjective conditions of what is communicated – is, in turn, divided in Boeckh's account into *individual* interpretation, i.e., understanding based on the subject *by itself*,[55] and generic interpretation,[56] i.e., understanding based on the subject *in connection with the subjective relations* that were set down as the subject's goal and direction.[57] We can now no longer expect from Boeckh a formulation of the fundamental problem of understanding. From what was said above, it is clear in which direction Boeckh

---

[53] Boeckh 1877: 82; cf. Boeckh 1877: 111ff.

[54] Boeckh 1877: 83.

[55] Boeckh 1877: 82, 124–140.

[56] [Reading with Špet 1993: 196 "*genericheskuju*" instead of "*geneticheskuju*" as in Shpet 2005: 354.]

[57] Boeckh 1877: 82f, 140–156.

must now proceed. There is but one object, and, consequently, he appeals again for fresh help at the point where grammatical understanding turns out to be insufficient to establish the objective sense of a word. If we look more closely at this "subjective" side of interpretation, we will discover certain new and interesting peculiarities of the hermeneutic problematic.

While we analyze a communication with respect to its objective conditions, its author, in Boeckh's words, is for us an "organ of language." However, language is also an "organ of the speaker" and, as long as we approach the word from this angle, we examine it as an expression of *individual subjectivity*. Every communicator uses speech in one's own special way and modifies it according to one's own individuality. This is not a matter of an interpretation of the personality of the communicator. For we have in mind one and the same object throughout, namely, a communication "about something." As it turns out, however, according to Boeckh this is not a subjectively psychological interpretation, i.e., one that reveals the ideas, intentions, or feelings of the communicator evoked by the content of what is communicated. Boeckh, together with Schleiermacher, refuses to call this kind of interpretation "psychological," since such a designation would be too broad here.[58] Individual interpretation cannot be derived from general psychological laws, since it abstracts precisely from the peculiarities of every given individual. Additionally, the individual places *his own* stamp on every literary work. This stamp affects the whole work – in the method used in its very composition – and is certainly reflected in every part of the whole and in all of its elements. This stamp is nothing other than an *individual style*.

Individual composition adds to the work a peculiar *external form* and therefore adapts to itself the *material element*, i.e., that which is objective in language. The result is not the form of a *logical* connection, something that is sometimes said to characterize a composition of the whole, since what is logical is again something general or normal. If we turn our attention merely to what is logical in the interpretation of the connection of ideas, we would understand the latter too one-sidedly, losing its rigorously individual moments. On the other hand, however, we would understand too much if we assume a logical connection where there is none. Furthermore, just as a grammatical interpretation is completed by a historical interpretation, to the extent that the sense of the word is itself modified by objective relations, so too an individual interpretation leads to a *generic* interpretation, to the extent that the communication is modified by *subjective* relations. That is, these relations are the goals of communication that are common to many people and by which its genus, the genus "speech," is predetermined. Thus, the character of the different kinds of poetry and prose is included in the subjective direction and in the subjective goal of the presentation. The individual goals of the specific authors are also included in these general differences.

Once again, Schleiermacher's designation of this type of interpretation as a *technical* interpretation seems to Boeckh to be too narrow. One can pursue some single goal in a simple conversation, which provides a livelier scope to the freedom of the

---

[58] Boeckh 1877: 127.

individual than the technique of a literary work would allow. Since we are concerned, above all, with the distinction between the genera and the species of literary works, what catches the eye is the discipline from which hermeneutics should here expect energetic and authoritative help, namely, *poetics* – or, more generally, *aesthetics*, which at the same time provides broader perspectives. Boeckh, himself, in any case, recognizes that a generic[59] interpretation is a kind of "aesthetic" interpretation.[60]

Therefore, strictly speaking, even in this subjective interpretation we still do not have a psychological interpretation. However, if in Boeckh's conception psychologism had earlier excluded historical interpretation, just as it had a personal or a strictly psychological interpretation, one can say that here psychologism is simply contraband. Questions of style and literary form are questions of psychology only to the same extent that questions of logic can be questions of psychology. Everything beyond that is contraband. It would be far more interesting to formulate directly the problem of aesthetic form, logical form, and, perhaps, even other *forms*, along with grammatical and syntactical forms, all of which should in fact be clearly revealed by an interpreter really *as a condition* of the understanding and the interpretation of a literary work as a genus of communication. It would then be clear, for example, that hermeneutics itself did not begin until the establishing and clarifying of these forms was proceeding. That process would include grammatical, stylistic, logical, and other kinds of analyses or inquiries. Hermeneutics itself, with its new techniques and methods, should be joined to these analyses. If it would turn out that hermeneutics not only introduces something new of its own, but even unifies in a unique way the aesthetic, logical, and other demands that we make upon understandable words, upon communication, then the fundamental role of hermeneutics and its universally logical nature would appear in a wonderful, new light. However, there is none of this, and we can again repeat our doubts. Does not such a definition of the kinds of interpretation, as we find in Boeckh, reduce all understanding, as *sui generis* knowledge, to *familiarity* with the mentioned disciplines as well as with still others that the philological encyclopedias refer to as auxiliary disciplines and stores of information for philology? Are not, then, Blass and Birt right in their narrowly practical understanding of the tasks of hermeneutics?

Of course – I will repeat once more – it would be impossible to expect from Boeckh, as a philologist, a fundamentally philosophical resolution of the problem of understanding. His great merit lies in the fact that he noticed the importance of this problem for philology and noticed how philology, in assimilating this problem, itself acquires a fundamental philosophical significance. Nevertheless, what strikes the eye is the lack of correspondence between the determination of the tasks of philology on this broad level and the narrowly empirical execution of these tasks.

Just the same, one could expect that if philology is a *sui generis* kind of knowledge – knowledge of what has been known – and such knowledge is understanding,

---

[59] [Reading with Boeckh 1877: 16 and Špet 1993: 198 "*genericheskaja*" for "*geneticheskaja*" as in Shpet 2005: 355.]

[60] Boeckh 1877: 156.

then at least we will have an indication of the place and the role of understanding. It turned out that although philology is almost identical with history, we, nevertheless, still did not get to know what, strictly speaking, historical understanding and historical interpretation are. Philology has swallowed up history and also psychology at the same time. If we do not investigate the very act of understanding, then we must at least show all of its kinds, being guided precisely by the objective distinction of these acts. However, it is impossible to deny the great value of what we have obtained. Grammatical and other *formal* types of interpretation are necessary conditions of understanding. Understanding itself, operating in these forms, is something "material," just as the *sense* itself that understanding aims to extract from a communication is material. It is precisely historical and psychological interpretations that promise us more in this sense, since they are in essence material interpretations. But if a word actually requires understanding, and not just acquaintance with the lexical material and its manifold forms, then there is something in it too that requires material understanding, since there must be a material sense in it. One should be able to extract this sense, not in a psychologized form, but in a pure form, as it is – as a real or an ideal quality, which, in the given case, are one and the same. It is not difficult to anticipate from this still one more thing, a development that will be of concern in a further investigation. Hermeneutics in its methodologically philosophical role should serve as a material-logical foundation for the historical sciences in the broadest sense. That this cannot help but have a transformative effect on the whole of logic, as we now know it, is also self-evident.

Thus, let us return again from possible philosophical generalizations to the elaboration of hermeneutic problematics on an empirical basis. We are convinced, then, that if a narrowly philological interpretation does not require a special and clear participation of *understanding* as a *sui generis* cognitive act, but reduces primarily to a "familiarity" with certain formal disciplines and to knowledge of a certain reserve of "realia," then we will, nevertheless, have to search further for the answer to the question what the essence and the role of understanding is by way of an analysis of a broadly conceived philological, *historical* interpretation.

We also sensed this whole time an inadequate clarification of psychological interpretation as a special type. It is time, however, to pose the question: is this concern with a single thing? Is not a historical interpretation, in the final analysis, really the same as a psychological interpretation, or vice versa? It would seem that Schleiermacher had already come to this conclusion. Moreover, is the psychologism in Boeckh's definition of historical interpretation not accidental? I have this entire time upheld the position that they are distinct, but in order to have this issue come to an end I will focus more on Steinthal, who addressed this issue not only as a philologist, but also as a psychologist.

# [Hermeneutical Moments of Historical Methodology]

## 1 [Heymann] Steinthal

Undoubtedly, the place that Steinthal assigns to philology undermines its pretentions to play the penetrating role that it did in Boeckh's account. For us, therefore, Steinthal's solution to this problem is of no interest. The place of philology (or history) here is a modest one, as a particular human science along with psychology and in opposition to the natural sciences and mathematics. In turn, all of these sciences, as material sciences, stand in opposition to philosophy, understood as formal and *a priori* knowledge.[1] However, philology cannot, in Steinthal, claim this independent place for itself alongside psychology. Psychology begins to dominate, appearing as the explanatory science among the human sciences.[2] Steinthal turns out to be one of the most outspoken psychologists arising from the school of Herbart. In one respect, however, such a position can be of interest to us. It commits us, as it were, to a more careful and precise definition of what precisely a *psychological* interpretation is. On the other hand, Steinthal retains Boeckh's identification of philology and history. Consequently, we can also hope to obtain here a more precise answer to the question as to what is special about *historical* interpretation as a *sui generis* interpretation.

Steinthal starts from the idea that the methodological part of philology is not limited to interpretation and critique and that the method of *constructing* the philological disciplines should be joined to those two methods, thereby resolving problems that go beyond the bounds of interpretation. An interpretation always has as its object a *single* work, whereas a construction goes beyond the bounds of a single work – to the aggregate of works of a single kind, works that form a certain

---

[1] Steinthal 1880b: 322–323. See also in the same volume the first article, Steinthal 1880a, and also his review of Boeckh's *Encyklopädie*, Steinthal 1878b. Steinthal developed his general views more fully in Steinthal 1855: 137ff and in Steinthal 1864. I have already mentioned his lecture 1878a.

[2] See, for example, Steinthal 1864: 16: "Because psychology is for history the doctrine of special principles …." [Clearly in error, Shpet's text has the quotation speaking of philology, not psychology. It also mistakenly has the quotation appearing on page 15, not page 16.]

© Springer Nature Switzerland AG 2019
G. Shpet, T. Nemeth, *Hermeneutics and Its Problems*, Contributions
To Phenomenology 98, https://doi.org/10.1007/978-3-319-98941-9_7

closed circle.[3] Despite the obvious conventionality of this distinction, it can be taken and justified without difficulty if we know *why* such a further sub-distinction is made. In any case, having limited the tasks of interpretation in this way, Steinthal, like Boeckh, considers *understanding* to be the goal of interpretation. Consequently, interpretation or exegesis is the path to this goal. We interpret in order to understand. Our natural understanding is necessarily coordinated with speech and is immediately conditioned by human organization and our social life. Philological understanding and, consequently, interpretation, which can be regarded as an artificial understanding, already requires a certain mediation. As such, it is not simply a "result," but a certain activity, directed to revealing the conditions under which what is understandable is given. The latter is not the mental content that immediately follows the perception of a sound complex, but a certain $x$ that still must be clarified. Therefore, the sought $x$ cannot be obtained from the sound complex by means of analysis. Its disclosure presupposes, on the contrary, a certain kind of synthetic activity that connects a particular communication with the general forces that constitute consciousness. Thus, a word amounts to a general root, which is the source of many other words, and to a general grammatical formation, which is the source of other forms. Finally, a philological interpretation can be traced back to the entire mental content and all the linguistic forms that lie in the consciousness of the speaker or of the one communicating, who tries to understand a given communication based on those forms and content as the conditions of the communication. On the whole, philological understanding is more or less rich, synthetic, deductive knowledge.[4]

Certainly, Steinthal himself cannot think that, with these suggestions, he reveals the nature of the act and activity of understanding as they should be revealed if, in their analysis, we want to find a fundamental foundation for, among other things, the construction of a hermeneutics. Nevertheless, one thing should be kept in mind here. The attempt in itself to *distinguish* between "natural" and "artificial" understanding, or, we can say, understanding in the proper sense and interpretation, is, above all, worthy of attention. The first step was taken, a step that inevitably had to be taken. However, neither Schleiermacher, as we saw, nor even after him Boeckh was aware of the necessity of this step. Secondly, I believe one must note that although he expressed himself quite vaguely, nevertheless, it is Steinthal's indubitable conviction that a "natural" understanding is a certain *immediate* psychological process or act that is closely connected with the very nature of speech and in general of human communication. It is not resolvable so simply or superficially as is often done by means of elementary associationism.

Interpretation in general begins with a clarification of the sense of a word and then passes on to the sense of a sentence and to the connection between sentences. This is a grammatical interpretation, which, according to Steinthal, forms the foundation for all further philological operations. Unfortunately, Steinthal does not provide definitions either of what such a "sense" is or of how we come to it, i.e., of what

---

[3] Steinthal 1864: 27–28.
[4] Steinthal 1864: 28–29.

such an understanding itself is as a specific cognitive act. There remains the suspicion that, perhaps, the entire concern of interpretation amounts here again to one of "familiarity" with a dictionary and a grammar. In this direction, he distinguishes a second type of interpretation, which is also unsatisfactory. Real or *factual* interpretation (*die sachliche Interpretation*) is a clarification of the external and internal circumstances and, in general, of the real connections to which the communication refers. More precisely, the concern here, consequently, is with both the subjective as well as the objective elements of a people's spirit: conceptions and concepts, the means of representation, views, opinions and judgments; then the surrounding natural objects and relations; and, finally, historical events, institutions, and mores, the states and the activity of a people's spirit. Precisely this type of interpretation should seem to us to be particularly important since it, apparently, also leads to the "historical" interpretation that we seek. However, in reality, for Steinthal the point here is neither the understanding of the circumstances themselves, which could also be called "historical circumstances" or "historical facts," nor their interpretation, but only in their usage, as in Boeckh, as conditions *for* a philological understanding of some passage that has attracted our attention in some given monument, document, or, in general, communication.

We are not now abandoning this communication as a means that has already been used and is no longer needed in order to comprehend the communicated fact itself. On the contrary, we looked upon this fact only as a means that serves the goal of understanding the communication itself as the document of a literary source. Steinthal himself sees that he faces a certain barrier here, and he appeals, for justification of the limitation he has accepted, to the already indicated distinction between interpretation (with a critique) and *construction*. He says, "An *Interpretatio rerum* should not develop and depict antiquarian and historical knowledge, since this is the task of construction. It should explain the given passage of a literary work on the basis of the acquired knowledge of the life of the peoples in antiquity – precisely just as an *interpretatio verborum* should not construe etymology and grammar, but should find the sense of the given word and sentence in them and in the use of words."[5]

One can agree that there is a difference between interpretation and construction, as Steinthal understands it. However, the deeper we begin to ponder over the sense of this distinction, the clearer it becomes that a special task stands out for the historian as such, and consequently for the philologist, precisely from this distinction insofar as the identification of the two is correct. If a construction itself is not a special kind of interpretation, it, in any case, presupposes one. What then are its characteristic features? It is sufficient for now to mention, as it were, simply that the historical object (a social object in the broad sense) is not construed like some machine, the whole and every part of which can be touched and, in general, sensibly perceived. It is also like neither a stone nor an organism that can be immediately

---

[5] Steinthal 1878a: 30–31. In another place, Steinthal also calls the general theory of construction (*Konstruktionslehre*), as well as the second part of the philological encyclopedia, a "*Historik*." Steinthal 1880a: 93 f.

sensed. Rather, it is something that is given in a construction as a sign or a symbol. Such a construction has an essentially symbolic and interpretive character. However, issues arise here: Are we concerned, then, with a fundamentally new "sign"? Is the interpretation of such a sign of the same order as a grammatical interpretation? What is its specific difference with the latter, etc.? These questions contain the very essence of what we call *historical* interpretation as distinguished from grammatical interpretation. Steinthal neither posed these questions nor did he answer them – it seems to me – for the same reason as Boeckh. Namely, he did not want to enter into an analysis of the objective distinctions in the act of understanding.

The third kind of interpretation, according to Steinthal, viz., *stylistic* interpretation, is not of direct interest to us now. Its task is to examine the general composition of a work, the basic idea in it, the tendency of the whole, its unity, etc. It is related to grammatical interpretation as stylistics is related to grammar. Of great interest, however, are the following two types of interpretation: *individual* interpretation and *historical* interpretation, chiefly in their relation to the first three. In them, we interpret only what is *given* to us, and interpret it according to its content and its form, but exclusively in terms of the national spirit of the language, in terms of the nation's practical and theoretical life, and in terms of that nation's artistic forms. Consequently, we have paid no attention to the question of *who* is speaking, but *duo cum dicunt idem, non est idem* ("when two say the same thing, it is not the same thing").[6] To reveal this is, above all, the task of an individual interpretation, which should be an interpretation based on the peculiarities of the very communicator, on one's personal worldview and that person's understanding of the world. Historical interpretation also proceeds in an analogous direction, inquiring about the time when the work being interpreted was written, a time that leaves its stamp on everything, including on the very individual as the author of a given work ("the young Plato is not yet the old Plato; in his old age he is no longer young"[7]). It is not difficult to see that both of these types correspond to Boeckh's "subjective" conditions. However, what is new and important in Steinthal's account of them is a *situating*. While the first three types represent, as it were, successive levels of interpretation, each of which goes deeper into the given text with respect to its content as well as its form, these two types approach the text as though from outside, namely, with respect to the *attitude* toward what is being communicated by the authors themselves.

What we have is not a new level, but a new direction that demands a new turning of the interpreter's vision and attention. Each of the first three levels can now be illuminated in a new light one after another, so that one can speak accordingly of an individually grammatical interpretation, of an individually real interpretation, and of an individually stylistic or historically grammatical interpretation, etc.[8] It is evident here that, even from Steinthal's own viewpoint, the concern is with a new *object* and, moreover, with exactly what we would want to see as the object of a

---

[6] [The Latin expression appears in Steinthal 1878a: 31. Shpet here is closely paraphrasing Steinthal.]

[7] [Steinthal 1878a: 32.]

[8] Steinthal 1878a: 31–32.

*strictly psychological* – both individually and socially psychological – interpretation. Despite the cursory and formal character of Steinthal's remarks, despite the absence of even the most general fundamental analysis of this direction of interpretation, we are, nevertheless, ready to see here, finally, a definition, or at least a situating, of this type of interpretation, which could be recognized as being at least provisionally satisfactory.

Unfortunately, the sixth type of interpretation that Steinthal distinguished and that he himself calls a *psychological* interpretation can arouse only misunderstandings, as happened with Blass, who fused Steinthal's individual and psychological interpretations into one. What is essential to the psychological type of interpretation is that the interpreter not limit oneself to a clarification of the sense of a given work, but seek, further, a *causal* explanation of it. One's task now is to reveal the genesis of the work, to answer the question *why* the author uses these or those means of depiction, why that person turns precisely to a given form, etc. This type of interpretation allows us to understand the literary work based on the creative personality of the very writer, thereby making our understanding more complete. Although this type of interpretation is not independent, i.e., it is possible only in connection with the remaining types and chiefly with individual interpretation, nevertheless, in Steinthal's opinion, it crowns philology, for the first time, with a predominantly "scientific" character.

All of this has been a source of the greatest misunderstandings, which, unfortunately up until now, have not been fully resolved. Steinthal himself compares psychological interpretation to individual interpretation, and such a comparison, certainly, arises on its own. Their difference, however, is outwardly and formally clear. An individual interpretation does not explain. It answers the question: *how?*, but not the question: *why?* But one must not forget that there is still the question: *what?* Steinthal is convinced that "I understand (*Ich verstehe*) best what, and how, something is when I comprehend (*Ich begreife*) *why* it is so."[9] However, to understand the "*what*" means to understand what has been communicated, and to understand the "*how*" means to understand the communicator. Steinthal sensed the disparity in these two different directions of understanding and interpretation, when he placed the types of individual and historical interpretation in another setting in comparison to the first three types. In fact, it is quite incomprehensible how one can get the "best" possible understanding of what the Peloponnesian War was by knowing and "comprehending" the genesis of the work of Thucydides, who communicates it to us. The deepest penetration into the personality of an author – it goes without saying – cannot provide anything to explain the events that the author communicates if these events are not his own deeds. An attempt to understand the objective content of a work based on the psychological laws of the author's creativity is the crudest kind of *psychologism*. To a certain degree, we can understand how it arises if we have in mind, for example, the interpretation of a poetic work, but this semblance of a justification of psychologism should disappear when we turn to the interpretation of a historical record. However, the identification of philology and

---

[9] Steinthal 1878a: 33.

history remains a basic presupposition for Steinthal – as he himself repeats more than once.

However, there is yet another side to Steinthal's arguments, one that we should also clearly take into account. Steinthal is right that *explanation* should complete a philological interpretation and that an explanation should give the latter a definitive scientific stamp as an empirical science. This is a basic methodological issue of philology as well as of history. However, one must be especially careful with it, chiefly in order to avoid blindly transferring into the sphere of historical knowledge those techniques of explanation that are known in the logic of the other sciences, primarily the natural sciences. The blind transfer of the methodology of the natural sciences to history would be a new mistake, which one could call the mistake of "*logicism*," by which we mean the unjustified transfer of old logical techniques into a new sphere whose logic has not yet been adequately investigated. Steinthal, undoubtedly, makes this mistake, subordinating historical content to psychological explanation. Therefore, instead of a historical explanation we obtain a promissory note for a psychological explanation, which perhaps psychology needs but which history does not. This, however, still does not circumscribe the sphere of misunderstandings to which Steinthal's argument leads.

In saying that an individual interpretation answers only the questions: *what*? and *how*? and does not provide explanations, he himself connects all the kinds of interpretation – except, that is, for psychological interpretation – to description. However, is this connection not essential? And does he not sin against the logic of description and interpretation in forcing upon it the further task of causal explanation? Do we not, thereby, enter into a fundamentally new logical sphere? However, above all, it is striking that empirical natural science, which appeals to explanatory hypothesis and theory, does not rely by any means on the interpretation of signs and communications, but on experience and the observation of the phenomena themselves. If interpretation is the path that also leads us immediately to this kind of phenomena, it is clear that further on – where explanation begins – the role of interpretation ends. But if it does not end, our concern is, nevertheless, with some new kind of interpretation, one that does not coincide at all with explanation, but also does not resemble in all respects the earlier kinds and types of interpretation.

Therefore, we repeat once more: do we not have here a *special*, namely, a historical, interpretation, one that we have been seeking in vain? Clearly, however, there is at least a negative result from Steinthal's reflections and distinctions, namely, that *this* interpretation is not psychological, that this deviation in a new direction, which presupposes, as we have already explained, a psychological interpretation, is a *withdrawal* from a direct deepening into the objective content of what has been communicated. We wish to see in this the path of historical interpretation. In this sense, the issue of psychological interpretation becomes clear. But what is not so clear, and what requires further determination is the problem of the meaning, strictly speaking, of a historical interpretation as such, as a *sui generis* type of interpretation in which not only the sign, but also the very meaning of that sign is interpreted.

## 2   [Johann] Droysen

Philologists after Boeckh, following his lead, tended to bring together their discipline and history and even to identify them. Nevertheless, if the identification has serious methodological foundations behind it, it is important to elucidate the position of historical methodology itself concerning its role in the logical construction of understanding and interpretation. If I am not mistaken, Droysen, in his *History*, was the first to examine these methodological functions as defining principles for history as a science.[10] We can also see the immediate influence of German Idealism in Droysen's philosophical presuppositions. In the theoretical grounding of history, he himself refers, as his source, to Humboldt, whom he regards as the "Bacon of historical science." In accordance with the objects and the nature of human thinking, there are, in Droysen's opinion, three scientific methods[11]: the (philosophically and theologically) speculative method, the method of mathematical physics, and the historical method. This division reproduces exactly the division that we encountered in pre-Kantian rationalism. Droysen himself compares it to the ancient canon of the sciences: logic, physics, and ethics. History is compared in this way to ethics and, consequently, the Fichtean-Schleiermacherian formulation of the issue is reproduced. From the viewpoint of method, this distinction points to the various methodological essences of the mentioned methods and to their respective tasks: *to know*, *to explain*, and *to understand*. Droysen specifies, "The essence of the historical method is *understanding* by means of *investigation*."[12] Therefore, Droysen sharply contrasts the method of natural science, as an *explanatory* method, to the method of history, as a method of *understanding*. This point of view absolutely excludes formulating the problem so as to include the tasks of a psychological explanation – or any other type of explanation – among those of interpretation, such as we saw in Steinthal.

In order to avoid misunderstandings, I think it necessary to note here that a distinction, such as that above, between the explanatory and the interpretive methods should not be understood, however, in the sense that history cannot have its *own* explanations – of a type distinct from those in mathematical natural science. In the first place, the explanatory method of presentation can fit nicely with the interpretive method of investigation. As a historical method, it cannot simply replace the descriptive interpretation used in an investigation. Second, one ought to keep in mind the broader meaning of the term "explanation," when it is identified with establishing a causal connection, one that takes place in history, as Droysen himself recognizes, and a narrower and more precise meaning, when the mentioned causal

---

[10] Droysen 1897. This work is based on early manuscripts from 1858 and 1862 and meant as a textbook to accompany the lectures that Droysen gave in 1857 on the encyclopedia and methodology of history. [See Droysen 1897: ix.]

[11] Droysen 1897: 15 (§14).

[12] Droysen 1897: 12 (§8), 15 (§14), 26 (§37). See as appendices to the *History* the articles "The Elevation of History to the Rank of a Science," Droysen 1897: 61–89, and "Nature and History," Droysen 1897: 90–105.

connection is understood as a necessary logical connection. The latter usually is the case with the general, law-like explanations of mathematical natural science with its numerous, replicable objects and its predictions in connection with the character of those objects. Consequently, there can be a causal connection but without there being an inner logical relation of a cause, as a generic concept, to an effect, as a specific concept. In fact, we observe this in every concrete and individually given causal connection. It is possible that Droysen has in mind precisely this absence of a logical necessity in the historical sequence of phenomena when he declares, "A historical investigation does not want to explain, i.e., to derive the later from the earlier as though by logical necessity, but to understand."[13]

Historical understanding, according to Droysen, has, as its presupposition, discoveries of a kind that are congenial to us, discoveries provided to us by the historical material. Such a discovery, when perceived and projected into the inner being of the perceiver, arouses a similar inner process in the latter. Thus, for example, when we hear a fearful scream, we sense the fear of the person who is screaming. We understand an animal, a plant, or a thing only partially, not in the entirety of its individual existence. We feel ourselves directly akin only to human beings and manifestations of what is human. Only they can be fully understood by us. We understand an individual expression as a single manifestation of something inner and as a projection of what is inner, which is itself understood, on the basis of this manifestation, as some central force that expresses itself in each of its peripheral phenomena. The individual is understood within the whole, and the whole from the individual. One must distinguish a given *act of comprehension* (*der Akt des Verständnisses*) from the logical mechanism of understanding. Such an act arises, under the specified conditions as an immediate intuition, as a certain creative act, as a spark flashing between two electrified bodies approaching each other, or like "conception in sexual intercourse."[14] Furthermore, "a person becomes what one is in terms of one's inclinations, a totality in oneself, for the first time only in understanding others and being understood by them (*in dem Verstandenwerden*), in moral communities (family, nation, state, etc.). The individual (*der Einzelne*) becomes a totality only within relationships. Understanding and being understood, the individual is only an expression of some association (*Gemeinsamkeit*), as a member of which the individual both is and in the essence and development of which one participates. The individual is only a single expression of this essence and development. The aggregate of the times, nations, etc. is only a single expression of an absolute totality. From history and from this aggregate, we learn to understand God; and only in God can we understand history."[15] "History is humanity's knowledge of itself and self-certainty (*Selbstgewissheit*)."[16] It gives us an awareness of what we are and what we have.[17]

---

[13] Droysen 1868: 19 (§37). [Cf. Droysen 1897: 26.]

[14] [Droysen 1868: 10 (§11). Cf. Droysen 1897: 14 (§11).]

[15] Droysen 1868: 10–11 (§12). [Cf. Droysen 1897: 14 (§12).]

[16] Droysen 1868: 38 (§91). [Cf. Droysen 1897: 49 (§86).] [The Russian text omits the clearly needed quotation marks here. See Shpet 2005: 367.]

[17] Droysen 1868: 51.

All of this is quite fascinating and readily lends itself to philosophical development and deepening, but unfortunately in Droysen's account these ideas did not go beyond the concise sketch in which he presents them. Moreover, in this form they are excessively general and indefinite. Their principles are not evident: passing references to intuition, to the congeniality and the unity of human nature as a condition of understanding can also be found in Schleiermacher and Boeckh. However, these are, obviously, still only questions, which themselves need to be answered. Conversely, where they end obviously already leads us beyond the bounds of the tasks that historical hermeneutics can pose for itself. In the best case, we have here the opportunity simply to pose a new question. Is there not beyond the bounds of historical interpretation and historical understanding a new – a metaphysical or philosophical – type of interpretation that is directed at a new object? However, without touching the problem of a fundamental justification of what Droysen has said about this, it seems to me that we can still – unless I am putting more into his words than they contain – extract something from what has been said (in particular from the quotation I gave above).

The understanding, which is our concern here and which should form the methodological foundation of historical science as an understanding, above all, of the "human being," brings us back to the *psychological* type of interpretation that was our concern already in Schleiermacher and that has up to now only impeded a definition of *historical* interpretation properly speaking. However, if we consider what Droysen says in this matter, we will (1) as it were, find a transition from psychological interpretation to historical interpretation, and (2) grope for certain peculiarities of the latter.

(1) With a precise understanding of Droysen's words, psychological interpretation not only does not devour historical interpretation and is not its "culmination," but, on the contrary, itself culminates in an objectively historical interpretation. Psychological interpretation is psychological, because it is directed at psychic experiences, or the human soul, i.e., the psychological subject, as its object. However, if Droysen is right that a human being – let us say, as a *person* – realizes oneself only in communication, whatever be its form, then this person, in understanding, thereby, ceases to be a psychological subject and becomes, instead, a social and historical object. Interpretations that are acts of understanding directed toward a human being cease to be psychological and become historical. The person is now an objectively social phenomenon, a "thing," a factor among other phenomena, "things," and factors of the objectively same social or historical order. One only need go further and become aware of what kind of phenomena and things these are. Droysen himself places the "individual" on the same level as an age, a nation, etc. Perhaps, one should include everything that historians consider to be their subject matter, such as institutions, mores, economic and ecclesiastical organizations, etc., etc.?

(2) The problem arises again here, in all of its generality, regarding the specific interpretation directed toward *this* object – an object that is neither psychological nor metaphysical. The "individual" is not just a psychological subject. Consequently, in Droysen's words, the individual is "an expression" (*ein Ausdruck*) of a community.[18]

---

[18] [Droysen 1868: 24 (§47); Cf. Droysen 1897: 33 (§47).]

One must understand and interpret the individual in such a capacity now. We can pass from verbal "expression" to the "individual" as a meaning, and call this transition "understanding." However, in the case when this "meaning" is itself only another "expression," this means that we must speak of a new type of understanding and a new type of interpretation. Nevertheless, none of this is revealed in Droysen's account. What he actually does reveal in his own distinction between the different kinds of interpretation, in fact, adds little to what we have already learned from the philologists.

Having somewhat unexpectedly compared interpretation to the activity of walking, Droysen distinguishes four kinds of interpretation. (1) A *pragmatic* interpretation, which resting on the remnants of once real circumstances as established by a critique, intends the reconstruction of their external form according to a causal connection that lies in the nature of the things. This is carried out with the help of simple logical techniques: demonstration, analogy, comparison, and hypothesis.[19]

Such an attempt to correlate interpretation with known logical techniques is valuable and interesting in itself, but it is impossible even to enter into a discussion of Droysen's outline, since his assertions are brief and no motives for them are given. It is impossible even to say with certainty whether pragmatic interpretation is the historical interpretation that has been our concern or is something else. On the one hand, this would seem to be a historical interpretation, since, with its help, we pass from real parts ("remnants") to the real whole. On the other hand, however, it is unclear how this transition, which is based on a natural causal connection, differs as an understanding from the ordinary type of inference. Only one thing seems to me to be clear, viz., that Droysen's reference to this causal connection between a remnant and the whole of reality, which we have in mind to reconstruct, shows that, denying a logically explanatory function to understanding and historical science, he does not thereby exclude the causal depiction of historical reality.

(2) An interpretation of *conditions*, insofar as the conditions of the circumstances that once were real still remain in the remnants being studied. Among them are spatial (geographical) conditions, conditions of time and of the resources – both material and moral – in which and thanks to which this or that fact was realized.[20]

As I already indicated, one can hardly call this an interpretation in the strict sense, since it is a question of knowledge and "familiarity." But the reference to resources deserves special attention, because it prompts us to look upon historical reality itself as a certain *"realization."* The fundamental meaning of such a formulation of the issue will become clear below, when we will show that we should look upon every understandable and interpretable sign as a certain realization.

(3) The task of a *psychological* interpretation is to reveal the willful act that caused a given fact.[21] Insofar as we are not trying to explain here, but precisely to understand, and insofar as this interpretation leads to an analysis of the willful act itself as an objectively social factor, to that extent, one must classify this kind of

---

[19] Droysen 1868: 20 (§39). [Cf. Droysen 1897: 27 (§39).]

[20] Droysen 1868: 20 (§40). [Cf. Droysen 1897: 28 (§40).]

[21] Droysen 1868: 21 (§41). [Cf. Droysen 1897: 28 (§40).]

interpretation in accordance with the explanations already given as purely historical. That we really have no explanation here, such as, for example, Steinthal sought
in a psychological interpretation, is apparent from Droysen's following remark:
"Things take their course in spite of the good or bad will of those through whom
these things are realized."[22]

(4) The interpretation of *ideas* "fills the gaps that psychological interpretation
leaves."[23] This is as incomprehensible as it is brief. According to Droysen, these
ideas are those of the "moral" world. That is, this is the new type of interpretation
already indicated, which goes beyond the bounds of *scientific* history. Yet, how can
it fill the gaps of psychological interpretation, and what would it mean to do so?
Rather, one should perhaps compare this interpretation with the second type: when
it is a matter of resources, we can also speak of realized ideas. But in such a case we
would either have to proceed again beyond the bounds of a science of history into
the sphere of philosophy of history or else return to philological interpretation, in
the broadest sense, which, after all, also looks behind the verbal signs to ideas as the
sense of the signs. Therefore, despite Droysen's very broad and very promising
formulation of the problem concerning history and understanding, what we can
extract from Droysen's account gives the reader occasion for new intellectual explo-
rations and efforts, but does not thereby give any satisfying resolution to the expectations that were aroused at the beginning.

## 3  [Ernst] Bernheim

Despite the thoroughness of his presentation, Bernheim gives even less in all
respects than Droysen.[24] In terms of his philosophical vigor, Bernheim stands to the
latter in approximately the same relation as Blass and Birt stand to Boeckh.
Bernheim's goal is not the theoretical illumination of the problem, but primarily the
acquisition of practical guidelines. True, he loves to introduce psychological explanations, but they are as elementary as is his choice of appealing to Wundt's authority
for support is unfortunate.

---

[22] [Droysen 1897: 30 (§41). Cf. Droysen 1868: 21 (§41).]

[23] [Droysen 1897: 30 (§42). Cf. Droysen 1868: 21 (§42).]

[24] Bernheim 1908. Cf. also his Berngejm 1908: 115f. [A Russian translation of Bernheim 1905.] In
Meister's recent work, interpretation is allotted one page, supported by a reference to a "detailed"
presentation of Bernheim. See Meister 1913. Langlois and Seignobos correctly accuse Bernheim
of "being satisfied with a single reference to Boeckh." Langlua and Sen'obos 1899: 122. [This
work is a Russian translation of Langlois and Seignobos 1898.] Cf. also Sen'obos 1902. [A Russian
translation of Seignobos 1901.] However Langlois and Seignobos are themselves no less simplistic
in handling the issue of interpretation than Bernheim. For them, interpretation concerns (internal)
critique, and hermeneutics is nothing other than a critique of interpretation. They suppose that the
almost highest goal of such a critique is a "clarification of the secret sense" of the interpreted
document.

Bernheim asserts quite correctly that the material of history is unique and that its special quality, unlike the material of the natural sciences, lies in the fact that it is not given immediately to sense perception.[25] But he concludes from this merely that, as the chief task of the historical method, a critique is necessary to establish the factual nature of what is communicated. He assigns to interpretation, as a secondary task of the historical method, knowledge of the connections between the respective facts. That is, in terms of our elucidations here, interpretation lies within the sphere of explanation as the method of presentation. Moreover, Bernheim himself distinguished between the tasks of understanding and those of explanation, i.e., knowledge of "general causes and conditions (factors)."[26] Between these two moments of historical "conceptualization" (*Auffassung*), he introduced the additional moments of connecting (combining) and representation (reproduction).[27] For Bernheim too, the conviction that there is an "identity of human existence" serves as a presupposition of understanding, as does the presupposition that this identity allows us to know, on the basis of given sensory signs, the mental realm, which these signs serve to manifest.[28] The fact that in hearing a communication or reading a document, we, above all, understand *what* it is about, even if it should be about the rotation of the Earth, about an earthquake or about the law of the conservation of matter – this fact apparently bothers Bernheim as little as it does other psychologists who proclaim that in understanding we pass from sensory signs to the "psychological." In any case, Bernheim makes no attempt to deepen the issue concerning understanding even in connection with the tasks of historical methodology, or to justify his presuppositions. But, then, his own understanding of the tasks of interpretation is at odds with everything with which we are already familiar. In fact, so much so that in line with the point of view of the preceding discussion we can recognize that Bernheim has not raised the question of interpretation at all in this sense.[29]

Bernheim believes the task of interpretation is fulfilled already from the moment it is established that some object is the source of historical knowledge, and when it, consequently, has been subsumed under the concept of "source." However, he sees the proper task of interpretation to consist in recognizing the genus to which a given source belongs. Bernheim sees a certain broadening of the tasks of hermeneutics in such a determination of the tasks of interpretation, along with an interpretation of the sources already determined according to their order and character. Philologists, in his opinion, have indeed developed the concept of interpretation, although it is

---

[25] Bernheim 1908: 185. Bernheim himself presents a great number of clarifying and supplementary parallel references to his own book.

[26] [Bernheim 1908: 562.]

[27] Bernheim 1908: 562.

[28] Bernheim 1908: 567. Cf. Bernheim 1908: 110.

[29] When one is convinced that other authors of a "*Historik*" take a similar position, one might think that historical hermeneutics is of no interest to them at all, and therefore it would be useless to seek in their writings the clarifications we need concerning this issue. Besides the mentioned works of Seignobos and Langlois and Meister, N. Kareev also limits himself to a remark on hermeneutics, which, in his words, is "a theory of the means of explaining texts as close as possible to the sense that the author himself puts into them." Kareev 1913: 129.

not apparent that Bernheim has used the results of their work. They had in mind, however, only the evidence of tradition, whereas the historian also needs to interpret the "remnants" (*Überrest*). This arises from the central interest of philology in comprehending literary works as ends in themselves, whereas for the historian they are only one of the means of knowing events and their connections.[30]

Philologists would hardly agree to such a limitation of their tasks, but the important point is what Bernheim does to compensate for this supposed self-limitation of the historians. However much he widened the sphere of the concept of "source," it is not clear in which direction and in what sense he expanded the methodological significance of interpretation, but for our concern with methodology, this is the only important point. Moreover, Bernheim ascribes such significance to this expansion that he divides the types of interpretation according to the character of the sources: (1) interpretations of remnants, (2) of tradition, and (3) of one source through another.

According to the first point, one that "expands" the tasks of interpretation, we learn that the historian needs a very broad knowledge of linguistics, anthropology, ethnology, folklore, archaeology, political economy, statistics, and jurisprudence.[31] According to the second point, the task of interpretation is to "learn and understand an author's views, ideas, and thoughts about the relevant facts."[32] It is as if the historian is not concerned with understanding these very facts, i.e., the *object* of these thoughts, ideas, and views. Interpretation itself here consists of the following moments: interpretation of the work and of the outer aspect of the sources (with the help of paleography); interpretation of the language (with the help of philology); and interpretation based on the character of the source (primarily Boeckh's generic-stylistic interpretation and Blass's technical interpretation) based on the time and place of the work's appearance and the individuality of the author.

After everything that we know from the history of the hermeneutical problem, Bernheim's discussions appear to us as empty and blind in the extreme. One can, however, notice a tendency in them that is fatal to hermeneutics and simply destructive to both it itself and all of the broad problems connected with it. A passion for determining the place, character, and, in general, the conditions of the very *appearance* of a source or historical document pushes the problem of understanding that very source into the background. It seems as though the resolution of this problem is taken for granted and not even worth our methodological concern. One has only to be convinced of the authenticity of the document itself, of its real value – something that requires a special skill and a lot of work – and what remains then is simply the work of *reading* it. Understanding will come by itself. Critique, in other words, swallows up hermeneutics, leaving no trace behind. I do not think that the essence of the issue calls for such a result, but this is not the place to enter into an examination of the causes for such an attitude on the part of contemporary authors of history

---

[30] Bernheim 1908: 569.

[31] Bernheim 1908: 570ff. [Reading the reference here as in Shpet 2005: 372, not as given incorrectly in Špet 1993: 221.]

[32] Bernheim 1908: 575.

and historical methodologies. It is essential for us to note only that, at the moment, there is, apparently, a mature interest on the part of logic itself in the problem of understanding in general and, particularly, in historical interpretation in the historical discipline itself. Since it seeks to grasp the methodological principles of its work independently, logic and philosophy can find neither support nor instruction from it. I will pause on one more example, which, in some respects, is very indicative of this state of affairs.

# 4 [Aleksandr] Lappo-Danilevskij

A. S. Lappo-Danilevskij,[33] stating that for a long time the theory of historical interpretation was not granted any independent significance, but was swallowed up by critique and assigned to the methodology of construction (Bernheim), remarks: "Such an attitude toward historical interpretation is explained partly by the fact that the general concept of interpretation has not, until recently, been fully explained, and partly due to the fact that not all of its principles and methods have attracted sufficient attention by those who have discussed it."[34] Such a statement creates a commitment, and its author actually poses for himself the task: (1) "to explain the general concept of the historical interpretation of sources"[35] and (2) to examine the principles and techniques that characterize its separate methods.

Lappo-Danilevskij's general presupposition is that anyone who undertakes the study of historical material already starts from a recognition of the "other I," to whom he ascribes the origin of the given source.[36] The author devotes a series of pages[37] to the very problem of the "other I" as a presupposition of historical study. The content of this discussion can hardly be considered satisfactory given the contemporary state of philosophy. We will shorten our presentation significantly if we agree to admit that this problem does actually play the role indicated and that it has been satisfactorily resolved in a positive sense. We will simply start from the author's definition, which reads: "Interpretation consists in the generally recognized scientific understanding of a historical source."[38] To understand a historical source scientifically means "to establish the objectively given *psychic significance* that the interpreter should attribute to the source."[39] This is possible if one has a reason to assert that he/she "attributes to it the same significance that the creator (the author) gave to his work." This concept of interpretation, in Lappo-Danilevskij's words, "can be supplemented somewhat (sic!) if one pays attention to what precisely in the

---

[33] Lappo-Danilevskij 2006.

[34] Lappo-Danilevskij 2006: 316.

[35] Lappo-Danilevskij 2006: 316.

[36] Lappo-Danilevskij 2006: 317.

[37] See Lappo-Danilevskij 2006: 238–251.

[38] Lappo-Danilevskij 2006: 317.

[39] [Lappo-Danilevskij 2006: 317. Shpet notes he added the italics here.]

source is being interpreted. Of course, the historian, in interpreting, tries, above all, to find the psychic significance of the source that corresponds best of all to the data of sense perception, i.e., to the *material form* of the source."[40]

One cannot recognize the contrast between "psychic significance" and "material form" as terminologically very successful, to say nothing of the fact that, from the viewpoint of logical precision, both expressions contain a *contradictio in adjecto*. If I have correctly grasped the distinction that the author has in mind, it is a matter of an opposition of sense perception to representation in a narrower sense. It is incomprehensible what purpose such a distinction could serve, given the generally phenomenalistic tone of the author's presuppositions, which are called upon to clarify the process of knowing "the other I." But it is clear that there is no possibility of approaching the problem of understanding and interpretation as long as we are seeking the "meaning" in the "representations" of the communicator.

Lappo-Danilevskij himself senses certain difficulties here. In blatant contradiction with the demand for a "universally valid scientific understanding of a historical source,"[41] he asserts that "an interpretation of a source provides only a more or less approximate understanding of it, and the degree of such approximation," he adds, "can by no means always be established with the proper precision."[42] Finally, it only adds to the confusion when he claims that *what* is interpreted in the source can "somewhat (!) supplement" his concept of interpretation.

Naturally, with such a *subjectivistic* "general concept" of interpretation we can hardly hope to fill the gap in historical hermeneutics about which the author complains. One could agree – independently even of his presuppositions about the "other I" – that the interpretation of any source or document *begins* with a psychological interpretation.[43] However, his idea that psychological interpretation lies *at the foundation* of the other methods of interpretation does not seem so indisputable.[44] What, in fact, does "at the foundation" mean here? From a point of view that is not prejudiced in favor of psychologism or subjectivism, it should seem clear that, if the historian needs a psychological interpretation, this is chiefly in order to discard what is attributable to the subjectivity of the source and then to understand what was communicated by that source as an actually objective-historical relationship. But, certainly, this does not square with the conviction that the only interpretation that may be called objectively historical is an interpretation *of what* is communicated, which only "somewhat supplements" the psychological interpretation, or is reduced to the level of the "secondary (!) techniques" that establish the "real object."[45]

If the author himself does not notice the unnatural character of such a state of things, that can be explained by his phenomenalistic or subjectivistic presupposi-

---

[40] Lappo-Danilevskij 2006: 317. [Shpet notes he added the italics here.]

[41] Lappo-Danilevskij 2006: 317.

[42] Lappo-Danilevskij 2006: 318.

[43] Lappo-Danilevskij 2006: 319, 320f, 322ff.

[44] Lappo-Danilevskij 2006: 339.

[45] Lappo-Danilevskij 2006: 326.

tions. Although they do not justify it, they, nevertheless, make sense of his conclusion that a psychological interpretation should reveal "a certain unity to the other's consciousness,"[46] a consciousness that is displayed in the interpretable document. On the other hand, however, this means that our esteemed historian introduces psychologism not only into grounding hermeneutics, but also into *history itself*. For in asserting that the interpretation of the source as such – and not only of the author of that source – reveals to us "a certain unity of consciousness," he thereby forces us to think that the historical process or, in general, what historical science considers its object to be is nothing other than a psychological process or a psychological object.

We are convinced of the accuracy of this charge addressed to the author[47] of the *Metodologija istorii* [*Methodology of History*] and that, along with his "basic" psychological interpretation, he also admits a special "method" of interpretation – an *individualizing* method. It also concerns "the unity of the other's consciousness," but this unity is to be distinguished from a unity that is "personal" or "individual," where the historian penetrates into the "personality of the author," starting with biographical data about the latter and penetrating into the "recesses of his personal creativity," etc.[48] This unity, as personal, is now contrasted to a "systematic" unity and even sets the "psychological" against the "logical" – which is quite confusing to the reader.[49] However, it apparently must be so: subjectivism is subjectivism.

If, therefore, psychological interpretation drives philological and historical interpretation out of hermeneutics, the other "methods" of interpretation enumerated in Lappo-Danilevskij's book threaten the very existence of hermeneutics. Their common feature lies in the fact that, like Bernheim's kinds of interpretation, they are directed not toward the content of a document, *but toward the conditions of its appearance*. As we have already indicated, this is not even interpretation but, precisely as in Bernheim, an enlisting of auxiliary knowledge from the fields of paleography, archeology, diplomacy, etc., as a prelude to historical investigation itself. Thus, the *technical* method of interpretation should investigate, on the one hand, the "material" properties of the source (in the literal sense: *materia ex qua*) and, on the other hand, the style of the source. Furthermore, the *typological* method of interpretation is invoked to reveal the "cultural type" to which the source belongs, both with respect to the general state of culture at a given "location" as well as with respect to the peculiarities of the given time or given period of culture on which the examined source really depends.

Finally, we have already discussed the *individualizing* method. On the whole, it is now either one of two things. Either the fundamental type of interpretation is psychological interpretation, replacing historical interpretation. In that case, the disclosure, with the help of the methods enumerated, of the conditions of the document's appearance is simply preliminary work, after which the source is read and understood *by itself*. Or psychological interpretation – contrary to Lappo-

---

[46] Lappo-Danilevskij 2006: 319, 336 and passim.

[47] [That is, Lappo-Danilevskij.]

[48] Lappo-Danilevskij 2006: 385.

[49] Lappo-Danilevskij 2006: 384; cf. Lappo-Danilevskij 2006: 396.

Danilevskij – turns out not to be fundamental but preliminary. In this case, we should perhaps be concerned in the remaining three "methods" not only with the disclosure of the conditions of the document itself, but really with *historical* interpretation.

Somewhat unexpectedly, Lappo-Danilevskij asserts this *too*. In connection with the typifying method, he remarks that this method "gives interpretation a more (!) historical character. It starts with the concept of the cultural type to which the source belongs, and it understands *the source's content* in accordance with this type."[50] This still may not be clear, since it gives us the right to think that the essence lies not in the "*content*" of the document,[51] but in the conditions of its appearance. If this is the case, the inconsistency that we have revealed makes itself more clearly felt, as it were, in a new division of all four "methods" of interpretation into two special "kinds."[52] It turns out that we can distinguish two kinds of interpretation: a formal, or rationalistic, interpretation and a real, or, strictly speaking, historical interpretation. The former reveals the general sense of the source and is connected primarily with the psychological (formal, or rationalistic!) and technical methods of interpretation. The latter refers to the typifying and individualizing methods: "... these methods are primarily characteristic of a real or, in the strict sense, historical, interpretation of sources, i.e., the *interpretation of its content* as much as possible in *its* entirety, *in its* dependence on the given conditions of place, time, and person that produced the given source under just these conditions...."[53] Are they ultimately really one and the same thing: the interpretation of the *content* of a source, *what* it communicates, even if it stands in all possible and impossible relations of dependency, and the disclosure, for example, of the conditions of time and place of the manifestation or composition of the *source* that *communicates* this content or of the *person* who communicates it?

Thus, if we do not consider certain remarks – or rather hints – that we could find in Droysen, the authors of the historical methodologies enrich us with neither solutions nor formulations of the problems that could have fundamental significance in connection with, or based on, the fundamental general problem of *understanding*. We could conclude our survey with this. But before we pass to examine the essence of the philosophical problems and the fundamental problems that have accumulated in the history of hermeneutics, I believe it necessary to familiarize the reader with how these problems arose in recent philosophy and psychology, how they are formulated in these disciplines, and the significance that is now ascribed to them.

---

[50] Lappo-Danilevskij 2006: 360. [Shpet notes he added the italics here.]

[51] For example, it is not a matter of understanding what is stated in the "Chronicle of Nestor" for the years 6494–6496 (986–988 A.D.), but of clarifying the "cultural type" of the Kievan principality at the beginning of the twelfth century or, perhaps, even the end of the fourteenth century, if one has in mind, let us say, the "Laurentius Chronicle."

[52] Lappo-Danilevskij 2006: 359ff.

[53] Lappo-Danilevskij 2006: 393. [Shpet notes he added the italics here. Importantly, Shpet slightly misquotes Lappo-Danilevskij here. Instead of "in its entirety" Lappo-Danilevskij's text reads "in the entirety of its nuances."]

# [Dilthey's Development of Hermeneutics]

## 1  The Philosophers: [Carl] Prantl

The elucidation of the general causes, inherent in the development of philosophy itself and of historical science itself, aroused a lively interest in the elaboration of the "historical problem" in the second half of the nineteenth century. This elucidation will form the task of the second part of my investigations.[1] Our concern now is only with the special interest awakened in connection with this general movement in the problems of hermeneutics and its role in the methodology of historical knowledge. Apparently, the immediate causes of this were, on the one hand, Droysen's *Historik* and Boeckh's *Enzyklopädie* (Bratuscheck's edition appeared in 1877)[2] and, on the other hand, the study of Schleiermacher himself (by Dilthey).

Prantl was, apparently, the first to undertake a treatment of the problem in its fundamental, general form and to attribute a broad philosophical and methodological significance to it.[3] Unfortunately, the direction he took does not seem to me fruitful, at least from the point of view of the formulation of the question that is serving as the starting point in our present investigation. He states at the beginning of his

---

[1] [In all likelihood, Shpet had in mind here the second part of his *History as a Problem of Logic*, Shpet 2002: 546–1131.]

[2] Steinthal's previously cited lecture on the types of interpretation was given (in September) before the publication of Boeckh's book (in December). However, as the author himself relates, it was directly in response to the book, since Steinthal received a proof of it as it was being printed. Steinthal refers to Droysen in the [unpaginated] "Preface" to his *Philologie, Geschichte und Psychologie*. [Steinthal 1864: Preface.] The quotation he gives is taken from Droysen's article on Buckle: Droysen 1868: 61–62. [The full title of the piece is "Erhebung der Geschichte zum Rang einer Wissenschaft." See Droysen 1868: 41–62.]

[3] von Prantl 1877. Prantl does not refer to Boeckh. However, his very juxtaposition of "hermeneutics" and "critique," and equally his identification of philology and history indicate the influence of Boeckh and support the presupposition that Prantl, like Steinthal, familiarized himself with Boeckh's *Enzyklopädie* as the proofs became available.

© Springer Nature Switzerland AG 2019
G. Shpet, T. Nemeth, *Hermeneutics and Its Problems*, Contributions
To Phenomenology 98, https://doi.org/10.1007/978-3-319-98941-9_8

article that hermeneutics and critique remain "not only a sign (*ein Kennzeichen*), but truly a landmark (*das Wahrzeichen*) for all of philology and also – which, in terms of its inner essence, amounts to the same thing – of all historical investigation in general."[4]

He states that there are indications that the boast of natural scientists that they alone possess scientific methods is losing its significance as a universally binding dogma.[5] And he expresses the hope that perhaps philosophy will be allowed to pose the question whether hermeneutics and critique are not the methodological techniques to which, in a theory of science, an appropriate fundamental function should be assigned. The theory of science (logic) finds its true completion only when it shows how the "form" of knowledge that embraces a multitude of perceptions and phenomena finds its concrete embodiment in science.[6] "Therefore, a theory of science should, in the last analysis, function 'phenomenologically' as a 'theory of method,' the object of which consists precisely in understanding and critique (*Beurteilen*)."[7] The *formal* side (the theory of judgment, concept, inference, and definition), based on the principle of contradiction, does not yet provide *material* truth. In the latter, logic becomes possible only thanks to the scientific mastering of its phenomenological side, i.e., of understanding and critique.[8] Consequently, scientific analysis of the concrete realization of every science reveals a moment that is at the same time a plan for a corresponding investigation. Every science is realized: (1) through the immediacy of understanding, (2) through a mediate stage of critique, (3) through a further mediated, most profound union of understanding and critique.

However, Prantl provides neither a fundamental nor a psychological analysis of understanding. The three stages of understanding that he uncovers attest more to his attachment to the Hegelian dialectic than to his aspiration to reveal the genuine nature of the act of understanding. Prantl depicts these stages as follows.[9]

1. The immediate, lowest stage (accessible even to the animal world) is a certain indeterminate, general sense of the object (*Objekts-Sinn*) in things and in words. This immediate understanding contains two moments: (a) the subjectivity of an apprehension in which things are represented in the mind of the individual (a motif of Protagoras' viewpoint); (b) the *universality* that arises from the apprehension of what abides through the changes in the subjective apprehensions and that leads to universal validity and general agreement. At the first stage, this universality, nevertheless, remains preliminary and indeterminate.

2. Understanding proceeds from this indeterminacy to the second stage, where it enters into the manifold of particular definitions and attempts to seize the special

---

[4] [Prantl 1877: 1.]

[5] [Prantl 1877: 2.]

[6] In this formula, as well as from what follows, the reader will have no difficulty in noting the author's [i.e., Prantl's] Hegelianism.

[7] Prantl 1877: 3.

[8] Prantl 1877: 4.

[9] Prantl 1877: 8–20.

meaning of a word or the special role of an object. Prantl calls this stage the "understanding of what is individual" ("*Verständnis des Individuellen*").[10] The understanding of what is individual also applies to an understanding on the basis of a single example, in its concrete phenomenological significance, of the forms and laws of thought. This is where the theory of method and formal logic meet.

3. From the wealth of what is individual, the understanding rises further to the third stage from its former immediate and indeterminate universality, through the understanding of what is individual, to the determinately formed universal. This is the "understanding of the universal, which is contained in the particular."[11]

Here understanding plunges into the most intimate depths of the universal essence of the singular. Insofar as some universal is revealed at every stage of understanding, there is a basis for connecting critique to understanding, since critique consists precisely in a comparison of the particular with the universal. Critique, therefore, also passes through the three stages that correspond to the stages of understanding. As a result of understanding and critique, one obtains bits of knowledge that find their consistent development in the realization of science. This is why Prantl thinks that the word "knowledge" means nothing other than the most perfect union of understanding and critique.[12] Guided by those same techniques of understanding and critique, we pass from separate bits of knowledge to their connection and strive toward some ultimate principle, so that the explanation required by science arises on the basis of this process of knowing.

From this, the universal methodological significance of understanding as the principle of the "logic of material truth" is obvious. It serves as a counterweight and supplement to formal logic, which is founded on the principle of contradiction. Keeping in mind, on the one hand, the methodological tasks of such a material logic and, on the other hand, the explanatory results to which it leads in the realization, i.e., the presentation, of science, it is not difficult to convince ourselves that the broad perspectives that Prantl promises for constructing a scientific methodology based on hermeneutics, are due, in fact, not from a penetration into the specific peculiarities of understanding as such, but from an excessively broad interpretation of the very term "understanding."

According to Prantl's definition, *understanding* is an "immediate apprehension in thought" (*ein unmittelbares denkendes Erfassen*), accompanied by a certain instinctive feeling of accuracy independent of whether we really are concerned with something that is justifiable or not.[13] Prantl explains that this is why the meaning of the word "to understand" (*verstehen*) is also akin to "conceptually apprehend, find something clearly explained" (*begreifen, erklärlich finden*). Interpretation, accordingly, is an explicating facilitation of understanding, and hermeneutics is the technique of understanding and at the same time of explanation (*und zugleich des Erklärens*).

---

[10] [Prantl 1877: 14.]

[11] [Prantl 1877: 17.]

[12] Prantl 1877: 34–35.

[13] Prantl 1877: 6.

Nevertheless, understanding as an immediate apprehension appears to be decisive, since what serves as an explanation must itself still be understood in order to
lead to an understanding (*Verstehen*) that is synonymous with a conceptual apprehension (*Begreifen*). Similarly, "understanding" in the sense of an immediate apprehension is distinguished from that meaning of understanding (*Verstehen*) (skill?)
when it is taken as a synonym for "mental agility" (*geistige Tüchtigkeit*), or "dexter-
ity" (*Gewandtheit*), or even "cunning" (*Pfiffigkeit*). In the indicated sense, one can
speak equally of both immediate understanding and of so-called a posteriori intuitions and also of so-called a priori concepts. That is, since thinking is essentially
connected for us with a word, understanding extends equally to every thought
expressed in a word. It is all the same whether what is communicated in a word is a
sense perception or some act of an ideally endowed person. Something understandable lies in every fact, since the simple perception of a fact and the assimilation
(*Vernehmen*) of a communication of that fact immediately presupposes a certain
intellectual content that is also immediately understood.[14]

There is much that is interesting in these arguments: the idea of a logic of material truth along with formal logic, the enlisting of hermeneutics to carry out this
task, the definition of understanding as an *immediate* apprehension. However, as an
answer to the problems of hermeneutics in the direction in which we seek an answer,
Prantl's work leaves us unsatisfied. If his essay actually were an attempt to answer
the contemporaneous demand noted above, then one would have to recognize this
attempt as unsuccessful. Prantl takes the concept of "understanding" in an extremely
broad sense, despite certain restrictions, which he himself indicates. But his generalization, it seems to me, does not move in a genuinely interesting direction.
Considering understanding, *Verstehen*, to be a "kind" of thinking, a function of the
understanding (*Verstand*), Prantl ascribes the entire "material" side of thinking, i.e.,
its *content*, to this "kind" of thinking, in contrast to the formal functions of the
understanding: judgment, syllogism (which follows from and is based on judgment), and definition.[15] This all-encompassing form needs concrete embodiment,
which, in Prantl's opinion, as we saw, is achieved with the help of understanding
and critique as methodological techniques for the realization of science. Therefore,
Prantl's generalization only seems to be a generalization. He seeks a certain ana-
logue to the formal functions of the understanding in the rational assimilation of the
content of thinking. The dialectical schemas help him to arrange the stages of understanding itself. Nevertheless, he has no grasp at all even of what is *specific* to the act
of understanding. On the one hand, he compares it in a very general way with a
"concept" and a "conceptual apprehension." However, on the other hand, he compares it to words in a rather helpless and ineffectual manner. Ultimately, Prantl's
idea of a special theory of method is simply a theory of discursively rational knowledge. His juxtaposition of it with hermeneutics seems to be a baseless move.

Since the specificity of understanding itself eluded him, the specificity of the
problems of hermeneutics escaped Prantl's attention. He circumvented a particular

---

[14] Prantl 1877: 7.
[15] See Prantl 1877: 2–3. Prantl 1875: 159ff and 190.

stumbling block, namely, that of the need to distinguish between *Verstehen* and *Begreifen*, in a completely external way. He felt no need, in this regard, to look into the essence of *Verstehen* as a quite unique act. This is why every problem that Prantl examined from this direction was doomed in advance to fail. This also explains the failure, for example, of a whole series of attempts to approach the problem of understanding from the perspective of contemporary experimental psychology. However, the historical roots that brought forth this direction and path go back as far as Kant. Consequently, the sources of many of the failed attempts to solve our problem also go back, to a significant degree, to him. This is a matter that we will have the opportunity later to discuss in greater detail.

## 2   Dilthey[: The Middle Years]

*Dilthey* deserves credit for highlighting the fundamental significance of hermeneutical problems and diligently advocating for hermeneutics as the methodological foundation of the study of history and of the human sciences in general. In his broadly conceived *Introduction to the Human Sciences*,[16] he had not yet established the role of hermeneutics and the problems involved in understanding.[17] Apparently, his thought takes a definite form for the first time in his articles on "The Natural System of the Human Sciences in the Seventeenth Century," in which he declares, "that a starting point of the highest value for the modern foundation of the human sciences is given precisely in hermeneutics."[18] Dilthey presents his thoughts more fully in the article "The Rise of Hermeneutics."[19]

In Dilthey's view, the significance of hermeneutics for the human sciences is completely all-encompassing, but he approaches the matter somewhat one-sidedly. The direction from which he approaches it predetermines his entire presentation, limiting and narrowing it for no good reason. In his investigations on the theory and history of poetic creation, Dilthey comes to the same point where, in Schleiermacher's view, hermeneutics stopped and, in Droysen's view, the problem of understanding stopped. This is the question of the individual person, or individuality in general, as the source of creativity. In connection with this, Dilthey poses the quite legitimate and long-pondered question of the *scientific* knowledge of the individual person,

---

[16] Dilthey 1989.

[17] One casual remark of Dilthey's made on a particular occasion shows that his first thought was to relate understanding to the activity of *phantasy*. What actually connects Dilthey's "Introduction" with his subsequent works in the same direction is, rather, his understanding of reality as a "system of life-units" (cf. Dilthey 1989: 67ff) and his definition of the subject matter of the human sciences as against that of the natural sciences. (Cf., however, also Dilthey 1989: 80ff, 157ff.)

[18] Dilthey 1914b: 115. In essence, Dilthey's articles form a continuation of the work, which he began with the first volume of his *Introduction to the Human Sciences*. See Georg Misch's "Vorwort" to the second volume of Dilthey's collected works. Dilthey 1921: v–ix. In it, Misch informs us concerning Dilthey's remaining unpublished work on Schleiermacher's hermeneutics.

[19] Dilthey 1996.

asking whether such knowledge is possible, and what means we have available to us for acquiring it.[20] In his opinion, this question can have significance not only for our conduct and well-being, but also for "the entirety of the science of philology and of history," which are based on the presupposition that a re-understanding (*Nachverständniss*) of what is individual can be raised to objectivity. The one-sidedness of such a formulation of the question is obvious: the philological and historical sciences have as the object of their study and understanding not only the "individual person," i.e., the individual person as the one who communicates, but also what it is that is communicated. The presupposition that what is communicated is just the sum total of personal or individual components is a pure prejudice and, at best, can be accepted only as a methodologically explanatory hypothesis. On the other hand, the "elevation" of the individual person to the level of an objectively social object, which I mentioned in connection with my presentation of Droysen's views, acquires its sense only when we understand what an objectively social object in general is and how to proceed to a re-understanding of it.

In formulating Dilthey's problem, it is all too easy to lapse into a psychologism and even to reduce the very object of historical study, or of understanding, to some-thing purely psychological. In fact, Dilthey exhibits such a tendency. By his defini-tion, the subject matter of the human sciences, as against that of the natural sciences, is not sensory appearance, but "the most immediate inner reality, reality as an inwardly experienced connection."[21] However, Dilthey's psychologism is certainly not the naïve psychologism that we are accustomed to finding in the methodological elaboration of problems connected with the human sciences by Wundt and similar authors. Dilthey emphasizes that a simple appeal to *inner experience* does not resolve the problem of knowledge in this sphere, and can least of all lead to the satisfaction of demands for *objective* knowledge in the human sciences. However, it is also clear that, even if we limit the sphere of understanding to the understanding of the individual person, it will still be impossible to say that the object of our con-cern is then given in "inner experience." But Dilthey goes further – and this is what gives his theory its fundamental importance. He states that "inner experience" is insufficient for knowledge of even my own individuality. Only by comparing myself to others do I form the experience of what is individual in my own self.[22] Yet, the problem of knowledge of the individual person, in such a case, remains an independent problem, one that cannot be reduced to the methods of introspective psychology. Moreover, if this kind of knowledge is precisely what is meant by understanding, then the problem of understanding is, thereby, simply being posed in its fundamental and methodological essence.

---

[20] Dilthey 1996: 235.

[21] Cf. Dilthey 1996: 236.

[22] Cf. the earlier quotation from Droysen: "What a person is, one learns only in history." [Contrary to this claim, Shpet did not provide such a quotation earlier. However, in his discussion of Droysen he quoted words that could be understood as having the same meaning as this quotation.] Spranger also compares Droysen's thought, in another connection, with Dilthey's views: Spranger 1912: 14–15. See also Erdmann 1912b: 14.

The existence of the other is not exhausted by sensibly given appearances, since, as was said, it is an inner reality or an inwardly experienced connection. Nevertheless, however, it is given from outside, above all, in sensible facts, gestures, sounds, and action – in other words, in signs of various kinds. Dilthey writes, "*Understanding* is what we call the process by which we know something internal based on sensibly given external signs."[23] It extends from apprehending the babbling of a child to penetrating into *Hamlet* or the *Critique of Pure Reason*. The human spirit speaks to us from marble stones, musical sounds, gestures, words, and letters; from actions, economic organizations and institutions. All of these require interpretation. Nevertheless, Dilthey sees only individual persons behind all of these. Since even the most intense attention to understanding cannot ensure us that this understanding is complete and objective, we turn to certain artificial and rule-guided techniques. "Such *a systematic understanding of vivid manifestations that have imprinted themselves over a protracted period is what we call exegesis or interpretation.*"[24] The human "inner being" finds its complete, exhaustive, and objectively understandable expression solely in language. Thus, the art of understanding centers its application precisely in the interpretation of written monuments – and this is the starting point for philology. The art of interpretation, to which philologists applied their talent and virtuosity, led to their techniques being fixed in the form of *rules*. The dispute about these rules and the struggle over the directions produced a need to ground the rules in a hermeneutical science, which manifested itself, therefore, *as the art of the exegesis of written monuments.*[25]

In Dilthey's view, hermeneutics so defined should fulfill the chief task of historical knowledge, viz., to contrast a universal obligatory and objective interpretation to romantic caprice and skeptical subjectivity.[26] In connection with the theory of knowledge, logic, and the methodology of the human sciences, hermeneutics is an important link between philosophy and the historical sciences and the principal element in the grounding of the human sciences.

Thus, Dilthey's formulation of the problem is really nothing other than a sharpening of the final point that Schleiermacher had already reached. However, like Schleiermacher, Dilthey only *poses* the problem.[27] He takes it more broadly, seeing in it the foundation of all the human sciences. However, this is by no means enough to overcome the narrowness that characterizes the psychologism inherent in his definitions. On the other hand, Dilthey did not formulate the reverse problem, which in many respects is the decisive one, concerning the *logical* expression of interpretation and understanding. This is the general problem concerning a *sign*. In it, we express not only ourselves, but something is communicated that is not merely personal but also objective. It is impossible to deny that this logically semasiological problem, which is correlated with a hermeneutical investigation, eludes Dilthey.

---

[23] Cf. Dilthey 1996: 236.

[24] Cf. Dilthey 1996: 237.

[25] Dilthey 1996: 237–238.

[26] Dilthey 1996: 250.

[27] See Spranger's address cited above. Spranger 1912: 18.

This is the result of the same psychological contraction of his fundamental presuppositions in determining the subject matter and tasks of the human sciences and, consequently, also of understanding as a specific "kind of knowledge" within those sciences.

# 3   [Eduard] Spranger

As we will see below, Dilthey himself later somewhat corrected his presuppositions and thereby freed them from psychologism. Nevertheless, his original definitions managed to have an influence, the results of which could hardly be accepted in their entirety given the positive development of the problems he raised. Spranger[28] undertook the laudable task of further developing the principles that Dilthey had formulated. And although his "epistemologically psychological investigation" closely adjoins Dilthey's idea of a *descriptive* psychology with its ultimate goal of constructing "types" and "structures" of spiritual life, he happily avoids the inadequacies of a Wundtian type of *explanatory* psychologism. Nevertheless, he is very close to such psychologically explanatory theories as that, for example, of Sigwart. Even the originality of Dilthey's inadequately formulated problems simply fades even further in Spranger's treatment. If, after this, we should find certain particulars in Spranger's ideas that are useful for the theory of understanding, we, nevertheless, would have no right to say that Spranger either solved the problem of understanding or even that he threw sufficient light on its truly all-encompassing fundamental and methodological significance. I will still have to deal with some of the details of Spranger's arguments concerning understanding below. Now, however, I will focus only on his views of the role that the problem of understanding can and should play in the methodological resolution of the problem of the nature and the tasks of historical science.[29]

---

[28] Spranger 1905.

[29] I will not focus, in this survey, on the views of Wundt or Sigwart concerning the role of understanding and interpretation, since these authors do not ascribe to understanding the fundamental and universal significance that interests me. After what was said on this issue by Dilthey, Spranger, Simmel, and Erdmann, Wundt's and Sigwart's discussions are of little interest. Furthermore, to the extent that it is a matter of their views on the logical nature of history in general, they will be of concern in the second part of my investigations, but I will use some of their points below with critical intents. I note only that in each of the authors mentioned there are deficiencies, which, from our point of view, devalue their theories. Sigwart approaches the analysis of propositions and their sense with respect to the "speaker" and not that of the "hearer" (Sigwart 1873: 28ff). He considers the latter to be of importance only for grammar and hermeneutics, not for logic. From the viewpoint of a narrow understanding of logic – since it is a matter of "presentation" without entering into a fundamental analysis of its dependence on "investigation" – we can consider him to be correct. However, when he then reduces the entirety of "understanding" to explanatory inference (Sigwart 1878: 483 (§99)), he simply eliminates the problem – not only of its philosophical and logical significance, but even of its psychological significance, which is the most important for him given his psychologism.

Spranger provides an overtly psychological foundation for the theory of knowledge in general and, consequently, for the methodology of the historical sciences in particular. However, as mentioned, he does not appeal to an abstract explanatory psychology for this purpose, but to the type of descriptive psychology *sui generis* that Dilthey conceptually defended. One of its essential characteristics is that, for its analysis, it takes psychic states immediately from *lived experience*, and always in connection with it, i.e., as a certain integral psychic process, the integrity of which we immediately experience. This givenness of the individual in the whole and their immediately given inner connection also predetermines the nature of *understanding* – both of ourselves as well as of others. In a purely intellectual process, we "explain," but in such an interaction of all of our psychic forces we "understand." Proceeding from the integrity of our lived experiences to each individual process, we understand the latter only because we live within an awareness of the integrity of the whole. This is why the immediately experienced integrity of psychic life must also remain the "firm, experienced, and immediately reliable foundation of psychology."[30]

Naturally, whatever advantages it might have in other respects, this kind of psychology must unilaterally predetermine the theory of interpretation constructed upon it in the individual-personalistic direction that we already encountered in Dilthey himself. Therefore, when Spranger declares, in quite general terms, "history, as a science, attempts to provide a psychological comprehension of outward actions, events, and states,"[31] we already know that the object of all of the manifestations of what will be comprehended will be nothing other than the individual person. Moreover, in those cases where history, "as a science," speaks not of the individual person, the psychological interpretation will attempt to understand the impersonal facts of history by analogy with an understanding of the individual person.

As against Rickert, Spranger stresses that an epistemological investigation of the historical discipline should not attempt the construction of an *a priori* logical ideal, but should investigate historical knowledge itself factually. Even as a *logic of understanding,* based on a psychological understanding, the theory of knowledge recedes into the background behind the essential problem of the methodological grounding of a psychology that will satisfy the logical demands of historical knowledge.[32] However, these demands are also demands for a fundamental analysis of under-

---

As for Wundt, his own psychologism, which leads him to a hopeless confusion of "interpretation" and "explanation" (Wundt 1908: 54; nevertheless, cf. Wundt 1908: 79) together with an unoriginal compilatory-eclectic presentation, will clearly convince the reader that Wundt did not grasp the original and fresh spirit that the problems of hermeneutics present. Wundt's discussions convey the impression of judgments about music made by someone who has no ear for music. He tirelessly repeats the words: induction, deduction, analogy, comparison. More than to anyone, what Dilthey said about Mill is applicable to Wundt: "Especially in Mill, we hear the monotonous and tedious clatter of the words 'induction' and 'deduction' ...." (Dilthey 1989: 158.)

[30] Dilthey 1894: 34.

[31] Spranger 1905: 18.

[32] Spranger 1905: 19.

standing itself, which, consequently for Spranger, is a psychological analysis. Once we recognize that the active principle in history is a matter of psychological relations, our task is thereby directly dictated, namely, to push the investigation as far as possible. The problem of how far these relations extend is, in accordance with the presuppositions of Dilthey and Spranger, also a matter of *how far understanding extends*.[33] This formulation of the problem separates Spranger not only from Rickert and Windelband but, on the other hand, also from the overt psychologism of Wundt, Sigwart, and Lamprecht insofar as these three theorists seek a causal explanation of historical phenomena in psychology. Spranger does not think that he is restricting the scientific tasks of history. On the contrary, he is convinced that the *understandable* (*verständliche*) necessity of each individual process, which arises from its relation to an integral structure and in connection with it, extends beyond the *explanatory* (*erklärende*) causal order. The historian, as well as anyone who is interested in knowledge of cultural and psychic life, bears within oneself an awareness of the whole and *understands* each individual process in terms of its inclusion in the general system and in terms of its significance for that system.[34]

In this way, the fundamental significance of the problem of understanding in all of the human sciences is exhibited more deeply. This significance is ultimately so great that the assertion of the fundamental character of psychology with respect to history, which has up until now played the role of a presupposition, can itself be revealed, it turns out, only after we have answered the question: "What is understanding?" (*Was heisst Verstehen?*).[35] Spranger's definition here clearly reveals the mentioned one-sided nature of his own understanding of understanding. "We 'understand' ourselves or anyone else," he writes, "only when we know the other person's motives, which are partly conscious and partly involuntary (*triebhaften*), and examine the person in connection with the motives exerting an influence on him. Consequently, the task and essence of understanding consists in revealing and becoming aware of these psychological connections, which to a certain degree are concealed or in general are still not identified."[36] It is not hard to see that we are dealing here with the unfolding of the same definition that we already encountered in Dilthey. Its merits and shortcomings are the same. It is important that Spranger pays attention to the specificity of the act of understanding. However, his fatal shortcoming lies in his one-sidedness. Whether it rightly or wrongly grasps the aspect of understanding that he noted, we are dealing with an understanding of the *individual person*. Nevertheless, if we must take this definition to be a *general* definition, it is obvious that Spranger forces us to understand every historical fact by analogy with an understanding of the individual person. The important contribution of Dilthey's descriptive psychology lies in the attention it paid to "types," "structures," and "relations." They, however, lose in this case their *sui generis* significance as social "things."

---

[33] Spranger 1905: 39.

[34] Spranger 1905: 21.

[35] Spranger 1905: 75.

[36] [Spranger 1905: 75.]

The result of such one-sidedness is something with which it is impossible to reconcile ourselves. Whether the socio-historical "things" be individual things or types of things ultimately makes no difference. In history "as a given science," in the historical facts with which the works of historians acquaint us, these "things" are *neither* purely psychological things *nor* psychological phenomena. The "individual person," for the historian, is a social *thing*. This is a fact. Apparently, one can free oneself from the pressure of *psychologistic* theory without renouncing the theory itself in only two ways: either by taking the path of least intellectual effort, i.e., proclaiming a psychological explanation for the historical facts and phenomena in the manner, for example, of Wundt,[37] or, under the influence of the skeptical "sub-foundation" of psychologism, by way of consigning the historical object proper to the spheres of metaphysics, to the sphere of the transcendent, to the sphere of things in themselves. In general, Spranger prefers the latter way. The development of the psychology of understanding, in his opinion, should begin, strictly speaking, with the problem of interpretation. A developed teleological psychology should start with the development of *typical* social and individual forms of psychic life and the relationships that can be established between them. The psychology of these types and relations, however, has strict limits in the form of *metaphysical* facts. Thus, even our I (*das Selbst*), which forms the sub-foundation of our own life experiences, cannot fully rise to the sphere of understanding insofar as it is intertwined with its metaphysical roots. The same applies to social formations as well.

"The state," Spranger says, "evokes a certain psychic reflection in its members, a certain determinate feeling of the state, which can be experienced (*nacherlebt werden kann*); but the state itself cannot be experienced."[38] Spranger's point is quite correct, and it necessarily follows from this that the state cannot be studied, explained, or understood by psychology. Either another science can do this – and evidently, then, Spranger has identified the problem of understanding in a one-sided fashion – or the state really is transcendent in a metaphysical sense. It also follows from this that psychological understanding and psychological interpretation are not the only kinds of understanding and interpretation.

Spranger thinks "the individual always remains the sole arena of psychological experience."[39] And although the individual stands in objective relations that are intertwined with one's teleological system, it is, nevertheless, impossible to derive any *objective* teleology from this. For otherwise we would abandon the psychological point of view and the ground of its reliable method. Hegel's objective spirit, Baer's rational nature, the soul of the people in Herder and the historical school of law – none of these are psychological concepts, but instead are metaphysical con-

---

[37] Wundt 1908: 400ff, particularly 412. Spranger's own comparison of his concept of "understanding" with Wundt's "psychic causality" makes a strange impression. [Spranger 1905: 49.]

[38] Spranger 1905: 27.

[39] Spranger 1905: 76. [This page reference follows the German translation, Špet 1993: 245. The Russian text, used as the basis for this translation, gives Spranger 1905: 77. See Shpet 2005: 389. Moreover, Shpet somewhat incorrectly translates Spranger, for the latter wrote, "Mental life is always immediately given to us only in one's own psychic experiencing."]

cepts. It is characteristic of the psychological method that it reduces everything to the given consciousness of a single psyche. "The state, law, religion, history exist only insofar as they are experienced. Their '*an sich*,' for psychology, is transcendent."[40]

Thus, the psychological interpretation is consistent: to understand means to "co-experience." The individual understands and is understood. Descriptive psychology does as little to solve the problem of strictly *historical* interpretation as does explanatory psychology. Its sole advantage over the latter is that, out of fear of metaphysics, it abstains from hypothesizing, something to which psychological explanation nurtures a strong tendency. Nonetheless, as I have said, an impossible situation arises. The "theory of knowledge" applied to history leads to skepticism instead of providing methodological support for history. So, just as a theory of knowledge and a corresponding type of skepticism did not prevent the work of the physicist, in spite of all the assertions of phenomenalism and intimidations of engaging in metaphysics, so – one must think – the historian too will not stop his work, regardless of whether a psychological theory of knowledge reduces the facts of history to psychic experiences or frightens the historian with that same metaphysics. In any case, in the knowledge of historical reality, there is in this connection for philosophy the same *scandal* that once threatened it in connection with the knowledge of natural reality. This scandal, by the way, is very instructive, since it reveals once again the enormous and fundamental philosophical significance of the historical problem itself.

# 4   Dilthey[: The Later Years]

One must recognize Dilthey's great philosophical sensitivity, because the impossible state of affairs that resulted from psychologism in historical methodology did not, in the final analysis, escape his attention. In his last published work, which appeared a year before his death, he again returned to the theme of methodology in history and the human sciences. However, this time the object of history, namely, the object of understanding, appears in a somewhat different light than it had previously in his own work and in that of his disciple, Spranger.[41]

The hermeneutical circle – *lived experience, expression,* and *understanding*[42] – appears, as before, to be in his eyes the distinctive characteristic of the human sciences and is the topic that attracts his attention. "From the perspective of perception and cognition," he says, "humanity would be for us a physical fact,[43] and, as such, it would be accessible only to natural scientific cognition. But, as an object of the

---

[40] Spranger 1905: 78.

[41] Dilthey 2010.

[42] Dilthey 2010. 109, 153. Cf. Spranger 1912: 17.

[43] [Reading with Špet 1993: 247 and Dilthey 2010: 108 "fact" instead of "act" as in Shpet 2005: 390.]

human sciences, it appears only insofar as human states are experienced, insofar as they are expressed in life's manifestations, and insofar as these expressions are understood."[44] A person, on the other hand, is defined by nature, whose laws we study as though we were excluding thereby ourselves in our lived experiences. Nature itself appears as the center here in relation to us. However, as soon as a person turns from nature to life, to oneself, a second center arises. Here *understanding* comes into its rights. Understanding turns from what is given to the senses in human history to what is inaccessible to the senses but that, nevertheless, is realized and expresses itself externally.[45]

As can be seen from this discussion, Dilthey is not renouncing here his earlier definition of understanding in terms of a transition from the external to the internal. However, this "internal" something, as the object to which understanding is directed, presents itself to him in a new light compared to what it was earlier. "Here," he writes, "it is a common error to substitute the psychic process of life – psychology – for our knowledge of this inner aspect."[46] Two examples will clarify our concern here.

(a) The apparatus of legal books, ideas, litigants, and defendants at a given time and place is the expression of a certain goal-directed system of legal definitions that organizes a certain collective will. The form of law is an imperative behind which stands the coercive power of society. The historical *understanding* of law requires passing beyond this external apparatus, penetrating to the general will that realizes it. In this sense, for example, Jhering says of the spirit of Roman law: "The understanding of that spirit is not psychological knowledge. It is a return to a spiritual formation that has its own structure and lawfulness."[47] All jurisprudence rests on this – from the interpretation of some passage in the *Corpus juris* to a knowledge of Roman law in comparison to the laws of other states.

(b) Aesthetics. The poet's work is given to us in the form of letters set in type by a typesetter and mechanically printed. Poetics and the history of literature seek in them the "inner" sense of what is expressed by these signs. It is important that the latter not be inner processes within the poet, but, rather, a connection created in him/her though separable from him/her. The connection of a drama, for example, consists in the *distinctive* relation of the material, of the poetic mood, motif, plot, and means of presentation. "The object that literary history or poetics has to deal with at first is completely different from the psychic processes in the poet or his readers."[48]

---

[44] Cf. Dilthey 2010: 108.

[45] Dilthey 2010: 105. Cf. Dilthey 2010: 104.

[46] Cf. Dilthey 2010: 106. Cf. Dilthey 2010: 173. See Erdmann 1912b: 15, where he contrasts Dilthey's new "epistemological-logical" viewpoint to the earlier epistemological-psychological viewpoint.

[47] [Dilthey 2010: 106–107.]

[48] Cf. Dilthey 2010: 107.

Clearly, we now have an entirely new formulation of the problem of understanding. Even if one retains Dilthey's earlier definition of understanding, one must, nevertheless, give it a new sense – in any case a broader and more versatile sense than before. Only now, one may hope, are we approaching the problem in its full scope. And it is obvious that the earlier psychological interpretation needs essential supplementation with respect to an objectively historical interpretation. Unfortunately, this time as well, Dilthey fails to provide an answer to the question that once again arises before him, namely, what, properly speaking, is the essence of understanding as a *sui generis* source of knowledge in the human sciences. However, one can find in Dilthey at least certain more precise indications as to what an *expression* (or "sign") is. The understanding of an expression forms the task of these sciences. Moreover, since these indications can facilitate certain subsequent formulations of the problems, it is not superfluous to mention them now.

They are interesting, above all, in that they determine more precisely the subject matter of the human sciences and of history from its *positive* side. For the question is now quite legitimate: since we come to what is "inner" by way of understanding and it is *not* something psychic, then what is it? We say that nature is given to us "externally." If nature also enters as a constituent element in history, then it is only in that nature has effects and insofar as one can influence it. However, the proper realm of history, Dilthey stresses, is also something *external*. This externality, whether it be musical notes, the canvas of a painting, a courtroom, a prison, etc., receives its material only from nature. What is important for the human sciences in these instances is their *sense*, their *significance*, the *spirit* acting in them. For spirit is what is *objectified* in this externality.[49] In this sense, the subjectivity of a "lived experience" is objectified by means of an "expression." The individual, societies, works of art, in which life and spirit are invested – all of these are the external realm of the spirit, manifestations of life, standing before understanding. "This great external reality of human spirit always surrounds us. It is the realization of the human spirit in the sensible world – from a fleeting expression to the rule of an institution or legislative authority that lasts for centuries. *Each single manifestation of life represents* something *common (ein Gemeinsames)* in the realm of this objective spirit. Every word or sentence, every gesture or polite formula, every work of art and political deed is intelligible because a commonality connects those manifesting themselves in them and those who are understanding. The individual (*der Einzelne*) always experiences, thinks, and acts within a sphere of commonality, and only in such a sphere does he understand. Everything understood carries, as it were, the stamp of familiarity derived from such commonality. We live in this atmosphere; it surrounds us constantly; we are immersed in it. We are at home everywhere in this historical and understood world; we understand the sense and meaning of everything. We ourselves are woven into this commonality."[50] Thus, the subject matter of the human sciences with their distinctive concept is delineated in a new way: "The

---

[49] Dilthey 2010: 108.
[50] Cf. Dilthey 2010: 168–169.

scope of the human sciences extends just as far as does the understanding, and understanding has its sole object in objective life."[51]

In addition, all of this contains something new and that is fundamentally different from the subject matter of psychology and from what a psychological interpretation, properly speaking, can reveal to us. However, what draws attention to itself in all this is the special significance that must be paid to *commonality* and *communication*, both for the objectification of the spirit, which forms the subject matter of the human sciences, and for understanding as the path that leads to the apprehension of this subject matter – both in the life of the spirit and in the sciences that study that spirit. This is a very important factor, and in light of it the problem of understanding acquires a new significance and occupies a special place. Through this factor, the problem acquires significance not just for the problem of the reality of the external world and for the problem of psychic activity in the other person, of the so-called other I. But, certainly, above all, this problem is revealed in its fundamental depth, a depth that hides from us its most secret and intimate roots. Understanding is most closely connected with commonality; they mutually condition each other. Is it truly difficult to say which of them is first? "Understanding alone," Dilthey quite correctly attests, "first eliminates this limitation of individual lived experience and, at the same time, imparts the character of life-experience to personal lived experiences."[52] On the one hand, mutual understanding assures us of the commonality (*Gemeinsamkeit*) existing between individuals, and, on the other hand, this commonality itself forms a presupposition for understanding.[53]

As for the essence of Dilthey's definition of the subject matter of the human sciences to be objectified spirit, one might say that there is little new in it. Such a definition comes, as is well known, from Hegel and has been frequently repeated since. Although Dilthey himself often[54] declares his conscious opposition to Hegel, there still can be no doubt that this definition is closely related to Hegel's concept. However, for Hegel the concept of objective spirit was, above all, merely a stage in the development of the spirit and a metaphysical and speculative concept, whereas for Dilthey it is an empirical and historical concept. For Hegel, commonality was the universal rational will, whereas for Dilthey it is life in its real full scope, lived experience, understanding, the historical context of life, the power of the irrational within it. In short, it is precisely what makes the very possibility of a historical science a problem.[55] "Today, we must proceed from the reality of life in which the integrity of the psychic connection is active. Hegel constructs metaphysically; we analyze what is given. A contemporary analysis of human existence fills all of us with a sense of fragility, with the power of dark instincts, with the suffering caused by mysteries and illusions, and with the finitude shown by all that is living, even where the highest creations of communal life arise from it. Therefore, we cannot

---

[51] Cf. Dilthey 2010: 170.

[52] Cf. Dilthey 2010: 162.

[53] Dilthey 2010: 163.

[54] Cf. Misch's "Preface" to the second volume of Dilthey's *Collected Works*. [Dilthey 1921: v-ix.]

[55] Dilthey 2010: 173.

understand objective spirit through reason, but must turn to the structural nexus of life-units that finds its extension in social nexuses. We cannot include objective spirit in an ideal construction. On the contrary, we must ground its reality in history."[56] Therefore, Dilthey is, above all, to a significantly greater degree more of a *rationalist* than Hegel.

Dilthey turns out to be absolutely and undoubtedly original, however, in that he connects the problem of objectified spirit, taken as the subject matter of history, with the problem of understanding, taken as the specific source of the comprehension of this subject matter. Once Dilthey took this step in the direction of distinguishing the subject matter of history from that of psychology, a second step was now urgently required. Namely, he had to recognize that historical understanding and historical interpretation are distinguished just as much from psychological interpretation as the respective sciences are different with respect to their subject matter. In his last work, Dilthey was overly concerned with the *logical* aspect of the problem, and he failed to undertake, properly speaking, a fundamental analysis of understanding, just as he had failed to undertake it earlier when he was convinced that psychological interpretation alone exists in the human sciences.

In addition, not only should Dilthey's own examples (law, poetry) have convinced him of the need for such an analysis – since they prove the objectivity of the understood spirit – but, in particular, his fundamental, quite correct, methodological idea about the mutual relationship between the human sciences and the role of understanding in this relationship. The connection between the human sciences, in his opinion, rests on the relationship between lived experience and understanding. However, this relationship is controlled by three fundamental principles[57]:

1. the expansion of our knowledge beyond the bounds of what is given in lived experience is carried out by means of an interpretation of the objectifications of life. But this interpretation, for its part, is possible only from the subjective depth of lived experience;
2. likewise, understanding of what is singular is possible only thanks to the presence in it of general knowledge, but the latter in turn presupposes understanding[58];
3. the understanding of a part of the historical process attains its completion only by relating that part to the whole; and the universal-historical survey of the whole presupposes an understanding of the parts, which are unified in it.[59]

It is not hard to see that these fundamental principles reveal and specify the methodological application of the most general principles of hermeneutics, which have in fact guided hermeneutics with its very first steps and which the authors of modern

---

[56] Cf. Dilthey 2010: 172–173.

[57] Dilthey 2010: 174.

[58] On this cf. also Dilthey 2010: 208ff.

[59] Dilthey 2010: 174.

hermeneutics – from Flacius to Schleiermacher inclusive – have tried to formulate theoretically. Dilthey's own formulations show not just a continuity in the problems of hermeneutics itself and introduce not just an organizing principle thereby into the general system of the human sciences. They also demonstrate with indubitable clarity the *objective* character of the tasks of a hermeneutics that corresponds to these fundamental principles. To this extent, its role here is so decisive in every interpretive investigation that the question can now concern not the rights and the principles of historical interpretation, but precisely the place and the role of psychological interpretation. Is it not the sense of these fundamental principles, taken as a consistent whole, that an objective understanding immediately, even with its first movement, leads us beyond the bounds of the subjective?

Finally, however much Dilthey stressed his difference with Hegel, and even if the integrity of lived experiences, which he puts in place of speculative spirit, is distinguished by the most strident irrationality, it is, nevertheless, clear that the function of comprehending the sense of history is a function of *reason*. The second principle above asserts this with respect to its abstract activity, and the third principle concerns its concrete and completed activity. The correlativity of the problems of concrete rationalism and historical understanding forms the two lines of a single philosophical track, which rests on a single fundamental foundation. The problem of understanding in essence, therefore, is the problem of rationalism itself. Thus, the place, the role, and the significance of every rationally objective interpretation should be shown based on it. Questions concerning the kinds of interpretation – including the historical and the psychological – implicitly lie in this problem. They need to be revealed and explicitly presented. Consequently, Dilthey is the highest point that the formulation of hermeneutical problems has attained – at least up until now. The hermeneutical circle (lived experience – expression – understanding) is the point from which we must now move forward.

## 5   [Georg] Simmel

In recognizing the *autonomy* of "spirit," and presupposing the specificity of the method of studying spiritual processes, both social and historical, Dilthey stands alongside the greatest sociologists of our era, along with Durkheim and Simmel. A general comparison of Dilthey with Simmel seems to me especially instructive, since it immediately reveals a number of interesting themes connected with his kind of recognition. The concept of *spirit* as the subject matter of the human sciences, and, consequently, as the subject matter of understanding, requires a more precise definition through a delimitation of its possible different meanings. Dilthey attempted to distinguish his understanding of this concept from Hegel's speculative, *metaphysical* concept. It cannot satisfy us. Above all, it is indubitable that we often use the concept of "spirit" as synonymous with that of "*psyche*," i.e., we take it in a psychological and not an objective sense, especially in so-called social and ethnic psychology.[60] Thus Simmel, though using the term "spirit" only modestly, tries to effect a definitive demarcation of sociology with its objective subject matter from social psychology.[61] The problem of the latter runs: "What modifications are experienced by the psychic process of an individual when that process proceeds under the definite influences of the social milieu?"[62] Unlike social psychology, the objects of the human sciences – language, law, cultural formations, etc. – being separated from the individual processes of their realization, are not products of the subject: neither of the individual spirit, or psyche, nor of the social spirit. "There is still a third thing: the objective spiritual *content* is no more psychological than the logical sense of a judgment is something psychological, although it can come to a reality in consciousness only within the dynamics of the psyche and thanks to it."[63] If, therefore, the objects are distinguished, the techniques of comprehending them must also be distinguished. Moreover, if these techniques are the techniques of understanding and interpretation, one must also distinguish their kinds and types.

The quoted definition shows, furthermore, yet another distinction that should also exert an influence on the division of the types of understanding. Dilthey, who contrasts "lived experience" to Hegel's speculative spirit, thereby implies with his concept of "spirit" a certain *reality* that is by no means of a metaphysical kind. In this respect, he should be compared not with Simmel but with Durkheim, for whom the "social fact" as the subject matter of sociology is a special kind of reality, along with the reality of individual – biological and psychological – life. In Durkheim's words, a social fact has its own existence "independent of the individual forms it assumes,"[64] from which follows the first rule for the observation of this kind of facts, namely, *consider them as things (comme choses).*[65]

Simmel's position is somewhat more complex. Distinguishing the psychological from the social, and in general from the spiritual, he is apparently not inclined to attribute an independent reality to the latter. Nevertheless, the psychic realm remains for him such a reality. However, as he himself declares – ascribing extreme methodological significance to this declaration and viewing it as "nothing less than decisive for the principles of the human sciences" – *a scientific examination of psychic facts is still by no means psychology.*[66]

---

[60] For several suggestions for distinguishing these meanings of the term "spirit," see my article "The Subject Matter and Task of Ethnic Psychology." Shpet 1917–18: vol. 1, no. 1; cf. in particular Shpet 1917–1918: vol. 1, no. 2, 245–251.

[61] Simmel 1908: 21ff. (*Exkurs über Sozialpsychologie*: 556–563.)

[62] Simmel 1908: 561.

[63] Simmel 1908: 559.

[64] Durkheim 1964: 10.

[65] [Durkheim 1964: 7.]

[66] Simmel 1908: 21. Cf. Simmel 1907: 4. (This second edition of the work from 1907 is greatly expanded in comparison to the first from 1892.) Simmel writes, "An interest in a psychic process by itself is not yet a psychological interest." [The Russian text used here, Shpet 2005: 397, gives as the reference the second edition. However, that second edition of Simmel's work dates from 1905, whereas the third edition was from 1907. Moreover, the quotation appeared on the indicated page in the third edition, but not in the second.]

Thus, putting aside these particular problems of the human sciences, we find that, for Simmel, the concern of sociology as a fundamental science – a science that studies the *forms* of social unity – is not with *really existing* objects, but with objects of an *ideal* order. However, it is equally the case that the subject matter of the particular human sciences, e. g., language, the state, law, religion, and mores, as well as the sciences that study the general forms of the spirit, considerably transgress the bounds of any single psyche, at least in its forms and also insofar as these forms are distinguished by their ideal character. Thus, the inventory of words in a language and the forms that express their connection, e.g., those found in a dictionary and a grammar book; in legal norms, as they are presented in codes of law (*Gesetzbuch*); in the dogmatic content of religion – all of these, strictly speaking, have no real existence, but are merely, as the Germans say, *gilt* – they have validity. "However, this *validity (Gültigkeit)*," Simmel writes, "of the content is not a psychic existence that requires an empirical bearer any more than the Pythagorean Theorem needs it to maintain the same distinction."[67] Nevertheless, how we come to it is, for us, the chief question. As in mathematics, is it by means of an intellectual intuition from sensibly given examples (*exempla*), or is it also by means of a *sui generis* understanding and interpretation of signs, both verbal and material? Simmel gives us reason to think that he would answer the first of these questions affirmatively.

With this, Simmel shows that he does not recognize the universal and fundamental significance that really belongs to understanding. The entire problem for him comes down to the usual problem of the extent to which understanding plays a role in history. However, while he rejects the autonomous reality of the social apart from the psychological, Simmel sheds little light on this problem compared to his predecessors. He equally does no more than merely formulate the problems, which are enveloped in a very dense fog as a result of his psychologistic sympathies.[68]

Simmel is convinced that the direct object of history is the *psyche*, and its subject matter is the representations, the desires, and the feelings of individual persons.[69] One must think that he has Boeckh's formula in mind and wants to expand it: "If the task of philology is to know what is known, historiography is merely an extension of this, in that in addition to the known, i.e., what is theoretically represented, it seeks to know what was desired and felt."[70] However, we also encounter here the

---

[67] Simmel 1908: 558.

[68] Simmel holds a different opinion about his contribution to the theory of historical knowledge. "I am well aware," he declares, "that this suggestion to solve the psychological-epistemological problem of historical understanding is only a first attempt. Perhaps, it is justified only because it clarifies the presence of the problem in general in its profundity." Simmel 1907: 41. Indisputably, from Simmel's viewpoint, his "suggestion" is a first attempt, but it is disputable whether he succeeded in clarifying the profundity of the very existence of the problem.

[69] Simmel 1907: 1.

[70] This quotation is taken from the first edition (Simmel 1892: 2). I did not find these words in the third edition. Nevertheless, there is in it a further development of the same idea connected with these words: "If the task of *history* is not only knowledge of what has been known, but also of what has been desired and felt, then this task is resolved only when, in some mode of psychic transformation, what has been desired is co-desired, what has been felt is co-felt." Simmel 1907: 307; Simmel 1892: 15.

important caveat cited above. An interest in psychic processes is still not a psychological interest. Sociology, as we saw, in working with psychic material, approaches
it with a special kind of *method* – it itself is this method.[71] Sociology, extracting the
ideal *forms* of socialization from it, is also the science of these forms. History is not
an ideal science.[72] According to Simmel's definition, it studies the ideas, etc., of
individual persons. It is concrete and studies what is singular and individual.[73]
However, it is not a method. On the contrary, it itself requires a special method.

Unlike psychology, for which a process is essential simply because it is a psychic
process, history is interested in the *content* of the process, something toward which,
inversely, psychology is indifferent. "For history it is not so much a matter of the
*development* of psychological contents as it is of the psychological development of
those *contents*...."[74] The content, in any case, is the "starting point" of a historical
examination. Additionally, communication (*aller Verkehr*) itself between people is
possible only on the presupposition that well-known physical movements of the
individual, e.g., gestures, mimicry, sounds, are based on psychic processes that form
for us the psychic unity of "the other." This presupposition also forms the a priori of
the relation of a subject to a subject.[75] Therefore, in historical knowledge we need a
methodological presupposition about the unity of the person – whether it be an
individual (real) person or a social (fictitious) party[76] – forming the a priori of history and making it possible.[77]

One can hardly call a presupposition of this kind anything other than psychological. In addition, if history is interested in "content," it should have its special paths
to such "content" and special presuppositions from which we could proceed to an
*objective* diversity and, in all probability, also to an objective unity. Evidently,
Simmel recognizes this too, but things immediately begin to become unclear after
this. At least, he himself asserts that if one presupposes a spiritual (psychological)
substantiation of events, the isolation of their contents poses additional epistemo-

---

[71] Simmel 1908: 3.

[72] [The German translation omits this entire sentence. By doing so, Shpet appears to be claiming
that sociology studies what is singular and individual! See Špet 1993: 258. Simmel writes,
"History, however, has to do at least in part – whether it is more than in part we will not go into –
with the individual, with absolutely unique personalities." Simmel 1907: 2].

[73] Simmel 1907: 2. However, [History studies what is singular and individual] not in its "reality,"
as *naïve realism* understands this, with its formulation of the historical task as a determination of
"how it really was" (Simmel 1907: 42), since history is neither a copy of reality (Simmel 1907: 51)
nor a reflection of historical reality (Simmel 1907: 55), but is a certain [...] of the communicated
content, where the psychic processes themselves accept the "form of history." Simmel 1907:
40–41. [The ellipsis here is to show that Shpet's manuscript text has a word missing.]

[74] Simmel 1907: 4; cf. Simmel 1907: 47ff.

[75] Simmel 1907: 7–9.

[76] Simmel allows also "impersonal forces" to serve as operative factors in history: law and mores,
language and ways of thinking, culture and forms of communication. Simmel 1907: 18. Curiously,
in the third edition, Simmel is not prepared to call these factors *objective* (*die objektiven Gebilde*)
as he did in the first edition of this work. Simmel 1892: 12.

[77] Simmel 1907: 27.

logical problems for us. The latter need a "very general presupposition." In this connection, based on Simmel's own words, one might think that *this* presupposition should precede the others. Moreover, if one is free of psychological prejudices, it would be impossible to think otherwise. "Whether the psychological connecting links that the historian introduces into the events are objectively true, i.e., whether they really express (*nachzeichnen*) the psychic acts of the persons in question, would be of no interest to us if we did not *understand* these processes in terms of their content and their development."[78] It seems clear that this objective understanding, as, strictly speaking, a historical understanding, must be the fundamental problem of the theory of historical knowledge. We only need to pose the question now: what is this understanding and what are its conditions?

Actually, Simmel does pose this question.[79] The general answer that he gives to it is interesting only in the sense that, unlike what was done earlier, he does not reduce understanding to a "clear" idea, but takes it in a broad sense, just as Dilthey did, namely, in the sense of an integral and original lived experience that copies (*nachbilden*) the corresponding acts of consciousness of the person who is understood. This copying is taken in the sense of a *transporting* of oneself into the psyche of the other person. However, this answer also immediately binds Simmel so that he fails to see other "ways" of understanding. In particular, the independent significance of understanding a *sign* disappears for him. In other words, his "general" answer in fact is merely a reference to the psychological type of understanding. Certainly, a simple mention of "copying" in no way reveals much about the essence or the content of understanding. In this regard, Simmel's conception is just as fruitless as was that of his predecessors. From another angle, though, his "answer" is more interesting in view of the difficulties that Schleiermacher had already experienced in thinking to connect grammatical and psychological interpretation by reducing both to a single type of interpretation, that of the "individual person."

Simmel explains the understanding of "the speaker" and the understanding of "what was spoken." He illustrates this distinction by referring to the distinction between our understanding of the law of gravitation or the *chorus mysticus*, on the one hand, and Newton's or Goethe's understanding, on the other.[80] However, his explanations of this distinction are not very profound. For one thing, his concern is with the *theoretical content of thinking*, and yet, strangely, it does not present a puzzle for him. It seems to him something that stands to reason. The whole point is that the same words that express the psychic processes of the speaker also arouse those processes in the listener. If there is an essential difference between the representations of the two, then the words of the one are poorly understood or not understood at all by the other. This is rather too simple. The actual puzzle for Simmel is an understanding not of what is objective, but precisely of what is *subjective*. "This sensation of what I, strictly speaking, do not sense, this copying of a subjectivity, which is again only possible within subjectivity, is at the same time given to it

---

[78] Simmel 1907: 27.

[79] Simmel 1907: 28.

[80] Simmel 1907: 29–30.

objectively. This is the puzzle of historical knowledge, a solution for which has so far hardly been attempted in terms of our logical and psychological categories."[81] There is no doubt that there is a puzzle here that hitherto has not been solved.[82] However, it is doubtful that the problem of historical and objective understanding has hereby been resolved.

It would seem natural to look for the "subjectivity" of which Simmel speaks in a sphere separate from sociology under the designation *social psychology*. The latter, as we saw, has to do with the modifications of the psychic processes of the individual under the influence of the social environment.[83] However, there still remains the problem of the historical understanding of the social environment itself as an objective fact. More precisely, the problem would, then, be more sharply outlined. However, Simmel does not see this. He envelops us here us in the fog that I complained about above. Consequently, the subjectivity of the individual person still remains for him, in the final analysis, the object of historical understanding. On the one hand, though, this subjectivity – as we already saw – is something peculiar, something ineffable, mysterious, and hard-to-reach. On the other hand, in Simmel's account it looks simpler and not of such wide scope. He contrasts the "speaker" to "what is said." The latter is objective and represents the "theoretical content of thinking." In one way or another, we understand them. If, however, we note that the speaker communicates his/her message under the influence of a personal goal, a prejudice, fear, irritation, etc., we, then, turn to another *kind* of understanding (*die Art des Verstehens*[84]), which, it turns out, is an understanding of the "historical person" that is important for historical knowledge. It is quite obvious that by combining two different meanings of the term "person," Simmel, thereby, simply achieves a reduction of several problems to one. In general, Simmel does not suffer from any predilection for clear thought or for precisely defining terms. However, here he has hopelessly confused different strands of thought, attempting to spin them into one, to such an extent that he himself cannot distinguish where each of them goes.

The individual person is an object and a term of both psychology and history. We can leave aside other meanings here without examining them. As an object of psychology, the individual person is examined also in social and historical psychology: the individual person, individual self-consciousness in a given social and historical setting. We always take the individual person in this sense as something *typical* in

---

[81] Simmel 1907: 32. [The Russian text, Shpet 2005: 401, incorrectly refers this quotation to page 33.]

[82] Simmel's own "solution," Kantian in spirit, is a conception of the historical as a "form" of psychic processes and is hardly acceptable. More about this, however, in another place.

[83] Concerning the method of the interpretive approach to this subject matter, see my already mentioned article, "Predmet i zadachi etnicheskoj psikhologii" ["The Object and the Tasks of Ethnic Psychology"], Shpet 1917–18: 1–4.

[84] Simmel 1907: 29.

given spatial and temporal conditions.[85] The individual person is not a historical reality in this sense. Such a person does not know any *institution*, constitution, or other social organization. Socially, there are the historical categories of citizen, a man, a juridical person, a political subject, an adult, a legally responsible person, etc., etc. However, there is no "individual person." It is another matter when the human being, as a psychologically – a psycho-physically – defined individual person, is the bearer or expresser of a certain aggregate of objectifiable social and historical potencies, that is, is oneself a sign, the interpretation of which reveals to us specific social and historical institutions and organizations.

The individual person speaks and acts here as a social factor, a social and historical reality. As Droysen (see above) explained, "The individual is only a relative totality. Understanding and being understood, the individual is only, as it were, an expression of a community of which he is a member, both in the essence and in the development of which he participates. He himself is only, as it were, one expression of this essence and development."[86] Such an individual person actually is the object of the historian's study and understanding. Simmel speaks of "historical individuals" and presents them very well.[87] However, it is clear, then, that psychological understanding contributes nothing to our comprehension of *this* individual person. Such a person must be understood in terms of the "essence and development" of the *community*. In other words, precisely what is needed is not a psychological, but a historical understanding.

Simmel tries to convince[88] us that psychological understanding is genuine historical understanding. But it is difficult to believe him when we know that psychologism is his fundamental presupposition and that, before proceeding to his "epistemological study," he already knew that there is only one historical reality, viz., the *psyche*, ideas, wishes, and feelings of "individual persons." Therefore, his "non-psychological" interest in the psychic could not save the situation. Simmel staked out sociology, assigning "forms" to it, but apart from this he found no sources for a psychological investigation of the psychic. Thus, it is remarkable that, having distinguished between the "speaker" and "what is said," he found nothing to assign to the latter except the "contents of thought" and ascribed objectivity to them.[89] However, this objectivity is not empirically historical, but only *logical*, i.e., it is also ideal and, in a certain sense, formal.

---

[85] See Shpet 1917–18.

[86] [Droysen 1868: 10.]

[87] Simmel 1907: 29–30; 36–37.

[88] He reproaches "historicism" for not understanding precisely this. Cf. Simmel 1907: 28–29 f.

[89] See Simmel 1907: 29: "in the case of objective knowledge" (*"bei objektiven Erkenntnisse"*). In the first edition, we find "in the case of objective and logical knowledge" (*"bei objektiven und logischen Erkenntnissen"*). Simmel 1892: 14.

What is the result? Simmel wanted to drive all of the kinds of understanding into the dead end of psychology alone, but they all slipped away from him and scattered in various directions: ideal understanding, the fundamental significance of which Simmel failed to grasp; historical understanding, the objective significance of which he did not value; psychological understanding, which he waved off as "copying" (*nachbilden*) and the, properly speaking, hermeneutic nature of which he also passed by with his eyes closed. He did not advance the problems of interpretation, and he did not notice the problems of the expressive sign. On the other hand, his separation of sociology from social psychology as well as his idea of a non-psychological interest in the psychic must not be forgotten in the future.

# The Contemporary Situation

## 1 [The Problems Awaiting Us]

However critically we may evaluate Simmel's arguments, it is impossible to deny the significance of his attempt to solve the problem of understanding from a certain novel and radical point of view. In comparing him with Dilthey, we are convinced that the problem in fact is more complex and multifaceted than it seemed to Dilthey. We are convinced that a large number of the basic problems of contemporary philosophy and methodology are clustered around the fundamental principles of hermeneutics. Following behind philology, and with the help of history and the recognition of the universal significance of the historical method in the "human sciences," the latter as a whole have already begun to pin their hopes on the theory of knowledge as their philosophical foundation. The theory of historical knowledge in the most all-encompassing sense is emerging not as an appendage to the theory of natural-scientific knowledge, but at least as a rightful and independent division of the fundamental principles of our knowledge.

Moreover, the works of Dilthey and, in part, of Simmel as well lead us to suspect that the philosophical principles of all knowledge as they are presented in widespread philosophical systems, particularly those oriented toward mathematical and natural-scientific knowledge, are not only incomplete and one-sided, but are in many respects simply erroneous, given their ignorance of the independent foundations of historical knowledge. Additionally, the increased attention that for some time now philosophy has again begun to devote to the problem of history testifies even more clearly to this. However, the very failure and fruitlessness of the attempts undertaken to solve this problem – insofar as they were directly or indirectly connected with the ideas of natural-scientific knowledge and their philosophical foundations – should have turned the attention of investigators toward the original hermeneutical path of knowing. All attempts to ground historical knowledge have turned out to be equally unsuccessful, regardless of whether they were modeled on empirical natural science by empiricists and positivists; on mathematical knowl-

© Springer Nature Switzerland AG 2019
G. Shpet, T. Nemeth, *Hermeneutics and Its Problems*, Contributions
To Phenomenology 98, https://doi.org/10.1007/978-3-319-98941-9_9

edge by Kantians; or on psychology by eclectic thinkers. Likewise, the attempts by another group of Kantians – from Schopenhauer up to and including Rickert – who had a skeptical attitude toward historical knowledge have turned out to be unconvincing.[1]

However, all of these attempts are very instructive in one respect. The very possibility of comparing historical knowledge with such diverse types of knowledge shows that the authentic foundation of historical knowledge, viz., understanding, must have a reciprocal influence on the philosophical foundations of both natural science and psychology, and even of ideal knowledge. In addition, insofar as the philosophical foundations of knowledge with respect to their object are motifs of reality itself, the very formulations of the problem of reality itself, as the root and ultimate problem of philosophy, should undergo significant modifications. These modifications should obviously be made toward expanding its formulation and freeing it from the abstract schemas of mathematical natural science. From here on, pressure is exerted on philosophy itself to realize at last the intention it had within it from the start of becoming concrete and historically real in the deepest and most fundamental sense of these terms. In short, it is clear from all of this that we now face the fully matured problem of understanding. Its solution confronts us in the form of three problems: (a) the independent problem of empirical psychology; (b) the problem of logical methodology; and (c) the problem of fundamental philosophy. Indeed, we can state that at least with regard to the first two aspects of the problem of understanding the elaboration has already begun.

## 2    [Hermann] Swoboda[, Erdmann, Et Al.]

(a) However strange, the psychology of *understanding* was not recognized as an independent problem until recently. H[ermann] Swoboda was profoundly right in beginning his investigation of understanding with the distinctive aphorism: "to understand" and "to grasp" are not scientific terms.[2] Psychology simply considered understanding to be a function of the mind or of the intellect, without pausing to clarify the specific nature of this process in greater detail. Sometimes, it identified this process with a clear idea and sometimes with a "concept" and its formation. Only the comparison of thinking, as a function of the mind, with speech reminded us sometimes of the special role of understanding, which usually was easily defined in the terms of associationalist psychology or apperceptive psychology, or, at best, was compared to reasoning "by analogy." There was no problem. Perhaps this was due to the general abstractly schematic tendencies of the explanatory psychology

---

[1] An analysis of all these theories is the subject of the second volume of my Investigations. [This second volume of his *Istorija kak problema logiki* has been published posthumously. See Shpet 2002: 547–1131.]

[2] Swoboda 1903: 131 – "'Verstehen' und 'Begreifen' sind keine wissenschaftlichen Termini." ["Understanding and "apprehension" are not scientific terms."]

that prevailed until recently. In any case, one could insist that a freer approach to the concrete complexities of psychic experiences should have led investigators to the problem of understanding, particularly if purely depictive intentions accompanied that approach. At least as far as one can judge this was how the mentioned Swoboda approached it.

Finnbogason approaches the issue in this way in his interesting book *Sympathetic Understanding*, which is the most thorough treatment of this problem to date.[3] Lipps also encounters the problem constantly in his investigations of *Einfühlung* ("empathy"), particularly insofar as it is connected with the psychological and philosophical problem of other minds. Spranger too, as we saw, approached understanding partly in connection with the problem of description and partly in connection with the problem of history itself. It is precisely this connection with the tasks of a *descriptive* psychology that accounts for the possibility of formulating the psychological problem of understanding as a distinctive lived experience. It also accounts as well for the one-sidedness of this formulation, owing to which these investigators have concentrated their attention chiefly, or even exclusively, on the problem of *understanding the individual person*.

Elsenhans also came close to the position represented by the works above. His attempt to separate interpretation from understanding and even to contrast it to the latter is, as we already know from the preceding account, a quite legitimate attempt – if only he had not carried it out so naïvely and superficially. His psychological appeals to "a general feeling" are also elementary. Only his general idea of the significance of the problem of exegesis for the human sciences may really be of interest. True, Elsenhans expresses this idea quite vaguely and is prompted to do so more out of a sense of the importance of the problem than by a desire for further theoretical penetration into its content. Indeed, this idea has remained, as far as I know, without further development. Nevertheless, when he characterizes the status of hermeneutical problems in contemporary philosophy, it is impossible to pass over his remarks in silence. In a paper that he read at the Congress for Experimental Psychology in Giessen in 1904, Elsenhans[4] held that the immediate knowledge of our own psychic activity is alone insufficient for the human sciences. There is a need also for an indirect investigation of the psychic activity of others as well. In the interest of the latter, he went on to demand a study both of one's own psychic activity as well as of the process of *exegesis* (*Deutung*) as necessary preliminary work for the human sciences. He understands the process by which we know and reproduce something psychic based on a sensibly given sign to be an exegetic process. Such an exegesis, in his opinion, of sensibly-given signs is carried out by analogy with one's own psychic activity and must presuppose having something in common with this activity.[5]

---

[3] Finnbogason 1911.

[4] Elsenhans 1904. As the author himself notes in another place in this paper he, at certain points, comes close to Dilthey. Elsenhans 1906: 83 f.

[5] Elsenhans 1904: 7, 5. Cf. also Elsenhans 1912: 342–344.

Such a view of exegesis as that above must be distinguished from *empathy* by the fact that in the latter the *I* and the *not-I* merge immediately into one, which is not the case with exegesis. Exegesis must also be distinguished from *understanding* (*Verstehen*), which, contrary to Dilthey's view, is not a transition from sensibly-given signs to something internally-given, which is precisely what exegesis is. Rather, in accordance with the meaning of the word *Verstand*, exegesis is the inclusion of the object in the context of our knowledge, whether this object is a sensibly perceived sign or not. Moreover, exegesis is further distinguished from simple understanding by the fact that the former reproduces the given psychic content in verbal form.[6] The theory of exegesis, if it can be of help to the human sciences, must keep in mind the following three points: (1) the sensibly-given sign, mediating our knowledge of the psychic activity of other people; (2) the connection of this sensibly-given sign to psychic content; (3) the transmission of this psychic content in verbal form.[7] The most important of these points is obviously the second one. A simple associative connection is insufficient for its explication. In addition to the activity of phantasy, one must also have recourse to a special sense, to which Boeckh had already hinted and which makes itself known to the extent that we penetrate into the common world of representations of the entire given historical period that is under study, a sense which, together with Wundt, one could call an "*integral* feeling" or a "common historical feeling."[8]

Benno Erdmann handles the problem in the same psychological manner, but already more broadly.[9] He attempts to solve the problem by using the unoriginal means of explanatory psychology, i.e., with the help of all of the same associations, apperceptions, and inferences by analogy. Nevertheless, certain aspects of his work are quite significant precisely from the viewpoint of the present status of the problem. He not only raises the problem of understanding in connection with the division of the sciences into the natural sciences and the human sciences in terms of both their subject matter and methodology.[10] But he also regards understanding as a "kind" of knowledge,[11] at the same time recognizing its certain universal function in knowledge.[12]

On the other hand, Erdmann starts with the presupposition that knowledge of the psychic activity of other persons presupposes knowledge of one's own psychic activity, which is possible only through introspection. He adds that, in general, feeling, thinking, or in short, putting oneself (*Einfühlung, Eindenkung, Einstellung*) into another person's psychic life rests on the fact that the emotive and intellectual contents of consciousness, which reproduce the other person's psychic activity, are copies within ourselves, apropos the movements of the other person and the prod-

---

[6] Elsenhans 1904: 8, 10–11.

[7] Elsenhans 1904: 11.

[8] Elsenhans 1904: 20; Elsenhans 1912: 344.

[9] Erdmann 1912a: 1240–1241.

[10] Erdmann 1912a: 1241–1242.

[11] Erdmann 1912a: 1243–58, 1261, 1280.

[12] Erdmann 1912a: 1265–66, 1268.

ucts of the other's psychic activity.[13] Nevertheless, Erdmann managed to distinguish not only these motor reactions as expressions of mental activity from the products of these movements, as historical sources of every kind, but also to distinguish psychological understanding, properly speaking, from objective understanding. At least with regard to *speech*, its understanding, in Erdmann's view, fulfills a richer function than that of putting ourselves into the inner, psychic life of another person. It also serves – often even exclusively, so that the lived experience of the communicator, properly speaking, loses its significance for us – to transmit intellectual content that is objective, scientific, cultural, or practical. Thus, for example, history in the narrow sense, as economic, legal, and political history, history of the sciences and even of religion and of philosophical ideas, is directed not so much on creative individuals and the individual conditions of their development as on the historically efficacious structure of their works.[14] One can only regret that these nuggets, though quite valuable for a deeper penetration into the problem of understanding, remained undeveloped in Erdmann, even in their empirically psychological form. However, one cannot possibly deny that in expressing them, Erdmann stresses yet again the necessity and timeliness for philosophy to penetrate deeper into an analysis of all of these themes.

Finally, contemporary psychology, primarily in the Würzburg School of experimental psychology, also poses the problem of understanding in connection with the application of the experimental method to the study of the so-called "higher" mental processes in the sphere of thinking.[15] These investigations occupy a rather special and distinctive place with regard to our problem. As experimental investigations, they are, by their nature, quite removed from the above-mentioned type of work in descriptive psychology, which has to do with the depiction of lived experiences in their entirety and concrete nature. However, at the same time, they are freer from prejudiced hypotheses and theories than is explanatory psychology. In a certain sense, they also claim to have a descriptive character, at least for those lived experiences that accompany a subject's perception of the task facing him or her and that person's search for an answer to it. Consequently, this is not, as in descriptive psychology, a depiction of lived experience in its natural setting, but a certain extraction of the act from lived experience as a whole by means of analysis and preliminary definitions.

The very organization of the artificial conditions, in which the process proposed for study stands out in its purity, requires preliminary definitions. It followed from this that in the experiments devoted to the study of thinking, judging, etc., the process of understanding appeared as supplemental and an accessory to the other acts of this type of lived experience. However, even if that process had appeared as an object of special attention, it drowned in the general investigation of the same thinking as that prescribed by the preliminary definitions, which bound the subject

---

[13] Erdmann 1912a: 1258–59.

[14] Erdmann 1912a: 1265.

[15] The most important works of this direction, which are of immediate interest to us, are: Marbe 1901; Taylor 1905; Messer 1906, 1908; Bühler 1907; Koffka 1912; Selz 1913.

of the study by so-called "instructions." We obtain something similar to what we saw in Prantl. Understanding is a function of reason or of pure thinking and then the specificity of understanding, properly speaking, fades in the analysis of reason itself. Only certain very general and pale outlines remain. However, in these investigations there is a particular feature, which the psychologist *should* consider a shortcoming but which, in the hands of philosophers, can turn these investigations into useful material for them. It is understandable why psychologists greeted the works of the Würzburg School with distrust and even with some hostility: "pure" thinking, the *actus purus*, was not at all the empirical reality that they were used to dealing with. And the more the new investigators insisted on the reliability of the data they had gathered, the more apparent it became that they were importing non-psychological categories into psychology. Psychologists were called to approach psychic data with a non-psychological interest. It would have been easier for empirical psychologists to reconcile themselves even with importing metaphysical motifs into psychology, but such *irreal* psychic data was alien to them – as it *should be*.

On the other hand, philosophers could easily recognize something of their *own* in this "new" psychology – something not real, either empirically or metaphysically, but something of their own as being ideal. The innovators could be inspired by the hope that with new tools they were securing for psychology the fulfillment of its ancient, even if illegitimate, claims to the role of the fundamental science. Philosophers could not help but harden themselves against these unjustified claims. But, by the essence of the matter, the further and deeper the work of the new investigators proceeds, the clearer it will be to an impartial observer – whether one be a psychologist or a philosopher – that this work forsakes the ground of psychology, that its experiments are being ousted by *analysis*, and the introspection that accompanies its experiments is being replaced by *reflection*. These experimental psychologists are all the more borrowing the very terminological apparatus of philosophy. We will see that, as a result, philosophy too can now gain something from this "psychology" in exchange for the services that it happened to render to this new psychology.[16]

(b) Since the psychological examination of the problem of understanding exceeds the bounds of an empirical-psychological investigation, and since the motifs of a fundamental and logical investigation have moved into it, we are passing here to the second aspect in which hermeneutical problems appear to the contemporary philo-

---

[16] Therefore Husserl was incorrect in reprimanding experimental psychology for its tendency to assume the place of the fundamental philosophical science. If it displayed such tendencies, it is precisely because it ceased to be psychology. However, Messer was even more incorrect, in thinking to prove that a "pure" psychology, which does not study its object in a natural-science setting, is philosophy. Messer 1911. See Messer 1908: 11 and cf. Messer 1908: 33, 56, 147, 158, 164ff, 171. This is the "logicism" in psychology that was so fiercely contested by Wundt. In general, Wundt and the psychologists contest the very *technique* of the new experimental psychology. See Kornilov 1916. Here, neither force nor credibility are on their side, but their criticism, apparently, is evidently motivated by a correct sense of the loss of psychology itself and its *methodology*. Introspection and experiment, in essence and not just on account of the setting, are fundamentally different from reflection and analysis.

sophical consciousness. Above all, *linguistics* has rendered a great service to philosophy here.[17] As interest in questions of semasiology has developed and as the conviction has grown that linguistics cannot deal with these questions using either its own psychological resources or those at its disposal, it had to turn to psychology, logic, and philosophy at least for the principles to solve them. At first, however, linguistics could not find anything in these disciplines except for the general explanatory theories of associationism and apperceptivism. However, linguistics itself encouraged a more specialized examination of its semasiological themes. Martinak's book was almost the first direct response to such an inquiry on the part of psychology.[18] Even earlier, Stöhr advanced questions concerning sign and meaning.[19] However, the turning point philosophically was the appearance of Husserl's *Logical Investigations*,[20] which linked the elaboration of semasiological problems to the objective logic of truth in the spirit of Bolzano, on the one hand, and with the fundamental theory of *meaning* as an idea in Lotze's modified sense, on the other.[21] In the same year as Husserl's *Investigations*, another prominent student of Brentano's, namely Meinong, published a book,[22] in which the problem of the role of sign, meaning, and understanding was also held to be of philosophical importance, although the problem was examined there with far less subtlety and skill than in Husserl. However, we find the highest achievement in the fundamental elaboration of the problems of semasiology in the books of Marty and Gomperz, both books appearing in the same year (1908).[23] The first of these is striking with its elegance and subtle analysis, and the second with its thorough historical documentation and its ability, one might say, to display the entire history of philosophical quests in the light of semasiology.

We will depend on all of these works below to a significant degree when we will have to pass to an examination of strictly logical and methodological problems in our investigation of the fundamental problems of understanding.[24] In my view, these problems will complete our fundamental investigation and become suitably clear

---

[17] Regarding the literature, see Paul 1909: 74–75 f.

[18] Martinak 1901. Frege's article "On Sense and Reference" pursues different goals and stands apart from all the literature. See Frege 1980. In general, the introduction of semasiological problems and their psychological, logical, and philosophical elaboration within the general scope of philosophy is primarily the contribution of *Austrian* psychologists and philosophers. I explain this, above all, in terms of the powerful influence exerted on Austrian psychology and logic by English logic (in particular Mill's logic), which did not sever the connection between logic and the theory of terms and propositions or the connection between the psychological theory of thinking with the theory of language in contrast to Kantian and post-Kantian formalism in logic. The influence of a re-discovered Bolzano was secondary and fell on receptive but already prepared ground.

[19] Stöhr 1889. See his more recent book, Stöhr 1910.

[20] Husserl 1970. See, in particular, the "First Investigation": Husserl 1970: 269–333.

[21] Lotze 1880: 507, 521.

[22] Meinong 1902. Meinong 1910.

[23] Marty 1908; Gomperz 1908.

[24] [Shpet here is referring to a planned third volume of his *History as a Problem of Logic* that never was written. He had already mentioned this intention in the "Preface" above.]

and firm only on the basis of that investigation. For the immediate purposes of a fundamental analysis of understanding itself, they can render only a partial and for the most part indirect service. The greater the division and the filiation of the problems that arise on the basis of understanding, the more the essence of understanding itself is revealed. It is not so much a shortage of works in this respect, but their inadequacy. However, we must state that this inadequacy arises not just from the predetermined character of the themes suggested by the logical and epistemological aspect of these investigations. Indeed, it is impossible not to notice this. Here, we encounter the predetermined character of the themes of understanding by way of the more general themes of thought, knowledge, and so forth. The themes of understanding arise when seen from this angle, but they should be examined as an object from all sides, and, moreover, they should themselves be made the center from which there will diverge different points of view on different problems situated on the periphery of the problem of understanding.

There is also in these investigations another lacuna – generally speaking, a particular point, but one that is of paramount significance for us. The analysis of semasiological problems in these investigations is not closely and intimately tied to the methodological problems of the human sciences and of *history* that led us to them. This is a particular defect. However, it also has certain general consequences. For we expect that the light of understanding in illuminating the problems of historical methodology must illuminate all other methodological problems as well. It is precisely this freshness, the spirit of the spirit itself, that we still do not sense in many of the philosophical conclusions of contemporary semasiology. This creates a peculiar situation. Dilthey and others, who valued the vivifying role of understanding for history and the human sciences, did not discover in the whirling rotation expressed in the formula "experience-expression-understanding" a key to the cyclical nature of all philosophical thought on the whole. The authors of these fundamental semasiological investigations did not see that the latter should be conducted through the life of spirit itself in order to obtain philosophically vital and concrete embodiment.

With this last reproach, however, we ourselves cross beyond the bounds of that aspect to which our methodological search should logically be restricted. That is, we pass to a new aspect, which earlier we called "fundamental" but which was not yet posed as a task with sufficient distinctness. Nevertheless, there remains the fact of underestimating the role semasiology could play if its position with regard to the human sciences were taken into account. Semasiology remains, but only in its abstract significance. It is not even clear just what place it should occupy among philosophical problems. Thus in Husserl, for example, questions concerning semasiology drown among the other problems discussed in his *Logical Investigations*, and one senses that he feels freer when he passes from "expression" to an analysis of what is expressed, to an analysis of the activity of "pure" consciousness itself and the relations of "pure" ideas.

On the contrary, in Gomperz, for example, we find the apparently most radical solution to the problem of the place of semasiology: it is a fundamental part of his "Noology." This gives the impression of something artificial and strained. Such a "reform" in the organization of philosophical knowledge is felt to be unnecessary, forced, but, above all, completely groundless. Such a grounding that would rationally determine the place of semasiology itself in the system of philosophical thought, can be – in my view – achieved only by clarifying its role in the organization of the human sciences.

(c) We must repeat once more, however, what was just said. A clarification of all of these questions, in addition to the demands required for such a clarification, leads beyond the bounds of the strictly methodological aspect of the hermeneutical problem and presupposes a deeper, indeed the deepest, fundamental analysis of the act of understanding underlying all of these problems. One reason for this is the excessively static character of semasiology itself, which cannot find a place for itself within philosophical knowledge, and its excessive aridity, which cannot sense the significance of its very close contiguity and relationship with the vital spirit of the human sciences. This is the reason for the absence of a comprehensive philosophical analysis of understanding in its vital efficacy, its dynamic character, and its all-penetrating rational spirituality. Psychological analyses of understanding – however exhaustive they may seem – always carry the stamp of the empirical limitations and relative character that is inherent in them from the outset. They themselves need a philosophical grounding in principle. One must proceed from a fundamental analysis of understanding. Only then can one hope for a rigorous and complete construction of a methodology, grounded on it, of above all, the historical sciences and then for the entire logic of semasiology, as it will appear after a verification of its general theses in light of historical methodology. Such a historical logic, however, will be "historical" in a broad philosophical sense. Applied to the particular objects of the human sciences, it must undergo a new specification. The circle is complete: by way of the spirit, we break through to the concretely universal, on the basis of which we solve the special problems of that same spirit. These particular tasks, which, by the way, psychology can also pose, are, obviously, also its own tasks. Psychology itself must take care to extract what it needs from the general source that we see in a fundamental analysis of understanding.

Thus, we have, above all, here the most fundamental problem of understanding in its entire breadth. Then there is a logic in light of a semasiology animated by the spirit of hermeneutics. And finally there are the objective specifications of this logic. The problem of understanding in such a form is nothing other than the problem of the spirit itself: spirit and understanding are correlative, just as an object is correlative to the act directed toward it. The spirit, as object, is the bearer of content, which, for the understanding, is a rational content. Comprehension can be directed only toward reason. *Spirit as an object of understanding is a rational spirit.* As I understand it, the problem is posed here for the first time in such a form.[25] Moreover, I would still like to make some remarks, partly to clarify the problem, partly to justify the intrinsic consistency of a further presentation. In particular, I would like to call attention to the following. In both a fundamental and a logical analysis, given

---

[25] I made several remarks in my book *Appearance and Sense*, and I expressed several ideas more explicitly in my article "Wisdom or Reason?" in 1917. [See Appendix 2 below; Shpet 2006.]

such a general formulation of the theme, it is impossible to limit oneself merely to the *first* theses in order to skip immediately from them to the particulars of special historical objects.

We should also not neglect here the *axiomata media*, since, moreover, it is impossible to do so. But the essential thing, to which I attach the greatest significance – even the only thing that has significance – is not how I succeed in formulating them, but whether I show their *transformative* philosophical role with as much clarity as is possible. Perhaps their content will be completely rejected, but their organizational role must be justified. I consider the realization of the ideal to be the most important thing in this transformation. Understanding and comprehending are not simply a matter of the apprehension of ideas – this I consider to be firmly established – but the apprehension of realized ideas. Only in such a sense can we speak of reality itself as history, for history has to do only with what has been realized. The reason that comprehends is not an abstract reason, but a reason that has been realized in this history. Only in this sense can we speak further of a rational reality. The chief thing is that only in this sense can we speak of an *absolute reality*. Only with respect to what has become, what is historical, what has been realized, can we apply this concept without fear of a *contradictio in adjecto*. The absolute reality of the otherworldly is unconditional. The absolute reality of the ideal is a destruction of the ideal. The absolute reality of what is becoming is an illusion; only the absolute reality of the historical is truth. We proceed from sensuous reality, as a riddle, to its ideal foundation in order to solve this riddle through sense-bestowal upon reality, through the insight of reason in what is realized and embodied in reality itself.

If understanding is the path toward the apprehension of spirit, then questions about the reality of the "external world," the reality of "other people," and the reality "of my own self" all are equally on the same level for philosophy. Ultimately – and consequently for our investigation from the very start – all of this is a single problem: the problem of a spiritual and cultural historical reality. Historical reality, as we have said, is something realized, but at the same time it is also being realized and is subject to realization. In short, it is a continuous process. However, the process is not mechanical, but theoretical. It is the fulfillment, the embodiment, the realization of the idea. I do not think that from our knowledge of how it was realized, and our knowledge of its rationality, we can learn how history should be further realized. I even think the reverse is the case, namely, that if we would attempt to realize it based on such knowledge, we would commit an evil deed: we would cease our free and unlimited creativity. We would simply eliminate the possibility of the further realization of history. We would stop it.

The sole lesson that we could learn from this would be that we should advance and realize what has not yet been realized. But this is tantamount to the fact that from all this we would learn merely the lesson that one cannot and should not learn any lesson from it. Therefore, from beginning to end, everything in philosophy remains pure: intuition, thinking, and comprehension. Our only concern, which is as much a human concern as a philosophical one, is to protect this purity. Dogma and opinion are inclined to transform it into an instrument, to pragmatize its reassurances. However, this is itself a matter of opinion. Philosophy, on the contrary, should defend the freedom of opinion itself, for the pragmaticization of any single opinion constrains the freedom of all the others, imposes upon them pragmatic legal restrictions, and then also brings moral condemnation on them. Philosophy protects the freedom of every opinion, and therefore, when an opinion arises, it should proclaim: "Opinion!" in order not to let that opinion drape itself in something that is alien to it, something that is not a garment of knowledge and not allow it to pretend to be something that can claim a recognition that excludes all other opinions. It is not opinions that are dangerous, but opinions masquerading as knowledge. Whoever truly values knowledge will not call it opinion. All this is particularly applicable to assertions of every kind about reality. Philosophy itself does not err in distinguishing opinion from knowledge, nor does the philosopher. However, a human being can err. Simple philosophical honesty therefore demands that we, at least, warn others. Perhaps I myself err and take my own opinion for knowledge. Be careful, watch out, and do not take my opinion for knowledge. But also please do not take knowledge for my opinion!

6 July 1918

# Appendix 1: Consciousness and Its Owner

## Editor's Introduction to "Consciousness and Its Owner"

The following essay originally appeared in a "Festschrift" in 1916 for G. I. Chelpanov,[1] Shpet's professor first in Kiev during the early years of the twentieth century and then in Moscow, where Shpet completed his studies after Chelpanov assumed a professorship there in 1907. However, originally in conjunction with acquiring material for his *magister*'s thesis in Western Europe he settled during the academic year 1912–13 in Göttingen, where he matriculated at the University and studied with Husserl, who greatly impressed him. When Husserl's *Ideen I* appeared in 1913, Shpet, by all indications, immediately set out to write an explanatory and critical account of it. The resulting work, *Appearance and Sense*, appeared in Russia already in the first half of 1914 and thrust Shpet into the forefront as the leading Russian representative and advocate for phenomenology in general and Husserl's latest transcendental turn in particular.

The essay that follows marks one of Shpet's few technical contributions to philosophy in the narrow sense.[2] In it, Shpet takes exception, among other things, with Husserl's abandoning in *Ideen I* of his own earlier non-egological conception of consciousness set forth in the *Logische Untersuchungen* from 1900/1. There, in his fifth investigation "On Intentional Experiences and their 'Contents,'" Husserl started his discussion much as Shpet will with the ego, or I, as understood in everyday language. The I is like any particular physical object, e.g., a book, a tree, etc. The unity that it has is that given "through its unified phenomenal properties."[3] If we conceptually eliminate (*abscheiden*) the body from the I, as given empirically, limiting ourselves to the purely mental I, we have a unity of consciousness, but this reduced

---

[1] *Georgiju* 1916.

[2] Molchanov remarks that with this essay Shpet "was one of the first, if not the first, at least in Russian philosophy who attempted to combine the problematic and the semantic aspects of an investigation of the I." Molchanov 2009: 11.

[3] Husserl 1970: 541; Husserl 1901: 331.

© Springer Nature Switzerland AG 2019
G. Shpet, T. Nemeth, *Hermeneutics and Its Problems*, Contributions To Phenomenology 98, https://doi.org/10.1007/978-3-319-98941-9

I is not some special thing hovering, as it will, over and above the various experiences. No, it is simply the interconnected unity (*Verknüpfungseinheit*) of these experiences. In short, then, the I is the unified totality of the content of experience (*einheitliche Inhaltsgesammtheit*). These contents come together, i.e., unite, in ways that are law-governed, and as united they form or constitute the I, or unity of consciousness. Thus, there is no need for an additional principle to unite or provide the basis for these contents. The postulation of any such additional principle is superfluous.

In his presentation, Husserl singled out for criticism, in particular, the Marburg neo-Kantian Paul Natorp, another figure Shpet will pointedly rebuke. Natorp claimed that we can distinguish three "moments" in consciousness, although they are actually inseparably united. There is, of course, the content, the consciousness itself and, through further abstraction, the I, "which, as a common reference point for all conscious content, cannot itself be the content of consciousness. The I simply stands opposite everything that can be content."[4] Both Shpet in 1916 and Husserl in 1900/01 were puzzled by this assertion: if the I cannot be a content of consciousness, it cannot be thought. If it cannot be thought, what is the basis for singling it out and even for acknowledging it in the first place? Yet, this is precisely what Natorp has done. Further on in his work, Natorp reiterated that the I cannot be a content of consciousness, and, in fact, it does not even resemble such a content. Therefore, it cannot be described, since description can only be done using terms drawn from the content of consciousness. Natorp, despite his own declared prohibition, characterized the I as the "subjective center of relations."[5] Shpet, as we shall see, will ask of Natorp whether he is not introducing here a lot of "theory," i.e., presuppositions.

Shpet was well aware that Husserl changed his position on the I in *Ideen I*, namely, that in 1913 he exclaimed he had managed to find it in the interval after publishing the *Untersuchungen*. Already in *Appearance and Sense*, Shpet expressed this change as "interesting" without a hint of any significant alarm or disagreement with Husserl's altered stand. Indeed, he alerts the reader that Husserl's earlier work represented an incomplete idea of phenomenology. During the intervening years, Husserl struggled with determining just what is excluded by the phenomenological reduction. His conclusion, as Shpet saw it, is that there is an I that remains constant and identical throughout the constant flow of lived experiences or processes. All belong to this I and emanate from it. Nonetheless, the I cannot itself be found in the flow of such experiences. Therefore, although necessary the I, the pure I, cannot be an object of investigation. It is, in Husserl's own language, a "transcendence in immanence."[6] Although Shpet does not refer to Natorp here, it certainly must have seemed to him that Husserl completely reversed himself, accepting Natorp's stand *in toto* for no apparent reason.[7]

---

[4] Natorp 1888: 11.

[5] Natorp 1888: 13.

[6] Shpet 1991: 58. Cf. Husserl 2014: 105.

[7] Marbach has suggested that Husserl altered his position in grappling with the problem of intersubjectivity. If *Erlebnisse* belonged to no one, i.e., were anonymous, how would it be possible to

Despite his fervent desire in 1914 to follow Husserl's trajectory, a certain unease pervades Shpet's defense of this new train of thought. How is it that phenomenology, calling for a "reduction" to the immanent and the exclusion of all transcendence, yet retains the pure I, which admittedly is transcendent? In *Appearance and Sense*, Shpet begs off the question, saying that a complete answer would require a phenomenological investigation that he cannot undertake at the time. All he can do, then, is suggest the path along which the question can be answered.

Shpet argued that the transcendence of the I and that of objects of consciousness are not the same. In conflating the two, the temptation arises to endow one with the properties of the other, leading to such metaphysical positions as spiritualism, on the one hand, or materialism, on the other. The being of the I is *essentially* not transitory, and whereas an intentional object is correlative to consciousness the I is in consciousness absolutely. That is, everything subject to bracketing in the phenomenological reduction is correlative to consciousness, but if we would try to bracket the I, attempting to see it purely in relation to consciousness, we get nothing. For "there would be nobody directing consciousness itself."[8] Every lived experience (*Erlebnis*) is a mental experience *of* the I, and consciousness belongs to the I, without which it, the I, is nothing.

Obviously in light of the position he upheld in the essay before us, Shpet himself hardly remained convinced of the position he himself valiantly tried to defend in 1914. The key, or at least the only key we have, that sheds light on Shpet's thinking at this time is a letter to Husserl from 14 December 1913, in which he thanked the latter for sending him the new edition of the *Logische Untersuchungen*, but that as a result he would have to re-work his entire presentation.[9] Of course, in the absence of any possible drafts for *Appearance and Sense* we cannot say to what extent, if any, Shpet did re-work the final version to reflect this new reading of the *Untersuchungen*. His editing could not have been extensive, for in the essay that follows Shpet sharply departed from Husserl's 1913 position as well as that of his own defense of it the following year. Now in 1916, Shpet took exception with what he regarded as Husserl's fundamental thesis regarding the I, namely that every *cogitatio* effected is of the form *cogito*. But what, or who, is this *Ego cogito*? And is it something other than the stream of lived experiences and, unlike the ever changing stream of experiences, something numerically identical in those experiences or, even more fundamentally, that to which these experiences belong? Husserl admitted

---

distinguish my consciousness from yours? Marbach 1974: 100. Unfortunately, Husserl only in the most cursory manner addressed the topic of intersubjectivity in *Ideen I*. In any case, Shpet, conceivably, would have found Husserl's treatment deficient by its reliance on the exclusivity of merely two types of intuition: experiencing and essential. It is owing to that exclusivity that Husserl's problem arises in the first place. Miller has suggested that Husserl's "change of mind about the notion of ego was primarily motivated by his theory of time consciousness." Miller 1986: 157. Again, the issue of time consciousness is barely broached in Husserl's *Ideen I* and found no response in Shpet's writings.

[8] Shpet 1991: 62.

[9] Husserl 1994: 529.

that the pure I is not "in" lived experiences. That is, this I is not one such experience among others.

Shpet endeavored to follow Husserl along the path of his new "discovered" phenomenological reduction, but unlike the latter Shpet finds that that path emphatically excludes the pure, or transcendental, I, as Husserl understood it. Husserl provided no new evidence in 1913 that warranted an alteration of his 1900/01 stance. There is no basis, after effecting the reduction, to hold that the stream of experiences that makes up the pure consciousness belongs to a pure I. Having excluded everything empirical, including the empirical I, we could, conceivably, retain the "transcendental residuum" as an I, but it would be ideal. Since the pure I is not a real (*reelles*) part of the lived experiences nor "behind" them as their subject, it must be merely a form, namely, the very unity of those experiences.

The denial of the unity of consciousness as the I and the concomitant positing of some pure I "behind" the individual consciousness, in Shpet's eyes, leads directly to subjectivism and with it the skepticism at least implicit in psychologism. Even stronger, taking merely the Cartesian *Ego cogito* as the starting point of philosophy itself leads to contradictions. However, just what is Shpet hereby suggesting? Does he hold that there is such a thing as an impersonal consciousness, a consciousness, albeit unified, that is neither yours nor mine, a consciousness that hovers, as it were, in some ethereal world yet observes this world of buildings, trees and people, a consciousness that is no one's?

Shpet does not deny that there can be a personal consciousness, but there can also be a multipersonal or shared one. There are times or cases where my consciousness is at least similar, if not identical, to another's. Moreover, just as Shpet in *Appearance and Sense* alluded to the possibility of a third form of intuition in addition to Husserl's experiencing intuition and eidetic intuition, one that provides access to a region of being that those forms do not, viz., social being, there is a consciousness belonging, as it were, to society as a whole, a united whole, viz., a communal consciousness. In other words, Shpet believed Husserl in 1913–14 had omitted from his gaze the entire realm of the social, or, better still, the communal. Whereas my lived experiences (*meine Erlebnisse*) are mine and only mine, the I, phenomenologically considered, can not only be distinguished from my experiences, but also not be exclusively mine. If we take consciousness ideally, i.e., phenomenologically, can we, then, ask whose consciousness it is? Such, at least, are the lines along which Shpet examined this theme and initiated his non-egological conception of consciousness.

Rather amazingly, Shpet articulated his position years earlier than both Sartre and Gurwitsch, both of whom almost certainly elaborated their respective criticisms of Husserl in ignorance of Shpet's work. In his 1936 article "La transcendence de l'égo," Sartre too questioned the need for a transcendental I within the phenomenological reduction. The field opened up by the epoché is in itself impersonal, or, to use Sartre's own expression, "pre-personal."[10] Admittedly, Sartre pointedly proceeded further than did the more cautious Shpet. Sartre, for one, appeared more

---

[10] Sartre 2004: 3.

willing to acknowledge the role of consciousness or consciousnesses in the process of the constitution of an object. However, for his part, Shpet was far more concerned than was Sartre with the notion of "sense." The two men most strikingly departed in different directions from this common non-egological conception. Sartre would go on to emphasize the sheer freedom of a consciousness that arises from its encounter with the world leading to the extreme subjectivism and nihilism of his *L'Être et le néant*. Shpet, on the other hand, would go on to emphasize human sociality and the role of language as an instrument in that sociality.

Gurwitsch, with full knowledge of Sartre's position, also rejected in 1940/1 Husserl's stand. In the phenomenological attitude, there is no center of activity, no pure I, from which conscious acts emanate. For Gurwitsch, to speak of an I is to speak of a mundane I, which is itself constituted. Concomitantly, there is no transcendental consciousness apart from that consciousness with which we are familiar, though it can have transcendental functions including constitution.[11] The difference here with Shpet's conception is more elusive, though again Shpet's emphasis lies elsewhere than Gurwitsch's, which was centered on the psychology of the mundane human individual.

Shpet's essay, as so many others of his, makes for difficult reading not least owing to his adoption of Husserl's technical vocabulary. Standard English translations of that terminology have been retained where possible and wherever it is clear that Shpet has the corresponding terms in mind. The appearance of a new English translation of Husserl's *Ideen I* by Professor Dahlstrom in 2014 has introduced a partial alternative to the terminology employed in the Kersten edition. Since the two translations are in print a choice had to be made which set of terms was to be used when the two differ: the established edition of Kersten or the new, but more natural terms Dahlstrom introduced. References in the text that follows are provided to the latter. Familiarity with the former over many years, however, may have made a consistent switch just about impossible. There are, of course, special issues that a reader versed in German philosophical literature will know only too well. The Russian word *perezhivanie*, which corresponds to the German word *Erlebnis*, has been translated variously in existing translations of Husserl. Here, that word is rendered as "lived experience." The Russian word *predmet* is consistently rendered as "object" and *ob"ekt* as "Object," except in those cases where such usage conflicts with an accepted English translation of a particular work that Shpet quotes. The Russian word *urazumenie* is given as "comprehension," in keeping with the terminology used in the translation of Shpet's *Appearance and Sense*, even though the word "understanding" may seem more fluid. The several uses of ellipsis in the text are found in the Russian original and do not indicate any omission of passages or words.

The Anglophone reader will also find that Shpet draws from a wealth of literature, making allusions to much material not typically found in technical philosophical pieces as well as, of course, to a number of philosophers, who, for one reason or

---

[11] Gurwitsch 1966: 287–300.

another, are largely unknown today but whom Shpet clearly regarded as significant.

The translator certainly wishes to express a deep sense of gratitude to two sets of anonymous reviewers' extensive comments and suggestions on earlier versions of this essay. Whereas almost all of the suggestions, being insightful, helpful, and correct, have been incorporated into this version of the translation, any and all inaccuracies and imperfections that remain are the responsibility of the translator alone. Finally but certainly not least, the translator would like to express his heart-felt thanks to The North American Society For Early Phenomenology, and in particular to Dr. Rodney Parker, for posting an earlier version of this work on the Society's website. It also appeared in the Polish philosophy journal *Kronos* in 2015. Heartfelt thanks go to its editor Piotr Nowak. The present version of the translation represents many changes and corrections over the previous versions.

As with all the essays in this collection, footnotes in square brackets [ ] are editorial additions, whereas those without such brackets indicate references/notes found in Shpet's original text.

## Consciousness and Its Owner (Notes)

### Gustav Shpet

1. Our thinking not infrequently gets us into trouble. Our enemy is our language. As if lying in ambush, a *homonym* hides behind almost every word that we express or apprehend. We cannot completely prevent others from misunderstanding our thoughts and, in particular, the expression of these thoughts. In fact, we ourselves occasionally fall into errors of expression. However, one group in particular stands out for its paradoxicality: Errors arise when we initiate a search for the *general* meaning or the *common* origin of homonyms. Perhaps from a psychological or linguistic perspective such a problem is of some interest, but logically it is paradoxical. Of course, a generalization is logically permitted when there is a subsumption of species, designated by various terms, under one genus. But what are we to make of a generalization that subsumes different things bearing an identical name under a single genus? Homonyms should not be generalized, but differentiated and determined. The meaning of each term should be rigorously delimited; the intended meaning should be specified and precisely stated. "If, then, the definition applies in a like manner to the whole range of the ambiguous term, it is not true of any one of the objects described by the term."[12]

   Among the homonyms that play an important role in philosophy is the pronoun "I."[13] The customary way of distinguishing the various meanings of this

---

[12] [Aristotle 1984: 102 (*Topics*, Book VI, §10). Shpet provides the original Greek.]

[13] [Unlike in English where the German "*das Ich*" has been variously rendered as "self," "ego," and "I," Russian uses only one word. Except when providing quotations from other works, the term "I" is used in this translation for Shpet's Russian word "*ja*."]

word lies in some supposedly consistent transition from a relatively general meaning to an ever more specialized one. It is said that we are to understand the word "I" or "self" as designating a *thing*, like one of the many things in the world around us: for example, I live on such and such street, I have a certain social standing, I am exhausted, I am wearing shabby clothes, I am bankrupt, etc. We pass from this first sense to the so-called psychophysical I, or self, when we understand that term as designating a psychophysical *organism* that reacts to irritations arising in its environment and in turn displays activity and movement produced by the organism's inner powers. Regardless of whether they are directly perceived or merely inferred on the basis of actions, the facts demonstrating the presence of mental activity in a person are attributed to a *psyche*, understood as the bearer of a person's mental powers and states. This, in turn, leads to the psyche being defined as a new meaning of the "I."[14]

It is easy to see an *analogy* between these various meanings, which consists of limiting the sphere of the I while concomitantly enlarging the "surroundings" to which it is contrasted. Extending the analogy further, the term "I" sometimes takes on yet another new meaning – anchored "within" the psychic I – as the source again of a new activity. New and quite varied senses appear as meanings of the I. Self-consciousness is now spoken of as the "I" of consciousness. We also hear talk of the [human] spirit, of a generic I, of a transcendental I or ego, etc. Not all of these meanings of "I" are synonymous. Our "spirit," for example, is taken to be a concrete object, and the earlier contrast between the I and its surroundings is preserved even when the term "I" is understood in this sense. Even here, it is used to designate the specific source of an arbitrary activity. In the other cases mentioned, an unoriginal, abstract meaning is usually ascribed to the term "I," a meaning that is clarified only on the basis of the well-known theoretical presuppositions of philosophical *subjectivism*. In such a case, the I, conceived as the subject, is invariably set against the Object of cognition or of behavior or of a consciousness in general. In each instance, there is either no consistent transition from one meaning to another, or the transition turns out to be merely imaginary. Although in the first three cases the use of the term "I" is somehow justified on the basis of an analogy – albeit only in a figurative or a metaphorical sense – using it to mean "the subject of cognition"[15] cannot be justified in the same manner. We have even less justification for using the term "I" to designate some abstract property. For in doing so we strip the I not only of its sense as the source of my activity, or of my suffering, but even of its sense as the "bearer" of my individual characteristics and traits. Instead, the I is transformed into a *quality*.

---

[14] One of the keenest analyses of the various meanings of the term "I," [or "self,"] is given by F. H. Bradley. Bradley 1969: 74–102.

[15] [Schopenhauer 1969: 207. Payne, however, translates Schopenhauer's *"Subjekt des Erkennens"* as "subject of knowing."]

2. What we have just seen is merely the reverse side of taking the ambiguous term "I" as synonymous with the words "person," "individual," "psyche," "subject," "understanding," etc. Let us put aside for now the question of the legitimacy of these and other, similar identifications. If we look solely at the formal relationships between these concepts, we can see that, on the whole, all of these meanings of the term "I" have to do either with the sphere of an empirical object, such as a person, a psyche, etc., or with that of an ideal object, conceived as a "subject," a (logically) generic or general I, etc. Such a position could be considered normal if we could establish a natural correlation between a "thing" and an "idea," something that would, of course, be revealed from the fact that the concepts within this or that order had a single sense. However, let us assume that the concept of the empirical I is actually "formed" by opposing it to its *surroundings*, while the concept of the ideal I is "formed" by opposing it to its *Object*. We would, then, have to recognize that in moving from the one concept to the other the substitution precludes any correlation like the one just mentioned.

3. This substitution can easily be seen if we form a clear idea of the character of the actual correlation. Since the empirical I is always a single, concrete "thing," a simple reference to it can take the place of a definition. Every attempt to describe this thing starts with an explicit recognition of its empirical existence, that is, the fact of its *presence* in the real world. No feature or collection of features could adequately express the "sense" of the proper name that an I so described in this way bears. We can get an indirect determination of the proper name only through a concrete reference to the surroundings, the situation and the conditions in which we find this I. If we examine these conditions, we will convince ourselves that the precise reference we need requires more than the mere specification of the "thing's" unique time and place and even of its unique birth as a living being. We also have to state explicitly its social and historical uniqueness. In other words, we simply return to its proper name – the one designation that points to the presence of the described I. And apparently only the demonstrative pronouns *this* and *that* can serve as a substitute for the proper name.

On the other hand, every direct reference to the properties, traits, characteristic features, etc., of this particular I presupposes knowledge and an understanding of his or her unique circumstances and surroundings. For example, we could say that Ivanov wrote a beautiful piece, but such a judgment would be unintelligible if there were no explicit reference or mutually understood context to our "sphere of conversation." In this way, the words "a beautiful piece" in connection with Ivanov acquires a different sense depending on which Ivanov we are speaking of: whether it be Nicholas, Eugene, Ivan, or Vjacheslav Ivanov. In exactly the same way, such determinations as "I am the one you heard,"[16] and so forth, serve as references only by way of mentioning the unique nature of the "circumstances" or of the "sphere of conversation," since this is sufficient to understand what is being said. Therefore, it actually seems that in our attempt

---

[16] [From the poem "Demon" by Mikhail Lermontov, Part 2, §10.]

to determine the I we end up with nothing but tautological judgments, such as "I am I," or "I am so-and-so," etc. Any reference to a characteristic, an activity, a feature, etc. of the I alone simply amounts to mentioning his or her proper name. A reference to the unique nature of the circumstances and the conditions leads inevitably to the same conclusion: A collection of common nouns is only a lengthy formula for the proper name. In spite of its subjective origin, it seems as though a simple pointing out (*haecceitas*[17]) is an exhaustive determination.

Certainly, there are significant difficulties here – or am I artificially magnifying them? Would it not be simpler, following the usual procedure, to begin with a portrayal of my "own I" and establish my distinctiveness "on the basis of what is given in self-observation"? I do insist, however, that each I is "personal," and if I would want to depict my own I, i.e., *myself*, I would have to present my autobiography, which, in any case, is not of philosophical interest even to me. This accepted procedure commits a sin at the very start. Avoiding biography, it proceeds from a description based on a fundamentally false assumption about the *identity of the I* of the writer who is being described, of the reader who is reading, and of the Ivan or the Socrates who figure as examples. If there is something similar in all of these, it is only that each I is an individual, a unicum, and this is exactly why we must see how they are *dissimilar*. Instead, seeking what is similar and "common" to all of them, the writer speaks not about the I, not about one's own individual self, not about oneself, but about "man," about "a person," a "subject," a "psyche," etc. In the best case, such a procedure involves a useless multiplication of terminology, and in the worst case it invokes the homonym we mentioned.

Do we not encounter, however, the same difficulties in describing *any* single, concrete object? Do these obstacles, perhaps, spring not from the peculiarities of the I, as the object of our study, but from those of a concrete thing as such? There is something, though, that empirically singles out the I in a decisive fashion from its surroundings populated with other concrete things: Only an I can be taken as a synonym for a proper name. We can give proper names to other single, concrete things, e.g., "Man's Best Friend," "Sans Souci," "The Count of Monte Cristo," the "Atlantic," "New York," "Mercury," the "Sun," etc. In some of these cases, we proceed from the possession of a thing to some I (*my* "Best Friend," *Al. Dumas*'s "The Count of Monte Cristo," etc.); in others there is no possession. In *none* of these cases, however, is there a synonymous identification of the proper name with the I. Grammarians (for example, Buslaev[18]) state that, properly speaking, the pronoun I refers to animate objects and *primarily to people*. Logic, which deals with the sense and the content of an expression, can more pointedly emphasize that the pronoun "I" simply acts as a substitute for the name of a particular person or "individual."

---

[17] ["thisness" – a central concept in the medieval philosopher Duns Scotus, for whom it is the principle of individuation.]

[18] [Fedor Ivanovich Buslaev (1818–1897), philologist and disciple of Grimm.]

When studying a single, concrete thing in general, we take it to be an example, a model, a specimen, i.e., as something "impersonal." That we immediately move on to an even more impersonalized "generalization" clearly shows that we are studying not this particular thing, conceived as a *unicum*. Although hidden in the guise of a "generality," we are, all the same, studying the thing as something concrete. In other words, that my particular "Best Friend" underwent a vivisection in the veterinarian's office provided me with the opportunity to make a judgment about "dogs in general." Nevertheless, he lost *nothing* in terms of being an object of study. When the vivisection is carried out on the I, however, the result is different: the I loses *everything*, since such a "generalized" judgment about the I that goes beyond this given I is essentially impossible. If we do, this I ceases to be this I, i.e., a *unicum*. In fact, we do speak about the "psyche," "a person" and other generalized scientific objects, but not about the I. In short, the I stands out among concrete things by the fact that general concepts concerning it are inadmissible if the concepts overstep the bounds of the individual. Indeed, it is impossible to say that this restriction is due to a "desire" or any "interest" on my part. On the contrary, it is due entirely to the I itself, conceived as an object. By virtue of the very peculiarities of the I, which permit no generalization to be made in studying it, about the I, as such, there can be no theories. As such, then, the I is *inexplicable*. It is subject to interpretation alone, i.e., to a "translation" into the language of another I or into the conventional, "artificial" language of poetic creation.

4. A doubt, however, automatically arises with such a restrictive characterization of the I, taken as an object: Is it possible to think and speak of an *idea* or *eidos* of the I? Since an eidos must be conceived as a "universal," a doubt was raised already long ago concerning the possibility of speaking of the eidos of a concrete, singular or "individual" thing without falling into contradiction. Today, we encounter categorical rejections of the notion of an "individual universal" just as we do of the idea of a given single, concrete thing as such. In particular, the assumption *of an idea of the I*, i.e., of the idea of a given so-and-so, may seem strange and unacceptable! Nevertheless, it seems to me that we must recognize such a thing as necessary. We should not forget that there is a contradiction here only if we accept a particular psychological theory according to which concepts are formed through a process of "generalization." Yet, the inadequacy of this theory has been adequately demonstrated even within the psychological sphere, i.e., within the sphere of the processes it was specifically invoked to explain. Nevertheless, if in "first philosophy" we encounter the conviction that the content of an eidos, taken as the aggregate of the essential predeterminations of a concept, is necessarily a universal, then this is surely due simply to the influence of just such a psychological theory. There is absolutely no basis for identifying an abstract universal with the "essential," except to deny the possibility of an individual universal. If the problem is formulated in a manner that

is unprejudiced in favor of any particular theory, then such a denial simply by itself constitutes an *ignoratio elenchi*.[19]

In fact, the only serious obstacle to accepting the *idea* of an I, taken as an object designated by a proper name, is our own Aristotelian logic. In spite of the fact that it proclaims on its first pages that there is a correlation between the extension and the content of concepts, it turns out further on to be entirely a logic of extension. But even if we allow our attention to be drawn to the content of a concept, our logic remains too much a product of the *understanding* to find in it a place for the rational explication of concepts as logical instruments. Being two-dimensional, it does not allow for movement from the *plane* of the understanding into the depths, a penetration into the intimate object by means of a comprehension of this intimacy. From a logical standpoint, the "content" is a simple aggregate of features, internally united and formed in such a way that in it the essential by itself already appears as a universal. Sense and meaning ultimately turn out to be for logic a "hindrance" that obscures its formal *purity*. This logic senses itself to be free only in the sphere of "species" and "genus." Any "singularity," and, even more so, the uniqueness of the I in its realm is simply an anarchic element that undermines its foundations and substructures. For this reason it is subject to all of the corresponding limitations and reductions. Nowhere is this so clearly expressed as in the distinction of the meanings of "the same," *το ταύτόν*, which Aristotle introduces and which remains a "fundamental law" of logic.[20] For "the same" has greater scope and has all kinds of rights within the sphere of "species" and "genus." However, within the sphere of the individual there is only the "numerically one."[21]

Actually, if traditional logic would wish to explain more than just the numerical identity of the individual, this could be done in only one way given its understanding of the "universal," namely, by dividing up the individual, temporally-enduring being into more or less arbitrary parts or "bits," viewing them as new individuals, which could then be generalized by its usual methods. A universal concept of the genus, for example, of Napoleon and of Socrates would result, where once again, however, the character and the individuality would be destroyed. Indeed, this is why traditional logic sooner agrees to accept an "abstract" Julius Caesar (as does, for example, Höfler[22]) than to doubt its theory of generalization and recognize a concrete *idea* of the same Caesar.[23]

---

[19] [Literally, ignorance of the refutation, i.e., drawing an irrelevant conclusion or missing the point of an argument.]

[20] [See Aristotle 1984: 7–8 (*Topics*, Book I, §7).]

[21] [See Aristotle 1984: 7–8 (*Topics*, Book I, §7); Aristotle 1984: 110 (*Topics*, Book VII, §1).]

[22] [Alois Höfler (1853–1922), a student of Brentano's and disciple of Meinong. See Höfler 1897 and Höfler 1906.]

[23] James frankly speaks of the "generic identity" and the "generic unity" of the person. James 1890: 335. [Although James does use the expression "generic unity" on the mentioned page, he never writes of the "generic identity" of the person in this work. On the page Shpet references, however, we find "generic similarity of different individuals."]

Nevertheless, such relations, as that of whole to part, organism to organ, person to his/her experiences, organization to members, etc., would have to provide the basis for a reconsideration of the relations of genus and species, which absorb everything into logic. Finally, "the typical," taken as a logical problem, is either silently passed over or is examined extremely superficially. Logic persistently remains two-dimensional, on a single plane, and because of this we encounter the difficulties we saw in explaining the "idea of an individual."[24] Essentially, it remains for us to recognize without prejudice that there is no contradiction in this concept. In any event, if logic in one way or another, i.e., regardless of this or that theory of generalization, accepts the possibility that "extension," which ultimately is always the "real," is *assimilated* into an idea, thereby surmounting the spatial extension of things, it is impossible to reject the possibility of the same "assimilation into an idea" of the temporal protraction of any thing. Each person or I completely lends itself to such a transformation into an "idea." Just as there is absolutely nothing absurd in seeing in, for example, Nikolaj Stankevich or Oliver Cromwell both a social (i.e., concrete) phenomenon and an idea (of this concrete phenomenon), so there is nothing absurd in raising the question of his idea along with the real empirical I, say, of Stankevich. And we do this each time we want to find and establish what is *typical* of it and of it alone and uniquely. We do this precisely when we want to incarnate a certain I in poetical form. And, finally, we do this when we want to picture to ourselves the idea of a concrete person as an ideal and a rule of personal or universal moral behavior or for religious worship and imitation.

Thus, it seems quite legitimate to speak not only about this actual, empirical, existing I, but also about its ideal correlate, about the constant, enduring I and therefore seen as outside the *empirical,* temporal order of its actual manifestation. The ideal I, like any object of an essential investigation, is characterized by ascertaining what is "the same" in its changing, unstable content. The identity of the I, which determines the essence of the empirical I, consequently is not a contradictory concept. On the other hand, however, it would be a contradiction to posit the empirical I as lying outside temporal change and ascribe a "real identity" to it. In this lies the actual reason why it is impossible to assert that the personal I is established solely by ascertaining the identity of this I or "self-consciousness" as, for example, Locke thinks. On the contrary, Leibniz was right in saying that identity is an adequate indication of the "moral person," but inadequate for the "real person." Indeed, Leibniz's reference to the fact that for the latter certain signs are still necessary, the "testimony of others" being of particular importance, deserves the most profound attention.[25]

---

[24] [Cf. "The formation of a Concept does not consist in separating the attributes which are said to compose it from all other attributes of the same object, and enabling us to conceive those attributes, disjoined from any others. We neither conceive them, nor think them, nor cognize them in any way, as a thing apart, but solely as forming, in combination with numerous other attributes, the idea of an individual object." Mill 1979: 309. James quotes this passage from Mill in James 1890: 470.]

[25] Locke 1968: 212–13: "For it being the same consciousness that makes a man be himself to himself, personal identity depends on that only." (The word "consciousness" here ought to be translated as "self-consciousness" or "consciousness of one's own self.")

5.  From everything we have said, it is clear that we are taking the I as an *object*,
    i.e., as the "bearer" of a certain content and imparting a necessary unity to that
    content. And it is as a unity that any object appears before us. If we were to stop
    our inquiry at this point, we could say nothing more about the I than about any
    other object. To stop our inquiry here would mean that we are satisfied with this
    quite formal characteristic of the I, viz., its *unity*. The sense and the meaning of
    an object, however, is revealed only when it ceases to be "empty." Only the
    object's content reveals the object, and, in general, apart from that content, we
    cannot say anything about it. That content, the unity of which we call the I,
    however, must be distinguished from the content of other concrete objects,
    which, as we pointed out, play for us the role of "exemplars." Therefore, at the
    very start we must point out what about the I prevents it from serving as an
    "exemplar" and essentially distinguishes it from all other concrete units.

    A *unity of lived experiences* is, in many respects, a satisfactory characteriza-
    tion of the I as an empirical unity, or, to put it another way, a *unity of conscious-
    ness*. In this case, the peculiar nature of the I, as a unity, is clarified by how we
    portray lived experiences, or consciousness, and what place we assign to them.
    Not for a minute, however, should we lose sight of the conditions under which
    such a characterization is created, for these conditions are precisely what makes
    the characterization inadequate. The first and most essential fact, by which this
    characterization is formed, is that we get it in answer to the question: What is
    the I? Consequently, proceeding from a recognition of the unity, we then ask:
    Of what is this a unity? In other words, the *path* before us is restricted in the
    sense that we must get an *irreversible* judgment as a result. Nevertheless, hav-
    ing said that the I is a unity of lived experiences, or of consciousness, we natu-
    rally begin to think that the I itself is essential for any unity of consciousness,
    whereas our assertion made no such no claim. Secondly, the homonymy of the
    term "I," with which we began on a path leading from a statement of a unity to
    a characterization of the manifold, makes itself felt particularly in the interpre-
    tation of both this very unity as well as of the unified content. In this way, it
    turns out that the I is the unity of psychic life, of the spirit, of a human being
    (i.e., the unity of a psyche and a body), of a person, etc. Nevertheless, we still
    need to find the genuine meaning of the I that would clarify its unique position
    among concrete things and that prevents it from being regarded as an "exem-
    plar." For it is not clear from the concepts of a psyche, a person, a human being,
    etc., per se why the objects designated by them are not considered to be exem-

---

Leibniz: "*Je suis aussi de cette opinion, que la consciosité ou le sentiment du moi prouve une
identité morale ou personelle. … Ainsi la conscience n'est pas le seul moyen de constituer l'identité
personelle, et le rapport d'autrui ou même d'autres marques y peuvent suppléer.*" ["I also hold this
opinion that consciousness or the sense of I proves moral or personal identity. … Thus, consciousness is not the only means of establishing personal identity, and its deficiencies may be made up
by other people's accounts or even by other indications." Leibniz 1996: 238.]

plars.[26] Finally, based on the above considerations, the I designates the same so-and-so as any proper name of a person. A reference to the unity of consciousness is only a reference to the meaning of a generic name. But again we come back to the question: Wherein lies the uniqueness of the I, as a particular so-and-so?

6. Ever since the era of ancient philosophy, "matter" has almost unanimously served as the individuating principle in determining what is individual and concrete. However, several voices expressed support instead in favor of "form" (Duns Scotus) as such a principle. In modernity, we more often come across claims that the real sources of individuality lie in "activity," "self-activity," the "will," etc., or that the determining relations have to do with spatiality and temporality. It is clear, however, that all such means of determining the individual are too general for the I. Besides, we want to approach the problem from a completely different angle. The means of determination just mentioned clearly bear either a pronounced metaphysical character or by referring only to determining relations they suffer from an extreme formalism. Moreover, we found that, generally speaking, the I is a unity of lived experiences or of consciousness, and it is precisely in this that we must seek the exclusive conditions determining its absolute uniqueness.

7. Nevertheless, despite the quite general nature of our remarks we believe that there is a need to introduce one division. The need for this will become clear from what follows. We have been speaking of a "unity of lived experiences" and now we seek to characterize this unity in terms of the peculiarities of the "lived experiences" united into an I. However, in general, if a "lived experience," as such, is correctly revealed to us to be first and foremost an activity, it is no less important to note that not all lived experiences without exception – or perhaps it is better to say not everything in a lived experience – appears *originarily* as an activity, and we have every right also to call our experience or something we "undergo" a lived experience. It is also quite clear – because this is a fact of immediate consciousness – that something we undergo is not simply a non-actual or potential lived experience understood as an activity. Rather, it is

---

[26] In his book Stern 1906, W. Stern bases his entire philosophical outlook on a distinction between "person" and "thing." But of all the definitions known to me his definition seems to me the least successful. "The person," he says, "is an existing being which despite (? – GS) its great number (and what unity is not the unity of a great number? – GS) of parts, forms a real, unique and intrinsically valuable unity, and as such, despite (! – GS) its great number of different functions, fulfills a unified, purposeful spontaneous action. A thing is the contradictory antithesis of a person. It is also an existing thing (How is one "existing thing" contradictorily opposed to another also "existing thing"? – GS), which consisting of many parts, does not form a real, unique and independent unity and which, functioning (How does something that is "non-real" function? – GS) in many different functions, does not accomplish a unified, purposeful spontaneous action." Stern 1906: 16. If this definition is not completely devoid of sense, then according to it a "thing" is an ideal or abstract object, e.g., a decagon, virtue, etc., and a "person" is what is usually called a thing, e.g., the Sun, the Earth's magnetic pole, etc. Other definitions either limit the concept of "person" by an attribution of moral and juridical features or expand the concept by a reference to their inadequate number, such as, e.g., identity, self-activity, etc.

originarily a distinctive feature given in the lived experience along with the activity, even though a subsequent analysis reveals that an "experience" also demands an active bearer.[27] Passing to an analysis of pure consciousness, we accordingly distinguish the states or "structures" of consciousness, which we can call, on the one hand, an aesthetic or, primarily, *phenomenal* (Stumpf's phenomenological, Husserl's hyletic) consciousness, and, on the other hand, a primarily *intentional* or functional consciousness.[28]

This division concerns the very essence of consciousness, and the distinguishing features that we found obviously must be given in both directions of consciousness. Hence, this division necessarily has to do with determining the absolute uniqueness of the I as opposed to the exemplar-like character of other concrete objects. The purely "subjective" haecceity of the subject of a proposition, objectively understood, is revealed as both a phenomenal structure and a functional productivity. Nevertheless, in the history of philosophy, as a rule, the importance of only one of these moments was stressed. In this way, the individual turned out to be either something completely predetermined, *omnimode determinatum*,[29] (e.g., Aristotle, the Scholastics, Wolff, et al.) or a pure creation from nothing (= from itself), a spontaneity, or, in the broad sense, a being *for itself* (Lotze's *für Sich*, Krause's *Sich-selbst-für-sich-selbst-Sein*[30]). A combination of both characteristics was considered to be internally contradictory and antinomical. In fact, however, just such a combination is a *conditio sine qua non*[31] and is an immediately recognized fact. Merely one of the mentioned moments is insufficient, and to assert such a thing is to countenance a deprivation. To affirm predetermination, or predestination, alone is insufficient for the reason that the absolute uniqueness of each individual remains incomprehensible. This is clear from the existence of theories of the absolute circularity or recurrence, etc. of events and things in time and from the existence of theories of metempsychosis – particularly with regard to the I when it is interpreted as a "soul." A reference to freedom is also insufficient, since it leads ultimately to the idea of a single source (in the genre of Schopenhauer's *Wille zum Leben*), and, consequently, makes the inner distinguishability of individuals and the I inconceivable.

The only way out that I see lies, above all, in recognizing the fact of the matter just as it is, i.e., the presence of both predetermination and freedom, or, combining these into one term, the presence of *rational motivation*. What makes this I, this so-and-so, absolutely unique? Its uniqueness lies neither in its unity in itself nor the in itself presence of a coordinated predetermination and

---

[27] [Husserl 2014: 69–73 (§35).]

[28] [Cf. Husserl 2014: 164–65 (§85).]

[29] [For example, Wolff 1983: 152 (part I, sec. 1, Chap. 2, par. 74, Band 1.2) – "*Apparet hinc, Individuum esse ens* omnimode determinatum, *seu in quo determinata sunt omnia, quae eidem insunt.*"]

[30] [See, for example, Krause 1892: 74.]

[31] [Latin: absolutely essential condition.]

freedom, the unification of which is manifested in an individualizing goal-directedness. Rather, its uniqueness lies only in a distinctive interpretation of this entire unity. Interpretation is the detection of sense, a construal as a manifestation of comprehension. That is, it is the way out into a third dimension that we spoke of earlier. Here, we find that the I is not cut off or restricted in scope, but is intertwined as a "member" of some "community" in which it occupies a place *predestined* for it alone and which cannot be taken by anyone else. On the whole, the predestination of a so-and-so – ultimately in the whole, in the "world" – predetermines its haecceity, although this still does not solve the problem of the impossibility of its quiddity. Imagine now the following: Let us take the I of Robinson Crusoe or that of Selkirk, not with regard to what is typical of them as individuals or in their individual essences, but with regard to what they have in common. We find between them a "similarity," which leads us, so to speak, to a "Robinson in general." According to what we have determined, this similarity should be a similarity of predestination, and a generalization of the I would actually be permitted. However, it is subsequently found out that in spite of the similarity of the predestinations, Selkirk "degenerated" and became "crude," whereas Robinson Crusoe acquired great virtues. How can we speak of a "Robinson in general" without depriving these two cases of what is essential in each of them? How do we accept the essential difference between these two I's if we assume that in both cases the "predestination" is the same? We must conclude that in order to recognize the uniqueness of Robinson and that of Selkirk there is a need for the creative freedom that each of these "members" in the vast whole retains and that, consequently, turns out to be far from unique. However, if this freedom did not suddenly burn out but from the start abided in each I, then we would have to think that it is precisely this freedom that determines them from the start in their absolute uniqueness and makes them mutually irreplaceable.

Thus, the I is an irreplaceable and absolutely unique member of the world as a whole. The I, as Leibniz said, "expresses the entire universe,"[32] and it is predetermined by its predetermination. However, the I expresses the universe from "its point of view," which can actually remain *its* point of view only by being essentially free and arbitrary. For a freedom repeated in the entire universe ceases to be free and arbitrary but becomes automatic or an imitation. The I, as an identity, i.e., the I in its essential meaning is a unity and "bearer" of consciousness, characterizable by its predetermination and by its freedom. Empirically, as we saw, we must speak of the relation of the I, or of each unique "subject," to the environment or surroundings. Indeed, the uniqueness of each I leads to the impossibility of a generalized I, just like the impossibility of a "general subject." However, this is a *conclusion*, as I indicated, based ultimately on the specific premises of the Aristotelian theory of generalization. But the

---

[32] Or Plotinus: "since then the Kosmos contains the Reason-Principles not merely of man, but also of all living individual things, so must the Soul." Plotinus 1962: 419–20. [Shpet provides the citation in Greek.]

immediate givenness of "the same" in the unique I should have given rise to a doubt in this very theory. Actually, Plotinus already closely approaches this problem of the "idea of the one" and the support for his doubts seems to be unshakeable: "man in general" is a prototype of the human "exemplar," but not of "*each*" in its infinite variety[33] – this is not at all a mere numerical identity. As a result, therefore, it turns out that the individual I in essence is indeed conceivable, is an auto-Socrates, an auto-Ivanov, etc., and yet it has a proper and not a general generic name.

8. In light of the considerations we have now seen which of the different senses of the term "I" do we take? The most interesting and important of these, of course, is that which accepts the "general" I as a (logically, not ontologically) "generic" I, a "transcendental," or an "epistemological" I. All of the preceding amounts to a rejection of the validity or "meaningfulness," in short, the intelligibility, of such a concept. Nevertheless, it can still be accepted either as an arbitrary conditional designation for some object *sui generis* or as a fiction, useful for one reason or another in clarifying the problem of the unity of consciousness. As we indicated, however, one way of forming this concept evokes bewilderment. For in it, we find that a certain "substitution" took place in the transition to this "I." We now want to pause on this.

For each of us, the "natural" and direct way of designating ourselves is through our name. We disclose the sense of our name or the meaning of the term "I" either by a direct reference or through an immediate recognition of "self-consciousness" or a "sensation of oneself." Since the "I" is replaced in this determination with some general or figurative meaning, such as psyche, man, etc., what we need to establish for a determination is not something common to several I's, but what distinguishes them. The external sign through which we get the latter is its *hic et nunc*, which is concretely revealed in the content of its "surroundings." Guiding this determination, the ideal sense of the I, as a concrete object, justifies such an empirical determination in establishing the rational motivation, combining predetermination and freedom. Hence, it turns out that when such unusual privative meanings as soul, man, and person are imparted to the I, the shift in terminology can still find its justification *analogously* to the way the definitions of these "things" are obtained through their relationship to the surroundings and to the conditions under which they are realized. However, we should not thereby ignore the fact that all of the meanings mentioned retain their sense, and the analogy itself finds its justification only by observing the *absolute* meaning of the term "I." The concept "surroundings" is no more correlative to that of "soul," "person," etc. than is the correlation between the I and the not-I.

---

[33] "one Reason-Principle cannot account for distinct and differing individuals: one human being does not suffice as the exemplar for many distinct each for the other not merely in material constituents but by innumerable variations of ideal type." Plotinus 1962: 420. [Shpet provides the citation in Greek.]

This much is clear as long as we do not introduce into our reasoning any philosophical presuppositions or theories, and consequently as long as we limit our examinations to what is actually given to us, i.e., to our own I and to that of others, but taken also as unique I's. The situation is obscured only if starting with certain presuppositions we introduce a "generalization," which (abstractly) accepts a "generic" or (abstractly) some other *general* I. In fact, what sense and meaning can the latter have? If not all, then in any case the overwhelming majority of philosophical writers take the "general I" to be the *subject*, which is conceived as correlative to the *Object*. However, strictly speaking, if this is not already included in the presuppositions of the corresponding philosophical theory, then there is no need of this correlation. In other words, if the "subject" is actually what the "I" designates, then *the subject is also an absolute concept*, and not a correlative one (namely, to the Object). It is a "concept of the Object" (as Drobisch[34] defines "absolute concept"). A preconceived interpretation of the I, as subject, conceals as well another counterfeit one – namely that in place of the "surroundings" an "Object" is posited, one supposedly correlative to the "subject." In this way a substitution takes place which further virtually accustoms us to conceive our surroundings as correlative to the I (for example, the surroundings to the individual). Above all, however, an understanding of the "Object" in general begins to be extended broadly to everything, where there is only some kind of sense of the I. Consequently, the "Object" becomes a completely universal correlate of the I, which is also understood as the subject in the universal sense of the word. We begin to speak of the "subject" and the "Object" in psychology, and from then on this correlation is extended to all other meanings of the I. Ultimately, a habit is formed, obscuring even the absurdity in the assertion of a correlativity simpliciter between the I and the not-I.

9. In this way, the source of the falsification lies in the substitution of the I with a general subject. And the source of the theoretical superstition is the instilled habit in *contemporary* philosophy to conceive the subject as if it were correlative to an Object. Fichte, apparently, more than all others, is responsible for implanting this superstition. Without going into superfluous detail, let us simply note the following. Although the term "subject" in general is now recognized as correlative to an "Object," it is, nevertheless, sometimes used in an absolute sense, in particular in the sense of an indefinite person. In fact, in such a case, unlike the "I," it designates something *impersonal*. But this sense, as well as other senses of the term, such as the "(grammatical) subject," the "(national) subject," the "(thematic) subject," in general the "content (subject)," etc. are obviously not the reason why we turned to this concept. The original, medieval meaning of the term "subject" points precisely to the "substratum" i.e., that with which we are concerned. Such a meaning of the term, of course, is not correlative, but *absolute*. The meaning of this term is retained in modern philosophy, where the term "subject" still has the meaning of "that with which we are dealing." Along with this broad "logical" sense, the term, however, also

---

[34] [Moritz Drobisch (1802–1896). German mathematician and philosopher. Professor in Leipzig.]

conveys a narrower "ontological" meaning of the "thing" that appears as the bearer or source of certain faculties and possibilities, both active as well as passive. (A stone is the *subject* of warmth; humans are the *subject* of knowledge, etc.). A subject is the *materia in qua* (or *id in quo*), whereas the material proper is the *materia ex qua,* and the Object is the *materia circa quam* (*id circa quod*). Only in *German philosophy*[35] from the mid-eighteenth century does the term receive a new, even more constrictive meaning, in some respects one directly opposed to the earlier one. From the time of Kant, the word "subject" in its new sense has become a necessary implement of philosophical language. The ordinary usage of the word, however, in many languages (e.g. French, English, Italian) up to now has resisted and poorly assimilated this new meaning of the word. However, if it has been assimilated, then it has been primarily in the *absolute* meaning of "man." (In the Russian language, the word is also ordinarily used absolutely: "the suspicious subject," the "unknown subject," etc.) It is quite possible that the "subject" in this new sense, stems ultimately from "man" (or "self" or "mind," etc.) as the *object* of our concern and which appears as the bearer of consciousness and the source of its *activity,* i.e., as the bearer of certain "faculties," – in general of all that in our earlier terminology (e.g., still Wolffian) we would call "adjuncts" of the subject.

In all this, the most essential thing for us is that the history of the term does not provide bases for understanding it as a term that has to do with some correlativity. On the contrary, it appears before us in its absolute sense even when it is incredibly constrained to designate merely the psychological subject. It is a clear fact that if we now generalize the concept of the individual I, which, as we said, we have no right to do, and on the other hand, limit the concept of the subject to mean the animate and thereby the human subject, we thereby to a certain degree justify the identification of the generalized I with the restricted subject. Yet, we still must use the term "I" as an absolute one. We can go further and agree to call the single, individual I the subject, but the question certainly is not only whether there is an inner justification not only for this identification, but even simply for a comparison of the I with the subject. Or is this simply a matter of a linguistic agreement? In any case, if there is a basis for this comparison, i.e., if in general it makes sense, then it is only that the I, as the individual unity of consciousness, *as the conceived and discussed object,* is called a subject.

10. Having reverted, therefore, to the I as a unity of consciousness and seeing it as a "subject," i.e., an object *sui generis* among other objects, let us now turn to an examination of this substitution, which is our concern, in its essence. We saw that there is a basis to speak of the ideal I as an essence, which we can see in the concrete and individual I, in some so-and-so, and that this ideal I retains all its

---

[35] Apparently for the first time in Baumgarten, though not just in German, but also, as Eucken observes, in Latin. [See Eucken 1880: 2.] Cf., for example, Baumgarten 1770: Prolegomena, 12 (§32) – *"Certum subiective tale est, cuius veritas a determinatis subiectis seu cognoscentibus clare cognoscitur."*

uniqueness, contrary to traditional theories of generalization. In this connection, it is found, on the other hand, that the idea of a "general I," of an "I in general," either contains a conditional form or is an absurdity. Nevertheless, this idea has begun to play a quite extraordinary role in philosophy since Kant's time. It is true, Kant himself gives anyone who does not want to confuse philosophical terminology the right to ignore him on this point. For he calls one and the same thing by several names that since long ago belonged to some other thing. By Kant's own admission, his "transcendental I" or "synthetic unity of apperception" is nothing other than the *understanding*.[36] And on the assurance of a contemporary commentator of Kant, it "would be less ambiguous and would more closely correspond to the fact" to say that it is a matter of a "scientific understanding" (Cohen).[37] Possibly! But where in this is the I in its indisputable singularity and absolute irreplaceability? In any case, it seems to me smarter to speak of a "scientific understanding" than of a "*universal self-consciousness.*"[38]

11. Nevertheless, however capricious the Kantian terminology may be, I am prepared to recognize in the identification of the I with the understanding, at least, the appearance of an analogy with other definitions of the I by its opposition to its "surroundings," since in singling out the understanding as the I, we can still interpret the remaining content of the "psyche" as the "surroundings" for this "I." However, how are we, then, to understand or make sense of Fichte's venture, i.e., of his empty and sterile deductions of the I and from the I? ... Fichte roared, screamed, angered and intimidated many, though not everyone. One who was not frightened was, for example, Schopenhauer, who also dispensed his own unique names for Fichte. Another one who was not frightened was a *personalist* metaphysician, who exhaustively characterized the philosophy of the "brave" Fichte with the words: "As an energetic character, he had a particular taste for the command doctrine (*Commandodoctrin*) of Kant's practical reason" (Teichmüller).[39] Let me quote one remarkable passage from Fichte: "If you do what I tell you," – he commands – "you will think what I think. ... Perhaps you would have no objection to including in the concept of the self something that I would not include, e. g. the concept of your individuality, since this concept is designated by the same word. All this is now left to you: Only what is established by means of the simple appeal of your thought to itself is the

---

[36] "And thus the synthetic unity of apperception is the highest point to which one must affix all use of the understanding, even the whole of logic and, after it, transcendental philosophy; indeed this faculty is the understanding itself." Kant 1997: 247f (B134f). [Shpet provides the citation in German.]

[37] [A reference to the Marburg neo-Kantian Hermann Cohen (1842–1918).]

[38] [Kant 1997: 247 (B132). Shpet's emphasis on "universal."]

[39] Teichmüller 1882: 7.

self of which I am here speaking."[40] Philosophy in the imperative mood! ... Apparently all that remains is to obey...[41]

I have quoted this passage in order above all to focus our attention on Fichte's new bias, compared with Kant, in understanding the "general I." The "understanding" in Kant "prescribes laws" and commands, but among other things it is concerned with its own business, viz., to think. In any case, Kant himself comes to it by thinking. The I in Fichte is obtained as the result of an activity and itself acts! "The *self posits itself*, and by virtue of this mere self-assertion it exists; and conversely, the self *exists* and *posits* its own existence by virtue of merely existing. It is at once the agent and the product of action; the active, and what the activity brings about; action and deed are one and the same, and hence the 'I am' expresses an Act."[42] This is worthy of attention in all respects. Above all, Fichte excludes "individuality" from the I, and yet his I "acts." It seems that God Himself, who can make what happened not to have happened, cannot force an abstract concept to "act" but Fichte can. On the other hand, if we are not quibbling over the word "action," it is impossible even for an individual to think in the form of an action, but for Fichte "to think" means "to act." "Your thinking is, for you, an *acting*. ... I am speaking of nothing but the activity of which you are immediately conscious when you are in this state – and only insofar as you are conscious of this activity. If, however, you should find yourself to be conscious of no activity at all in this case (and many celebrated philosophers of our own day find themselves in just this situation), then let us part from each other in peace at this point, for you will be unable to understand anything I say from now on."[43]

Having parted with Fichte on *this* point, let us recall another order he issues, which again illuminates subjectivism from a new angle. One of the numerous experiments in his exposition of the *Science of Knowledge* begins: "Attend to yourself: turn your attention away from everything that surrounds you and towards your inner life; this is the first demand that philosophy makes of its disciple. Our concern is not with anything that lies outside you, but only with yourself."[44] Who is this going to deceive? I personally know very well that our concern will not be *myself*, this so-and-so. If some so-and-so should by chance discover his presence here, he commits a great philosophical mistake. But this can also be forgiven, since at the moment something else interests us in Fichte's

---

[40] Fichte 1971: 523. [Not page 513 as in Shpet's text.]

[41] However history notes that among Fichte's auditors there was one who dared to ask: "Is this individual determination now something foreign in the I, by which it is contaminated and distorted?" [Herbart 1824: 86.]

[42] [Fichte 1970: 97] The word "*Thathandlung*" is now somewhat out-of-date. Originally and even in Fichte's day, it meant a *forced action*, but then in general the execution of any act. Fichte's play with concepts could be translated very well by the expression "executed act." The sense of an *actual, realized action* fully conveys Fichte's idea.

[43] Fichte 1994: 106–07.

[44] Fichte 1970: 6.

*Introduction.* Let us in fact follow Fichte's invitation and start to deduce a philosophy from the I, however we take it, whether in Fichte's sense or in mine or in whatever sense. For example, let us agree that the term "I" designates "water" or a "stone." Then as long as we are consistent and do not exceed the bounds of our first fundamental thesis is it any wonder if it then turns out that *everything is an I or in the I* and that yet we are not overstepping the bounds of the I? Therefore, if we find that the I is the unity of consciousness, then clearly adhering to elementary consistency, we next find that consciousness is merely unique to the I and that outside the I there is no consciousness. Starting from the I, we come to this position and everything that we find along the way will belong to the *I*, everything will be "*mine*" and will be "given to *me*." *I* will possess it, etc. – whatever expression we can devise here. And if this I is still a "subject," then everything necessary for "subjectivism" is now guaranteed.

12. Thus, on the basis of everything said we take a step forward here in revealing something fraudulent: finding that the I, some so-and-so, is a unity of consciousness, the unity of consciousness is proclaimed to be the I! Is it this so-and-so? But where is common sense here? It is right where it should be! A so-and-so is surely only a contingency, a *phenomenon*, a thoughtless act of the Creator,[45] a pretentious nothingness! There is a genuine, authentic transcendental I. All we have to do is remove from this so-and-so *his* "mask" and a *certain subject* is obtained which is indistinguishable from its neighbors to the right and to the left. Moreover, since in the higher spheres there is no "right" or "left," it is the "universal subject" alone guaranteeing everything and vouching for everything.

13. If the entire issue amounted simply to the fact that the conditions under which a *conversio pura*[46] is achieved are so easily forgotten, we would suffer little, since we also gain little if they are observed. The assertion that the "unity of consciousness" is nothing other than the I seeks corroboration in the pure evidence with which the fact of consciousness itself is ascertained. Consequently, it is neither a matter of deductions *nor of theories* but of an immediate, obvious and undeniable fact. While it is true that Hume doubted some of the things here, he was a skeptic by vocation and by specialty. The same holds for Mill as well as for perhaps a few others. But, on the other hand, as is well-known neither Mill nor Hume hid the fact that with their doubts they were not able to make the ends meet. As a result, there is an impressive unanimity of opinion in contemporary philosophy concerning the question of the immediate presence of the I in every lived experience and in every act of consciousness. Consequently, there is also an essential necessity for consciousness to be a consciousness of

---

[45] Sergej Trubeckoj interprets the relationship between the "absolute subject" and an "individual consciousness" in the absolute idealism of German philosophy in this way: "Individual consciousness emerges by means of some unfathomable error of the absolute subject, its original sin. The individual consciousness is recognized as essentially false, that need not exist and is subject to elimination." Trubeckoj 1994: 490.

[46] [pure or simple conversion.]

the I. In order to check such an assertion we could limit ourselves to the analysis of a particular example, but since I have to object "to the evidence" and consequently must proceed with particular caution, I will select three representatives of three *different* philosophical *theories*. All three, however, display a great degree of solidarity on our issue.

14. Teichmüller[47] was one of the most subtle thinkers of the late nineteenth century, a defender of transcendent metaphysics, a personalist and a most vicious *"Kanttödter,"* if I may so express myself. Taking Lotze as his point of departure, Teichmüller resolves the entire content of consciousness into relations and analyzes the "material of consciousness" in the following way: "Let us take a simple relational unit, for example, the judgment 'I see a green field' or 'I hear the soft music,' etc. We need only eliminate the relational forms – therefore the article "a," the representation of the object, such as 'field' or 'music,' and the grammatical endings – in order to obtain three spheres of simple relational points. (1) In the 'I' we have an immediate singular self-consciousness, which cannot be put together from other simpler representations; (2) In 'seeing' and 'hearing' we have a consciousness of our activities or states; (3) In the 'green' or the 'soft' we have sensations or feelings. Nothing here is obtained through inference or mediated in any way. It is a simple, relationless consciousness."[48]

Therefore, what we have here is not a "theory," but the pure depiction of an actual lived experience. Doubts concerning the "purity" of the depicted experience, however, arise already with a preliminary "elimination" of certain parts of the "judgment," the removal of which, in my view, does not always leave something to be analyzed. Let me take other judgments: "The Earth revolves around the Sun"; "The relation of the circumference of a circle to its diameter = $\pi$," etc. If we eliminate here the "relational forms," then what remains for determining the "relational points"? We must appeal to *theory* and *deductions* in order to explain that "in fact," i.e., psychologically, every judgment of such a sort is implicitly accompanied by some mental supplementation, for example, "I see that…"; "I hear that…"; "I find that…"; "I doubt that …"; "I am convinced, am glad, etc., etc., that…." That is, it is a matter of either a so-called modality or simply of "my" relationship to something that is ascertained irrespective of me, in which the I, this so-and-so, concerning the specific issue of my relationship to it simply "does not participate." Of course, however, since Teichmüller in one way or another took or takes part in some "relational whole" and if thereupon he analyzes this whole starting with himself, it simply would be an astonishing lack of attention or unnecessary modesty on his part were he not to find himself and not to mention his own name. Once some so-and-so introduces himself, it is clear that in all of the events in which he does participate, he must be mentioned as one of the "relational points." Let us suppose some so-and-so now imagines himself to be the center and "subject" of all the correlations

---

[47] [Gustav Teichmüller (1832–1888) taught philosophy at the Universities of Basel and later Dorpat, now Tartu in Estonia, which at the time was part of the Russian Empire.]

[48] Teichmüller 1882: 18.

introduced. In that event, even if he refused to give his name and identity in order to preserve his honored place in the universe, this would be on his part only a form of conceit which can, perhaps, also be categorized as a modality of the respective judgment. However, it is quite impossible to recognize it as a "representation of the subject" or of what truly exists. Let us assume, though, that to some so-and-so it really *seems* to be so, and let us restrict ourselves only to what *seems* to be the case. Again, we are left with *just what* seems to be the case. Perhaps, it is dubitable, but the fact that it *seems* to be is inescapable. Is it not clear, then, that this "seems to be" is correlative to an I, and that the latter is just as indubitable as the very process of "it seems to be the case"? Nevertheless, I think that this is neither clear nor simple. It is a matter of the experiential or conscious process, of a "stream of consciousness," as we are used to saying now, and of the evidence or of immediate givenness. However, if it is correct that the experiential process is obvious in its immediate givenness, then the I does not lie in *this* piece of evidence. For it is impossible to find the I unequivocally as a part or moment in the changing lived experiences. The "green" changes to "yellow," the "delicate" becomes a "screeching," a "delight" becomes a "revulsion," etc., but it is not clear where the "I" enters in these changes nor again what its role would be. If it is given, it is given somehow *differently* and not as experiences themselves are given. Nevertheless, if the I is given evidently and immediately, this evidentness and immediacy are of a different sort than the evidentness of a lived experience or of an act of consciousness. And if we accept Teichmüller's opposition of the "material of a relation" to the "form of a relation,"[49] the "representations of the object" necessarily belonging to the "forms," then I am ready to assert that the I, this so-and-so, has precisely the givenness of an object and has, of course, its immediacy and primacy. In any case, though, this is just not the evidentness of a lived experience. Along with other "objects," the "I" is also ascertained in consciousness as an object, perhaps, even as an object *sui generis*, but that already is a secondary issue. It is, above all, an *object*. Correlatively, consciousness itself can be *sui generis*, as Leibniz already said (and as Lipps also said), a "feeling of the I," a self-consciousness, as an object-consciousness *sui generis*. This too, however, is a secondary issue. In any case, since we are thinking of Leibniz, I recall his remark about the necessity of the testimony of *others* in order to establish "personal identity," e.g., the identity of some so-and-so, e. g. from the cradle, through the battlefield and finally onto the island of St. Helena. The testimony of the so-and-so himself, consequently, is insufficient, and my preceding observations evoke the question: *Who* is this who is conscious of this object *sui generis*, of "his very self," of this so-and-so? For the time being, I will answer that in any case it is *not only* I myself, *not only* the so-and-so himself. This is enough to emphasize the difference between the evident givenness of the I, of a so-and-so, and the givenness of a lived experience, which belongs *only* to the I

---

[49] [Teichmüller 1882: 19.]

as in Teichmüller's example. One must not only connect one's thoughts by grammatical forms and relationships.

15. Let us turn to a second example. *N. Losskij* is a representative of immanent philosophy, a staunch advocate of, as he himself calls it, the "intuitivism of N. O. Losskij." In examining the issue before us, he holds that we must "begin simply *with an analysis of the structure of consciousness* and with a precise description of the elements and of the relationships found within it, without relying on any preconceived theories of the relationship between the I and the world."[50] He carries out the analysis itself in the following way: "Let us discard all of our preconceptions of the world, the psyche, the human body, etc. and concentrate on an examination of the factual structure of the manifestations of consciousness expressed by the words 'I am glad,' 'I want to listen to music,' 'I see stars in the sky,' 'I am touching something coarse,' 'I know that $2 \times 2 = 4$.' In each of these examples, the object of consciousness – whether it be a sense of joy, the desired listening to music, the seen stars, etc. – is very different, but in each case there is *something* that stands in a certain special *relationship to the I*. It is impossible to describe or define this relationship by means of an analysis of its elements, since it is both simple and elementary. The only thing we can do is allude to the relationship with the aid of the following vivid expression, which must not be taken literally: Everything that the I 'possesses' enters into the sphere of consciousness."

It is not hard to see that almost everything that was said above with regard to Teichmüller's analysis is applicable here as well, and if we were to judge solely on the basis of the passages cited, the ways in which "transcendent metaphysics" and "immanent philosophy" approach this problem are not so different. Do they perhaps have just a different understanding of the "I"? Nevertheless, how would this be possible if both authors have in mind the same piece of evidence and the same immediate givenness? And if they do not, then already this alone speaks against the supposed givenness of the I, conceived not as an "object," but as a moment or part of *every* manifestation of consciousness. In addition, however, I do not understand how Losskij can speak as though he does not rely "on any preconceived theories of the relationship between the I and the world." He proposes to discard "all of our preconceived ideas of the world, of the psyche, of the human body, etc." However, is it not really the case that behind

---

[50] Losskij 1911: 231ff. In his article "Reforma ponjatija soznanija," Losskij gives the following definition: "Consciousness is the aggregate of all that stands in a certain distinctive *relationship* to the I." However, the "I" is to be understood here not as an "individual I," but, in our terminology, as a "fraudulent" I, so that it is impossible to object to it by arguing that, for example, the "religious consciousness of paganism" is a consciousness, while "paganism" is not an I. Of course, it seems that either the "I" or "consciousness" must be understood "differently" here. On the whole, though, it is clear that if "consciousness" is *defined* as that which stands in a certain relationship to the I, then, as we saw, simple consistency demands that every consciousness be a consciousness belonging to an I. Losskij's argument, which I am examining now, is, on the contrary, of special interest as it is an attempt to discover the I not by means of deductive reasoning from a definition, but by means of a direct reference.

the expression "etc." there hides, among other things, a thoroughly "preconceived" idea of some "general I," which in Losskij is in a direct line of succession from Kant's "transcendental apperception" and from Fichte's vacuous "I"?
Therefore, the most important point of all is that the "I" is then called on in
Losskij's philosophy to play the role of the "epistemological subject."
Consequently, it also plays the role of the "subject" which must be correlated
with the "Object," or which stands, to use Losskij's own terminology, in an
"epistemological coordination" with its "Object."[51] In this regard, Losskij's
analysis is of particular interest to us now for the following reason. Since the
subject and the Object, the I and the not-I, or (as Losskij puts it) the I and the
content of consciousness, are correlative concepts, we must be able to characterize the relationship between the two in some way, just as we can all correlative concepts. (For example, the marriage relation is between a husband and a
wife; between a servant and a master the relation is termed "service," etc.)
Losskij, indeed, makes an attempt to designate this *relationship*. He vividly
characterizes it as "possession."

We must admit that this portrayal is not very successful. The kinship between
this possession to the German word "*Haben*" is obvious. A great admirer and
defender of the latter is [Johannes] Remke, who uses this term to characterize
the "activity" of consciousness, which should not be understood as an operation
or an efficacious act.[52] This purely negative characterization seems to me quite
correct, but how can we then find a positive characterization of consciousness?
The term "possession" or "*Haben*" is inadequate in that it leads us to interpret
the "acts" of consciousness as "belongings" or "property," but whose "property" or "belongings" would they be? We would have to say "of the 'I'."
However, if we actually discard every idea of the "body," of the "psyche," etc.
and know the "I" only as the "unity of consciousness," what sense does it make
to speak of consciousness as a "belonging" of the I or as something that the "I"
possesses?[53] The unsuccessful nature of this portrayal is also revealed from
another side: If we can put up with such cacophonical expressions as "I am
happy" = "I possess happiness," "I feel" = "I possess a feeling," etc., what, then,
does it mean to say "I possess stars in the sky," "I possess the fact that $2 \times 2 = 4$"?
Or are these improper questions, because it is impossible to speak of "stars in
the sky," but only of "my vision of stars in the sky"? Surely, though, Losskij
also wants to avoid at all costs just such a "subjectivism." Therefore, he must

---

[51] In order not to complicate our exposition we do not want to leap from a fundamental analysis of
consciousness to a theory of knowledge, but it is certainly impossible to ignore it.

[52] Lipps also uses the word "*Haben*," and it seems to me that Losskij is closer to Lipps than to
Remke on this point. However, I mention Remke in order to stress the positive meaning of this
term. Cf. also Mill: "mind may be described as the sentient *subject* (in the scholastic sense of this
term) of all feelings; that which has or feels them." Mill has a right to speak in this way because he
considers his I "as distinct from these sensations, thoughts, etc." Mill 2009: 40.

[53] Lipps speaks about "belongings" (*Zugehörigkeit*), but for him "the proper meaning of the word
'consciousness' is the I." [Lipps 1909: 5f.] This is why he starts his "description" with the "I." Is it
so amazing that his analysis of the "experience of consciousness" refers only to the I?

distinguish the two sorts of the "possessive" relationship that depend on the two sorts of "the content of consciousness." Such a division, consequently, ought to save us from "subjectivism." How is this possible, though, if in both instances the other member of the relationship is always the same "I"?

Losskij says, "This 'possession' is of two sorts, each sharply distinguished from the other. Certain contents of consciousness are immediately experienced as *manifestations of my I* (happiness, desire, etc.). On the other hand, other contents of consciousness (the observed 'blue' color of the sky, the 'rigidity' of iron, the 'oscillation of a pendulum,' etc.) are immediately experienced as something that is *foreign to my I*. They enter into the sphere of my consciousness only as 'given to me,' only so long as I direct my attention to them, only so long as I 'have them in mind.' There is no dispute that the contents of the first sort are always recognized as *psychic* and belong to the *inner* world of the subject. On the other hand, those of the second sort are seen immediately, without the help of any theory, as belonging to the *external* (transsubjective) world, similar to the way naive realism construes them...." Thus, the *"foreign to my I"* is at the same time what the I "possesses," and so the I "possesses," for example, the "rigidity" of iron, etc. Furthermore, this *"foreign to my I"* is "given to me" as long as "I have them in mind." However, with the *psychic*, it seems, this is not the case? But, then, what kind of liberation from "psychologism" and "geneticism" is this? The "psychic," as the object of psychology, is as "transsubjective" as is the "physical." And if Losskij understands the "psychic" as pure consciousness, what does he mean by the "subject" with its *inner* world? Surely, here is our *fraudulent* "I"! And why are "ideas of the world, of the psyche," etc. "theories," while an idea of the "subject" is not? Finally, why does Losskij hold that there are only *two sorts* of contents of consciousness? Truly, the division appears quite irreproachable, a pure dichotomy: "mine" and "not-mine" or "foreign to me." The error lies elsewhere: It is envisioned not by the logic of the division, but precisely in the preconceived theory. Losskij wants to divide up the "content of consciousness," but in fact he severed *the content of consciousness that is united in the I*. Naturally in his view the "I" is present in both members of the division. For this reason there remain quite unforeseen problems: (1) Can we, perhaps, ascertain consciousness apart from the I? (2) Can we, perhaps, find consciousness elsewhere besides in the I? Accordingly, Losskij selected his examples so that they all plainly begin with the "I." However, even in Losskij's adduced examples one thing sharply breaks the harmony of the entire construction: "I know that $2 \times 2 = 4$." "Twice two is four" is a certain "content" of consciousness. However, where do we assign it? Do we assign it to the first sort along with "happiness," "desire," etc. or to the second sort along with "the blue color of the sky," "the rigidity of iron," etc., i.e., to the *psychic* or to the *transsubjective*? In any case, it is, apparently, not a "manifestation of my I," but what basis do we have to refer it to the *"external* (transsubjective) world"? In general, it does not belong to any subject; $2 \times 2 = 4$ is a relation that holds apart from any subject. If we undertake to analyze this expression as a judgment that is a part of consciousness, we are not duty bound to justify any theory. In our analysis, we do not even think of the existence of a "subject," and, consequently, we do not have to turn to any "transsubjectivity." A philosophical and logical analysis of this expression will be as "impersonal" as a mathematical analysis of it, as impersonal as a multiplication table. This is probably why Losskij does not say "$2 \times 2 = 4$," but says "I know that this is so." However, the question arises: What is the importance to the relationship, to two times two, whether N. Losskij or any genuine or phony "I" knows it or not? Another so-and-so might indeed find such knowledge to be laudable. However, such knowledge is of absolutely no importance to the relationship itself, just as it is of no importance that it is *not only* Losskij who knows this relationship, but others also know it or in any case *could* know it. There is only one "I" that cannot know about this, namely, the general, transcendental, epistemological, fraudulent I. It cannot know anything, for otherwise it would not be fraudulent.

There is something else in Losskij's example that we cannot silently overlook. "I am happy" = "I have happiness"; "I want to listen to music" = "I have a desire to listen to music," etc. Or we can continue with Losskij's examples: "the felt happiness, the desired listening to music, the seen stars, and so forth." It is unfortunate that Losskij stops with "the seen stars," since it is not easy to ascertain what this "and so forth" is without his help. How does one analyze: "It is known that $2 \times 2 = 4$"? ... I will now turn to the direct objects of the expression "I have." "I know that $2 \times 2 = 4$" = "I have knowledge..." – Here our rephrasing *breaks down*. Instead of "twice two is four" we have to say "I have knowledge that $2 \times 2 = 4$." Are these two truly only a matter of syntax? *In terms of meaning*, is it really the same to say, "I know Alexander Ivanovich," or "I know the multiplication tables," and "I know *that* Alexander Ivanovich is something, e.g., my mentor," or "I know *that* the multiplication tables are foreign (or not foreign) to my I"? This little word "that" plays a rather large role. (I will simply remind you that by means of it Meinong defines his notion of "Objective.") Among other things, it is precisely this little word that signals an entry into the topic to be under discussion – even though it be *my* discussion. Such a relationship by itself has nothing to do with my I.

I will repeat once again that, of course, if we begin our analysis of consciousness with an analysis of the I, we will come to the fact that we find the I to be present everywhere, provided we simply remember enough not to forget just what it is we are investigating. If we are investigating consciousness itself, we will find that it is always a consciousness of *something*. This "something" is found to be a system of relations in which the presence of the I is optional. It may be present here, but it may also not be. However what is particularly important is that since this is an investigation of pure consciousness, of pure directedness to something, or pure intentionality, we are not obligated to begin with the I as the unique form of the unity of consciousness. Without saying anything about the complete intelligibility of such expressions as the "moral consciousness of humanity," "the religious consciousness of the first Christians," "the scientific consciousness of the Enlightenment era," "the political consciousness of the Russian nation," etc., let us turn our attention simply to such descriptions as "the evening at NN's place was boring," "it was terrifying in the city," "the audience was excited," "all of Russia is amazed at the news of the treasonous act," etc. What these expressions want to convey in this way are not the judgments of some so-and-so, who happens, for example, to "notice," "find," or "hear" this, but something quite different. Whereas the "boredom," "dismay," "amazement," etc. that are mentioned are "states of consciousness," the unity of this consciousness is sometimes directly indicated (that of the "audience," or of "Russia"), only it is not the unity of an "I." So, at least a fact is ascertained, and one can now *ad majorem Meimet gloriam* concoct as many theories as one wants including theories, I venture to say, of some sort about cellular psychology or theory of knowledge. However, a fact remains a fact.

16. Finally, let us turn to a third example. *Paul Natorp* is one of the most prominent representatives of contemporary transcendental idealism and a most industrious disciple of the so-called "Marburg School," which has done so much to overcome Kant and his subjective philosophy. We begin directly with the assertion: "Nothing can be an Object except to a subject or consciousness. To every Objective thing that is cognized or accepted there lies a contrasting subjectivity (*das Gegenverhältnis zur Subjektivität*). For every subject, there must be an Object (*dem Subjekt soll das Objekt gelten*). The Objective is indeed set against the subjective and at the same time is placed in an inseparable relation to it."[54] Therefore, from the very start it is all the same to Natorp whether it is the "subject or consciousness." Likewise, the correlativity of the subject, as consciousness, to the Object or of the subject, as the epistemological and cognizing subject, to the "cognized and accepted" Object makes no difference to him. However, let us drop all talk of a theory of cognition – which is a separate philosophical fraud – and stick simply to an analysis of *consciousness*. It is indisputable that consciousness is correlative to what is intended, and if we agree to call consciousness the "subject" and what is intended the "Object," then certainly there is no Object without a subject and no subject without an Object. However, you know one is supposed to compile the "conditions" "correctly" and "without any trickery." In any case, they are supposed to be observed. Natorp's "trick" is revealed when it turns out that his "subject" is also the "I" and as such is not "consciousness" but only a moment within consciousness. We then end up fundamentally with everything that we saw in Teichmüller and Losskij. In fact, that "something is an object of consciousness" Natorp sees as a hidden indication of "an I (or You or He, etc.)" and states "on the whole there are three moments which are closely connected into one in the term 'consciousness,' but which nevertheless can be distinguished through abstraction: (1) the something that someone is conscious of; (2) the something or someone who is conscious of something; (3) the relation between the two: that someone is conscious of something. Simply for brevity, I call the first the *content*, the second the *I*, and the third *awareness* (*Bewusstheit*)."[55] I will not start arguing that it so *happens*,

---

[54] Natorp 1912: 22. Cf. Natorp 1888: 11ff; Natorp 1904 and Natorp 1910.

[55] [Natorp 1912: 24.]

as Natorp depicts, that we can distinguish the mentioned moments in some lived experiences or in some acts of consciousness, but I do doubt that his analysis is an adequate expression of *every* act, indeed, of *every* unity of consciousness. This, indeed, is certainly the entire issue. Natorp himself glosses over his doubts by his very courageous parenthetical clarification, namely "(or You or He, etc.)," even though he should have recognized it as fatal. Does this mean his "I" is not universal? Or is it the very same universal "You" or "He"? And is not the "I" present in the "You" as a necessary moment and the "He" in the "I"? This would be a surprising result for subjectivism! And what does the "etc." mean here? Does it mean "She" and "It" or also "We"? Should we not then expect the appearance of some neotero- or neotato-Kantians,[56] who reveal to us that subjectivism proper is a *communality*? But the fact of the matter it seems is not so pretentious. It is simply a matter of terminological scope. The word "or" does not have here an explanatory but an exclusionary sense: today you, but tomorrow me. However, if it is *not* the case that *every* act of consciousness reveals the presence of the "I," then the first question that arises is: *When* does this happen? I gave examples above where I could find no presence of the I. It is essential in all of these cases that consciousness be directed toward some content, the "subject" or the bearer of which, however, cannot be called an I. Conversely, is it now impossible to say that the I is found in a lived experience or in an act of consciousness when it serves as the "object" toward which consciousness is directed at a given moment? But it is precisely here that we encounter the chief stumbling block on the part of Natorp, which must be subjected to a special examination. Therefore, we will put this question aside for now in order to return to it later.

17. Now let us turn once again to Natorp's analysis. He also makes an attempt to designate the relation between "being conscious" and the "object of consciousness" as one of "awareness." This may be more subtle than "possession," but such a designation loses all of its charm, if we recall that "under our condition" consciousness is a subject. Consequently, it simply here is a matter of *subjectivity*. Owing to the general sense of Natorp's division, which brooks no exceptions, every relation between consciousness and its content is subjective. This is the theory from which Natorp starts out, and it is therefore pointless when he speaks as though an immediate lived experience is found here. The condition itself was formed "incorrectly": consciousness, the subject and the I are quite different things, and it is impossible to substitute one for the other. What can actually be found in every lived experience is a correlation between consciousness and the object of consciousness, something that is immanent and something that is transcendent. Further analysis reveals the specific features of each side. We can examine one or the other absolutely, but once we come upon their

---

[56] [The suffixes *–tero* and *–tato* were added to Greek words to make comparative forms of the adjective stem. Shpet is here, most likely, writing facetiously as though we could speak of neo-Kantians (or new-Kantians), then neotero-Kantians (or newer Kantians), and then neotato-Kantians (or most recent Kantians).]

correlation, we are obliged to carry out our analysis on the basis of this correlation so that each statement about one side of the correlation necessarily has a corresponding statement about the other side. In finding such a simple and originarily given thing as the manifold of some "consciousness," we thereby find the manifold of the "object of consciousness" and vice versa. Each manifold is, in turn, correlative to a unity, and we start speaking of a "unity of consciousness." Do we need a special term for this unity? Let us take any manifold: the table, the dog, the world, the Thirty Years' War, Tatiana's letter, Roman Law – all of these are unities, unities of manifolds. Why, when we speak of the unity of consciousness, do we have to have a separate designation for it? Because in one way or another subjectivism as a theory must be justified. There can be no other answer. A table is a unity of a manifold, but who would think to assert that this *unity* "possesses" its features, or that this unity stands to its features in a relation of "tableness," etc.? Obviously, some will understand this "unity" to be not a simple "union" of features, but something that evokes, causes, obtains or bears them. In short, some want to justify a *theory* of substantiality, of subjectivity or some such thing. I am not saying anything against these theories, as theories, for example that certain ones are better and others worse. What I am saying is that it is impossible to claim that these are not theories, but an immediate lived experience. Furthermore, as soon as a "subject" appears, it is immediately qualified as the correlate of an Object: There is no subject without an Object, and there is no Object without a subject. We recognized that a consciousness is correlative to the Object of consciousness. However, what is the subject here? And what is the Object? If we could actually establish some subject as the bearer or originator and so forth of consciousness, then its content would also amount to consciousness itself, i.e., acts of consciousness, and not the object of consciousness. Surely, it is precisely what is intended that is called the "Object" here! Pure subjectivism, i.e., illusionism, is logically more honest: There is the I (the subject) and my consciousness (the Object) and nothing more. Subjectivism in disguise: the I (the subject) and my consciousness (+ that which is intended = the Object). A correlation is obtained between the I and what is intended, which also perhaps, in some senses, cannot be denied insofar as it is a matter of the I, as a so-and-so, provided only that such a correlation does not overstep the bounds of the so-and-so. Here, the reverse is established. What is happening is the already mentioned *conversio simplex*: The intended belongs to the I. In order to avoid "solipsism," the I must be taken not as a so-and-so, but as the I, which amounts to a moment in any consciousness. However, it is not enough to say "a moment in consciousness." No, consciousness itself is the I! A so-and-so is already unnecessary. It can be eliminated. Psychologism is overcome. One thing is true: It is impossible to cut the hair of someone who is wearing a wig. But no matter how much subjectivism disguises every so-and-so under a single "general I," it fails to achieve one thing. Although perhaps the subjectivists do manage to get used to the idea that this "wig" amounts to a necessary accessory of every lived experience and that they see it as immediately present in every lived experience, this does not make us see every so-and-so as being born wearing such a wig.

18. However, am I not myself eliminating the so-and-so? Surely, if all that is originarily given is consciousness and the object of consciousness, without any relation to an I, a kind of "impersonal" consciousness, is this not a monstrous paradox, something grotesque, as though there could be a consciousness belonging to *no one*, and as though an analysis of consciousness and what is intended gives us everything in the world except their owner, the I: the Object alone with no subject whatever? Certainly, this question is only rhetorical on my part. I dare not suspect the reader of misunderstanding everything said above, just as I dare not suspect the reader of harboring a skepticism concerning my sanity. In fact, I only want to say that consciousness is not "no one's," since every so-and-so finds it within oneself. However, it is merely the consciousness of a so-and-so, and this so-and-so is mistaken if he or she thinks that one's own consciousness is the only one possible. It is *not only* this so-and-so who has consciousness, nor is it merely his neighbor's. There can be and still are consciousnesses which, like that of this so-and-so, are unities but which do not belong to an I and which – if the I is the subject – cannot be called subjective. It is not some "general I," built entirely on the basis of the elimination and negation of the I, of this so-and-so, and which would therefore be in the full sense *no one's*. The so-and-so has one's own consciousness, which is not reducible to anyone else's and which is, on occasion, even inaccessible, or "inexpressible," to others. Likewise, these unities can each also have their own, "expressible" consciousness, though it is not accessible and not comprehensible to any so-and-so. This does not amount to the fact, though, that consciousness belongs *only* to a so-and-so. A so-and-so can know about something, but at the same time he also knows that it is *not his* or *not only his*, that, in any case, he is not in such an instance the subject of consciousness in the sense of a *materia in qua*. This is the essential point. However, although I do not believe in the dogma of subjectivism, as though there is no Object without a subject, it is clear that speaking in this way about some so-and-so and about other unities of consciousness, I also cannot accept a "bare" Object *in se*. The subject, *id in quo*, is itself an object. It must be sought in the objective, i.e., in what is intended. To transfer it into another member of the correlation, as the foundation, source and principle of consciousness deprives it, above all, of the distinctive features that are uniquely peculiar to it. Inasmuch as they do not "pity" it, take away from it its special features, they perpetrate an inadmissible *substitution* and force it to live with the forged passport of a *Kannitverstan*.[57]

19. Let us pause a bit longer on the question of "whose" consciousness consciousness is. However obvious the legitimacy of this question may seem, there is no need for us to hurry to answer it. I should simply remind you of Vladimir Solovyov's warning: "The fact is that not only must every answer be examined

---

[57] [A reference to a character in Zhukovskij 1907: 115–124. The character Zhukovskij is drawn from a German short story, "Kannitverstan," by Johann Peter Hebel from 1808.]

by rigorous thought – the same is required for every question. In everyday life we can ask, without giving it a second thought: whose coat? or, whose galoshes? But by what right may we ask in philosophy: whose consciousness? – thereby assuming the real presence of various selves to which we must give consciousness as private or communal property? The very question is simply a philosophically inadmissible expression of dogmatic certainty as to the independent and self-identical existence of individual beings. But it is precisely this certainty that needs examination and justification by indisputable logical deductions from self-evident data. ... In the present state of affairs, to the question *whose* consciousness is this or *to whom* do the given psychic facts (the facts which form the starting point of philosophical discussion) belong, one can and should answer: *it is not known;...*"[58] This really must be our starting point. The I is, precisely speaking, a problem, and it is in no way either a foundation or a principle. On the contrary, taken as the starting point of philosophy, concern for the I can only distort the analysis of consciousness itself, anticipating a pure description of the facts by preconceived theories. It does not matter whether the I is understood to be a "general" I, a transcendental I or a single, individual I, that is, this so-and-so. Again, I will appeal to another Russian philosopher: "Therefore, having proclaimed the individual to be the supreme principle in philosophy and regardless of whether we take it as an individuality or as universal subjectivity, we come to illusionism and fall into a host of opposing contradictions. *Having posited personal self-consciousness as the starting point and at the same time the supreme principle and criterion of philosophy, we are unable to explain to ourselves our consciousness of ourselves.*"[59]

Clearly, once there are arguments against the allegedly immediately given fact that every consciousness is a consciousness belonging to an I, the "personal" character of consciousness is not a self-evident thing. And the ironic question "*Whose* consciousness is this?" does not, in any case, then, carry such deadly force. In claiming that consciousness can be non-personal, we are not asserting its impersonality. We are only saying that it can also be superpersonal, multipersonal and even individual. To put it simply and briefly, consciousness can be *not just* personal. The opposite assertion is not obvious, and demands proof. Natorp, incidentally, has an argument: "The phrase 'to be an object of consciousness' contains, as it were, the condensed general sense of the expression: 'Something is an object of consciousness for me or for someone'."[60]

---

[58] Solovyov 1965: 130. Solovyov examines this question in close connection with that of the *reality* of the unity of consciousness. For the time being, I am intentionally not dealing with this question, inserting here only a portion of my notes on the question of the unity of consciousness. However, I still want to return to this theme and examine in detail the articles by Solovyov and L. M. Lopatin's response to them. E. N. Trubeckoj, who has recently revived this dispute, has not, in my view, provided *all* the conclusions that can still be drawn from the presuppositions of Solovyov's unfinished work.

[59] Trubeckoj 1994: 489. Emphasis added.

[60] Natorp 1912: 24. Konstantin Oesterreich in his very informative and interesting book, Oesterreich 1910: 225, quite categorically asserts: "...it is impossible to evade the question: 'Who perceives?,'

However, for us, the entire puzzle lies here in the words "for someone." To whom does Natorp cede a right to consciousness? After everything that subjective philosophy has told us, this is a pointless question. However, does it follow from the "infinitive" above that *only* the I is conscious? Or is the grammatical word "we" philosophically the same I?

In the article cited above, S.N. Trubeckoj connects subjectivism's appearance and its successes with the dissemination of Protestant philosophy and finds a completely different understanding of consciousness in ancient and medieval philosophy. "Medieval scholasticism, just like Greek philosophy, did not directly raise the issue of the individuality of consciousness... Therefore, the logical and psychological principle of medieval, or more precisely general Christian, thought was exceptionally broader than Protestant subjectivism. Along with the personal basis of human consciousness the possible communal nature of this consciousness was also recognized as obvious."[61] Whatever the connection between subjectivism and Protestantism may be, only the latter fact is important to us. In philosophy, a recognition of the specifically personal nature of consciousness, its subjective character and that it belongs only to an I, is by no means universal. The matter would certainly be different if consciousness essentially had to belong to an I and if this were an immediately given and obvious fact. Modern philosophy begins simply with an analysis of consciousness – cogitatio, but there is no obvious data that would entitle its leading names, Descartes, Spinoza and Leibniz, to connect it with subjectivist theories or for "rationalism" on the whole to recognize the I as essential for consciousness. It is true that in the eighteenth century we can find some insignificant figures whose theories were at the time characterized as an "egoism," but the genuine start of a fundamental subjectivism – albeit with a fraudulent subject – is with Kant and Fichte. The problem, properly speaking, of the "individual" was posed, of course, earlier, and post-Lockean philosophy allotted a prominent place to it. We might also think that ancient and medieval philosophy were blind, but once the problem was raised philosophy, as it were, "saw the light." Nevertheless, we encounter the facts regarding a categorical rejection of the immediate givenness of a self-identical I. Already Leibniz, as we saw, pointed to the fact that for him to be convinced of the identity of his I "while in the cradle" as well as at the moment of his polemic with Locke, he had to recall "relations with others."[62]

In any case, this should not be misunderstood. Neither Leibniz nor any other so-and-so of the ancient, medieval or contemporary world would be troubled by

---

'Who apperceives?,' 'Who represents?,' etc. Invariably, the only answer can be to say: Some I perceives, apperceives, etc. Essentially, a moment of the subject is inseparable from all these processes." If this were so, then in my view it, nevertheless, means only that it is essential for the "subject" to perceive, etc. but in no way that an "I" is essential for "consciousness."

[61] [Trubeckoj 1994: 492–3.]

[62] In one of his letters to Arno (June 1686), Leibniz additionally insists on the necessity of a "proof" and of an "a priori foundation" to the identity of the I.

the problem whether he is aware of himself. The answer would be an indubitable "*yes*." But when he begins to tell us about his I, he already cannot say that it is given to him also immediately in its entirety. On the contrary, it presents itself to him as an "object," the content of which is revealed in a very complicated way and by no means through some immediate ascertaining. But what's more, analyzing one's own consciousness, a so-and-so will have to recognize that *not everything* in it is essentially connected with the I. Finally, in wishing to express one's "idea" of oneself, this so-and-so must also treat it in the same way as in the transition from what is empirically given in an object to its idea. Whereas consciousness itself in its essence stands before oneself, it is only in its ideal givenness, and in this sense it is not one's own consciousness, the consciousness of this empirical so-and-so. The question now is whether an ideal I, an ideal so-and-so, is essential for this consciousness. We answer "No." It is not essential, because the consciousness of an ideal I is not only one's own consciousness and not entirely only his entire consciousness. Precisely here we find intruding the idea of a "general I," of a "subject" belonging to no one, which, transgressing the individuality of the so-and-so, pretends to embrace the "entire" consciousness. In this way, the authentic I, the so-and-so, is eliminated, and the fraudulent "I" begins to play a role that the so-and-so cannot pretend to do, namely, the role of a philosophical foundation and principle. Now, we are faced with verifying whether it is correct that only this so-and-so is an I, and there is no other I whatever. But, then, are the other unities of consciousness of another type and sense than the I, as a so-and-so?

20. The classical expression of a doubt in the immediate givenness and evidence of the I – taken not simply as the "I" of a *moment*, but precisely as something stable that is ascertained to be the "bearer" or "subject" of consciousness – is found in Hume. Hume certainly harbored not the slightest doubt that *his* consciousness is precisely *his* consciousness, and that consequently our idea of ourselves is always within us and immediately present to us.[63] Nevertheless, his well-known chapter "Of personal identity" begins with the words: "There are some philosophers, who imagine we are every moment intimately conscious of what we call our SELF; that we feel its existence and its continuance in existence; and are certain, beyond the evidence of a demonstration, both of its perfect identity and simplicity."[64] In place of this, he advances his theory of the "connexion of perceptions." Certainly more important than this, however, is his testimony from immediate experience: "I never can catch *myself* at any time without a perception, and never can observe any thing but the perception."[65] Actually what Hume doubts, above all, is the substantiality of the I and its separation from lived experiences. The question of substantiality is of no interest to

---

[63] "Ourself is always intimately present to us." Hume 1968: 329. Cf. Hume 1968, in particular part II, Of the Passions (According to the Selby-Bigge edition, Hume 1968: 307, 320, 339, 340, 354, 427).

[64] [Hume 1968: 251.]

[65] [Hume 1968: 252.]

us at the moment, but such a "separation" is either a theoretical problem or a problem with the definition of the concept of substance. As the literature noted and, in particular, as L.M. Lopatin clearly showed, there is nothing contradictory in the indivisibility of a substance. More importantly, Hume also doubted the identity and the continuity of the I. As we recognized based on Leibniz's observations, there are grounds for such a doubt. However, we would now like to push to the foreground one consequence of this doubt. Since for the I, which finds itself in each of its lived experiences, a doubt in the identity and the continuity of this I is possible, and since the sole means to verify it lies in an appeal to another's experience, we recognize that the *object* of this doubt is an object *not only* for the doubting I. That is, this object is also "another's" consciousness or those of "others." There are no grounds to think that these other consciousnesses, as unities, are identical or even similar to the doubting consciousness. On the contrary, even if we are convinced that the other's I is always similar in appearance to mine, then already the simple fact of our *communal consciousness* speaks of some new, peculiar form of consciousness. Consequently, my I turns out to be an object *not only* for me. From the very start, the I is decisively distinguished from my lived experiences, which can *only* be mine.

Hume did not draw these conclusions although he had grounds for directing his thought in this direction.[66] He preferred to seek substantiation for his theory of the "connexion of perceptions." However, it was in essence only a matter of ascertaining an isolated moment within the stream of consciousness, of an isolated lived experience. As soon as Hume sought to pass beyond these limited confines and resorted to "memory" he fell into a difficulty from which he could not escape but which he honestly recognized: "But upon a more strict review of the section concerning personal identity, I find myself involv'd in such a labyrinth, that, I must confess, I neither know how to correct my former opinions, nor how to render them consistent."[67] Remarkably, however, Hume, in spite of this, did not think it possible to accept the views that he had opposed. In his eyes, the *arguments* of the advocates of an *immediate* recognition of the I's identity remain unconvincing. Consequently, for Hume the "I" ultimately cannot be established even to be the so-and-so – although, of course, Hume could not deny its reality. However, in all likelihood he would in return rise up against our "ideal I." From the point of view of such an extreme nominalist, like Hume, this would only be a matter of consistency. In any case, Hume, on the whole, rejects the I as a subject but does not reject the I as an Object. Consequently, if there is any immediate givenness of the I, this givenness would be of another

---

[66] Namely, in his theory of sympathy. For example, he says: "Tis also evident, that the ideas of affections of others are converted into the very impressions they represent, and that the passions arise in conformity to the images we form of them" (Hume 1968: 319, Cf. Hume 1968: 369 and other places). This conversion is already a theory and explanation, and we can argue against it, but it is indisputable that the mentioned conformity is indicative of some "communal consciousness" in the feeling of "sympathy" but not of a new "I."

[67] [Hume 1968: 633.]

sort than that which is found by the subjectivists who recognize that every consciousness is a consciousness belonging to the I alone.

21. Mill quite correctly recognized that once we speak of the "I" as a *subject*, and of lived experiences as its "possession," the I is thereby placed "outside" the processes of consciousness. This alone already means that it cannot be the object of an immediate givenness, but that it appears to be the result of a hypothetical or deductive construction. In *An Examination of Sir William Hamilton's Philosophy*, Mill insists that we not only do not have a conception of the I distinct from the phenomena of consciousness, but in general he also rejects the view that in our experience we have from the outset a conception of the I as continuously existing. He asserts that there is no basis for holding, along with Hamilton and Mansel, that the I (ego) is the original conception of consciousness. However, in declaring that there is no more basis to assert the presence of the I in each moment of consciousness than there is in asserting the presence of some non-I, Mill goes too far. For by doing so Mill rejects not only the *subjectivity of the I* but its *objectivity* as well. This is simply a consistent result of Mill's phenomenalism, but ultimately he, like Hume, is conscientiously aware that phenomenalism is not equal to the task. Nevertheless, he shows no greater inclination than did Hume to recognize the arguments of the opposing viewpoint as convincing.

22. Let us pause briefly on one example which is particularly instructive, because: (1) it concerns our own era in which subjectivism reigns as the dominant philosophical trend; and (2) with it we once again encounter an exceptionally conscientious investigator, who really undertakes his work free of "theories"[68] – and yet nevertheless succumbs to theory. There is reason for us to think that in opposing Natorp's well-known analysis, Husserl was to some extent under the influence of Mill's *Examination*. In the first edition of his *Logical Investigations*, Husserl categorically asserts: "I must frankly confess, however, that I am quite unable to find this ego, this primitive, necessary centre of relations. The only thing I can take note of, and therefore perceive, are the empirical ego and its empirical relations to its own experiences, or to such external objects as are receiving special attention at the moment, while much remains, whether 'without' or 'within,' which has no such relation to the ego."[69] This much is clear.

---

[68] [Cf. Husserl 2014: 52 (§30) – "In these investigations we keep theories, that is to say, pre-conceptions of every kind, strictly at a distance."]

[69] Husserl 1970: 549–550. Oesterreich replies to Husserl's argument with the following analogy: We are not always conscious of the I as the center point of an act, just as in hearing music we do not always notice the rustle of pages being turned and so forth, although undoubtedly we do hear it (Oesterreich 1910: 235). In such an observation, however, there is obviously a confusion of an *empirical* situation and the *essential* moments in that very act. Who can dispute that the empirical I is present in every experiential act of the I? But what is disputable is Oesterreich's statement (Oesterreich 1910: 236): "To perceive, to read and to ponder are conceivable only as the acts of perceiving, reading and thinking of some subject." These examples by no means exhaust the sphere of consciousness. However, even among them, "reading" is essentially an "overstepping" of the bounds of "subjective" consciousness, and is a purely "social" act or process. Moreover, how do

Here, he can only raise the issue of the "empirical I" and of its "eidos." Yet, in the second edition Husserl already recognizes a special "I" as the "necessary centre of relations" and writes, "I have since managed to find it."[70] This "pure ego," as Husserl now calls it, is nothing other than "the subject of a pure experience of the type *cogito*."[71] The latter proviso, as we will see, is very important. Nevertheless, can we avoid lumping Husserl among the "subjectivists" and as a representative of that Ego psychology which Stumpf so energetically dismisses?

We find some clarification in Husserl's *Ideas*. He writes, "In reflection, every implemented cogitatio takes on the explicit form of the cogito" (§57).[72] We must understand what the expression *Ego cogito* means. Indeed, it turns out that in reflection consciousness belongs to the I. We recognized this, because it is self-evident. Hume did not deny it; Husserl himself earlier also probably recognized it. However, Husserl later asserts that in the stream of lived experiences something remains as the object of phenomenology, i.e., after the so-called phenomenological reduction of everything empirical and real. Although nowhere in this stream do we come upon the pure I as a lived experience like the others, it, nevertheless, belongs to every lived experience that flows by. *The I is an identical something.* In principle, every cogitatio *can* change – even though we doubt that it presents itself as *necessarily* ephemeral and not just *factually* ephemeral. On the contrary, the pure I is necessary *in principle*; it is absolutely identical throughout all the real and possible changes in lived experiences, and *in no sense can it appear to be a real part or moment* of a lived experience. But how then did Husserl come to this identical I? Contrary to his habit and contrary to his own "principle of all principles," which demands evidence of originary givenness, Husserl does not provide any evidence. Here, to me, is how the matter stands: Having excluded the empirical I in the phenomenological reduction, Husserl can retain the ideal (eidetic) I only as an *object*, but by no means as the subject of consciousness. And then in the "transcendental residuum," as the object of phenomenology, a pure consciousness would remain, but it would be, so to speak, *no one's*. This indefiniteness now introduces the temptation of subjectivism: A positing of the I at the *foundation* of consciousness itself, as its condition or as the condition of its unity. For Husserl, in other words, this means an alteration of his principles and an introduction of theory where there is no need of it.

---

we explain, for example, a "joint" reading? Or if we say, for example, "*Quel giorno piu non leggemmo avante,*" ["*That day we read no further....*"]. Dante 2012: Canto 5, line 138] do we concur with Oesterreich that "all psychic life is the life of an I and there is no bridge from one subject to another" (Oesterreich 1910: 250)?

[70] Husserl 1970: 549f. Nevertheless, it turns out that the problem of the "pure ego" *is irrelevant* to any of the "logical investigations." Husserl 1970: 551. How could this be possible if the "ego," or "I," actually is the *necessary center* of relations in consciousness?

[71] Husserl 1970: 544f.

[72] Husserl 2014: 105.

23. Perhaps, however, another consideration is even more important here. The empirical I, as a so-and-so, is one "thing" among the other things in our real world. An ideal I must also be correspondingly coordinated. It happens here, though, that the I turns out to be, as it were, on the same level as a "physical thing" and consequently, in accordance with Husserl's definition, is a *transcendence*. Just why does this conclusion stop Husserl?[73] After all, not only is there nothing paradoxical in this, but it is something that had to be recognized long ago! Certainly to be precise there is a difference between a *physical* thing and the so-and-so, but to elucidate this difference is not as easy as it seems. The point is not that the I, this so-and-so, is necessarily a "physical thing." Rather, the point is that a "physical thing" is a certain convention and is in any case an *abstraction* or a *part of a whole*. So as not to be verbose, let me explain it this way: in seeking an example of a "physical thing," we turn to the *things surrounding us*, and the favorite examples of philosophical mediations are our everyday objects – a table, a book, an apple, a block of wood, etc. Leaving aside, however, the difference between those that are organic and those that are inorganic, *all are, above all, social objects*. They are the products of work, culture, exchange, purchase and sale, etc., etc. The state of things is such that we do not even know *another* reality than social reality: Sirius, Vega and the most remote stars and nebuli are also for us social objects. For otherwise we not only would not have a name for them, but we could not call them "stars" or "nebulae." Actually, we can obtain a physical thing from this only as a result of abstraction or by separating a "part" from the "whole." It is thought that one has shown God knows what generosity by allowing oneself to call the "I" not only a "psyche," but also a "psycho-physical organism," and even on occasion an organism draped in clothes. Except in the last case, however, as the thorough Dr. Teufelsdröckh[74] already showed, everything else is an abstraction and is referred to by a common noun. This is why it cannot also be called an I, a so-and-so.

Therefore, the I is actually a "thing" alongside other things, although it is not the same as a physical thing. Nevertheless, it does precisely appear as a transcendence *sui generis*. Husserl himself says that the "pure Ego" is in no sense a part or moment of a lived experience. Consequently, it is not a moment of consciousness, but can be characterized then only as an objective transcendence. Husserl calls this *"peculiar"* transcendence a *"transcendence in immanence."*[75] But does this ornate combination of Latin terms provide any clarification of the matter? And if we are convinced that the I, the so-and-so, is a social thing, then for us it is only a matter of a generalization. For is not every social thing a transcendence in immanence?[76] In any case, the problem remains

---

[73] Cf. Husserl 1970: 544f.

[74] [The fictional character in Thomas Carlyle's work *Sartor Resartus*.]

[75] [Husserl 2014: 105.]

[76] As is well-known, the idea that the "social" is an objectivized subjective something (Spirit) comes chiefly from Hegel. At the present time, some defend this idea. I personally think that the

a problem and is not resolved by combining Latin terms. One thing, however, is clear, and it is that even with his altered formulation of the problem Husserl has no basis for recognizing, along with Natorp, that the I is a "foundation." That it is not a problem, as Natorp asserts, but the foundation and premise of every problem is, properly speaking, consistent subjectivism.

24. Let us return to Husserl's above-mentioned proviso that the I is the subject of lived experiences of the type *cogito*. Are all lived experiences of this type? Earlier, we contrasted the field of the intentional to the sphere of the "predetermined," and in analyzing Losskij's division we provided examples in which we believe the object does not always refer without fail to an I and only to an I. Husserl, actually, elaborates on his proviso. Other lived experiences (those not of the type *cogito*) that form a general milieu for the actuality of the I certainly do not have a distinctive relatedness to the I, but they do participate in the pure I and the latter in them. They "belong" to it as "its" lived experiences. They make up *its* background of consciousness, *its* field of freedom. However, by virtue of the peculiar interweaving of all lived experiences with the I, the latter cannot be taken *by itself* and made the Object *proper* of an investigation. Apart from its "relations," the I is empty; it has no explicable content and in itself is indescribable: the pure I and nothing more.[77] Above all, we can assert that this still does not exhaust the types of cogitatio itself, since along with the form *cogito* we find the form *cogitamus*, which is irreducible to the former either by means of addition or multiplication. However, even within the bounds of the *cogito* and, consequently, *committing* ourselves in the name of consistency to stick with the I, we still come upon "other lived experiences," which we cannot possibly avoid, experiences that, Husserl says, have their "share" in the I and the I its share in them. *This holds not merely for an I.* That is, there must be other unities of consciousness, since the I is a unity of the type *cogito*. However, another side in all of this is particularly worthy of attention. Husserl, certainly, is correct in holding that the I by itself cannot be described and cannot be the Object of an investigation. For it is a unity of consciousness and nothing more, though consciousness itself can be subjected to an investigation. However, the truly empirical I, the so-and-so, as well as the ideal I, though it be individual, concrete and indispensable, a unicum, can also be such an Object. In this way, Husserl obtained his "pure Ego," but not as the I appears in its direct givenness. It is clear from his explanations that Husserl's "pure Ego" is actually formed through an analogy with the actual I so far as there is a determination of the I's *milieu* (to use Husserl's term). In such a case, the I is not merely a "unity," but is subject to an all-round determination. It must be an *omnimode determinatum*. In accordance with what we determined earlier, the I must be determined in line with its predetermination as well as with its freedom. It must

---

relation here is actually mutual: The social is an objectivized subjectivity, but it is also a subjectivized objectivity. I am simply repeating the word "subject" for others, and I think that "the unity of consciousness" can be both subjective as well as collective.

[77] Husserl 2014: 153–55 (§80).

be rationally motivated. Husserl himself recognizes that his "pure Ego" must be "intrinsically different for each stream of lived experiences."[78] We obtain here a striking paradox[79]: the I, the so-and-so, is something individual, concrete, particular and even ungeneralizable. Consequently, reality in its immensity presents an infinite plenitude of content, an inexhaustible wealth. This is the case not only empirically, but essentially and fundamentally. Then suddenly Husserl has nothing to say about this I by itself, i.e., the I in its particularity and singularity: the pure Ego and nothing more! Would it not be more correct to say that there simply is nothing? That is, that nothing can be said, that nothing need be said and simply that there is *nothing* to say about this I, because it is not an I at all. The real, genuine I, the so-and-so, is, as we saw, a social "thing." It is, just like the social "we," an "object of consciousness." It is, for example, Ivan Ivanovich, both as an empirical being together with his narrowly construed way of life as well as his ideal and enduring essence. He is not some intentional subject. Consequently, the I has its own content, its object and its sense. Philosophically, it is a problem and not a foundation or presupposition.

25. Of course, from the point of view of subjectivism, which recognizes its fictitious I to be a foundation, this I cannot itself be a problem. Natorp quite persistently defends this position, apparently without noticing the contradictions and difficulties into which his own presuppositions plunge him. This much seems clear. Although we cannot understand how we can speak about the I, a fact remains a fact. This is something basic. If our presuppositions can lead us nowhere, we must either repudiate them or frankly acknowledge, as Hume and Mill did, that no resolution of this aporetic problem is to be had. However, after Kant can we really speak of insoluble problems? ... Natorp says, "To be an I means not to be an object, but to stand in a relationship to objects without which something cannot be an object."[80] If this is meant to be a *definition*, an objection could be leveled against its narrow scope. For it is incomprehensible why something is an object with respect to the I, but with respect to another object, it seems, it will not be an object. However, even for Natorp this is not a definition, but a "thesis," which he tries to prove. It would seem here, though, that since the I cannot be an object of consciousness, it cannot be the object of a proof, a discussion, or a conversation. It also cannot be the object of a fraud or even of an hallucination. Regarding the I, Natorp argues: "Consciousness, as we said, is a relation which, as such, needs two terms. It cannot be satisfied by one alone. Consequently, if we say that we have a consciousness of ourselves, we artificially double what nevertheless by itself must be absolutely one; we (artificially) make ourselves into an object. This means, then, that what we are conscious of in this act is no longer the original I, which is conscious of this fact. For the original I is precisely the subject (i.e., that which has a conscious-

---

[78] Husserl 2014: 105. [Translation slightly modified.]

[79] Many contemporary thinkers do not notice this paradox. Cf., for example, Schuppe 1878: 82 and Messer 1914: 359.

[80] Natorp 1912: 29.

ness of something). It cannot be at the same time also an object of the same act of consciousness (i.e., what we are conscious of in it). I conclude from this that the object of the act that we call self-consciousness must no longer be the original I, but a derivative one."[81] What we get here as the Object is merely a fiction. "However, the subject is not fictional. In any case, the I is the one who is distinguishing. Consequently, the object must be purely fictional. That is to say, it is not the original I but something else, some 'content,' through which the I is represented."[82] Just as the retina cannot see itself except in a reflection from a mirror, so we can speak of the I, as an Object, but not in the literal sense: as in a mirror, the I is reflected through its content.

Natorp's reference to the correlativity of consciousness is a reference to an actual and indisputable fact. It is quite correct that every consciousness is a consciousness of *something*. However, we saw how a substitution can take place here: The I as a hypothetical subject (in the contemporary sense of the word, i.e., as a "general I") takes the place of consciousness; and this I then turns out to be correlative to what is intended as its Object (also in the contemporary sense, i.e., Object = not-I). In precisely this way, it turns out that consciousness is not merely the consciousness of *something*, but also *one's* consciousness, not any *someone's* but precisely *one's*, specifically that of the "general I." However, leaving aside this substitution we must recognize that because consciousness is a consciousness *of something*, it is necessarily directed to an object, and if we pause on this affirmation of *self-consciousness*, this "self" makes sense only as an object, whatever peculiarities it may show in comparison to other objects and whatever peculiarities are revealed in the correlative description of consciousness itself. In any case, the analogy with a "mirror" and "retina" is quite inappropriate here. We can make an analogy when the comparisons deal with whole items that have similar parts. A comparison of consciousness with the object of consciousness has by itself no more of a basis than the expression "it rained cats and dogs." And the only thing that Natorp's analogy can prove is the conclusion that there is no basis for comparing self-consciousness to a retina's seeing of itself in a mirror.

Examining the essence of Natorp's argument and even ignoring the fact that he *sometimes* identifies the I with consciousness, we must recognize that his argument goes too far, *nimium probat*.[83] For if it is correct, not only can the I not be an "object," but consciousness itself, as such, cannot be an object. "Experience," Natorp says, "is more original than any concept. Consequently,

---

[81] Natorp 1912: 30.

[82] Natorp 1912: 31. It is worth our while here to notice the truly Copernican approach of Natorp's thought. The experience that gives us the I is a fiction, but this I, as a "condition," is not a fiction! Nevertheless, this condition is constructed along a notorious pattern: If we do not accept this fact, then we cannot explain or demonstrate that fact. Where is the "fiction"? According to the quite competent definition of Hans Vaihinger, the author of the *Philosophy of As If*, a "fiction" is nothing other than "*a scientific invention with practical intent*" (*eine wissenschaftliche Erdichtung zu praktischen Zwecken*). Where, then, in Natorp is the "as if"?

[83] [Latin: "proves too much."]

from the very start it was absurd to demand a concept of it" (p. 32). Clearly, Bergson is forcing an already open door! However, we would contend just the reverse: Precisely because a lived experience is "more original" than its expression, it is in need of concepts. And if, as Natorp thinks, with a logical concept we "withdraw from the ultimate immediacy and originality of lived experience," this means only that we have *very bad* concepts that cannot express what is necessary. Is it simply incomprehensible how and why those same concepts become *good* when we need to express the thought that the I is not a problem and an object, but is the foundation and the subject? However, Natorp's reasoning is *nimium probant* still in other respects. Above all, all of his arguments actually are expressed using poor "modern" concepts. As for their content, the arguments are quite respectable given the age of the participants in the old campaigns against the possibility of "self-observation," "reflection," etc. I do not think that they are like useless invalids. On the contrary, the question is very serious, but since it is, as we saw, somewhat "excessive" I will limit myself simply to pointing this out. The only thing that I will venture to note is the extreme *nominalism* of Natorp's deduction. He operates with a "consciousness in general," and with the same ease with which he successfully deprives consciousness of objectivity he could object to the objectivity of a "horse in general" or an "auto-horse," or "auto-person" ($\alpha\dot{\upsilon}\tau o\dot{\alpha}\nu\theta\rho\omega\pi o\varsigma$), etc.

26. On the whole, however, it is necessary to recognize that in spite of the extreme banality of the assertion that there cannot be a "consciousness of consciousness," just as of course there cannot be a "movement of a movement," or an "oscillation of an oscillation," etc., the assertion itself is not nonsensical. In no way does it follow from this that "consciousness" cannot be "the Object of an investigation." If we do not make *two* different problems out of this, we can meet the natural objection: inasmuch as an "investigation" is a lived experience and a consciousness, it turns out that a "consciousness of consciousness" is possible. And if we actually do not want to admit here a secret *quaternio terminorum*, then we need only reveal the sense of the conditions under which this is possible. It appears that precisely because a "consciousness of consciousness" is impossible we speak of self-consciousness, i.e., we ascribe to consciousness some *subject* (in the old sense) as the object or the "bearer," as an *id in quo*. This is already sufficient in order to say that consciousness can be an "object" and is an "object." But in order for it to become an Object (taken also in the old sense: *Objectum est subject, circa quod aliquid versatur*[84]) we need only point out its "limits." We need to *terminate* it (because again: in *objecto terminantur actiones agentis*[85]). Therefore, it turns out that if we turn to consciousness, regardless of whether we take it in its parts or as a whole, as a disjunctive or as a collective unity, this "unity" appears as an object – not a "fictitious" but a *given* object. This is why there is a play on words here when we say "the subject is not fictitious. In any case, the I is the one who is distinguishing. Consequently, the

---

[84] [Micraelius 1679: column 729.]
[85] [Wolff 1736: 684 (§950).]

Object must be purely fictional."[86] But surely this also means that the "distinguishing" is a fiction! Well, with a fictional "condition" and "foundation," what is surprising about having a fictitious "Object"?

27. The result here is that if the I, in some sense, can be taken or defined as a "unity of consciousness," then it certainly is as an *object* of consciousness. Moreover, it is not difficult to see that the I, the so-and-so, in the actual, concrete sense of something individual and irreplaceable, just like any concrete unity of consciousness, simply lies within the sphere of what is intended and consequently appears as an *object* – and from a certain, for example, metaphysical point of view – appears even as an object *par excellence*. Consequently, "subjects" certainly are objects whether in the old or the new sense, and even the Fichtean formula "there is no subject without an Object, no Object without a subject" makes sense in terms of the assertion of a correlation between the objects themselves: *There is no object without another object.* An object is an object or becomes an object only with respect to another object or other objects. The I, the so-and-so, only exists as an object among objects – Pavel Ivanovich (Chichikov) in his nourishing and illustrious surroundings or "milieu," which is lit and warmed by his presence.[87] The I is an object, and there is nothing that would force it to conceive the correlative non-I as a non-object. However, the I by itself is not correlative to another object. The I simply does not exist without surroundings, without a milieu. Yet these are not logical but *real* relations, which correspondingly must be examined. If, as is obvious, the I is a social "thing," then its milieu is also a social milieu. The I, the so-and-so, and the milieu exist in a real relation or interaction, but obviously these surroundings can be conceived without the I just as the I can be conceived in changing surroundings. What we have here ideally is a social theme, whose resolution subjectivism was most responsible for obstructing. Instead of a transition to an analysis of the sense of the ideal I, the ideal so-and-so, as the object of consciousness, subjectivism proceeded to the I, written with a capital letter, positing it, as if it were, an absolute ruler, legislator and the owner of every kind of consciousness and of everything that is an object of consciousness.

28. I just said that the I, for example, can be looked at from a metaphysical point of view even as an object *par excellence*. The metaphysical point of view is the point of view of real explanation, and we only need to find the substantial nature of the I in order to explain why it can be called in metaphysics an object *par excellence*. However, we need to consider the empirical and ideal proforms of the concept of substance both in empirical reality and in their ideal essence in order to get to the corresponding relationship of the I and the object. The anthropomorphic interpretations of nature are no less a misuse of the I as an object than is a psychological interpretation of the I as a psyche. The I in the concrete sense is a social "thing," but it does not need to prove that it is a *"thing" par excellence*, whereas even such "things" as a house, a street, a book,

---

[86] [Natorp 1912: 31.]

[87] [Pavel Chichikov is the main character in Nikolai Gogol's novel *Dead Souls*.]

a judge, a gentleman, and so forth, are "relations" and are reducible to "relations." An analysis of pure consciousness, as such, reveals to us the ideal source of such a division. The most fundamental distinction carried out on the intended, as such, is that between "content" and "object" (K. Twardowski and in general the school of Brentano). It is difficult for subjectivism to accept this distinction, because for it the entire object of consciousness is "content."[88] However, if we adopt this distinction, it is not hard to agree that the I, the so-and-so, is an object *par excellence*, because it is impossible to say about it what is said about an object in general, viz., that it is an X, that it is an *indefinite* object. The I is precisely a definite object; it has a proper name. Its objectivity is not a matter of theory, but an immediate lived experience even though the "content" of this object has to be established, as we saw, with the help of communal or collective evidence. Although situated among and in connection with other objects, the I, as an object, could, nevertheless, with good reason be called absolute, because there is no correlation that could serve as the basis for its unique and necessary determination. Furthermore, the very concept of an I, as unique and irreplaceable, even excludes the possibility of any correlation whatsoever, since the latter bears a general character. In other words, if there were such a correlation, it would also be new and irreplaceable each time, and this already deprives the correlative determination of sense. The I, as a social object with a proper name, is absolute in the sense that the I is not only a "bearer" but also a "source," not only "predetermined" but also "free." However, since along with the I we find also other "unities of consciousness" including also collective "unities" that "are connected" only by "bonds" of freedom, freedom itself is found here both as something communal and also as something *common*. Consequently, a complete definition, or better, a self-definition of the I, of the so-and-so, still demands something that, as we already casually indicated, is "inexpressible." "The divine is God's concern; the human, man's. My concern is neither the divine nor the human, not the true, good, just, free, etc., but solely what is *mine*, and it is not a general one, but is – unique, as I am unique."[89] And what is sin, if, starting from oneself, such an I, a so-and-so, for example Kaspar Schmidt, then attests: "And now I take the world as what it is to me, as mine, as my property; I refer all to myself."[90] The I, the so-and-so, is absolutely right here, because there is no one even to challenge its rights.

29. But if the I wishes to secure one's right to property, wants to specify one's heirs and find one's ancestors, to point out one's mother and children, if one wants to find oneself and say one's name, wants to find one's place amidst one's possessions, he/she cannot manage without addressing someone with a "you" and without a recognition of "we." He/she is right. However, if one sets out from oneself, one's hands are tied, so that already he/she cannot say: "I," but "*also*

---

[88] Natorp's theory of "presentative consciousness" and "representative consciousness" tries to "cover up" this *originary* fact. Natorp 1912: 53ff. Cf. also Natorp 1912: 282ff.

[89] [Stirner 1971: 41.]

[90] [Stirner 1971: 49. Johann Kaspar Schmidt was the real name of Max Stirner, the anarchist philosopher.]

*not only I'* – give me a hand, friend, and brother! If he/she, nevertheless, one way or another came to say this, he/she must recognize oneself as having been *wrong*. One must hear and *understand* the voice of one's brother, a single assertion from some so-and-so already forces one to recognize a connection and a unity existing "outside" and "above" them both. *Διά νά ήναι πάντες έν...*[91] And any assertion in this regard, or even a thought about it, already testifies, as we said, that the judgment "I am a unity of consciousness" is irreversible. If, continuing on the basis of definitions in formal logic, we relinquish the idea or preconception that the "individual" is the minimal type, then it is clear that judgments with the subject I cannot be general judgments, because the I cannot be *generalized*. Strictly speaking, it is impossible even to say that "every" I is a "unity of consciousness," because there is already a generalization here. The I, the so-and-so, is pushed into the background. Consequently, the I, the so-and-so, is, at least, not *only* a unity of lived experiences and of consciousness, but is rather what distinguishes a unity of consciousness from another unity. In "collecting" consciousnesses, we do not generalize them, but rather *multiply* them, passing from an *I* to a *we*. Without encroaching in the least on the individuality and irreplaceability of the so-and-so, we, nevertheless, clearly see in this "multitude" not a unity of consciousness, but a *unity* all the same. The I, the so-and-so, necessarily appears as predestined, which establishes and sets its boundaries, its "definition": *an I cannot not be itself*. Its boundaries are also the boundaries of other so-and-so's. Within these boundaries, each is free: *The I is free, since in everything it remains itself*. The "community" is what eliminates these boundaries, i.e., the boundaries of each so-and-so. It is what eliminates separation and distributiveness. In other words, it is what leads to absolute freedom. In this, the I is liberated from predestination. *It can also not be itself.*

30. So *whose* unity is it, the unity of consciousness? The unity of a single consciousness certainly is the unity of *this* consciousness, but the unity of a multitude or of a collective or of a communal consciousness is a unity of the collective consciousness! I am not playing with words but am distinguishing a meaning which has a *genetivus subjectivus* and a *genetivus objectivus*. I deliberately wish to stress merely that since such a question is being posed, the only possible answer is to refer to its ambiguity. A "unity of consciousness" belongs to no one, because in general it is not a "possession" or a "property." It is only a *unity of consciousness*. That is, it is consciousness itself. But in answer to "Whose consciousness?" it is its own. It is free! In other words, this means that it is *no one's*! Perhaps, some Ivan Ivanovich will claim: I am a unity of consciousness. What are we to make of this? In my view, he will be right but only that Ivan Petrovich is also a unity of consciousness. ... Here is the origin of our tendency to identify consciousness with the "psyche" or the "spirit." Such expressions as "I, this so-and-so, am conscious of my body, my social position, my immortal-

---

[91] [John 17:21 – "that they all may be one."]

ity, etc." deprive *me* of a body, of social connections, but the *I* still remains. However this same so-and-so can say:

When I die, bury me
In a grave amid the vast expanse of the steppe
In my beloved Ukraine[92]

Does the "*me*" here mean consciousness and its unity? Certainly not. It only means that "I" am a social thing who also determines his social relations. Ultimately, it is as impossible to say *whose* consciousness as it is to say *whose* space or *whose* air this is, even though everyone is convinced that the air that one breathes is *one's own* air and the space that one occupies is *one's own* space.[93] They are "natural." They make up "nature" and refer to it. They "belong" to it. However, these examples, it seems, reveal the sense of the question: *Whose* is this consciousness? The word "whose" is itself here a social category, and Solovyov was profoundly correct in comparing this question with that of "Whose coat?", "Whose galoshes?"[94] If we understand consciousness and its unity to be an *ideal* object, i.e., examine it in its essence, then it makes no sense to ask *whose* it is. Consciousness can belong to the essence of the I, but it is not clear that it belongs to the essence of consciousness to be the consciousness of an I or of another "subject."[95] The I itself, as a unity of a multitude of other "unities of consciousness," is collective and communal. If we have in mind some aggregate of empirical experiences, then of course being empirical they are pinned to a specific time and place just as well as to a specific geographic, social and historical moment. The word "whose" here is only a request to indicate the "thing" with the help of which certain social relations must be revealed to us. To answer the question "Whose?" means to specify the point in the social whole where we must refer the given problem, which we can call, as above, an "Objectification" or an "utterance." In a discussion of the corresponding

---

[92] [Cf. Shevchenko 1964: 25. The poem is better known under the title "My Testament." Shpet provides the original Ukrainian.]

[93] "We are so accustomed to the thought that everything is for us, that the earth is mine, that when we have to die, we are surprised that my earth, something belonging to me, will remain and I won't. Here the principal mistake is in thinking the earth as something acquired and complementary to me, when it is I who am acquired by the earth, an appendage to it." Tolstoi 1917: 147. As though this is not applicable *mutatis mutandis* to consciousness....

[94] [See Solovyov 1965: 130.]

[95] The problem of "no one's" consciousness has risen in various forms. In the treatments of it known to me, their "critical" part is of more value than their "constructive" part, which concludes either with abstract definitions of the "I" or with very stupid "psychophysical" hypotheses. "One should say, 'There is thinking' just as one says, 'There is lightning.' To say '*cogito*' is already to say too much as soon as it is translated as 'I think'." Lichtenberg 1844: 99. Mach's position on this issue is well-known. The "actual I" of Zschimmer is also interesting from a critical direction. See Zschimmer 1909: 54ff.

problems, then, there definitely are no obstacles to referring to any so-and-so
as such a point.

31. Continuing, however, with our empirical analysis, we can find other "points" of
consciousness as well to which it is impossible to direct our question, as we can
to a so-and-so, but which if they would answer could not always say "my" but
would say "our," as in such examples as: "Our epoch," "Pushkin is our pride
and glory," "our victories and defeats," etc. Here the word is "our," but by no
means does it mean belonging to each of us. The author of the brilliant work
"Ojcze Nasz"[96] (Count Cieszkowski) points out that we say "our Father" but
not "my Father." We speak of "our" common Father, who is *our* Father only
insofar as we consider ourselves brothers. He writes, "Live! But live in fullness.
Live in one love with family and nation, with Church and Humanity, even with
our mother the Earth, who is not dead as you suppose, but also lives and shares
in the fellowship of the universe. Live in love unceasing; for in so doing you
will be living in God, and with God."[97] Since such thoughts and feelings, such
experiences, are possible, what does it mean to speak of *my* consciousness in
this context? But it is interesting that in purely *personal* utterances we quite
often mean not *just* ourselves. Such expressions, as "*my* homeland," "*my* moral
consciousness," "*my* duty," "*my* political convictions," etc., not only do not
point to me as their "owner," but directly suggest the idea of my participation in
collective relations, which are characterized by reference to "points," "unifying" some *communal consciousness*.[98] We hardly need to dwell on this aspect
of the problem. In his time, Sergej Trubeckoj in the article mentioned above
selected many empirical arguments in favor of a collective or communal consciousness. We have a science – whatever it may be called – whose object is
consciousness, "the existence of which does not depend upon the individual;
not because the contents of this consciousness presuppose a collective subject
(*un sujet collectif*) distinct from the individuals composing the social group, but
because they are characterized by features that cannot be found solely by examining individuals as such."[99] In short, it is a matter of the "ways of acting, think-

---

[96] [Polish: "Our Father."]

[97] [Cieszkowski 1919: 127.]

[98] Sometimes we speak directly of a "social psyche" or of a "collective I," for example, in the ethnic
psychology of Lazarus and Steinthal. In general, much attention is also given to this question in
contemporary French "sociology" (the school of Durkheim) and in American "social psychology"
(Baldwin). Cf. also Balicki 1912: 63, 141 (*jaźń zbiorowa, jaźń społeczn*
[collective I, social I – TN]).

[99] Lévy-Bruhl 1966: 3. [Shpet references Lévy-Bruhl's work but without giving a page reference
here. I have translated Shpet's Russian, which serves his own purposes, rather than providing the
English translation of Lévy-Bruhl, which runs: "their existence does not depend upon the individual; not that they imply a collective unity distinct from the individuals composing the social
group, but because they present themselves in aspects which cannot be accounted for by considering individuals merely as such."]

ing, and feeling that present the noteworthy property of existing outside the individual consciousness."[100] But *whose* are they?

32. Analyzing consciousness as such and not clearly realizing the fact that an I, a so-and-so, is solely a concrete, social thing, extraordinary significance is attributed to it only because, as we pointed out, in this analysis one proceeds from oneself. Striving then to establish such an important thing, there is no resolve, however, for it to be introduced – probably owing to the pressure of the collective consciousness – as "the sole problem of philosophy," and the quest begins for a universal representative: psyche, spirit, transcendental apperception, absolute I, etc. All of these serve as cloaks of philosophical modesty. Subjectivism, in this sense, is a proof of this exceptional philosophical modesty and timidity and by no means of conceit and swagger as it can seem to the superficial observer. But since the subject, in fact, is both impersonal and unpretentious, our observation, amounting to the fact that the I is an object along with other objects, can hardly seem paradoxical to anyone. The nature of the I, by the way, still remains a completely open question. Consequently, to say that this object is a "unity of consciousness," is the perfect truth. The proviso that the unity of consciousness is *not only the I* does not destroy this perfection in the least. Unfortunately, like many other "perfect truths" this truth is quite empty. The fact is that a "unity of consciousness" – by virtue of the correlativity, which is difficult to deny, between consciousness and its object – will always also be a unity of the object. Does this mean that the unity of the object of consciousness is a unity of consciousness? In order to show the unity of the object of consciousness, of the "world," of "nature," it is necessary to resort to different kinds of "substances," "forces," "things in themselves" and other devices of dogmatic metaphysics. Would it not correspond more to the dignity of philosophy to designate the unity of consciousness as the "subject" and through it guarantee the possibility of philosophy itself and of all kinds of knowledge about it – except for the disgraced metaphysical knowledge? Here, we have the trump card of subjectivism! But the trouble in this case is that this "ace" was not pulled from the playing deck, but turned out to be provided beforehand. For this reason it is said to be *fraudulent*. This is what we were talking about.

33. What we have determined to be the unity of consciousness, or respectively of the object of consciousness, is extraordinarily varied. Any "thing," "content" or "object," – whether it be named, conceived, represented, imagined, or whatever – is a *unity*, a unity as much of the object of consciousness as of consciousness itself. In this *general* description, no individual I or collection of I's enjoys any special rights or privileges. The problem concerning them arises, as we saw, in the form of the more specific one of the "social object," which must, above all, be coordinated with other objects. If we now concentrate on this "object," we discover in it not only its "predetermination" but also what realizes it, viz., a certain entelechic principle, which is the "source" of lived experiences and of consciousness, namely *freedom* – the source of its concrete nature and

---

[100] Durkheim 1966: 2. [Shpet references Durkheim's work but without giving a page reference.]

individuality. "Consciousness" itself appears here as an object of consciousness, and the unities of consciousness *sui generis* are revealed to us as "bearers" *sui generis*, though not as "X's" but as proper names that are a symbolic expression of the "inexpressible." Here lies the genuine source and prototype of any concept of a "bearer," a "substance," an "hypostasis," etc. Refraining, however, from any metaphysical theory of this source, we see that the sole path to comprehending it lies in a pure explication of these symbols, in exposing them and, consequently, in revealing their secret. Every instance of comprehension is by its essence not simply an instance of "participation," but one of "co-participation," "co-involvement," and com-plicity.[101] This by itself is already a new object of consciousness in its unity: a unity of consciousness that is an object of consciousness. The unique and irreplaceable nature of each participant or co-participant in this unity cannot be destroyed by it. Were it otherwise, it would be internally contradictory and consequently in essence impossible, because it would reduce the individual to nothing, and of course from a collection of nothings a new unity could not arise. The unique nature of the individual is not destroyed if, glancing into its essence, we establish what is "typical" about him and describe him with particular reference to his uniquely peculiar structure. Without anticipating any theories or analogies, we cannot in any case assert that what is typical of an individual in some relation can predetermine for us the relations and what is "typically" collective. The essence of the communal and its essential types form an independent sphere of investigation. Such expressions as the "moral consciousness," the "aesthetic consciousness," the "religious consciousness," the "scientific consciousness," etc., already show the directions from which corresponding problems arise, although it is only an abstract field, and in such a form are merely titles for whole "disciplines." These are not "types," but generalizations. We must not forget, however, that the concrete, as such, has its own special "community," which is attained not by means of a "generalization," but by means of "communication." A consciousness, for example a religious consciousness, can be looked upon not only as a common consciousness, but also as a *communal* consciousness. It has its own concrete form of *community*; it has its, let us say, "faith organizations." The aesthetic consciousness has a concrete communal form of art or "beauty organizations." The same holds for "science," and so forth. All of these necessarily should have their own "form" so that they can be designated and then the sense of that *designation*, its logos, could be revealed.

34. Our analysis of a "consciousness that is the object of a consciousness," as a collective object, shows that the I itself, the so-and-so, is the "bearer" not only of its own "personal" consciousness, but also of a communal one. The analysis itself, certainly, distinguishes – although this is not always easy – the instances in which this so-and-so presents *himself "as himself,"* and those in which he presents himself *"as his community."* S. N. Trubeckoj, speaking of "cognition,"

---

[101] Finnbogason in his book, *Den sympatiske Forstaaelse*, collects some interesting facts. Finnbogason 1911.

states: "in fact the I holds within himself a council about everything with everyone."[102] It is not just a matter of *cognition*, and not of the "criterion" of the matter, which Trubeckoj finds here.[103] I even think that there simply is no criterion here. Trubeckoj hastens to make use of a *fact* that he noticed already for his theory. We simply pause before this very "fact." What is important to us is simply to pay attention to its peculiarity. If we need "conclusions," each of us can draw them to our heart's content: A fact does not guarantee them and does not answer for them. There can be no criteria here already simply, because *otherwise* no one comes to this council. There is no "unanimity" nor was there one. Ultimately, what is ingenious is not to hold "a council with all" but to conceive *oneself* as a pseudo-council, to conceive *oneself in one's* own freedom as a so-and-so, and not in a communal freedom. Is it in essence possible to answer this? No one else's experience can convince me, not because it is improbable, but because it is irrational, i.e., inexpressible. On the basis of reason and comprehension, such a "personal" thing already will not be "mine," because the "thing possessed" is not the I, not this so-and-so but "Ward No. N."[104] ... In any case, all these are problems above all for a fundamental analysis of pure consciousness in its essence.

Moscow, January 1916

# Bibliography to "Consciousness and Its Owner"

Aristotle. 1984. *The Complete Works of Aristotle*. ed. J. Barnes. Princeton: Princeton University Press.
Balicki, Zygmunt. 1912. *Psychologia spoleczna*. Warsaw: Gebethner i Wolff.
Baumgarten, Alexander Gottlieb. 1770. *Philosophia generalis*. Halle: Carl Hermann Hemmende.
Bradley, F. H. 1969. *Appearance and Reality*. Oxford: Oxford University Press.
Cieszkowski, August. 1919. *The Desire of All Nations*. Trans. William John Rose. London: Student Christian Movement.
Dante, Alighieri. 2012. *The Divine Comedy*. Trans. and ed. Robin Kirkpatrick. London: Penguin Books.
Durkheim, Emile. 1966. *The Rules of Sociological Method*. Trans. John Mueller. New York: The Free Press.
Eucken, Rudolf. 1880. *The Fundamental Concepts of Modern Philosophic Thought*. Trans. M. Stuart Phelps. New York: D. Appleton.

---

[102] [Trubeckoj 1994: 495.]

[103] "Our general agreement, the possible unanimity, which I immediately see in my consciousness, is for me the absolute inner criterion, precisely just as an external, empirical agreement concerning some identified generally accepted truths is the external criterion, the authority of which depends on the former." Trubeckoj 1994: 99. It is quite incomprehensible why Trubeckoj in his analysis of *consciousness* needed to provide the criterion of *cognition*. This is surely the heresy of "Protestant subjectivism," namely, epistemologism. Did Trubeckoj recall that with such a "criterion" he stands closest of all to ... Feuerbach?

[104] [Possibly an allusion to Anton Chekhov's short story "Ward No. 6" about the occupants of a provincial hospital ward 6 devoted to the mentally ill.]

Fichte, Johann Gottlieb. 1971. *Fichtes Werke*, vol. 1. Berlin: Walter de Gruyter & Co.
Fichte, Johann Gottlieb. 1994: *Introductions to the Wissenschaftslehre and Other Writings*. Trans. Daniel Breazeale. Indianapolis: Hackett.
Fichte, Johann Gottlieb. 1970. *Science of Knowledge (Wissenschaftslehre)*. ed. and Trans. by Peter Heath and John Lachs. New York: Meredith Corporation.
Finnbogason, G. 1911. *Den sympatiske Forstaaelse*. Copenhagen: Gyldendalske boghandel.
*Georgiju Ivanovichu Chelpanovu ot uchastnikov ego seminariev v Kieve i Moskve 1891–1916*. 1916. Moscow: Typ. A. I. Mamontova.
Gurwitsch, Aron. 1966. A Non-egological Conception of Consciousness. In *Studies in Phenomenology and Psychology*, 287–300. Evanston: Northwestern University Press.
Herbart, Johann Friedrich. 1824. *Psychologie als Wissenschaft: neue gegründet auf Erfahrung, Metaphysik und Mathematik*, vol. 1. Königsberg: August Wilhelm Unzer. .
Höfler, Alois. 1897. *Psychologie*. Vienna: F. Tempsky.
Höfler, Alois. 1906. *Grundlehren der Logik und Psychologie*. Vienna: F. Tempsky.
Hume, David. 1968. *A Treatise of Human Nature*, ed. L.A. Selby-Bigge. Oxford: Clarendon Press.
Husserl, Edmund. 1994. *Briefwechsel*, vol. 3: *Die Göttinger Schule*, ed. Karl Schuhmann. Dordrecht: Kluwer Academic Publishers.
Husserl, Edmund. 1970. *Logical Investigations*, vol. 2, Trans. J.N. Findlay. New York: Humanities Press.
Husserl, Edmund. 1901. *Logische Untersuchungen, Zweiter Teil: Untersuchungen zur Phänomenologie und Theorie der Erkenntnis*. Halle: Max Niemeyer.
Husserl, Edmund. 2014. *Ideas for a Pure Phenomenology and Phenomenological Philosophy*. Trans. Daniel O. Dahlstrom. Indianapolis: Hackett.
Lipps, Theodor. 1909. *Leitfaden der Psychologie*. Leipzig: W. Engelmann.
Losskij, N. O. 1911. *Vvedenie v filosofiju*. St. Petersburg: Stasjulevich.
James, William. 1890. *The Principles of Psychology*, vol. 1. New York: Henry Hold and Company.
Kant, Immanuel. 1997. *Critique of Pure Reason*. Trans. Paul Guyer and Allen W. Wood. New York: Cambridge University Press.
Krause, Karl Christian Friedrich. 1892. *Vorlesungen über Naturrecht oder Philosophie des Rechtes und des Staates*. Leipzig: Otto Schulze.
Leibniz, Gottfried Wilhelm. 1996. *New Essays on Human Understanding*. Ed. and Trans. Peter Remnant and Jonathan Francis Bennett. Cambridge: Cambridge University Press.
Lévy-Bruhl, Lucien. 1966. *How Natives Think*. Trans. Lilian Ada Clare. New York: Washington Square Press.
Lichtenberg, Georg Christoph. 1844. *Vermischte Schriften*, vol. 1. Göttingen: Dieterichschen Buchhandlung.
Locke, John. 1968. *An Essay Concerning Human Understanding*. New York: Meridian Books.
Marbach, Eduard. 1974. *Das Problem des Ich in der Phänomenologie Husserls*. Den Haag: Martinus Nijhoff.
Messer, August. 1914. *Psychologie*. Berlin: Deutsche Verlags-Anstalt.
Mill, John Stuart. 1979. *An Examination of Sir William Hamilton's Philosophy*. Toronto: University of Toronto Press.
Micraelius, Johannes. 1679. *Lexicon philosophicum terminorum philosophis*. Jena: Mamphrasii.
Mill, John Stuart. 2009. *System of Logic, Ratiocinative and Inductive*. New York: Cosimo, Inc.
Miller, Izchak. 1986. Husserl on the Ego. *Topoi*, 5(1986) 2: 157–62.
Molchanov, Viktor. 2009. Ot chistogo soznanija k social'noj veshchi. *Issledovanija po istorii russ- koj mysli: Ezhegodnik za 2006–2007 god*. Moscow: Modest Kolerov.
Natorp, Paul. 1912. *Allgemeine Psychologie. Erstes Buch*. Tübingen: J.C.B. Mohr.
Natorp, Paul. 1904. *Allgemeine Psychologie in Leitsätzen*. Marburg: N. G. Elwert.
Natorp, Paul. 1910. *Allgemeine Psychologie in Leitsätzen*. 2. Aufl. Marburg: N. G. Elwert.
Natorp, Paul. 1888. *Einleitung in die Psychologie nach kritischer Methode*. Freiburg: J.C.B. Mohr.
Oesterreich, Konstantin. 1910. *Die Phänomenologie des Ich*. Leipzig: J.A. Barth.
Plotinus. 1962. *The Enneads*. Trans. Stephen MacKenna. London: Faber and Faber.

Sartre, Jean-Paul. 2004. *The Transcendence of the Ego*. Trans. Andrew Brown. London: Routledge.

Schopenhauer, Arthur. 1969. *The World as Will and Representation*, vol. 1. Trans. E.F.J. Payne. New York: Dover Publications.

Schuppe, Wilhelm. 1878. *Erkenntnistheoretische Logik*. Bonn: Eduard Weber.

Shevchenko, Taras. 1964. My Legacy. Trans. C.H. Andrusychyn and W. Kirconnel. In *Taras Shevchenko Memorial Book*. Washington, D.C.: The Shevchenko Memorial Committee of America, Inc.

Shpet, Gustav. 1991. *Appearance and Sense*. Trans. Thomas Nemeth. Dordrecht: Kluwer Academic Publishers.

Solovyov, Vladimir. 1965. Foundations of Theoretical Philosophy. In *Russian Philosophy*, ed. J.M. Edie, J.P. Scanlan and M.B. Zeldin, vol. 3, 99–134. Chicago: Quadrangle Books. .

Stern, L. William. 1906. *Person und Sache*. Leipzig: Johann Ambrosius Barth.

Teichmüller, Gustav. 1882. *Die wirkliche und scheinbare Welt*. Breslau: Wilhelm Koebner.

Tolstoi, Leo. 1917. *The Journal of Leo Tolstoi (First Volume – 1895–1899)*. Trans. Rose Strunsky. New York: Alfred A. Knopf.

Trubeckoj, Sergej Nikolaevich. 1994. O prirode celovecheskago soznaniia. In *Sochinenija*. Moscow: Mysl'.

Stirner, Max. 1971. *The Ego and His Own*, ed. J. Carroll. New York: Harper & Row.

Wolff, Christian. 1736. *Philosophia prima sive ontologia*. Frankfurt und Leipzig: Renger.

Wolff, Christian. 1983. *Philosophia rationalis sive logica*, ed. J. Ecole. New York: Georg Olms.

Zhukovskij, Vasilij A. 1907. Dve byla i eshche odna. In *Ballady*. St. Petersburg: Glazunov.

Zschimmer, Eberhard. 1909. *Das Welterlebnis*. Leipzig: Wilhelm Engelmann.

# Appendix 2: Wisdom or Reason?

## Editor's Introduction to "Wisdom or Reason?"

Gustav Shpet completed the following essay in January 1917 and published it as the opening essay in the first volume of his own unfortunately short-lived philosophical yearbook *Mysl' i slovo* [*Thought and Word*]. As with many such essays, there is a considerable "backstory" to its composition, much of it now familiar and some much less so. As is generally well-known, Shpet had attended at least some of Husserl's lectures and seminars during the 1912–13 academic year in Göttingen. He had come to this German university town initially in conjunction with acquiring material for his planned thesis *Istorija kak problema logiki* [*History as a Problem of Logic*], which he would go on to defend and publish in Moscow in 1916. Within a remarkably short time after his acquaintance with Husserl, the two developed a friendship and a high estimation for each other's philosophical talents and dedication.

The work that follows can in large part be read as an affirmation, a defense, and an elaboration on Husserl's own lengthy and programmatic article from 1910–11 "Philosophy as Rigorous Science," which appeared in a Russian translation remarkably quite soon afterward. In it, Husserl expressed his conviction that the higher interests of human culture called for the establishment of a scientifically rigorous philosophy. He fully realized that in his own day various reductionist tendencies held a certain sway, claiming that they represented the realization of the very ideal of a "scientific philosophy." Husserl, however, maintained that they represented no such thing. These reductionisms all modeled themselves on an existing mathematical or physical method used in the natural sciences, thereby positing at the start the existence of contingent, natural "facts." Consistent with this method, they, for the most part, reified consciousness, and they thereby entered into the philosophical comedy of employing consciousness to *explain* consciousness. Husserl held that what we need to do is lay the groundwork for a new way of doing philosophy, one that does not avail itself of the existential positing of nature, of anything contingent, namely,

© Springer Nature Switzerland AG 2019
G. Shpet, T. Nemeth, *Hermeneutics and Its Problems*, Contributions
To Phenomenology 98, https://doi.org/10.1007/978-3-319-98941-9

an investigation into the essential relationships between consciousness and its intended correlate, being. The import of this is that the sense of any talk of objectivity must become clear from consciousness itself in the manners in which it seizes objectivity, for example, as remembered, expected, or represented. This new approach, viz., phenomenology, calls for a study of the essentials of objectivity in the modes in which those essentials are presented. What is needed, then, is a patient and detailed study of the modes of the consciousness–object (as intended) relationship that must not rest until we have reached absolute clarity, the absolutely clear beginnings. It is with little exaggeration to say that Shpet's own understanding of phenomenology and his reading of Husserl's 1913 *Ideen* was via Husserl's 1910–11 essay.

In late January 1914, Shpet gave a talk in Moscow on "The Idea of a Fundamental Science."[1] This occasion afforded Shpet the opportunity to reiterate and elaborate on Husserl's theme of making philosophy into a rigorous or fundamental science. As had Husserl, Shpet claimed that the fundamental science was still only in the process of being constructed, not that the construction had already been completed. A crucial and foundational step in this construction is the diversion of our gaze from the contingent, the pragmatic, the transient, toward essences, toward ideal being. To the possible objection from a representative of *Lebensphilosophie*, such as Bergson, that such a procedure would lose what is most essential in life, namely, the timely, the vitality of the moment, Shpet replied that the objection is misplaced. The *fundamental* science accepts each science and each form within the respective science as it is without reducing one form or one science to another.

Shpet amplified and broadened his position in the essay presently before us. For one thing, instead of referring to the desired construct as "rigorous science," as had Husserl, Shpet saw it in early 1917 as "pure knowledge" (*chistoe znanie*), shortening this often enough here simply to "knowledge." Yet, even in this respect, we find Shpet, not unlike Husserl in 1910–11, at least mentioning humanity's historical quest for pure knowledge.[2] Additionally, as with Husserl, Shpet too saw this anticipated philosophy as standing in opposition to any form of reductionism and built on firm, non-theoretical foundations, i.e., without the incorporation of other ideas or conceptions. Moreover, unlike some other philosophies, Shpet's ideal would not delimit its boundaries from the outset, but would range as far as the methodological rigor stemming from our human resources allowed. Along with Husserl, but arguably more firmly and explicitly, Shpet recognized that, although this ideal has been historically present through the ages, even back into antiquity, it had compromised itself from time to time and to various degrees with what Shpet characterized as myths and tales. Whereas Husserl, albeit only much later than Shpet, in his 1935 so-called Vienna Lecture, traced the origin of philosophy proper to an amalgam of ancient Greek thinkers, Shpet saw philosophy originating specifically with Parmenides, whose prescient idea was passed on to Plato and others. The admixtures that historically came into play after this period pushed the purely "European" and rational idea of pure knowledge into the background for centuries to come. Nevertheless, Shpet here,

---

[1] For an English translation, see Shpet 1991: 175–180.
[2] See, for example, Husserl 2002: 250.

arguably far more audaciously than Husserl, set out through his discussion of Parmenides the view that phenomenology *in nuce* can be traced back to the pre-Socratics and represents the telos of Western philosophical thought.

The chief culprit, however, for philosophy's deviation from its path to truth was what Shpet called an "Eastern" element. In this, we have another of Shpet's audacious and controversial claims, one which such an established figure as Husserl would hardly have made with the poignant vehemence that Shpet expressed. This "Eastern" element in which philosophy as pure knowledge was submerged but not completely eviscerated was Christianity.[3] For Shpet, it is one type of "wisdom." Regrettably, Shpet provided no specific definition of "wisdom" – perhaps one cannot be had – but he contrasted the "wisdom" of the East to the "reason" of pure Europeanism as found in Plato, et al.: the East experiences, whereas Europe patiently reflects.

Shpet presented yet another contrast, one between opinion and knowledge. The former is concerned with the here and now – this empirical object perceived by my senses. It places the absolute in another realm, largely inaccessible to mere mortals. Knowledge, on the other hand, is concerned with truth, which is timeless. It arises from reflection on the thought of the object, in other words, on the Platonic ideas, shorn of any mysticism, but knowledge requires from us more than mere sense intuition for its apprehension. Moreover, an intellectual intuition is required to see the reason or sense of the essences themselves. To some, this distinction conjures in their minds a distinction between everyday knowledge, on the one hand, as against mathematics and philosophy, on the other. Shpet saw this mistaken fascination with "mathematical philosophy" in Bertrand Russell, and, with Shpet's critique, we see what amounts to an early phenomenological critique of positivism. Shpet admonished those who think like Russell, saying that mathematics – or, we might add, any other non-phenomenologically rigorous discipline – is an abstraction from consciousness, whereas philosophy, properly construed, views its objects precisely in their connection to consciousness. In this, Shpet thoroughly adhered to the cherished phenomenological dictum that consciousness is always a consciousness of something. However, most importantly, in Shpet's understanding of phenomenology as the fundamental science, the consciousness of something implies a consciousness. The "consciousness–something" relationship is fundamental to philosophy, properly conceived. Bereft of its relation to consciousness, an alleged study of the "something" parts company with phenomenology, i.e., pure knowledge.

Admittedly, much in Shpet's exposition in 1917 is itself couched in abstract, even at times metaphorical, language. His debt throughout to Husserl's programmatic 1910 article should be quite apparent including his notion of "wisdom" and "scientific philosophy." Still, whereas we can view Shpet as inspired by Husserl's views we can also contrast Shpet's positions in the essay before us to those enunciated by a compatriot and friend of Shpet's, namely, Yehuda Leyb Schwarzmann, better known under his pen name "Lev Shestov" which he adopted to help avoid a

---

[3] In the first of his *Aesthetic Fragments* from 1922–23, Shpet wrote, "The crisis of our present culture is a crisis of Christianity, because in the twentieth century there is no other culture." Shpet 2007: 197.

recognition of his Jewish roots. Shpet and Shestov not only knew each other in adulthood, but in all probability were already acquainted from their early days together in Kiev and remained friends even after the former relocated to Moscow and Shestov to Germany and Switzerland.[4] Both would in time come to know Husserl personally, and both engaged the other in their respective assessments of phenomenology. Shortly after the publication of Shpet's 1914 work *Appearance and Sense*, Shestov tried, albeit ultimately unsuccessfully, to convince Shpet to translate it into German.[5]

Although Shestov's essay "Memento mori" appeared only later in the September–October 1917 issue of the Russian philosophy journal *Voprosy filosofii i psikhologii* – and thus after the following essay by Shpet – Shpet's essay can be read in conjunction with Shestov's, even as if it were a reply to Shestov's.[6] In any case, given the similarities in topics covered and that many of the same historical figures are mentioned in a similar context, it is hard to believe that Shestov was unaware of Shpet's contribution, even though Shestov never so much as mentioned it. For example, both refer to Parmenides in strikingly similar ways, albeit for different ends.[7] Both make the determination of just what philosophy is a central theme of their respective essays. Additionally, both invoke a distinction between wisdom and reason despite the relatively minor role that distinction played in Husserl's article. Both illustrate how philosophy as formulated by the Greeks was from time to time compromised, for better or worse, over the centuries. However, unlike Shpet, Shestov pointedly sees both the opposition between reason and wisdom, which forms the central theme of Shpet's essay, and the historical compromises philosophy made to "wisdom" in Husserl's own work.

There are also, however, obvious differences. The most noticeable is the relative absence of Husserl's name from Shpet's essay. Whereas in Shestov's piece Husserl's conception of philosophy is explicitly at the center of attention, Shpet apparently

---

[4] Shchedrina 2004: 183–84.

[5] Shpet wrote to his wife in June 1914, "Shestov thinks that he [Husserl] will again insist on its translation and advises me to do this immediately, even though this would necessarily incur material sacrifices. But another thing troubles me. Something would have to be changed for a German translation, and I have no time for this. He says that I 'must find the time'." Shchedrina 2005: 191. Shpet possibly had in mind here Shestov's lament expressed in a letter already from March, "It is simply a pity … that you are not publishing it simultaneously in German. Think about it." Shchedrina 2005: 330. Quite possibly, Husserl suggested Shpet undertake such a translation already in October 1913, when Shpet showed Husserl the page proofs of his book. Such a conjecture makes Shpet's lines in a letter to Husserl from November all that more understandable: "I copied my treatise in Moscow, but I had no time to deal with it and revise it. But I see that careful revision would be necessary." Husserl 1994: 528.

[6] Shpet did not publish a formal reply to Shestov's interpretation and criticisms of Husserl. The editor of many of Shpet's works, T. G. Shchedrina, conjectures that this silence was out of courtesy to Shestov, who had lost his son, Sergej, fighting in World War I in 1915. Shchedrina 2004: 188.

[7] Shestov, quoting some of the same lines as Shpet had, wrote, "Parmenides already said the other sciences have only opinions; philosophy gives truth." Shestov 1917: 1.

fully assimilated Husserl's conception, making it his own, and expanded on it. There is also a difference in how each of the two regarded "theory of knowledge." Shestov clearly looked upon Husserl's phenomenology as such a theory, albeit one with uncommon rigor and clarity. Shpet, as it were, anticipated Shestov and offered a reply in advance, as it were. In Shpet's eyes, philosophy as knowledge, i.e., Husserlian, or, arguably better, Shpetian phenomenology, is not a theory of knowledge, because it is not a theory at all; it deals with descriptions of essences and the role of such descriptions in fundamental philosophy. Indeed, Shestov did recognize that Husserl had already in the sixth of his *Logical Investigations* declared that phenomenology was not concerned with theoretical constructions, i.e., with explanations. Yet, Shestov did not recognize that, as a consequence, phenomenology was not a "theoretical" philosophy at all. Whereas Shestov held that in phenomenology reality recedes from view, Shpet contended just the opposite – that philosophy as knowledge brings reality into clear view. It reveals the truth, i.e., being, without the presuppositions that theory introduces.

We surely could make many more comparisons and contrasts between the positions of Shestov, Husserl and Shpet. These are best left to the reader. It should hardly come as a surprise that, given Shpet's prolificacy, he not only knew of Shestov's article but also took notes, at least for himself, on it. These notes have only recently become available, but they reveal Shpet explicitly defending Husserl against many of Shestov's charges and ultimately leveling a quite damning assessment of Shestov's hostility to the secular and rational quest for truth, a quest which both Shpet and Shestov found in phenomenology. Shpet asks of Shestov, "In all the academic objections to Husserl one thing surprises me. Does the author seriously think that Husserl did not anticipate these elementary objections?"[8] Shpet charged Shestov with ultimately no sincere interest either in Husserl's positive message or, really, in philosophy in general. Shestov's concern was not with determining truth, but with finding God! Despite this evaluation of Shestov's attitude, Shpet was quite reluctant, what with their many years of friendship and the political situation within Russia itself after the appearance of their respective articles, to engage Shestov in the public arena. Shpet clearly preferred to remain silent even in light of Shestov's contentious position toward Husserl.[9]

Since the intent of the present translation is to convey Shpet's ideas, the translations of Greek authors is from Shpet's Russian, as found in his original text, rather than from standard English translations of those Greek authors. However, reference to an English-language translation is provided in the footnotes in the hope that they can be of some assistance to the reader. The items in square brackets "[]" are editorial additions, not found in the original Russian text.

---

[8] Shpet 2010b: 221.

[9] For Shpet's critical notes, see Shpet 2010b: 210–221. Unfortunately, we cannot be certain precisely when they were written, but since Shpet referenced the published version of Shestov's article, the notes must have been written sometime after September 1917.

# Wisdom or Reason?

## Gustav Shpet

*Quid ergo Athenis et Hierosolymis?*
*Quid academiae et ecclesiae?*
Tertullian

We must carefully distinguish *philosophy as pure knowledge* from *scientific philosophy*.[10] Scientific philosophy is defined negatively in strict opposition to non-scientific philosophy, where the latter is understood as "metaphysical" or inauthentic philosophy, i.e., *pseudo-philosophy*. Scientific modesty, at first, seems to dictate such a specification of philosophy's tasks. On closer examination, however, we easily see that what we have here is, in fact, a peculiar type of conceit. Behind its sham self-limitations, scientific philosophy actually harbors great pretensions. Desiring to be "scientific," it takes the techniques and methods of a certain, pure field of scientific knowledge as the norm, and then, by employing a parochial methodology, scientific philosophy sets out to solve universal problems. Measured simply in terms of the task it poses for itself, scientific philosophy, however, turns out to be bankrupt.

Two possibilities present themselves. Scientific philosophy can either: (1) pointlessly duplicate scientific solutions to problems; or (2) it can transgress the bounds of the individual sciences and undertake to solve by scientific means problems that cannot be solved scientifically. Simply as a matter of fact, it chooses the latter path. Having accepted a particular science as the model of scientific cognition, it immediately transgresses those bounds. First, it attempts to solve the problems of the other sciences in terms of this model and then it attacks problems that the other sciences have not attempted to solve owing either to a recognition of the empirical limitation of our knowledge or of the fundamental difficulty of these problems for those sciences. Regardless of which science it chooses as the model, "scientific philosophy" inevitably seeks to accomplish a job whose significance it denies. In this way, it itself becomes an inauthentic – a "metaphysical" – pseudo-philosophy. By "*pseudo-philosophy*," I mean: (1) positivistic phantasies of a "synthesis" of all knowledge modeled on a specialized science; (2) mythological and, in the narrow sense, metaphysical phantasies invested with a scientific form and constructed primarily along the lines of a specialized science; (3) theological phantasies encompassing religious beliefs and arbitrarily proclaimed dogmas expressed in a scientific

---

[10] [Although the contemporary reader, most likely, will associate "scientific philosophy" with the Viennese Logical Positivists, as Michael Friedman points out the expression was "first developed in the mid-nineteenth century, as a reaction against what was viewed as the excessively speculative and metaphysical character of post-Kantian German idealism." See Friedman 2001: 5. Shpet certainly has in mind here, for one, Wilhelm Wundt, who pointedly used the expression "*wissenschaftliche Philosophie*." See Wundt 1897: 17ff. For Shpet's direct reference to Wundt and "scientific philosophy," see Shpet's 1914 lecture notes on the "theory of cognition." Shpet 2010a: 237.]

form; (4) gnostic phantasies of every sort. All of these have one thing in common, viz., to give scientific form to the respective phantasies and call the result "philosophy." Since all of them transgress the rigorous bounds of science, all of them can be called "*metaphysical*" in the broad sense. As a free, individual creation, any of them can be the expression of a truly philosophical *experience*. In this sense, of course, none of them is bound by any restriction, since none claims "scientificity." Consequently, pseudo-philosophy is a metaphysics, in the broad sense, that pretends to be a precise science. Only in that rare case when the term "metaphysics" is intentionally, but arbitrarily, used as a *synonym* for philosophy as pure science does the term "metaphysics" not fit under this definition. Therefore, mechanism, dynamism, biologism (evolutionism), subjectivism (psychologism, epistemologism), historicism and such forms of scientific philosophy are basically no different from such metaphysical doctrines as, for example, materialism, spiritualism and monism, along with their privative sub-groups, such as mechanistic, evolutionary, and historical materialism; dynamistic, intellectualistic, and voluntaristic spiritualism; idealistic, realistic, and energetistic monism; etc., etc. The numerous directions that scientific philosophy takes deprive its foundations of any unity. The most we can speak of here is a unity of the model. With its variety of explanatory directions, scientific philosophy turns out to be divisive and privative. Each of its directions treats the others negatively. This is, for the most part, an intolerable position for philosophy to take.

On the other hand, *philosophy as pure knowledge* has positive tasks and is built upon solid foundations. A single philosophy by design, it is indeed uniform in its approach. It may seem pretentious when it declares that the object of its investigation is *everything*. However, the rigor of its method and the great demands made of it to fulfill its tasks precisely and reliably establish its bounds. These tasks are determined by its object, which is different from that of other sorts and types of cognition, be they scientific or unscientific. Its self-restraint is sincere and unambiguous. The reach of our human faculties empirically restrains it. Yet, in a sense, it is limitless – ideally as limitless as the possible development of these faculties or as limitless as the insight of genius. In principle, it is restrained by the fact that it cannot accept tasks that cannot be accomplished by its rigorous methods. Yet, it is also in that sense limitless – as limitless as the content of the object before it. From its unique position, philosophy as pure knowledge does not oppose itself to the other sciences, because it itself is a science. Additionally, as a constituent part, and not its contradiction, philosophy as pure knowledge occupies a definite place *within the entirety* of philosophy understood in a broad sense as including not just rigorous knowledge, but "metaphysics" and "life" as well.

"Wisdom," on the one hand, and pseudo-philosophy, on the other, present worldly temptations for philosophy as knowledge. But rigorously adhering to its own path, it takes a definite stand with respect to them. Yet, we can discover in history more than one occasion when philosophy as knowledge succumbed to these temptations, but it then turned out to be ridiculous, attempting to apply its rigor where that rigor was quite out of place. Of course, philosophy as knowledge can bolster its position, though not through a blind negation of pseudo-philosophy or wisdom, but through a positive clarification of its own content and its relation to the whole of "philosophy" and to its other parts, where "philosophy" is understood in the broad, everyday sense of the word.

In the history of human thought, we cannot find a single science that has managed without some kind of association with strange and mysterious fellow-travelers, such as seekers of the elixirs of life, wizards, sorcerers and even street-corner magicians and conjurers. Consistently and without compromising itself, the sciences have delivered society from the intrusion of such dubious imposters. In turn, philosophy has had its own share of alchemists, astrologers and magicians, who have contributed to giving it a bad name, who have smeared philosophy, as it were, with a coat of grime.

Philosophy as knowledge has a clear responsibility to cleanse itself of this filth and to reveal straightforwardly and honestly its true goals and intentions. In our own day with the reexamination of scientific paths and methods, we have heard on occasion expressions of regret that contemporary science has unjustly dismissed this or that "alchemical" problem as worthless. This regret stems from the fact that now with science's rigorous recognition of its responsibilities the same problems are again arising before us. There is, however, no need for science to be in a hurry, at least not the science that does not kneel before and is not based on the premises of that contemporary prestidigitator – *technology*, which now controls the destinies of science and human thought! It is said that problems that were once abandoned are emerging again. Well, then, regardless of the reason they are again emerging! If we must draw a moral from this, it is only that the cleansing of science must not proceed by bare negation alone. No, the cleansing must be even more rigorous and more circumspect. Philosophy as knowledge, therefore, confronts enormous constructive tasks, but these are also no less historical and critical. To start with, it must point out its goals precisely as well as the means at its disposal to achieve them. It must also point out its own structure, i.e., those organs that it must use to fulfill its designated goals. While being a part of a certain greater whole, philosophy as knowledge itself forms a single whole out of the several *philosophical sciences*.

# II

Our culture, by origin Mediterranean, though now universal, is oriented, generally speaking, by two elements: an Eastern and a European element. In this opposition, I use the term "*European*" in a narrow and proper sense to designate an independent creation of the peoples inhabiting Europe. In its *pure* form, we can trace this independent creation in European culture only *up to* the dissemination in Europe of Christianity, i.e., to put it more precisely, mainly up to the dissemination of the *idea* of Christianity, of Christian *ideology* and of the Christian "worldview." While there can hardly be a doubt that in pre-Christian Europe we can find vestiges and echoes that are of Eastern origin, there is also no doubt that in this new locale something new, something original sprang up. The European element during the course of the last 2000 years – taking "European" now in a broad sense – contains so much that is Eastern that our contrast of Eastern and European at times loses any sense. In any case, to isolate one thing or another from the elements that compose our culture is no easy matter but demands great attention and even then would remain only an approximation. For this reason, we must look on the following discussions as no more than a look at a trend.

The East is indeed the homeland of wisdom and of all sorts of tales, legends, and myths. The East *experiences* them, feeds on them, and expresses itself in them. It does not know such a thing as *reflection*. Intellectual life is something foreign to it. Only with difficulty does the East distinguish reflection from laborious physical work. The East relaxes when intellectual effort is not demanded of it. Intellectual laziness is both its nature and its virtue. Pure Europeanism arose when the first ray of reflection illuminated our own experience to ourselves. For Europe, this thing, intellectual effort, is not work, but a "leisure." It is one of life's delights and festivities. The creation of thought is the dearest thing to Europe, and no power – neither sword nor moral sermon – can destroy the European's *passion for thinking*. Europe has experienced tales and myths, wisdom and revelations no less than has the East. However, it has *not just* experienced them; it has also *thought through* them. How deeply it has experienced and how deeply it has thought through these experiences is testified by one of *its* creations, viz., *tragedy*, which is the highest form of artistic reflection. In general, the fundamental directions of reflection – rigorous art and rigorous pure knowledge – are Europe's creations. The expression "rigorous art" is not infrequently used as a synonym for "ancient art," i.e., European art. We came to "rigorous science," as it were, later when Europe was "oriented," when Christianity guided its history. However, do we need to remind martyrology of philosophy when philosophy began to exhibit the desire to be a science and martyrology of science when the latter became rigorous science?

Philosophy as pure knowledge is a product of ancient pagan Europe, i.e., of Europe in our narrow, more precise sense. For a long time, the Eastern element pushed such philosophy into the background of history, though it could not quite destroy it. On the contrary, the Eastern element itself absorbed more than just a smidgen from the Europeanism that was so foreign to it. Then came the Renaissance of the sciences and the arts, and Europe openly and fully began to reveal everything that had until then been secretly smoldering but had not died out even for a moment. Philosophy never ceased being philosophy, and the Middle Ages were no less imbued with it than later ages. In Medieval philosophy, we can find all of the same features as in both earlier and later philosophy. It is simply that with the Renaissance what was a purely European creation and was pushed into the background by Medieval Christianity again advanced to the foreground of history. In fact, what started with the Renaissance has still not ended. Modernity is the epoch of the conclusive struggle between Europe and the East. Toward which side is the whole of history leaning? European culture – taking European in the broad sense – is now the world culture, and the struggle we mentioned has already extended for quite some time far beyond the borders of that geographic area designated by the term "Europe." The East is all the less *experienced* and all the more *studied*. The East itself is acquiring the ability to reflect, and, in any case, all the more "practices" it.

Philosophy, in the European understanding, is becoming the property of the whole world. Accordingly, we must give as clear an answer as is possible of what its essential features and its proper meaning are.

Philosophy as pure knowledge is pure European philosophy, a child of Europe. It is amazing with what rigorous stability this philosophy has understood its tasks throughout all of its history, with what unswerving consistency it has carried them out, and finally with what straightforwardness it has returned to them when temptation, tales, and wisdom distracted it from its true path or when, through force and threats, the fanaticism of the East blocked it from its path. Already at the very instant of its emergence, it succeeded in determining its object and rather clearly designated the peculiar method that leads to revealing and clarifying this object. That moment when *thought* for the first time directed its reflective gaze *on thought itself* must be considered the inception of philosophy as knowledge, philosophy understood as and in the sense of pure European thought.

In Plato's estimation, *Parmenides* was the *first* European philosopher. We find in his thought a clearly elaborated distinction between philosophy, understood as pure knowledge, and pseudo-philosophy, understood as those tales, myths, and "opinions" that claim to be philosophy. In a precise manner, he established the proper object of philosophy and showed the path along which philosophy is called to solve the problem posed by this object. We can easily see an agreement between the two parts of Parmenides's poem if we view the first part as an expression of the principles of *philosophy as pure knowledge* and the second as a characterization of *pseudo-philosophy*, or at least as a presentation of one of the most original and widespread types of pseudo-philosophy. Just as neither one excludes the other, so neither part of the poem contradicts the other, as is sometimes thought. The truth is the truth; its connections and relations are true. An appearance is an appearance; the connections and relations within it are contingent, "probable," and of a hypothetical nature. To each his own. Only it is impossible to think that in the sphere of truth itself feebleness prevails in the way it does in those minds aspiring to this sphere. Additionally, it is impossible to think that we are the ones who introduce a rigorous and absolute order into the sphere of essentially contingent and incoherent appearance. In other words, it is impossible to look on "truth" as "opinion" and on "opinion" as "truth." It is *our* mistake when we proclaim "truth" to be relative and probable and "opinion" to be true. In reality, I repeat, the truth is true *in itself* and as such it *is*. However, an appearance is what seems to us, and this is why it is *for us* as it seems.

"You should know all things," Parmenides himself says, "both the unshakable heart of complete Truth and the opinions of mortals, in which there is no true trustworthiness."[11]

---

[11] [Cf. Robinson 1968: 108–109. I have modified the English translation of Parmenides's poem to bring it in line with Shpet's rendition. Whether Shpet himself translated from the Greek or used an available Russian translation is unclear. Shpet provided no references.]

# III

Consequently, the object of philosophy as knowledge is truth, i.e., what is, namely, *being*. Not this or that sort of being in particular, but being itself, as such, in its essence, that is to say, being as opposed to non-being. However "formal" such a conception of being may seem to us, it is, nevertheless, the independent and distinctive object of cognition. Being is what is; its opposite is not what is – above all, what is not. But then over and above what is is what still is not, but is occurring, arising or being manifested and again disappearing, in other words, what seems to be. "It is necessary to talk," Parmenides asserts, "and to think about the being of what is. Being is, and what is nothing is not."[12]

This much is clear, but it still does not fully define philosophy as knowledge, since it is still not obvious how we come to a philosophical cognition of *being*. Surely, it can be that in reality we attain such cognition from studying particular, "empirical" sorts of being, sorts that "seem to be," for example, through their generalization or through abstraction. However, this would obviously be a *non*-philosophical path. It would be the direct path of "opinion." As I indicated, philosophy as knowledge is realized when we direct our thought on thought itself. Being, understood as that which is, as truth, is then studied in an authentically philosophical manner when we direct our reflection on the very thought of being. For thought is revealed in itself to thought. It is revealed in its authentic essence and not as something that springs into being and passes away, something that "seems to us." We have here the authentically "unshakable heart of complete Truth." Being in itself is being and just that. Only through thought does being become an object of thought and, consequently, the object of philosophy as knowledge. We must come to the realization that philosophically being exists through thought, that the object of thought and the object of being are one and the same. They are a *single* object. According to Parmenides, "thinking and being are one and the same." Or, as he puts it even more clearly, "thinking and that toward which the thought is directed are one and the same; you will not find thinking without what is and what the thought expresses."[13] Thus, for philosophy not only is the object of being the object of thought, but the thought, toward which philosophy is directed, is also certainly a thought of an object. Consequently, there are no thoughts of "nothing." In this, philosophy as knowledge has a solid and reliable starting point.

Philosophy as knowledge does not exclude human "opinion," "the opinion of mortals," which admits only relative and conditional knowledge and is determined by its object, which, in turn, is different from the former's object, viz., "truth." "Opinion" in philosophy has a legitimate right to exist alongside philosophy as knowledge, but it cannot be identified with the latter. "Metaphysics" in the *narrow* sense is a part of philosophy on the whole, and in this way it certainly has contiguous points with philosophy as knowledge. Aristotle said, "even the lover of myth

---

[12] [Robinson 1968: 111.]

[13] [Robinson 1968: 110.]

($\varphi\upsilon\lambda\acute{o}\mu\upsilon\theta o\varsigma$) is in a sense a philosopher."[14] It can be said that the object of pseudo-philosophy is also a being. However, pseudo-philosophy grasps being not through thought and not in thought, but as if it were in itself and as it would then be. Consequently, pseudo-philosophy from the start supposes a certain hypothesis about being *as nature*, which it then attempts to justify, reducing being to this or that particular type of it. However, since human "opinion," guided now not by thought, but by "sense perception," holds one or another of these types as more fundamental or a more trustworthy "*it seems*," we have, as a result, as many pseudo-philosophical "theories" as we have types of distinguishable empirical nature. With this, our very method has decisively changed. Having begun with presuppositions about the real being of this or that nature, we continue on the road of our presuppositions about nature's origin, development, purpose, etc. Therefore, the "opinions of mortals" multiply and proliferate, each wishing to occupy the seat of truth. In reality, though, they are only "opinions," or *doxa*, and we can speak of them only as more or less "probable" and seek to investigate the respective "opinions."

If "opinion" wants to take its *true* place in philosophy as a whole, nothing other than philosophy as knowledge can determine what that place is. Philosophy as knowledge can make "opinion" itself an object of thought and draw, thereby, a clear distinction between "thought" and "opinion." The latter always remains an "opinion" and essentially distinct from thought however deeply thought might penetrate into its essence. Furthermore, the deeper philosophical reflection penetrates into the essence of "opinion," the brighter philosophical reflection reveals its unstable and fluctuating nature. Philosophy as knowledge can study pseudo-philosophy along with other issues but only as its object, as characterized above. It must be careful of only one thing in order not to depart from *its* path of truth. Philosophy must not follow the path of the pseudo-philosophy that it investigates. Parmenides warned, "Nevertheless, you will learn how opinion, which always pervades everything, must occupy an appropriate place. ... But restrain your thought from this path of investigation, and do not let habit born of many experiences force you onto this path."[15]

The East introduced many types of pseudo-philosophy into Europe already before Parmenides. However, as far as we can tell Parmenides primarily had in mind cosmogonical or cosmological theories and in general every sort of theory ("genetic theories") of the "origin." The object under scrutiny in these cases is not "being," but the "apparent order." The task in all of them was to find "nature" and "from whence the order came into being": the Earth, the Sun, the Moon, the ether, the stars and even the "outermost Olympos"[16] – indeed, if we believe the report of Diogenes Laertius, even human beings. Obviously, all of these are issues that in contemporary "Introductions to Philosophy," which is a modern invention, are labeled "ontological" and "cosmological problems." In line with the above discussion, they are not part of philosophy, understood as a science, but are one of the types of pseudo-

---

[14] [Cf. Aristotle 1984: 1554 (*Metaphysics* 982b 19). As with Parmenides, the translation has been slightly modified to bring it into conformity with Shpet's rendering.]

[15] [Cf. Robinson 1968: 111.]

[16] [Cf. Robinson 1968: 119.]

philosophy along with other Eastern imports, viz., wisdom, worldview, morals, etc. Precisely so far as the mentioned "problems" lay claim to a "scientific" solution, they actually form the main content of "pseudo-philosophy."

# IV

I have no intention to include myself among the interpreters of Parmenides. To me what is important are simply the fundamental guiding threads of his philosophical design, a design that I want to understand based on taking his own words literally and proceeding from the essence of philosophy itself. This is not the place to "prove" that my understanding is correct. Besides its general sense, I can simply refer to the first interpreter of Parmenides, that genius of European positive philosophy, *Plato*.

Plato deepens, strengthens, and develops the principles laid down by Parmenides. He elucidates in a more precise and more comprehensive manner the path of philosophy and at the same time demarcates philosophy, as knowledge, from pseudo-philosophy more definitively. Time and again, Plato expresses himself on this theme, but perhaps he most vividly develops the distinction between them, between "science" and "opinion" (*episteme* and *doxa*), in his most pseudo-philosophic dialogue, the *Timaeus*: "Above all, in my opinion," says Timaeus, "we must distinguish that which always is but has no becoming from that which is always becoming but never is. That which is grasped in thought with the help of concepts is always one and the same, but that which is presupposed with the help of alogical sensation, which is becoming and disappears, does not possess unconditional being. ... As essence is to becoming, so truth is to belief."[17] We find this opposition, with the same aphoristic expressiveness, in the *Republic*: "opinion (*doxa*) deals with becoming, and thinking (*noesis*) with essence."[18] Plato found a name for the lover of "opinion": to the philosopher, he contrasted the *doxaphilist*.[19]

Plato displays remarkable consistency and an unflinching spirit in the way he develops his thought. "Opinion" and "knowledge" are, we would say in contemporary terminology, states of consciousness. And since consciousness is necessarily consciousness *of something*, it is clear from this that necessity and possibility are *objective* characteristics of consciousness. Plato follows precisely this path. It would be a quite naïve *quid pro quo* to think that we could ascribe a contemporary understanding of philosophical issues and definitions to Plato. It is quite the contrary; contemporaneity is again being revived and inspired by him.

I realize the need to be brief, but in recalling the Platonic definition of philosophy, I cannot help but cite one passage from the *Republic*. Of course, I will present Plato's words as I understand them, but I will strive to be as faithful to the original as possible.

---

[17] [Cf. Plato 1969: 1161–1162 (*Timaeus* 27d–29c).]

[18] [Cf. Plato 1969: 765 (*Republic* 533e–534a).]

[19] [Cf. Plato 1969: 720 (*Republic* 479e–480a).]

Tell us here something: Does he who knows know something or nothing? Reply to me for him.

I will answer, he said, that he knows something.

Is it something that is or is not?

It is what is. How could what is not be known?

So, we are adequately assured of this, regardless of from which side we examine it, that what unconditionally exists is unconditionally knowable, and what does not exist is in no way knowable?

Quite adequately.

Let us suppose. And if something stands so that it both is and is not, would it not lie between what obviously is and what in no way is?

Between.

Then since knowledge is about what exists and ignorance of necessity is about what does not exist, with regard to this "between" we should seek something between ignorance and knowledge, if there is such a thing.

Certainly.

Is there not something that we call opinion?

Why not?

Is it a different faculty from knowledge or the same?

A different one.

Consequently, opinion is directed toward one thing and knowledge toward another, each by virtue of its own distinctive faculty.

Yes.

Thus, is not knowledge naturally related to what is, to know that what exists is? However, it seems to me necessary, if you please, to explain first how things are.

How things are?

We say that faculties are a certain sort of what is. Only thanks to it are we able to do what we are able to do. And everything else is a faculty of whatever it is a faculty. I call, for example, sight and hearing, faculties, if only you understand what I want to say by this concept.

Certainly, I understand, he said.

Hear, then, what seems to be the case concerning them. I cannot see any color in a faculty or a shape as in many other cases, in spite of the fact that I distinguish things around myself. One thing is such; another is different. In a faculty I see only that toward which it is directed and what it accomplishes. In this way, I call each of them a faculty, and what is directed toward one thing and what accomplishes the same thing I call by one name, and what is directed to another and accomplishes the other I call another name. How about you, what is your practice?[20]

We could dwell on this problem, but what we have said is enough. Do we need to translate it into contemporary terminology? We would surely get the same result. Perhaps our terms would be more precise, but the essential idea expressed by Plato is clear. Problems of the "origin," i.e., problems concerning an explanation of empirical activities, form the object of opinion. They are resolved on the basis of presuppositions and can be given only more or less probable answers, viz., "opinions." Knowledge has to do with another object, one that is fundamentally different from what is perceived by the senses and that seems to be true. There are some,

---

[20] [Cf. Plato 1969: 716–717 (*Republic* 476e–477d).]

however, who do not have a precise understanding of the positive tasks of philosophy that Plato formulated and who think that he viewed *all* of reality as an "illusion." Such an expression of "idealism," or more precisely, of phenomenalism and illusionism is an essentially negative expression and in no way positive. It is also an Eastern import.

On the contrary, the first task of philosophy, as knowledge, is to distinguish what is illusory (*ta phainomena*) from what is real or essential (*ousia*) in given reality itself (*ta onta*). This, incidentally, is the theme of Plato's *Sophist*. What remains, then, as the genuine object, or subject matter, of philosophy, as knowledge, what remains "the same" (*tavton*) in the unsteady fluctuation, is the mentioned essence, and we can grasp it in definite, logically and verbally fixed forms (*eidos*).[21] However, the most remarkable thing is that Plato, having so clearly shown what the object of philosophy, as knowledge, is and having sharply distinguished philosophy from pseudo-philosophy did not fall into the error so natural here and which is apparently becoming characteristic of philosophy *today*, as opposed to the psychologism of *yesterday's* philosophy. I mean the error of formal "ontologism."

For Plato, the distinction between objects is clearly a distinction in the ways in which consciousness is directed toward them: presupposing and thinking, sense intuition and "intellectual" intuition. The difference between them is a difference in the directedness itself. It is precisely this "discovery" that prescribes to philosophy its unique and true path. A reflection on directedness itself, probing deeper into it, proceeding through it back to the originarily given ("*anamnesis*"), rescues philosophical knowledge from the formalism of the purely ontological sciences, such as, for example, "mathematics," which, nevertheless, serves as an object of the understanding ("*dianoia*") or of "reasoning," though not of an intellectual grasping in the rigorous sense ("*noesis*") or of reason ("*nous*"). Being directed toward thinking itself in its directedness toward objects, philosophical thought seizes it in a pure intuition as an "*idea*," i.e., as the content, meaning, or sense of the objective forms. It is precisely this, the grasping of the sense, of the *reason* ("*logos*") of the *essence* itself, that properly raises philosophy, as knowledge, to *dialectic* – as opposed to "reasoning" – at the highest level, as Plato himself defines dialectic in the *Republic*. However, the doctrine of "ideas" is particularly in need of special clarification and of a deepening, since it has given rise to a number of distortions of a pseudo-philosophical character: ideas as "realities," ideas as "laws" and "methods,"[22] ideas as "immanent objects," and finally, in the least successful witticism of the East, ideas as "thoughts of God."[23] All of these are tempting but in no way present a deepening.

---

[21] [Whereas Shpet writes here of "fixed forms," he clearly writes "*eidos*," not "eidoi," the plural of "*eidos*."]

[22] [A reference, probably, to the Marburg neo-Kantian interpretation. See Natorp 2004.]

[23] [A reference, possibly, to an ancient and traditional interpretation of the Platonic Ideas, or Forms, as "thoughts of God." For more information on this interpretation, see Dillon 2011: 31–42.]

# V

If we ponder the sense of the adduced clarifications and recall the "history" of European philosophy, we will have to admit that there has been an amazing stability in our understanding and *feeling* of the methodological path of philosophy, as knowledge. Philosophical thought has continually addressed it and returned to it having satiated itself on worldly and pseudo-philosophical temptations, tiring of wisdom and morals. Philosophical thought found in it new sources for its creativity and drew new strength for its serious work. Not only positive but also negative philosophy detected the scent I have stressed, and we can easily discern a single thing under various designations: "consciousness," "memory," "thinking," "thought," "cogitatio," "perception" (Hume), "cognition" (Fichte), *Urwissen* (Schelling), "spirit," and many other names, among which there is even – *poenitendum est* – "soul." These terms have sheltered an honest allegiance to philosophy, as knowledge, along with a betrayal of it.

What understanding have we now reached of the tasks of philosophy as a result of so many centuries of philosophical work? Above all, we are convinced that truth, as the task of philosophy, is true and not conditional or relative. We know that the actual source of error and inconsistency is the human individual, who in his empirical being is conditioned by many things and is correlated with many things. We understand that, as a consequence, human errors and mistakes have only a conditional and relative significance, that their source lies in our own insufficiently resolute philosophical will, which succumbs to non-philosophical temptations. Furthermore, we have achieved great precision not just in our terminology, but also in our analyses, sometimes attaining an incomparable depth and dialectical force.

Occasionally, we happen to hear complaints about the "difficulty" of contemporary philosophical works and, oddly enough, these complaints often come from people who accept the legitimacy of such "difficulty" in other scientific fields. All of these complaints are vestiges of the *Enlightenment*. They look to philosophy seeking to be "enlightened." There is no dispute that there happen to be times when philosophy, fulfilling its *civic* duty, concerns itself with "enlightening." However, it would be an error to see this as the essence of philosophy, just as it would be to see *technical* applicability as the essence of mathematics or physics. Finally, there is one respect in which we have made great achievements, we have achieved great precision in our understanding of philosophy's tasks. This is, perhaps, our most important achievement.

When the talk turns to *precision*, we often understand it to be a kind of verbal paralysis or frostbite, forgetting that this would signify not progress in knowledge, but a halt in the development of language and of its creativity, a uniform hardening of previously created forms. When talking about "precision," philosophy is often compared with other sciences, in particular with mathematics. To the disgrace of philosophy, mathematics has supposedly made some, one would say, "progress." What, in comparison, has philosophy achieved? Let us leave aside the judgments of today's *obscurants* – *obscurorum virorum*[24] – who are guided by one particular pragmatic criterion, namely, technology. Nevertheless, there is no denying the legitimacy of a comparison from the standpoint of knowledge itself. A comparison can be conducted here from two angles: one with respect to the progress achieved and the other with respect to the distinctive features of the object of exact mathematics and of exact philosophy. In the first, the result of the comparison is negative; in the second it is positive. In the first, what is usually stressed is the difference, in the second it is the similarity. On the contrary, let us turn our attention in the first case to their similarity and in the second to their difference. If we do so, we will clearly see that the mentioned characterization of the results of such a comparison greatly simplifies the actual state of things.

In fact, however, is the *difference* we see in the second case not more important? Is it not better to discover the essential element in each of the types of knowledge we have compared? This difference arises from the fact that the results of mathematics are abstract. Mathematics abstracts from living experience, from the fact that everything given to us is given *via* consciousness. But an abstraction from consciousness is an abstraction from the content. Mathematics, therefore, is essentially *ontological*. As Plato precisely determined its place – understanding, the faculty of geometers, lying *between* opinion and the intellect – mathematics deals with objective essences, though not with the thought directed toward this object as such. On the contrary, philosophy must always remain concrete. To the extent that it is positive, even pseudo-philosophy is concrete, and the results of its work, therefore, are distinguished by an unusual complexity that mathematics does not know. Philosophy operates with the absolute plenitude of all that is given in living experience. It essentially concerns *principle* and is non-ontological. Philosophy, as knowledge, is the "fundamental" science in its most direct and originary sense.

Mathematics and philosophy are similar insofar as both deal with "essences" and not with "facts." Both yield, we would say, ousiological or eidetic knowledge. However, at this point they must be rigorously distinguished. An inability to see this distinction resulted in philosophy yielding to the general enthusiasm for mathematical precision. Imitating mathematics, philosophy became ontological, abstract, and lost its fundamental independence. Here again with regard to precision, it is more important to give an account of the difference than of the similarity. Precision in mathematics and precision in philosophy are not one and the same. Obviously in both types of knowledge there is a concern with logical techniques, but whereas in mathematics the concern centers on techniques for defining, proving, deducing, etc., in philosophy we demand precise references, descriptions, clarifications and a bringing to originary givenness. Mathematics is essentially discursive; philosophy is interpretive. The difference in the methodological techniques employed in the various spheres of knowledge leads to a "qualitative" difference in precision. Any viewpoint that sees the difference as limited only to degrees of precision is very primitive. Certainly, precision is not a stupefied formula established over centuries,

---

[24] [Most likely, a reference to the sixteenth century book *Epistolæ Obscurorum Virorum*, published in Germany, a satirical work aimed at the clergy and scholasticism.]

as if it were an incantation, in which not a single letter can be changed. Rather, precision is more or less an approximation to a logical ideal. It seems to me that to compare degrees of demonstrative-mathematical precision with degrees of dialectical-philosophical precision would actually make no more sense than to compare the value of the premises of some syllogism with that of the premises of a property owner.[25]

# VI

On the other hand, concerning the progress of both mathematics and philosophy, it would be important to understand their *similarity* as well. Perhaps then we would not come to such absolutely negative conclusions with regard to philosophy. I have not the slightest intention of denying or underestimating the progress made by mathematics, not because of the "practical" consideration that such a move would not serve to embellish philosophy, but above all because it would not be true. I value mathematical knowledge in the highest possible way and see it, as *pure* knowledge, one of the most glaring manifestations of the genuine European spirit. However, taking precisely the standpoint of understanding this purity, of comprehending its foundations as those of pure knowledge, it seems to me that the fortunes of mathematics are in many respects analogous to those of philosophy. Above all, I have in mind the opinion of one writer who is completely caught up in the "purification" of mathematics and who has expended quite some effort establishing its "principles." I am referring to Bertrand Russell, the author of *The Principles of Mathematics*, whose views Louis Couturat, the author of another book, albeit with the same title, characterizes in the following way: "They are the necessary conclusion and the crowning point of all the critical investigations mathematicians have devoted themselves to in the last 50 years."[26]

Those who fall into a cataleptic state upon hearing the words "mathematical precision" should ponder Russell's words. Many people are convinced that Euclidean geometry is, in general, notably privileged, unusual for a human artifact, with being outfitted after having just been discovered with the armor of undeviating precision. Here, for example, is what Russell has to say about this geometry: "...not only is it doubtful whether his [Euclid's] axioms are true, ... but it is certain that his propositions do not follow from the axioms which he enunciates. ... Thus Euclid fails entirely to prove his point in the very first proposition."[27] Alternatively, we can take another example, "Macauley, contrasting the certainty of mathematics with the uncertainty of philosophy, asks who ever heard of a reaction against Taylor's theorem. If he had lived now, he himself might have heard of such a reaction, for this is

---

[25] [Actually, Shpet here plays on the Russian world *posylka*, which can designate the premise of a syllogism as well as a parcel. I have modified the example to play on the dual meanings of the word "premises" in English.]

[26] [Couturat 1905: v.]

[27] [Russell 1918: 94.]

precisely one of the theorems which modern investigations have overthrown."[28] Of course, these "new," perhaps for some even futuristic, views on the nature of mathematics should be taken *cum grano salis*. Nevertheless, however, the magic of the conjurer's invocation of "mathematical precision" must be dispersed by the light of reason, which cannot look on it as if it were a museum piece that can be observed but must not be touched.

Turning to Russell again, I would like to note several unexpected features in the similarity between philosophy and mathematics. Instead of always proceeding forward, philosophy is sometimes blamed for too often turning around and going backward. It is blamed for being always ready – and particularly at the present time – to revive Scholasticism rather than appreciate our enlightened era. Russell, claiming that Kant's philosophy is incompatible with today's mathematics – by the way, let us note that Couturat sees the basis of Kant's failure in the fact that he was insufficiently *rationalistic* – and admitting that the Scholastics confused the imperfection and narrowmindedness of their logic, nevertheless, recognizes that "the Aristotelian doctrines of the schoolmen come nearer in spirit to the doctrines which modern mathematics inspire."[29]

In order to note what, in my view, is the most important similarity between the successes achieved by philosophy and by mathematics, let me cite one more of Russell's pronouncements. How many times have we heard that philosophers up to now have not even been able to agree on what philosophy is? Russell asserts, "... one of the chief triumphs of modern mathematics consists in having discovered what mathematics really is."[30] It is a pity that this was said about mathematics, for to some extent this holds for philosophy and precisely expresses its successes today.

Philosophy, though, has accomplished something else in our time: More clearly than mathematics, it knows how to explain the difference between the results of philosophical and mathematical knowledge. Russell defines mathematics in the following way: "Thus mathematics may be defined as the subject in which we never know what we are talking about, nor whether what we are saying is true."[31] Russell succeeded in presenting an accurate definition of mathematics, because he clearly understood its *purely formal* character, as a science. Of course, this is a great "triumph" for mathematics, namely, the realization of its true nature. However, only philosophy itself, which also starts with such an understanding of mathematics, can find the true place for this sort of knowledge along with other types of knowledge as well as itself. With this understanding of mathematics, philosophy clearly realizes that if we are to compare mathematics to logic, we must compare it to its special "kernel" and its logical foundation in the broad sense, i.e., to so-called "pure logic." For the latter, what is essential is its purely objective *ontological* character, owing to which alone it turns out to be merely a purely formal discipline. However, it follows from this that pure mathematics together with "pure" logic include their problems

---

[28] [Russell 1918: 95.]

[29] [Russell 1918: 96.]

[30] [Russell 1918: 75.]

[31] [Russell 1918: 75.]

within the sphere of a special philosophical discipline, namely, formal ontology. In other words, together with the latter they form a special closed sphere that was termed even by the old rationalism as *Mathesis universalis*. On the other hand, philosophy itself, as the fundamental science, the science of principles, filling objective forms with the content of living experiences, that is, with the content of an awareness of these objects, does not enter into this formal triumvirate, but with its "material" tasks carries out its own independent work.

Thus, philosophy's determination of the tasks of philosophical knowledge and its answer to the question of what philosophy is turns out to be a dual triumph for it. Philosophy not only points out the place of the various types of exact knowledge, but by determining this place it also points out the difference in the quality of this precision, the vague awareness of which gave rise to so many misunderstandings.

# VII

This, however, does not exhaust the achievements of philosophy today. It emancipated itself from "mathematism" and "ontologism," because it understood more profoundly both their formal as well as its own *sui generis* object. But philosophy achieved this very understanding as a result of penetrating more profoundly into the distinction between the objects that the fathers of European philosophy had already revealed. Today's philosophy has fundamentally succeeded in bringing out the distinction between "ideal" and "empirical" objects, between the objects of "knowledge" and those of "opinion." It has rigorously disassociated itself from the pseudo-philosophical temptations that would prove fatal for it and at the same time has dispelled the specter of a *unique scientific form*. It has successfully shown that "scientific" philosophy is just as much a pseudo-philosophy as is "metaphysical" philosophy, since both pose for themselves the task of resolving the issues of "origin" and "explanation."

Here in liberating itself from all *dogmas* of scientific and common sense, philosophy today stakes a claim to a rigor totally unknown in the past. Only now is it completely imbued with the grandeur of the two commandments of *philosophical rigor* – both having again originated with Plato – which any philosopher, having accepted them with sworn solemnity and sincerity, must follow.

*I. For philosophy as pure knowledge, there are no important or unimportant truths.*
*II. Philosophy as pure knowledge takes nothing for granted.*

Plato himself in his works implemented these commandments as though he had posed it as his own special task to reveal their significance: The first in the *Sophist*, and the second in the *Theaetetus*. However, it seems that we grasp their secret sense completely only now, when we demand that in philosophy as pure knowledge everything in our intuition be given originarily and immediately; when we demand that not just some particular theory, but all theories and all hypotheses be banished from philosophy as pure knowledge; finally when we demand the most careful and precise account be given in every turn of our intuitive gaze, in every movement of our reflection directed to even the most "insignificant" thought.

The more rigorous we become, however, in determining the tasks of philosophy as knowledge, the freer we apparently are in determining the other sorts and types of knowledge. We limit philosophy as knowledge not in order to restrain other types of knowledge, but, among other things, in order to gain a clearer understanding of the latter in their free "opinion" and also to emancipate them from pseudo-philosophy. Having unloaded what for it is the excessive burden of purity, pseudo-philosophy is now completely free to pursue its concern with "consoling" humanity and making "sense" of human destiny, as well as putting in order matters unforeseen by the Creator of the cosmic disorder, all of which trouble humanity. The sciences themselves, the "special" sciences, long ago won for themselves an unusual amount of freedom. Once upon a time, it seemed that lifeless "physical" nature was subordinated to the rigor of straightforward mathematical laws. This became a memory a long time ago. It turned out that the *empirical* world is much broader. Our "experience" far exceeds the bounds of "physical" experience, and one empirical object after another yielded to our growing scientific knowledge: living things, the psyche, and finally social and historical "nature." Indeed, the broader the field grasped by experience, the clearer it became that the rigor of the "laws of nature" are only pseudo-rigorous. However rigorous we want these laws to be, they are in fact only *empirical*. The "relativity of knowledge" has become a cliché; "relativism" is a refrain learned in the kindergarten of science. In this respect, one would think there are no reasons to restrain pseudo-philosophy except perhaps, and then only in certain cases, a pedagogical one.

The fact is that pseudo-philosophy, noted for its great imitativeness and suggestiveness, has always, given enough time, tried rather loyally to proceed in step with empirical science. For example, after Copernicus it realized quite well its awkwardness in justifying the caprices of Joshua, son of Nun.[32] On the other hand, however, after Joseph von Fraunhofer, pseudo-philosophy considered itself as having every right to talk about how matters stand on Sirius or Vega. And after Darwin it began to depict with great inspiration the origin of parliamentarianism from the obscurity that at one time the solar system occupied. Precisely in this way, pseudo-philosophy with all of its materialisms, spiritualisms, monisms, evolutionisms, sometimes lagging behind a bit and sometimes running ahead, nevertheless, on the whole strove to be on a par with "empirical knowledge." But now and then it was capricious and revealed a considerable amount of willfulness, appearing aloof and displaying scorn for experience. In its flights of phantasy, it lifted a veil from the deepest mysteries and with great thoroughness undertook to transmit to us the most detailed "knowledge" of all the designs, plans and activities of the worldly overlords whose names are usually written with capital letters: Fate, Demiurge, Jehovah, Love, Will, Unconscious, Energy, etc. Here – precisely here – I suppose, some restraint is pedagogically justified. Nevertheless, it would be necessary, as the Platonic Timaeus

---

[32] [See Joshua 10: 12–13.]

wanted, "to accept the tale which is probable and inquire no further."[33] We must recognize, however, that at just this point contemporary Europe, indeed in its purest expression, namely the English spirit, found an entirely adequate criterion in *pragmatism.*

Pragmatism provides broad scope for individual metaphysical creation, subordinating its appraisal to that of the creative individual: the richer, more versatile, and deeper is the author of a metaphysical system, as a depiction of *one's personal worldview*, the more interesting is this construction. The truly metaphysical constructions are honestly individual and personal. Their significance is directly proportional to the significance of their authors. Every genuinely metaphysical system is of the form: "How *I* perceive the world." This is exactly the reason, on the other hand, why metaphysical systems have no need of "disciples." They are philosophical *poems* of a sort. It is impossible to look on such systems as knowledge. Indeed, *my* perception and sense of the world are not even *my knowledge*. Of course, however, a personal metaphysical creation is not something unconditional. Rather, it is conditional, reiterating the conditions under which the "worldviews" of individuals are composed. These conditions provide the possibility of arranging the worldviews *by type*. A "religious" worldview, a "positive" worldview, a "mythological" and a "spiritual" worldview are such types. Their very name points to the source of their guiding ideas and schemas.

Yet regardless of what type of metaphysics we establish, the most essential characteristic of each is that they are, nevertheless, an individual creation. Therefore, the "struggle" against metaphysics is senseless. This "struggle" has its source in one and the same pseudo-philosophy, namely the aspiration to exclude the individual element and to substitute for it a seemingly scientific "universal" element. Regardless of whether we say metaphysics is exact knowledge or that metaphysics is not a science and therefore "scientific" positive knowledge must be substituted for it, both expressions advance the idea of pseudo-philosophy. Actually, philosophy, as pure knowledge, peacefully coexists with metaphysics as well as with a relative knowledge of reality, though only under the condition that complete autonomy be granted to the individual, the empirical and the pure. The infringement of one on the freedom of another is the unfailing source of pseudo-philosophic temptations.

Enough, however, about pseudo-philosophy. Let us return to the positive achievements of the philosophy that wants to be pure knowledge. We should note here another of its outstanding and essential achievements. Having secured a precise definition of the object of philosophy as knowledge and having determined its investigative path, we now have the possibility of illuminating anew the entire history of philosophy. This definition provides us with the criterion by which we can not only distinguish what belongs to positive philosophy and what to negative philosophy, but through it we also realize what negative philosophy, properly speaking, has introduced into the general history of thought and the very useful role it, as a matter of fact, played in the development of positive philosophy itself. Its doubt and even negation have often provided very interesting and profound problems for positive philosophy.

---

[33] [Plato 1969: 1162 (*Timaeus* 29d).]

Everyone understands that there is a distinction between the sincere doubt of Hume or of Mill, which, although amounting to a negation, nevertheless, poses many problems for philosophy, and the negation of Protagoras or of Kant. The positive role of the latter two perhaps lies solely in the reaction they evoked. Furthermore, seen from the viewpoint of the mentioned criterion the role of pseudo-philosophy becomes clear. Certainly, there is a distinction between a pseudo-philosophy presenting itself as magic and faith-healing, or an unraveller of "worldly riddles,"[34] and a pseudo-philosophy sincerely convinced of the educational, inspirational, aesthetic or some other value of its outright phantasies. There is also a distinction between a pseudo-philosophy that maintains that its "opinion" is true and a "worldview" that never forgets an "opinion" is just that, an "opinion." In this way, it is easy to distinguish between a Haeckel, on the one hand, and a Giordano Bruno or a Fechner, on the other. We can also easily grasp the difference between a Wundt, on the one hand, and a James, on the other. Yet, with this new criterion, we achieve even more. Namely, with it we can distinguish in every individual philosopher a positive and a negative philosophy, philosophy as knowledge and philosophy as opinion, an "honest" pseudo-philosophy and an oracle. This opposition between "knowledge" and "opinion" should not mislead us. If we encounter it in a Spencer, we can immediately set against him, for example, such a truly European philosopher as Hamilton.

Finally, we can distinguish where pseudo-philosophy came into close contact with philosophy as knowledge. Even though it there played a directly obstructionist role, pseudo-philosophy, giving crude answers as befitting its Eastern heritage, nevertheless helped contribute to philosophy's successes. Thus, for philosophy it certainly does matter when pseudo-philosophy treated philosophy as an abstract-scientific construction or when philosophy's essentially concrete character was simply not taken into account. Consequently, it does matter when philosophy fell into the hands of the likes of Spencer or Schelling. There was also a difference when philosophy ignored its true path "via" thought and consciousness and when, whether consciously or unconsciously, recalling the one rightful path it turned in this direction. This, for example, clearly shows us the significance of materialistic pseudo-philosophy, on the one hand, and spiritualistic pseudo-philosophy, on the other. We need not dwell any longer on the fact that our criterion with particular clarity reveals those moments in the development of philosophical thought when philosophy stood loyally behind its traditions and faithfully adhered to the first principle of positive European philosophy.

# VIII

Thus, with regard to all the points mentioned we can already speak of the achievements realized by philosophy as knowledge and even of some of its "triumphs." However, let us turn in the other direction, namely, to the future. We see that in rigorously adhering to its tasks, philosophy confronts an infinite field of serious and

---

[34] [A reference, most likely to Ernst Haeckel's *Die Welträthsel.*]

fascinating work. Here, in the realm of future perspectives we see the tasks facing our present philosophic epoch as well as tomorrow's. We can speak of neither ultimate solutions nor even the final formulations of the problems. In them, we certainly will find the stamp of time, of the interests of particular individuals, of inconclusive judgments and creations that have not been completely destroyed by criticism. Certainly no one can claim "finality," the "final word," when speaking of philosophy as knowledge. Indeed, hardly anyone would want to so long as one does not forget that philosophy as knowledge stands before us. Moreover, a faulty memory here, which is neither difficult nor unusual, would only be a wish for improvement. In any case, philosophy itself does not make a mistake; the philosopher does. And it is illogical for "negativists" and "positivists" to pretend that they do not notice the difference between the philosopher and his/her philosophy. The philosopher, in turn, is *obliged* to admit to his/her philosophical mistakes and to take responsibility for them.

Taking the tasks confronting philosophy as pure knowledge in the sense mentioned above, we stand, as I pointed out, on the only path predetermined by the very essence of such philosophy. What is revealed to us on this path as the ultimate goal of our efforts is reality itself in its genuine being, namely *that which is, that which exists*. Reality, that which is, always surrounds us; we *live* in and by it: we suffer, occasionally rejoice, fear, become indignant, struggle, love, and die. Among the numerous and wide diversity of experiences, there is one, or, more precisely, one group of experiences, that occupies in general an extremely modest place in human life but that sometimes expands to monstrous dimensions. This is that group of experiences designated by the term *philosophical*. In this group, what predominates is an interest that sometimes grows to a crushing size, an interest in reality itself, in what there is and consequently what we experience, on the whole, an interest in *everything*. As soon as we attempted to satisfy our interest, we were faced with the question: What is? – What is this everything? – as we called this *object*, which we then designate as the object, or subject matter, of philosophy. Therefore, with this question we set our experience against something "greater" than it. As long as we simply "live," we find this *everything* in our experience: One thing enters into it, another leaves; one is added, another is taken away. Nevertheless, we *experience everything* and only it.

Our question, as it were, however, removes us from the sphere of experience. What is not easy to "give up" is not easy to take away. Something comes to a stop before us and stands like an enigmatic question mark. It lurks "behind" everything and stops the continuous stream in which everything flows. The object is the question, and philosophy begins with the quest or expectation of an answer to it. We now look with *different* eyes on what there is. We look for solutions to the emerging problem in it. Sometimes it deceives us, and, at other times, our hopes are raised only to be disappointed and then again encouraged. We become more distrustful and suspicious. Not everything that we experience can help us in answering our question. Although we try to free ourselves of deception, we often fall into an even more delicate and intricate web of deception. Sometimes we completely trust – or pretend to trust – what "seems to be the case" in experience. Nevertheless, we do not find what we need. Perhaps there is nothing, and there is no need to seek and no need to expect anything, since there happen to be no "answers." This discussion about everything is already a matter of morals. Philosophy cannot and must not come to a stop. To stop would be its death, and morals would be a lethal poison. If there is "nothing," and no "answers" can be had, then philosophy will find *this answer* to be *its* answer and not a moral exhortation. But what here is *its* exhortation, its further path?

If there is something that "seems to be," then there is also something that does not seem to be. If there is something "fortuitous," then there is also something not fortuitous. Moreover, it is the same *with everything*, in what there is and what we experience. There is "something" *in addition* to "everything." If it is not "nothing," it is surely also a profoundly moral addition. The philosophical path leads along the border between what seems to be and what does not seem to be, namely to what is true. This is the path of philosophy, *its* path. But we do not always see it: Sometimes it is the darkness of night, sometimes it is because of blindness, and sometimes we did not want to see. But we must seek this path, must pave it ourselves. Not everything that is is "in fact." Not everything given in experience is "really" given[35]; not everything that exists is essential. We must distinguish the essential, the *essence*, in what exists from what is not essential. We can turn directly facing what is essential and say what it is, as we see it, if only our judgments about it were not so often mistaken, if we ourselves did not introduce into the essential judgments what is not essential. We can do things differently. We can concentrate our attention on what is not essential and "isolate" it from what is essential, carefully removing from the given what "seems" to be and what is "contrived," thereby "cleansing" it of what to us is "habitual," of presuppositions, conjectures, hypotheses, theories, and of what simply "happens," "occurs," or "takes place" in what there is but does not *abide* in it. The essential, what abides in being, stays itself, *"the same."* All this is one. Being is what it is only through the fact that it is, that in it an essence (*"ousia"*) abides. If we were told that variability and contingency are the essence of being, this would thereby be an acknowledgment that this variability, this "twinkling," is what abides, stays itself. Precisely this would be understood as the essence. Even Eastern wisdom cannot evade essence. Having recognized everything that is is illusory, it sees illusion to be the essence, "the same," of being. If we are told that we often take an essence to be an illusion and an illusion to be an essence, then we will have to repeat that our mistakes are not the mistakes of what is, but of how *we* perceive an essence. An essence does not cease to be an essence.

Therefore, although we are advancing along the path of philosophy, we have by no means embarked on the path that leads directly to philosophy as pure knowledge. We still are at that stage of philosophy where philosophy is taken as dealing with our *experience*. Yet staying within the sphere of experience, we can advance a bit further. Distinguishing the essence from the contingent, that which abides from that which is transitory, in what there is, we can be certain that we see each with a *differ-*

---

[35] [Shpet here employs the Husserlian distinction between "real" and "*reel*." For Husserl and for Shpet here, to say that not everything in experience is really given means, in brief, that not everything in experience is temporal and has distinguishable components.]

*ent gaze*. I noted above that the moment when we opened our eyes for the first time on reality, as on a riddle, when we looked on "everything" with *other* eyes, was the moment of the transition from the simple experience of "everything" to a philosophical experience of it. We took just one timid step, but again we must concern ourselves with enlightening our philosophical gaze. Just as earlier we passed from our usual view of our commonplace reality to an intuition of it as a kind of riddle, so now having recognized the contingent and the essential in what is, we recognize that we intuit these two "sorts" of being by means of two sorts of looking. Just as we passed in the first instance from a blind experience of reality to a more enlightened one, so we now proceed in the same direction, but reality is all one and the same, and our gaze is one.

It is easy to grasp the source of this distinction and identity. We do not find reality divided, as it were, into two parts, one positioned "alongside" the other, or one "behind" the other, or one "above" the other, or something else that a figure of speech could incorrectly convey to us. Instead, we do find a *single* reality. It is only that our gaze dwells sometimes on the contingent "surface" of reality and sometimes probes "deeper" through it to its essential "core." The two sorts of intuition directed on what is given to us are a *single* intuition, but only different degrees of seeing. We will not deviate far from customary terminological usage if we compare the two mentioned "sorts" of intuition with the usual opposition between an "inner" and an "outer" look, a "sensual" and an "intellectual" look, or simply a *look* and an *insight*. In any case, the sense of such oppositions benefits a lot from such a comparison.

# IX

Our results are, therefore, of the greatest importance, because they now earnestly provide us with the possibility of approaching the means by which philosophy can begin its work. On the one hand, we found that there is a fundamental distinction between the two sorts of objects we mentioned and toward which our experience or our consciousness is directed. On the other hand, we see that this distinction rigorously corresponds to one between the ways in which we arrive at these objects with their distinct sorts of givenness. It is not hard to see that this correlation between an object and the intuition directed toward it has a completely universal character not just in that every object refers to some consciousness, i.e., that consciousness is a consciousness of an object, but, more precisely, in that to every object of some particular sort, there corresponds a peculiar form or structure of consciousness, or – to put it in yet another way – an "attitude" of consciousness. Consciousness as a whole conforms to the sort of object before it, although we can easily pass from one attitude to another: from the contingent to the essential, from the factual to the eidetic, and vice versa.

Let us now turn our analysis toward consciousness itself as such, making it the object of our examination and study. In addition to the concrete unity of consciousness with its different sorts of attitudes and regardless of what kind of consciousness we have in mind, consciousness is always essentially characterized by its directedness toward an object. To use more commonly accepted terminology, we find that consciousness is always characterized by *intentionality*. We are now at the threshold of philosophy as pure knowledge, and in order to provide as clear an account as possible of where we are headed let us turn once again to the distinction between the factual and the eidetic. Let us now try to approach them philosophically, *through* a consciousness of the factual and the eidetic. In this way, we come to a clearer understanding of the essence of this issue and at the same time illustrate the way to approach the problem philosophically.

Citing examples, we have mentioned various sorts of experiential objects, and with them in mind immediately state the difference between two sorts of *givenness*. This givenness appears before us as the "content" of the intended objects that are the "indefinite bearers" of the given. This distinction, of which we are immediately aware, can seem so obvious that it "goes without saying." It can be taken as the basis – and actually relied upon – for classifying the sciences. An object given in this way can be taken as an object for science and even for ontology. Nevertheless, however, this is a "dogmatic" givenness, and not a philosophical givenness in the rigorous and precise sense. Consequently, it is necessary to turn to the respective differences in our consciousness of these objects with the content that is given in them. We notice at once here how consciousness through its intentionality "conducts" itself in different ways depending on this or that attitude. We will pause only on one aspect that is of paramount importance for our concern, an aspect that so struck St. Augustine, judging by his *Confessions*, and that allowed him to demarcate distinctly between a consciousness of the factual and a consciousness of the eidetic.

I have in mind the "aspect" that in the most general and broadest sense could be called the "reproduction" of the given in experience. When we observe the reality in which we live, we notice some things in it that "protractedly" remain an observed object, and along with them we notice other moving things that constantly change position, location, and form. A "motionless" house stands before us while people, animals and cars approach and pass by. We see how the trees sway and smoke billows from the chimneys. To put it succinctly, some of the things around us appear more or less stable and others moveable. By means of reflection and "theory," we conclude, however, that *everything* is moveable, everything is changing, and everything is dependent on its place, form, shape, etc. However, if in observing reality we take into account also our own selves, so-and-so's, as "bearers" and, as it were, centers of various sorts of processes – whether they be those of life, of the mental or of the social – that are given to us as our *experiences*, and if we consider the role they play in our act of observing, we easily get used to the idea of the universal mobility and instability of our given reality. Not just the color of the things in our surroundings depend on our own position and condition, but also the noise caused by these things, the relationship between them, and even the shape, form, size, etc. too to a considerable degree.

If we now concentrate solely on our very own experiences, we will thoroughly understand the meaning of the feature of reality that we so often repeat when we talk about reality as a continuous flux of "appearances," or a stream, a current and so forth, of experiences. It turns out precisely for this reason that in wishing to make some part or "piece" of reality the object of our study we not only extract it from the whole, as if tearing a thread that connects this piece to the whole, but even, it turns out, "freeze" this fixed "piece." At the same time as reality itself and all of our experiences have passed and are passing somewhere into the distance we remain, strictly speaking, in "the past," a past that *itself* is not given, so to speak, directly to us, but only *reproduced* by us. A reproduction of something at one time given and experienced can be repeated as a *new* experience an indefinite number of times. Moreover, we are not only conscious of this "novelty," but being unable to arouse in our consciousness the original givenness of precisely what was experienced we, nevertheless, are also conscious in a remarkable way that there is the distinction between this original givenness and all "copies" of it repeated in our experience.

No examination of the "thing" is conceivable without a reproduction of what already "has been," as well as a comparison and judgment about it, etc. In this respect, there is no *fundamental* difference between the "observation" of a thing and "self-observation," i.e., the observation of the vital and mental processes, of the psycho-physical processes, in the observer. In both cases, we are concerned with the "factual": a *factum*. Therefore, we always see the factually given as given mediately. It demands that it be the object of an examination, of a *representation*, and a descent to what is actually originarily given here, what is *presentatively* given, what, to put it another way, "remains" after removing everything that is introduced by our "imagination," "recollection," "understanding," "desire," "apperception," etc. – extending to the highest degree of difficulty.

*Phantasy* is what we call the activity of picturing to ourselves a free reproduction connected with a combining activity. We have in phantasy the most varied ways of re-grouping the data of reproduction including complete "arbitrariness" in doing so. In one respect, however, this arbitrariness seems to be limited. Namely, we cannot achieve a reproduction that would yield a *precise* copy of the originarily given. Such a thing is essentially impossible, and we are always conscious that *there is a difference*. Despite the fact that in reality we are often mistaken and accept some "similarity" to be an "identity," there fundamentally *must be* a difference, even though we have achieved – or so it "seems" to us – the maximum degree of "precision" and "adequacy."

# X

The eidetic stands in a correlative opposition to the factual. It is often depicted as a system closed unto itself, abiding in a state of static equilibrium, where each "idea" occupies a strictly determined and carefully doled out "spot." For this reason it cannot be "budged" without breaking its connection to the whole, without breaking certain "laws of logic," without creating – and this would be the kiss of death! – a "contradiction." It is forgotten, however, that "ideas" are not savage beasts that must be caged. Some imagine that an "idea" is responsible for a *natural* limitation on those who imagine. It is true that some are blind to the essential. Their intellectual gaze does not cleave the empirical envelope of an object and does not penetrate directly to the object's *eidos*, to its essential content, and, having difficulty "reaching" the "idea," then begins to "organize" it. As a result of these efforts, the respective "extensions," i.e., the concepts, are rounded-off and are arranged in some "order," like pictures hung on tacks one next to another and above another.

An *eidos*, however, is actually stable and "firm" – like truth itself. It is at rest, because it is free of worldly fuss, from the fuss of the wisdom found in the book of *Ecclesiastes*. This is, however, by no means a "statism" and a rejection of "dynamics" in it. It is not dynamic in the sense that it is not measured in horsepower or foot-pounds. Nothing moves it from its spot, and it does not contribute anything whatever to the quantity of force and energy in the world. However, its essential dynamism is easily grasped by those who not only measure "extension" by an "idea," but who *understand ideas*, those who see that an *eidos* not only always fills its forms with an active content, with a *sense*, but even in the most exacting manner reflects, by its own "movement," the slightest demands on the part of the object's formative content. An *eidos* disconnected from the whole, of which it is a necessary constituent part of the system, of the structure, is static, because it is lifeless, *devoid of sense*. As a part of the whole, it has sense and lives. Its dynamic is the dynamic of sense. What is genuinely nonsensical is to expect from it the mobility of a juggler, the strength of a locomotive or the explosion of dynamite.

Thus, as against the fussiness of the empirical, an *eidos* is actually stable and maintains its self-identity. If we apply to it the same criterion of "reproduction" that we applied above to the empirical, we will clearly see what this means. We find here what we rightly expect of an *eidos*, since we characterize it with respect to its "stability" and identity. What is revealed to our intellectual gaze in the intuition of an essence does not immediately run away from such a gaze, but remains before it in its originary givenness. It does not change *in the way* that an empirical experience changes. We do not determine it at those moments when there is a "succession"; there is no "later" and no "now" in it. In general, it has no temporal determination. Therefore, we can speak of a *reproduction* here only in an improper sense. What is recalled is not something "new" and altered every time in comparison with the originally given. The originally given is itself "personally" before us.[36] Consciousness can always be directed toward it or "averted" from it, but consciousness does not encounter it in a new "altered" form. An *essence* has no need of representation. It is given presentatively. An essential intuition is fundamentally adequate. In analyzing consciousness, our concern is not with alterable and "contingent" experience, but with the necessity correlative to it. We look on consciousness itself in its essential intentionality.

This certainly does not mean that consciousness itself, as such, is absolutely not subject to any modification at all. Consciousness is subject to it *as such*. That is,

---

[36] [Cf. Husserl 1970: 608–609 – "In perception the object seemed to achieve a full-bodied presence, to be there *in propria persona*."]

putting aside the "material" difference in acts of consciousness, we can notice in such acts certain modifications that concern not only their "qualitative" diversity but also a modification of consciousness itself, as such, "on the whole." Apart from such purely attentional alterations as concentrating our "attention" first on one and then on another "point," and apart from apperceptive "rearrangements" of it, we must above all mention the peculiar "fulfillment" or "absorption" of consciousness by some kind of "quality." In this way, we begin to see consciousness *as* consciousness, for example, as a rational consciousness, a deliberating consciousness, an evaluating consciousness, etc. Correspondingly, we approach an object as the object of "this or that" consciousness. We can say that along with the extensive alterability of consciousness we also ascertain its intensive "alterability," when we speak of an actional or non-actional state of consciousness. In an actual experience, as a process, we confront a constant change of such states. What is particularly striking here is the difference between empirical and essential objectivity.

Once an empirical object has left the field of an actional consciousness, we fundamentally cannot "restore" it, just like we cannot stop or turn back *time*. An *eidos*, an essence, remains "within our power." It stands "outside" time, and we can turn to it "whenever we please" and find it in its unconditional selfsameness. We can easily "transfer" an examined essence from one state of consciousness to another. It is always "at our command," and when we "need" it, it always turns up without fail before us. Whereas a fact "*appears*" and only then can be reproduced, an essence always "is" and is not reproduced. This modification of consciousness, as an intensive modification, fundamentally allows for "degrees" even though we also quite often notice "sudden" transitions from one state to another. These degrees can be characterized as greater or lesser degrees of *clarity* of consciousness.[37] The object toward which consciousness is directed is located at a distance of more or less *nearness*. It is found farther away or closer to the clearest "center" of consciousness. But with all of these modifications of consciousness, with quite varied degrees of "effort" or "vigor," the essence intuited in it remains invariably and calmly *one and the same*.

With regard to an essence, let us now assume we have complete freedom to phantasize and arbitrarily combine. However easy and simple it is for us then to change the content and form of an empirical object, we cannot achieve just one thing: the adequate precision we associate with the eidetic sphere. In an originally and immediately given essence, we are unable to change anything. It is as it is. Here we have the remarkable feature of the eidetic. We can have it even in our imagination and can study it as it is originarily given. We find in this, the originarily given, the source of the "precision" of eidetic knowledge. We "admit," we "imagine," we "present to ourselves" – all of these have in the eidetic sciences (formal ontology, mathematics, philosophy as knowledge) a quite special significance. The "inadmissible" and the "unimaginable" are here what is *inconceivable*, and the conceivable is everything that is simply possible. Such is the sphere of *pure possibility*; this sphere is governed by the "law of contradiction."

---

[37] [Cf. Husserl 2014: 122 (§67) – "The apprehension of an essence has accordingly its own levels of clarity just as does the individual hovering before us."]

The "law of contradiction" is not at all some kind of commandment that *must* not be violated and that, consequently, is always violated. It simply cannot be violated, and this turns out to be just the special characteristic of its very essence. The "law of identity" simply means that the essence (*essentiae entis*) is, as it is, and there is nothing that can be done about this. The "law of contradiction," however, modifies this very fact: an essence must be the way it is and again nothing can be done about it. An apparent violation of it in the empirical sphere is, on the other hand, a characteristic of the empirical itself. It is a sign that we have passed from "possibility" (*possibilitas*) to "actuality" (*actualitas*), from the "necessary" to the "contingent." Certain pseudo-philosophical attempts to hypostatize the empirical and, vice versa, to apply empirical determinations to what is essential are, properly speaking, not "contradictions," but simply *incongruencies*, which ultimately are deeply *comical* examples. Finally, "contradictions" in the presentation or expression of our thoughts and views are not, properly speaking, contradictions, but are a simple *inconsistency* in our presentation. Its presence says merely that we do not always notice an inconsistency between our words and our judgments and that we do not always even trouble ourselves with it.

# XI

Let us sum up and move on. Our "dogmatic" division of objects receives its critical justification in an analysis of the consciousness directed toward them. The advantages of such a philosophical method of studying "what is" is obvious. Since every consciousness is a consciousness of "something," this essential correlatively gives us the possibility, while studying consciousness itself, to expose the object in all of its wealth and its entire content completely. In any case, this is already obvious with respect to the formal side of the eidetic. If it may seem that the question is still not dealt with thoroughly with regard to its eidetic "content," this is due only to the fact that we have not yet adequately clarified the fundamental pillar on which philosophy as knowledge rests, namely that *consciousness itself in this study is given to us eidetically*. Here lies the *guarantee* that the philosophical knowledge of everything that is is rigorous and unconditional knowledge. In this, we find the *self-restraint* of philosophy as knowledge as against the boundless pretensions of pseudo-philosophy and wisdom.

We began our analysis with *our own* experience, having found *ourselves* to be a "thing" among the things in our surrounding world. Like any thing, like any condition or activity of a thing, our experience appears to be entirely an empirical fact, a "contingency." Forming some part of reality, the one who "experiences" implicitly reflects in oneself, perhaps, the whole of reality, as certain metaphysicians admit, and perhaps one of the paths to a cognition of the cosmos leads via this microcosmos. Such an *opinion*, like any opinion, is full of conjectures, presuppositions and images, but, although it *seems* probable to us, the mentioned possibility, in any case, cannot be excluded in principle. However, the realization of this possibility in all likelihood presents special difficulties, because although it was expressed quite long ago empirical science has continued to proceed along another path. It dogmatically divides the reality it accepted into a series of "objects" or "spheres," the study of which ultimately is to embrace all of empirical reality. Among these "spheres," a modest place is also allotted for an empirical science of "experiences" themselves as well as of the "experiencing subjects," namely psychology.

As such, i.e., as an empirical science, psychology does not, however, pretend to a cognition of the cosmos via a microcosmos. While it is true that there are many pseudo-philosophical – psychologistic and spiritualistic – attempts to revert it to the other path mentioned, that is not the path of "knowledge," but the path of the "opinions of mortals." As we heard from Parmenides, "you should learn" it, "but restrain your thought from this path of investigation."[38]

Experience, as such *furnishes* us with some purely empirical knowledge that in the course of a person's entire life accumulates passively or is actively enlarged, classified, ordered, etc., etc. In general, it is in one way or another *assimilated*. However, whether experience itself can be called cognition even in a broad, improper sense is doubtful. This means that it is impossible even to call it an "opinion." The issue is not the "conditionality," "relativity," etc., invoked in calling it empirical and contingent, but that only a single special sort of experience – and then only under special conditions – can be called "improper knowledge" or an "opinion." An experience in general is an "empirical consciousness." More precisely, it is a consciousness that belongs to the empirical human being as its "owner." In such a capacity, it is not cognition and in any case cannot be confused with cognition, since it itself is the empirical object of cognition. At most, it is only an *occasion* for an eidetic cognition.

Experience, as "opinion," which makes up "improper knowledge," is distinguished from other experience by the fact that being directed toward cognitive goals, it actively operates, though not in the sense of, for example, a volitional action on things in my surroundings and not in the sense of an attraction or repulsion of them by our senses, but in the sense of a "judgment" about them. The latter presupposes special conditions: an "opinion," as an experience, fulfills a cognitive function only when it is what is empirically given to us, when it begins to "process," i.e., summarize, explain, and grasp the given and supplement it with conjectures, hypotheses, theories, etc. In this form, an experience not only "furnishes" material for knowledge, but also itself appears against the backdrop of other experiences as the *cognizing* consciousness.

In such a form, an experience presents itself to us, as the empirical state of a "thing," i.e., of a human being, a living psycho-physical subject. It is studied in such a form by empirical science. And it necessarily remains so as long as we look at it as a state of the mentioned subject. We can attempt to pass from an examination of our own experiences or of some other subject to "experiences in general" or to the experiences of a "subject in general." We obtain a series of eidetic judgments about experience, which we include in a corresponding science under a, perhaps, corresponding title. For example, the corresponding science in psychology goes under

---

[38] [Cf. Robinson 1968: 111. Shpet already quoted these words from Parmenides in §3 above.]

the title "eidetic psychology." Nevertheless, we will be concerned, undoubtedly, with scientific or ontological knowledge, though not yet with philosophy as pure knowledge, not with the "fundamental science" in principle. In order to pass to the latter our eidetic judgments must speak not of "experiences" or of the "consciousness" of a subject, given as an empirical thing, but of *consciousness itself* in its essence.[39] For this, we must stop considering experience itself as a "dogmatically" given thing of the real world. We must look at it for its part *via* consciousness, as it is given in its essential givenness, originarily, immediately, and adequately in eidetic intuition. In other words, it is necessary to take consciousness not as an empirical experience of an individual, not as the data of "observation" or of "self-observation," but as a consciousness given to consciousness, *consciousness in a reflection on itself*. Since it is revealed to us here in its correlativity as pure intentionality, as the consciousness of any object and of any objective content, it is neither a hypothesis nor a metaphysical conjecture. It also shows that everything that is is via consciousness and that this is the path, and thereby the rigorous philosophical path, of studying "everything." There is no need to construct hypotheses and explanations here. Since nothing "depends" on consciousness in its essence, it neither "acts" on anything nor does anything "act" on it. It is not a "thing." It is not a "reality." Rather, it is an "essence" and an "idea." Any givenness is a givenness to consciousness, but it can be seen "dogmatically" as simply a "givenness" and philosophically as it is given via consciousness. Here, we need only to relate, without making any conjectures, presuppositions, and explanatory theories, and there is no need to fear that something can escape philosophical analysis. There are no details, nuances, or subtleties of the object and its content that would not be "reflected" in consciousness and that we could not reach via consciousness. Consciousness in reflection on itself reveals and intuits itself in its genuine essence, and this is why we are concerned here not with "opinion," as is the empirical experience of an individual, but with genuine knowledge.

As I already noted, "opinion" itself can be the object of rigorous knowledge. Likewise, any improper empirical knowledge can become the object of rigorous knowledge, although certainly these are only particular issues in which the task is to cognize "everything." However, from this alone it is clear, incidentally, how narrow are the attempts of privative philosophy to pass off *theory of cognition* as the "fundamental philosophical science" and even more so to turn a philosophy into "scientific philosophy." If philosophy must not be "formal" and "abstract," or "one-sided," ontology cannot be the fundamental philosophical science in the full sense. Proceeding to "everything" via consciousness, philosophy cannot help but be concrete. Every form in it is filled out; every one-sided feature is supplied, and nothing

---

[39] [Shpet's discussion here runs parallel to Husserl's talk of "eidetic sciences" that are not "transcendental" or truly "phenomenological" in that the investigations are not within the transcendental-phenomenological attitude. As Shpet makes clear here, *his* understanding of the phenomenological reduction includes an essential reflection on consciousness itself, taken eidetically, in its *essential* relation to its intended object. For Husserl's discussion of eidetic sciences, which includes eidetic psychology, see Husserl 2014: 18–20 (§§7–8).]

remains "empty." The entire *content* of an object is given exhaustively and completely with as much adequacy as is the object's form, since the content is itself composed of pure and essentially given "acts" of consciousness, from its pure intentions. It is clear from this that philosophy, being rigorous knowledge, like the ontological sciences and, in particular, like mathematics, is fundamentally different from those other sorts of knowledge in that philosophy happens to be concrete and "material" knowledge, whereas those other sorts of knowledge are abstract and formal.

The fact that philosophy as material knowledge loses so little in its eidetic nature can easily be checked by means of applying the mentioned criterion – reproduction – to its data, to its intentions. Let us say, for the sake of a psychological study, I reproduce a state I experienced yesterday, for example, that of aesthetic enjoyment. I recall in my memory not only myself as a psycho-physical organism reacting in a particular way that I can recall, but also the corresponding spatial and temporal situation of the experience. Concentrating on "myself," I can successively reproduce my every movement and gesture. I can reproduce even the tension in the muscles of my body, a distinctive "pounding in my breast," and other details of my experience. Yet despite all this, I am not repeating the experience itself precisely; I am only "reproducing" it. Furthermore, I can assemble a number of other "self-observations," and I can compare and generalize them. However, all of this is still not enough. I can even resort to a hypothesis of "physiological" and "mental" causes of my state and explain it by referring to these factors as real forces, etc. Something quite different, though, is necessary for a philosophical investigation.

Let us assume that I take that same experience as the subject of my philosophical analysis. I reproduce it, as I did earlier, but only I now direct my attention not toward "myself" as the given organism in a given setting, but, as it were, direct my attention past or "through" myself toward the very experience as an aesthetic consciousness given essentially. Not only am I immediately convinced that both the entire setting as well as I myself have no need of me for this analysis, let alone need me to increase the number of "examples" of an aesthetic impression. I also see that what I have as the "content" of consciousness – a certain unity of founded and unfounded intentions – are not "reproductions" at all. They are the *same* acts of perception, judgment, recognition, etc., that they were "yesterday" and not a new "example." Nothing has changed in them. I can even phantasize about some setting for the aesthetic experience that "did not exist." However, the conscious acts that I distinguish in reflecting on the experience are all the *same*. The more I ponder over them and want to discern their true nature, the "farther" I move away from the "fact" that gave rise to my investigation. To me, it turns out to be "unnecessary." And as I delve deeper into the aesthetic consciousness *itself*, I discover in it the quite complex structure of the various acts – some "simple" and some "complex," some "thetic" and some "synthetic," etc. – and their interrelationships. All this, I pose to myself as tasks to "reveal," to dissect, to establish and to describe. If I rigorously adhere to this purely ideal sphere of *eidos*, or the essential, in aesthetic consciousness, not the slightest urge can arise in me, not the slightest need, to construct any explanatory hypotheses or "theories." Conversely, the true sign that I have left this ideal sphere is when the urge arises in me to "explain" something, to introduce causes and effects as real connections. The conviction that in philosophy – which retains its *privilegium odiosum*, viz., purity – "explanation" must also follow after "description" is a typical trait of pseudo-philosophy. In reality, if "explanation" follows *behind* "description" in philosophy, then it undergoes the same transformation that it undergoes if explanation, due to our oversight, enters *into* the description itself. That is, philosophy is then transformed from "knowledge" into "opinion."

# XII

The most significant negative impact of this transformation on philosophy would be in that "opinion" would again play the role of "knowledge." The guarantee of philosophical rigor lies simply in the "purity" of its descriptions, in the actual communication of what "we see" in the essential analysis of consciousness. However, another question can quite legitimately be raised. Philosophy can indeed be rigorous, but the executions can be carried out badly. How can we be sure that the *philosopher* relates only what is "seen," adding and assuming nothing? History shows the most persuasive moral arguments. The threat of the Last Judgment and the death penalty could not stop philosophers, and they continued to pass off their opinions as knowledge. The freedom to express any opinion as well as to criticize that opinion had great success. Of course, this still is not a "guarantee," but apparently in philosophy there can be no other. It must carefully check its every step, every expression. It must root out every "presupposition" and every conjecture. Philosophy has nothing to fear from the length and duration of such an examination. In fact, its path is actually strewn with the victims of critical ruthlessness, but it fears nothing and is in no hurry. Its object is invariable and stands outside time. The human being, on the other hand, is in a hurry – perhaps not without reason. What remains, apparently, is to grant us complete freedom to express any opinion, even the issue of "probability" should not bind us. The same people who "confine" themselves and wish to have "knowledge" obviously must go for it without relying on the opinion of others. When we see what essentially is, what we get to know is not via some representation, but what we run into face to face. When we are convinced that it "itself" is right before us, we get to know also our fellow seekers of "knowledge." We get to know also their "personal" failings and are able to separate the one from the other. With this, the very critique of the philosophers ceases to be negative and becomes positive. A philosophical critique of knowledge consists not in the fact that knowledge "in general" is impossible, unattainable, relative, subjective, etc., but in the clarification that *what we actually see* in each given case can be discussed and that what we introduced into the *given* we can remove. A negative critique rejects the "everything" and the "in general" with the exception of "oneself." It is a pure self-affirmation. A positive critique is more difficult. It affirms *everything* but limits itself. It is a self-renunciation.

As the history of philosophy shows, even positive philosophy was not always able to accomplish this difficult act of "self-renunciation." One of the few points where negative philosophy has shown a certain consistency was its assertion of the "I" as the pivot that supports everything and the center around which everything moves. The "I" turned out to be the criterion, the measure, the source, the owner, and even – as it sometimes happened – the guarantee not only of its own arguments but also of "all things" and of *truth* itself. In those instances where in place of the name of the individual the "I" was inserted, quite often granting a law-giving function to it, relativism and negativism came naturally. Sometimes, however, this "I" is depicted with such power and omnipotence that it seemed *it* certainly must have arranged and put in order "everything," and that is why it also guarantees "knowledge" of everything. On closer examination, though, this "I" turns out to be a "self-asserting" non-entity: the gray shadow of an individual in whose pallor we saw its right to a pan-philosophical "meaningfulness" and on which a pronoun was conferred, because it itself forgot its "name." This anonymous "subject" appeared here with guarantees of not just philosophical, but of every kind of knowledge.

In my article "Consciousness and Its Owner,"[40] I tried to show that consciousness has no philosophical need of any owner, that consciousness, as such, seen in its essence, is *no one's*. If we actually analyze consciousness philosophically, we find in it, in its stream, no owner, but we do find as a special object of investigation unities of consciousness of various types and sorts: rigorously individual and collective unities. We find among these unities a "unity of cognition," but (1) under no condition can it serve as an "epistemological" guarantee; and (2) it cannot be called an "I." In reality, the "I" is always a unicum, a social "unit," a *so-and-so*. Certainly, each so-and-so is also a "unity" of consciousness, but this unity is surely a factual, empirical, and historical unity. If a unity of cognition, as essential, forms a certain "part" in the "whole" of consciousness, then obviously the *philosophical* problem of cognition simply goes past the so-and-so, "without touching" it. To an equal degree, it can neither give nor not give guarantees of knowledge. This will remain obscure only until it is clarified that consciousness in its essence – and consequently also that "part" of it that is united under the heading "cognition" – is not *my* consciousness, or that of any other so-and-so or in general, of any *real* being, that the essential, eidetic consciousness is *ideal and not real*. Just as the very idea of a real *dependence* of the real on the ideal is absurd, so is it absurd to think that a real individual can exert an *influence* on the essential consciousness.

The "ideal individual," not as an object, but as a subject, is an "epistemological" fiction. The same applies to the "pure I," the "transcendental I," etc. As an "ideal," it must be essential. Having conceded such a fiction, it would already be impossible to recognize the existence of mistakes and delusions. Let us say that in reality itself we come upon the *fact* of cognition and the fact of delusion. In order to explain this fact, it seems to me, we can assume one of two hypotheses. I, a so-and-so and an actual member of a given society, really cognize and make mistakes, and many of us also "cognize" and "imagine." Or there is one real subject of cognition in the world, and we, so-and-sos, are its organs. That is, it cognizes through us. In some unknown manner, our cognition is its cognition. It seems to me that the first hypothesis is

---

[40] [See Shpet 2006: 264–310 and of course the previous essay in this collection.]

more likely, since in the second we, living and breathing human beings, so-and-sos, still appear to be the immediate reality doing the cognizing. But if this is the case, then there are no guarantees nor can there be any in the "subject of cognition." The so-and-so, as the subject of cognition, is capricious, fragile, and mortal. Knowledge is knowledge, and the vanity surrounding a so-and-so no more guarantees or determines that knowledge than makes it waver.

Nevertheless, a so-and-so is interested in knowledge, and *he* needs to be able to separate *his* opinion from true knowledge. Finding the means for this neither within oneself nor in the fictional creations of negative philosophy, the philosopher seeks other means for protecting oneself from one's own contingent mistakes and delusions. As we know, in reflecting on itself consciousness "sees" its essence not through images or "reproductions," but unconditionally presentatively. That is, the essence of consciousness is present in reflection; the essence is "there" *in* the reflection. To put it in yet another way, this essence is *immanent* to consciousness itself. This is why there can be no "mistakes" here, because it would be a "mistake" of being itself, of *truth* itself. It would be the same as determining there is nothing here. That is, we must seek the source of any "mistakes" somewhere else. To find the source of the mistakes and find the means to eliminate them is just as much a philosophical demand. This demand must be met by philosophical means.

# XIII

Unfortunately, I do not have the opportunity here and now to enter into a detailed analysis of this problem, which is of the greatest importance for philosophy. I will only present some of the results of my analysis here.

When we say that our knowledge is obtained from *experience*, taking the concept of experience in its broadest sense, as that which we *live through*, we correctly indicate the source of our cognition, but upon a closer examination such a formula for the *principium cognoscendi* is too *crude*. To a certain extent, it conveys only the fact that our experience serves as the principle of cognition "for us," but it says nothing about how the matter stands "in nature." Here, there are two sorts of possible misunderstandings, which arise from prejudiced theories. As just noted, our cognition is constructed to conform to two fundamentally different objects: the empirical and the ideal. It begins to seem that one of these is "illegitimate," and attempts are made, on the one hand, to show the "origin" of the ideal from the empirical and, on the other hand, to "derive" the empirical from the ideal. In reality, as we already saw in part, the "object," as transcendent, toward which our consciousness is directed, is one and "the same," but it is presented to us with empirical or essential content depending on the attitude of consciousness with which we take it, whether we take it as the datum of sense intuition or as the datum of essential intuition.

In both cases, we certainly can speak about "experience," because in both cases we strive for the originarily and immediately given. Obviously, however, the formula does not express this. Furthermore, though, there is a lack of clarity in the fact that the essential content of the object is itself immanent to consciousness, that it, consequently, given presentatively, sometimes prompts us to seek in consciousness representatives of the transcendent object in the form of a special sort of "immanent object" or "idea," taken as a mental concept. These representatives "substitute" for the transcendent object in consciousness and therefore serve as the object and principle of cognition. Consequently, the identity that "permeates" the empirically given also remains as the essential foundation in the eidetically given. It is this foundation that, therefore, is taken as creating the "unity" of the object and which the adduced formula also does not reflect. Finally, in another respect this formula gives rise to misunderstanding. We speak of "experience" as a source of knowledge forgetting or ignoring the fact that when experience ceases to be a simple "experience" and our attention is fixed on it as the source of cognition, our concern with it is not as "bare" data, but with data *invested in a word* without fail, or in some other sign that substitutes for the word in principle and consequently is still a linguistic expression.[41]

Although it allows us to distinguish rigorously both the sense as well as the essential content terminologically or simply by the "context," a word can conceal both equally. Nevertheless, it forms a new basis for misunderstandings on the question concerning what is the actual starting point of cognition. Our formula also does not reflect its role. Yet, here lies precisely the means for the elimination of all the misunderstandings mentioned above. A word plays such a role in our cognition that I am ready to alter the formula to read: *a word is the principium cognoscendi of our cognition.*

Actually, analyzing our consciousness we cannot help but notice that a "word" lies in it like a special, though quite universal, stratum. As long as we simply live, our experiences flow one after another. Among these, there are "verbal experiences," but they occupy their place alongside the other experiences. They too appear and disappear, and their universal significance is little noted. However, it is worth our while to pause on whatever is involved in cognizing consciousness, and we find it to be immediately impressed in words. Henceforth, we cognize consciousness in the form of words. As Plato depicts in the *Theaetetus*, the mind talks with itself about what it is thinking. "When the mind is thinking, it is simply talking to itself, asking questions and answering them, affirming and denying."[42]

If we pause to analyze a word further in its distinctive forms, we will notice their great variety. There are grammatical, stylistic, aesthetic, and logical forms. The latter are particularly important to us. They are neither fortuitous nor empirical, but essential and necessary, as stable and uniform as the formative object is identical in itself. Analogous with Humboldt's "internal form of language," I call these logical forms the ideal inner forms of language.[43] They happen to be present in every process of cognition, and if we have them in mind, then all the misunderstandings

---

[41] [As pointed out in a note at the beginning of "Hermeneutics and Its Problems," Shpet's use of "word" can mean not only a single word but also a clause, a complex sentence, and even an entire text.]

[42] [Cf. Plato 1969: 895 (*Theaetetus* 189e–190a).]

[43] [Ten years later in 1927, Shpet published a study of Humboldt, *Vnutrennjaja forma slova.* Shpet 2007: 323–501.]

mentioned above cannot occur. They directly indicate the unity of the cognitive object. They render unnecessary any "immanent object" as the representative of the transcendent, and they advance the cognitive role of a word to its fitting place.

An even deeper philosophical analysis of a "word" in its ideal inner form shows us that such a word, a logical word, fulfills various functions in cognition. It names an object (a nominative function), it designates the meaning or sense in the context (a semasiological function), and it formally fixes it (a predicative function). Furthermore, a word in its comprehensive form is a sentence or clause; in its curtailed form it is a concept. We have already adduced enough examples in order to see how the sphere of logical forms develops. Philosophy as rigorous knowledge singles out *logic* as the special science that is concerned with the mentioned forms and that, consequently, studies a word precisely as the *principium cognoscendi*. Logic itself goes even further: cognition, as experience, only becomes science and knowledge when it is *expressed* in a word. Logic studies a word as the expression of cognition. If a word, as an ideal inner form, could be immediately transmitted, perhaps our science would be as error-free as the truth itself that science wants to transmit. However, the essential source of error and delusions lies in the fact that the ideal logical forms in a word itself are closely connected with other forms and that the final empirical impression of a word is itself empirical. Philosophy appeals to logic for checking and to establish the ways, means, and methods we use to express the truth. Logic, therefore, controls philosophy itself when the latter proceeds to state and depict what it has seen in its analysis of the essential consciousness. Logic is the final arbiter, since it can itself check even its own "expressions." It must find a means to do all this. There is no means greater or beyond this to "correct" and control the cognizing individual who makes mistakes.

# XIV

We need not imagine the issue as though philosophy invented "logic" ad hoc merely to check and control itself. The significance of logic is incomparably broader and more fundamental. It imposes such a powerful stamp on all our knowledge that for us the terms *knowledge* and *logical knowledge* essentially turn out to be synonymous. This is quite understandable once we recognize that the "logical stratum" in consciousness overlaps all of our cognition. We see all of our knowledge only through this stratum. Consequently, it, as knowledge, cannot be other than in the logical forms necessarily peculiar to it. Since these forms have their own regularity, we fix all knowledge in accordance with the laws of logic. The logical nature of knowledge is as much an essential characteristic of knowledge as intentionality is the essential characteristic of consciousness. However, again, this is not a "commandment" – just a statement of the way it is. This is why all the ruckus about logic by certain representatives of contemporary pseudo-philosophy is essentially absurd. A "protest" against the logical forms of thought is just as absurd as a protest against a solution to a mathematical problem using the principles and techniques of mathematics. The terms "alogism" and "arationalism" make sense when they express the inadequacy of certain logicians' narrow-mindedness and formalism. They prompt us to review and expand logic. But the attempts so characterized to overthrow logic as such – by logical means – are ridiculous. In place of logic, they wish to see "instinct," the "fullness of life," the "passion for life," and other advantages of pre-verbal animals. Best of all are the constructing insects found in *Creative Evolution*.[44] Others simply wish "nothing" in place of logic.

The deficiencies of logic were clarified long ago. As it should be, these deficiencies are not part of its essence, but are the results of certain "passions" and of the one-sidedness of logicians. Positive philosophy noticed them, and it took steps to eliminate them. These fundamental deficiencies of logic were: (1) to a fault, logic surrendered to the forms of "mathematical natural science," devoting little attention to the *concrete*; (2) concentrating on a study of "extension," it forgot the role of "content." Clearly, both of these points are connected. Negative philosophy did not proceed further in these directions. The so pompously proclaimed "antinomy" between "intuition" and "discourse" is really not an antinomy at all in the proper sense. It is as much an "antinomy" as that between a block of granite and the chisel that hews out a monument from it – between the material and the means of production.

It is one thing to admit to oneself and to others that *my* logical words, my concepts, are anemic, that *I* do not know how to use them adequately, that I see more than *I* can express in rigorous logical speech. And it is another thing to blame my own limitations on concepts and proclaim the poverty of logic. There is no need for any special subtlety in self-observation in order to notice that we do "see" more than we can express in a rigorous logical form, that time and again we resort to figurative speech to express our "experience." However, as I already indicated concerning "opinions" we must permit complete freedom to express anything that one pleases, just as one pleases and not hurry "truth." It will abide. A or B can say nothing about truth, but X or Y, who do possess logical forms of speech, will speak about it.

I certainly am not excluding the fact that truth can be expressed in a figurative form. Indeed, this probably often happens. But every figurative form in principle allows for a "translation" into a rigorously terminological form. The thought expressed in such a form may thereby lose its aesthetic or stylistic appeal, but it will be transformed from an "experience" into "knowledge." Who wants which? To some what is important is the soul's salvation; to others it is a multiplication table. However, one does not exclude the other. We may have need of both. Only, it is impossible in a multiplication table to seek recipes for saving the soul. But in fact for saving the soul, it, perhaps, does not matter whether $2 \times 2 = 4$ or 5. The "Christian Cicero" eloquently expressed this: "There remains that third part of philosophy that is called logic, in which the whole subject of dialectics and the whole art of speaking (*omnis loquendi ratio*) are contained. Divine learning does not need this, because wisdom is not in language, but in the heart; and it is of no importance what kind of language you employ, for the question is not of words, but of things. And we are not

---

[44] [A reference, of course, to Henri Bergson and his most famous work *L'Évolution créatrice* from 1907.]

disputing about grammar or oratory, the knowledge of which is concerned with the proper manner of speaking, but about wisdom, whose learning is concerned with how one must live."[45] It is my conviction, however, that the elegance of Lactantius is as little needed for this useful goal as is a multiplication table.

Today, certain pseudo-philosophical circles love to refer to a special sort of experience – *mystical experience* – as a source of knowledge, where not only logical but also figurative language is impotent, since in it the "ineffable" is given in a "vision." It is impossible to deny the *fact* of such experiences. To me personally, the claim that such experiences are not "accessible" to all seems even more dubious. However, the recognition of a "fact" of experience is quite far from a recognition in it of a *cognitive* experience. We see as quite crude the formula that knowledge is obtained from experience. What we must show is how we can speak of mystical experience as a source of knowledge. Although "ecstasy" and "prostration" are also experiences and, in addition, provide material for judgments about the corresponding states of consciousness, I do not see in what sense they could be called "principles of cognition." A mystical consciousness is a *sui generis* state of consciousness, and those who want to obtain a *philosophical* answer to the question what its nature is must turn to philosophy. After this, it will be clear whether mystical experience is a principle of knowledge or not.

An analysis of mystical consciousness presents to philosophy one of the most interesting problems, and there is no basis whatever to claim that the content of mystical experience cannot be expressed, in particular, that it cannot be expressed in a logical form. If it can just be expressed *somehow*, then a logical form will be found for it. But sometimes it is said it cannot be expressed at all. "*A dumb thought without words is a beast.*" If the issue were so hopeless, then we would know *nothing* about mystical consciousness. It would not be. But we do talk about it and not just a little, although not always intelligently. This is sometimes considered an indicator of its alogical or arational nature. I am aware that the "rationalization" of mystical experience that is presented to us in the form of such Eastern gifts as *gnosticism* or *theosophy* is a profoundly disgusting and aesthetically repulsive phenomenon, but I think it is also logically ugly as well. However, it no more follows from this that mystical experience cannot be expressed than that the illiteracy of a cinemagraphic libretto cannot be made literate.

I will not attempt to answer the question whether earlier writers who *depicted* mystical experiences knew about them only on hearsay or experienced them and in what way contemporary writers, who are informed about them, yet assert that such experiences cannot be depicted. In any case, however, I think that if they can be expressed – even if in disconnected ravings and mutterings – a meaningful logical form will be found for them. And as soon as philosophy as knowledge attempts to describe the peculiarities of mystical consciousness, to highlight it against the background of the rest of consciousness, philosophy will seek how it affects the whole and as a whole, whether such consciousness actually is a source of cognition or

---

[45] Cf. Lactantius 1905: 81.

whether it is a special type of interpretation of what is, and so forth, and so forth. Philosophy as knowledge cannot give answers to any of these questions except in a logical form.


# XV

When negative philosophers attack the infirmity of logic, they, at the same time, forget that precisely those who attack it are maintaining with all their might the idea of a restricted logic, since only owing to its formalistic character – and as long as it is formalistic – can the reproaches made against it have any significance. Therefore, logic must answer such attacks by emphasizing those aspects which the attackers ignore and continue its own positive work. The words used in logic, the terminology, are *concepts*. Concepts, according to logic's opponents, "destroy" the wealth of life's experiences. They are "boring," "static," "formalistic," "cinematographic," etc. All this is, to a certain extent, correct as long as it is a matter of the logic that looks on "concepts" as delimitations of one content from another purely in terms of their respective *extensions* and when it is concerned only with the relations between concepts in terms of their extension. However, we find the idea of such a narrowly formalistic logic in neither Aristotle nor the Stoics, in neither the Middle Ages nor the Port Royal logicians, in neither later rationalism nor modernity. In the entire course of the history of philosophy, we encounter the idea of such a logic only in the most brilliant negativist – Kant. This is why in their understanding of the tasks of logic contemporary alogicians are Kantians. There is certainly no riddle in this. Otherwise they would not have to reject logic wholesale, but only "parts" of it, and consequently they would have to be concerned along with positive philosophy with "improving" them. That is, they would have to pass from concerns with pure negation to positive creation.

If we designate the relations between concepts in terms of their extension as their *conceptual* aspect, then we see that all the attacks of the alogicians refer to conceptualism. However, it is worthwhile to recall that each word has a *meaning* in order to see what the alogistic critique does not touch in the least. The meaning of a word lies in its content, and the content is everything that is, everything that is experienced, that we are aware of. If we not only conceptualize concepts but also understand them, then through concepts as *signs* we apprehend everything that these signs designate. We can understand something well or poorly, but once again if the latter, if we understand something poorly, it is *our* fault and not the fault of logic. In terms of its meaning, a concept is concrete when it concerns a concrete concept, abstract when it is a matter of an abstract concept and general, particular, or single depending on what our concern is. It is necessary to kill everything in order for the concept to be dead. Perhaps, however, it will then be even more "boring," because then there will be no concepts. A concept considered semasiologically in essence cannot be characterized as "static" or as a "snippet." On the contrary, it is fundamentally dynamic, as dynamic as is its meaning. Such a concept is not a "snippet" but a living organ. An *understood* concept lives and moves. Any verbal particle is understood only in *connection* with others and with the greater whole. And this whole is understood again in a new whole of which it is a part. A word, a sentence, a period, a conversation, a book, an entire speech – there are no cessations here to endless penetrating acts of understanding. In every concept, therefore, all the connections and relations of what there is is implicit. This peculiarity of a concept, taken as a logical concept, which, as shown, overlays all of consciousness, gives a special character to philosophical knowledge, as primarily conceptual knowledge.

We have still another name for the *whole*, as the empirical whole, and it is *"history."* Historical cognition is an interpreting cognition, a *hermeneutic* cognition that demands understanding. The logic of historical cognition, speaking concretely, is a fundamentally semasiological, fundamentally all-encompassing, logic. However, through this, philosophy as knowledge, presented in accordance with this logic, becomes in a particularly profound sense *historical philosophy* or, to put it another way, a hermeneutic, comprehending philosophy. Such is the stamp of logic on philosophy. Historical science describes, and like empirical knowledge it explains. As we saw, philosophy is fundamentally in no need of explanation. It only describes, but we grasp the described as a meaning, and it becomes "pure history." Recalling what we clarified earlier, we can say that it becomes the *pure history of consciousness*. The logic of *this* history is the *dialectic*.

Sometimes, however, the opinion is expressed that "description" is a technique that is directly opposed to logical discourse. What is more, some see description as a means that is intended to replace logical operations with the help of rigorous concepts. A misunderstanding lies at the foundation of this opinion. Certainly, description is not a demonstration or an explanatory deduction, but it is not true that it is opposed to them by the fact that it does not use logical concepts as a means. Perhaps "description" is to be understood simply as vivid, figurative language. But what do we gain from substituting stylistics for logic? Let us imagine that figurative language is "richer" than logical language. But in what respect? Of course, there are more *images* in the former, but surely what is important to us is its meaning, its *sense*, and in order to extract it we must "translate" the images into concepts. However, concepts, some still say, express only the essence of things, and not their *empirical* richness. I think that there is no other way to express the richness of the empirical than by words. But for philosophy as knowledge nothing is needed except this "only," since its object is precisely the *essence*.

Here, we return to our starting point, and I again appeal to Plato: "Understand then, that by the other part of the intelligible, I mean that which reason itself lays hold of by the power of dialectic, treating its presuppositions not as beginnings, but actually as presuppositions, underpinnings, footings, and springboards, so to speak, to enable it to rise to that which requires no presupposition and is the starting point of all, and after attaining to that again taking hold of the first dependencies from it, so to proceed downward to the conclusion, making no use whatever of any object of sense but only of the *eidos* itself moving on through the *eidos* to the *eidos* and ending with the *eidos*."[46]

---

[46] [Cf. Plato 1969: 746 (*Republic*, book VI, 511b–511c).]

Some imagine such a dialectical ascending and descending as a formal and abstract "deduction" of pure "concepts" or as a formal-classificatory distribution of "sorts" and "types" in terms of their extension. That is, they see the dialectical process as actually establishing *such* logical relations between concepts in which "we do not care about the content." Clearly, such people see nothing but "formalism" and "statism," not because, apparently, they "can" in fact construct, as it were, such "pure" schemas, but precisely because they *pay no attention* to the "content." If our thinker "considers" that the concepts he disperses have a certain sense, that without understanding them it is impossible to perform the simplest operation on them, then he should also surmise that his idea of logic is very primitive and that "alogism" and "arationalism" are genuine nonsense on a par with being truly envious even of the "instinct of insects."

Let us take as an example the division of types of planar triangles. The division is performed on objects that are eidetic, formal, and, in terms of their characteristics, also essentially formal. We divide the triangles, let us say, into those that are acute, right, and obtuse. We immediately "see" in our ideal intuition of a triangle the essential characteristic of each class and name them. But however long we may "look" at triangles, we will not see that this division is exhaustive if we *do not understand* it. If a student, having approached the study of plane geometry, posed to the teacher the question whether in making a categorical claim about our division of triangles all triangles on Earth have been examined and whether there are still some unexamined planar triangles on the North Star, the teacher would say that the student *did not understand* geometry. The student's parents would say, of course, that the teacher failed to clarify to the student the *sense* of the geometric object.

As we saw, philosophy, as a pure science, is distinguished from mathematics and from the formal-ontological disciplines in general by the fact that it is "material."[47] That is, it is concerned with objective categories that form not its abstract, but its concrete content. This content is consciousness itself essentially and also completely. Perhaps here we can look and yet not understand. However, if even the slightest impulse, as it were, is aroused in our consciousness to *establish* "what is visible" or "what is in the visible" – even if it be in the form of a pure perceptiveness – "now I have a recollection," "now I have a doubt," etc. – understanding will immediately enter into the exercise of its duties. As contemporary investigations show, to "establish" something is part of the nature of every act of consciousness. It does not allow for a paralysis in some "extension." It impels passing beyond the borders of any extension, since it intuitively reveals any meaning and sense only in its living movement. The connection, which everything that exists reveals, forms its limiting moment. The fact that understanding is not a duplication of the "manifold," as a manifold, but is a quest for some "agreement" in it, a *consensus in varietate*,[48] does not make "everything" poorer and does not present the "sense" as less varied

---

[47] [Cf. Husserl 2014: 109 (§60) and 136 (§75).]

[48] [Latin: concordance in diversity. The expression can be found in Wolfio 1730: 390 (§530) – *"Perfectio est consensus in varietate, seu plurium a se invicem differentium in uno."* See also Wolff 1968: division II, vol. 3, §503.]

than it is. On the contrary, the "variety" in the content of philosophy, not only in "everything," as a whole, but also the intensive "variety" of each act of consciousness, accounts for the fact that philosophy cannot be satisfied with the logical forms and techniques that are adequate in the formal-ontological sciences. This is why philosophy incessantly demands variety from logic itself.

"Description" as a free and supple means in logic does not diminish and even less does it destroy the role and significance of logic. On the contrary, it strengthens the significance of logic and exalts its role. Therefore, the opinion that description "transcends" formalism and the schematism of concepts is completely without foundation. Description in philosophy uses concepts and only concepts precisely to the same extent as any other technique in logic. The descriptive dialectic has its rigorous methods of purifying knowledge of empirical mistakes, techniques of analysis, calculation, division, distinction, etc. The empirical cognizing subject – and there is no other – is too "hurried." Time and again, we take some feature that strikes our fancy as the essential feature, a feature of some sort as a feature of a genus. We yield to originary experiences and are not always sufficiently disciplined for the work of pure philosophy in the sphere of pure *eidos*. Description must adhere to the rigorous demands of the dialectic in order not to transfer "opinion" into the sphere of "knowledge." Certainly, "opinion" also has its dialectic, its "argument," its logic – a logic of the probable. And the succession of positive opinions has its dialectical guiding line, but only in the sphere of rigorous and pure philosophical knowledge does the dialectic play its truly prototypical role.

# XVI

Taking into account not only the cathartic but also the hegemonic role of logic in "knowledge," I will now venture to draw the final conclusion in the sphere of the perspectives that have opened up before philosophy. Cautiously approaching this conclusion, I feel trepidation owing to a shortage of words, but the "conclusion" before me is extremely fascinating and … *necessary*. The issue here is that in a concept, as an internally formed word, we see not only the "concept" but also – and this is essential – its eidetic content, which contains the sense or meaning of the concept. We penetrate to this sense not by means of a simple "conceptualization," but through an act of "establishing" that includes within itself – insofar as it is in itself only a formative act – a *sui generis* act of "intelligible intuition." It is this act that gives us an "understanding" of the corresponding sense. Therefore, a word-concept is for us not only an "extension" and a "class," but also a *sign*, which requires understanding. That is, it requires that we penetrate into its meaning, into, as it were, its "intimate something," into the "living soul" of the word-concept. In other words, this neologistic expression, the "word-concept," demands *interpretation*. For this reason, logic has for us an essentially hermeneutic character and puts its own stamp on the whole of philosophy as pure knowledge. From this, philosophy becomes *historical*, and we employ anew a principle once expressed: "*nihil est in intellectu, quod non fuerit in historia, et omne, quod fuit in historia, deberet esse in intellectu.*[49]

We now want to proceed further while keeping in mind the essentially "historical" character of philosophical cognition. We find the eidetic "content" of any objectivity in the sphere of pure consciousness. We take a step deeper in this sphere and try to penetrate into the *consensus in varietate*, seeking to comprehend the eidetic content itself as a new "sign." This idea, the crowning aspiration of philosophical quests, is not new. Some thinkers devoted a stunning and truly "maddening" effort to this end – Plato, Plotinus, Spinoza, Hegel. Such are the philosophical heights that only the rare head was spared from spinning, but not once did human cognition turn away from them. Someone who, having tried his hand, stops at the point he has reached acts in a more philosophical manner than does a person who considers what *he* has attained to be the "final word" and forbids *anyone* to go any further, passing off his "opinions" as the final summit of "knowledge." These "opinions" are the source of the most obscene pseudo-philosophical conjectures. At first, the "unknown God"[50] frightens us, but then his biography is recounted in detail, or we are simply bombarded with words written with a capital letter: Truth, Reason, Will, I, the Good. They once tried to comfort us: that "there" is the same as this "here." Pseudo-philosophy hypostatized morals itself – that the "there," it turns out, is the "moral world-order."

To avoid lapsing into fantastic pseudo-philosophical revelations, what we have to say about this further deepening of our philosophical understanding must – whether we like it or not – have a "purely" *instructional* character. How do we see the object of philosophy in this new deepening of knowledge, what *task* lies before us here – though neither by any means resolving the tasks nor "explaining" them – and, then, how do we discover the philosophical path before us leading to this object? The very object that is revealed here has been shown time and again with respect to its "formal" side, and in all probability we should not say anything more about it in advance. Even when Plato speaks in such a case of "beauty itself" or of "beauty in itself," he is perhaps saying more than can be said without the risk of succumbing to "temptation." We are satisfied, then, with the indefinite expression of the rationalists, viz., *perfectio,* or equally with the scholastics' indefinite allusion: *bonitas transcendentalis.*[51]

There is more that can and must be said when standing on the firm ground of the philosophical path, which logic, moreover, illuminates. Contemporary *patheticism* advances "anomalous" states of consciousness not only as the only valuable

---

[49] [Latin: Nothing is in the intellect that has not been in history, and everything that was in history should be in the intellect. This is Shpet's adaptation of the Scholastic doctrine that there is nothing in the intellect that does not come from the senses (*nihil est in intellectu quod non fuerit in sensu*). Leibniz amended the expression to read: "*Nihil est in intellectu, quod non fuerit in sensu, excipe: nisi ipse intellectus.*" Leibniz 1996: 111 (Book 2, Chapter 1). Curiously, Baader already in a letter from April 1836 gave Shpet's exact expression. See Baader 1857: 539.]

[50] [Shpet here probably alludes to Paul's visit to Athens in Acts 17: 23.]

[51] [Shpet's claim here is, most likely, again based on Wolfio 1730: 390 (§530): "*Dicitur perfectio a Scholasticus bonitas transcendentalis.*"]

"source" of knowledge, but also stresses the *regularity* of such cognition. Coming from the lips of representatives of "pathetic philosophy," this sounds particularly coquettish.[52] However, this very "regularity" is "*our*" argument, the argument of philosophy as pure knowledge, and "*we*" certainly do not agree to call what is "regular" "anomalous." We only have to indicate the place they actually occupy. Once again, in order to avoid the reproach of modernism, I agree with Plato. There are two different "modes" of consciousness: on the one hand, wisdom, or common sense (σωφροσύνη), and, on the other hand, madness, inspiration or "mania" (μανία). The last is, therefore, a special "sphere" of consciousness, a truly philosophical analysis of which not only points to the "common" object of the directedness of this consciousness, but which must also carry out the examination and, above all, a severing of the "types," as the dialectic that controls the analysis demands. In the *Phaedrus*, Plato separated "mania," which can give nothing worthwhile, from what can provide the "greatest of blessings."[53] He, then, in the latter distinguishes inspiration that comes "from God" and that is manifested in religious prophecy from inspiration of a moral character, which is connected also with prophecy in the sphere of healing and purification, and both from poetic inspiration. Finally, there is *philosophical* rapture or enthusiasm. To be embraced by philosophical rapture is characterized by Plato as being "in love." Of course, a philosophical "intellectual love," *amor intellectualis*, is directed toward the highest "comprehension" and "wisdom" (σοφία). A "philosopher" is a philosopher, because he strives to comprehend the truth, even though this striving still cannot be said to be a comprehending (σοφος) of it. As this idea is revealed in the *Symposium*, the philosopher occupies a spot *between* comprehending and ignorance.[54]

However, we would be incorrectly interpreting Plato and incorrectly understanding the philosophical path were we to see the source of philosophical cognition in the depicted "state" of consciousness. Our depiction is that of a "type" of experience as concrete and complete with an indication of the "features" that accompany a particular "mode of cognition" but not the very "act" of cognition. The latter as such is always the same, namely, *reason*. However, in the various "attitudes" of consciousness reason, penetrating into the various layers of the "given," discovers or sees various things. The state of consciousness that we call philosophical enthusiasm or *amor intellectualis* is an aggregate of experiences based on a rational cognitive act. The latter in its purity also describes the absolute purity of the object toward which it is directed and which, consequently, is itself the "reason of things" taken in their essence. The general effort of consciousness, which is our concern, can attain its highest level, surpassing the "norm of common sense." Enthusiasm can rise to *ecstasy* – clearly not in the sense of Eastern "twiddle" or "zeal" but in the sense of an absolute *repose*, corresponding to a calm abiding of the essence of the object. Nevertheless, the cognitive act is essentially the entire "self-same" rational act. However, just as in one and the same act of reason we can distinguish the moments

---

[52] [Most likely, a reference to Bergson and his disciples. See, for example, Benda 1913.]

[53] [Plato 1969: 492 (*Phaedrus* 245b).]

[54] [Plato 1969: 556 (*Symposium* 204b).]

of its empirical and essential seeing, the moments of a sense intuition and of an intellectual intuition, depending on the depth of the act's penetration, so in this new deepening we can see a yet third moment, which in my book *Appearance and Sense* I called *intelligible intuition*.[55] Here, we find the possibility not only of an intellectual understanding but also of a rational comprehension of the very "reason of things," of their rational foundations. As Spinoza characterized his "third source of cognition," with its help, we cognitively grasp the essential causes of a "thing" or its uniquely proper essence – *per solam suam essentiam*[56] – (if it is a *causa sui.*).

# XVII

If we do not want our "conclusion" to bear the stamp of a "theoretical conclusion" forestalling a hypothetical conjecture, it must be a pure description of the very act of comprehension at this final stage of the deepening of reason. In looking at the eidetic content of the word-concept, as a "signifying" sign, we found *the meaning of a concept*. We recognized, thereby, that it is not enough for philosophy to see the "*eidos*" in a reflection on consciousness. It is also necessary to understand it, to understand what is attained in the act of determining (judging) it. The same demand that we posed to the "word" we now pose to the *eidos*: we look upon an essence itself as a sign. Passing from a sign to its sense is not a "deduction" at all, but there is at least in its foundation an originary and immediate act that is an "insight" into the sense. We look for the sense in this originariness. A semasiological acceptance of the essence *eo ipso* forces us to seek in it, as the "beginning," the *sense*, which is revealed to us as the *rational foundation* inherent within the essence itself. The content of the essence arises from reason, as its beginning. Ultimately, we can say that the object appears not as a "task" in the proper sense, but as a *sign* of what *here* is the task. Consequently, the very formulation of the task is not directly given, but "will be" found in the process of deciphering its sign. Thus, we saw that mathematics only "now" comes to comprehend its object, although from the start it went under its "sign." We spoke analogously about philosophy. However, this "now" certainly is a "process" and a process that is far from being complete. What are its bounds? Here we have a question for those who love endless work.

So, ideally speaking, in the final analysis as well as on the whole, hermeneutic philosophy remains essentially a rational philosophy, a philosophy of reason. *Rationalism* is the first word, the enduring word, and the final word of European philosophy. *Everything that is, that exists, in its essence is rational. Reason is the ultimate foundation and the first mark of the essential.* Such is the formula of rationalism. However, we must already ask the question: Is this assertion not an "opinion"? My answer is "No." It is not an opinion, but knowledge, even though it may perhaps be expressed very imperfectly. An "opinion," though a very unlikely one, would go: the empirical reality in which I live is rational. But even this is not the

---

[55] [See Shpet 1991: 158ff.]

[56] [See Spinoza 1958: 7 – "solely through its essence."]

"opinion" of philosophy, but an opinion of wisdom. In such a case, I, at least, would have difficulty distinguishing such an "opinion" from the no less profound "opinion" of the same wisdom, which states: "This also is vanity and vexation of spirit."[57]

However, reason with its inescapable logic – so goes contemporary wisdom – is the coffin of creativity, tightly confined within it. For what kind of creativity? For the creativity of wisdom itself, the decrepit wisdom, like in the East? Any alarm on our part is in vain: it turns out to be tailor-made for wisdom. However, this fear of reason, a "logo-phobia," is quite indicative of the wisdom that endures to this day. Is it not because on the very eve of "our era" the most powerful weapon was tested against reason? Until the moral poisoners did their work, there was no such "fear," but then someone started "to philosophize with a hammer."[58] It seemed to be according to "reason," and it turned out to be according to "reason" – only "reason" was the anvil, and between it and the hammer morality itself was hit. Here is the fear: is it not the case that only reason itself is effective against reason, and where is it to go having ruined it for itself? The man who philosophized with a hammer summarized his "new view" of "Reason in philosophy" in the following four theses:

> *First thesis.* The bases on which 'this' world has been characterized as apparent affirm, on the contrary, its reality; a reality of *another* sort is absolutely unprovable.
>
> *Second thesis.* The features that have been endowed on the 'true being' of things are the features of non-being, of *nothing*; the 'true world' has been constructed out of contradiction to the real world: the genuinely apparent world, insofar as it is merely a *moral-optical* illusion.
>
> *Third thesis.* There is no sense at all in creating fables about 'another' world, if an instinct of slander, detraction, and suspicion against life has not gained possession of us. In such a case, we *avenge* ourselves against life with a phantasmagoria of 'another,' a 'better' life.
>
> *Fourth thesis.* To divide the world between the 'true' and the 'apparent' – whether in the Christian manner or in the manner of Kant (in the end, a *perfidious* Christian) – is only a suggestion of decadence – a symptom of a *decline* of life.[59]

I have quoted these four theses of Nietzsche's, wishing only to stress that positive European philosophy alone, philosophy as pure knowledge, as a *rationalism* logically and consistently carried out, can accept and hold them without any reservations, restrictions, and circumlocutions. A new interpretation is unnecessary. Everything said above may serve as a commentary.

# XVIII

I could conclude on this point, but keeping in mind the popular character of this article I would like to pause on certain especially aidotic (η αιδώς) or, in popular terminology, pedagogical considerations. (By *pedagogical*, I, coming from philosophy, understand a rational *theory of means*, which still does not exist, but which

---

[57] [Shpet here quotes from Ecclesiastes 2: 26.]

[58] [An allusion to Nietzsche.]

[59] [Cf. Nietzsche 1982: 484.]

arises from contemporary morals and wisdom. We can find something of this theory in Baltasar Gracián's *The Art of Worldly Wisdom*, but also even in Ovid.)

Aristotle, the author and source of many pseudo-philosophical theories, correctly, however, grasped the idea of European philosophy as pure knowledge: "Clearly, we seek philosophy not for the sake of some other use at all, for something outside of it. Just as we say the human being is free when the goal is oneself and not someone else, so also with regard to philosophy. It alone is free knowledge, since it alone has it itself as its goal."[60] This is just what the East cannot understand. It accepts knowledge only *for* the sake of wisdom. The idea of philosophy as pure knowledge is what contemporary capitalist Europe and its nation-states forget to understand. This Europe accepts knowledge only *for* its usefulness. An "isolation from life," "uselessness," "ivory-tower scholarship," "scholasticism," "metaphysics" and many other reproaches pour from the lips of the in general honorable figures, the contemporary ideologues of wisdom, who have counted on finding in philosophy the means for settling their moral, spiritual, religious, and other concerns. Behind the ideologues, there is a series of "controllers," who actually are not isolated but deeply attached to life. These are the bureaucrats, the engineers, the deputies, the monks. Unfortunately, we must state that not only pseudo-philosophy, but even philosophy itself has made strange and unjustified concessions in this regard.

Two opinions, in particular, are widespread. One of them would have us think that the fundamentally general theses of philosophy are only the "first" theses from which philosophy will then proceed to arrive one day at "life itself." These theses are general and far removed from life, but by means of derivations and deductions we pass to the concrete and empirical itself. At the basis of this assertion is an old psychologistic mistake that the "single," the "individual" is the "minimal type," the final point in the process of the specification of concepts. Apart from that fact, however, such an opinion is simply a mystification.

Even if it were true that philosophy can be *expressed* in the form of a deductive system, there would, nevertheless, still be the fundamentally wrong presupposition that there is an analytic transition from ideal theses concerning what is "possible" to what is "real." As was beautifully expressed earlier, the real, in comparison to the "possible," always demands a certain *complementum*, which by means of a pure analysis of what is "possible" is not revealed at all if we ourselves do not put it there in the first place. Ultimately, this mystification is simply naïve. It springs from the fact that up to now many were convinced that we *come* to our thoughts as we *express* them, that is, in the order, for example, of a rigorous deduction or "proof." In philosophy, we proceed from the "given" and can say about the empirically given only what is given empirically and about the essential what is given in an essence. It is simply absurd to think that from knowledge of what is essential we also obtain knowledge of what is contingent in its contingency, just as it is absurd to think that from an opinion about the contingent we get knowledge of what is essential in its essentiality.

---

[60] [Cf. Aristotle 1984: 1554–1555 (*Metaphysics* 982 24–27).]

There is yet another view that to me is no less strange. Philosophy is sometimes taken to be an "art," the art of living. This expressed less elegantly means that philosophy is to be understood simply as wisdom. I do not deny that there is a special "art" of philosophical life and that the philosopher is not only a representative of knowledge, but also can be a representative of a way of life characterized by a special state of consciousness. We already encountered this above. However, the deceiver is one who says and the deceived is one who believes that philosophy as knowledge provides lessons on how one *should* live. Philosophy contains neither recipes for living nor the means to save the soul. We sometimes imagine to ourselves that philosophy consists of "two parts": one that is "theoretical" far removed from "life," and another a "practical" or "applicable" part that solves the highest questions, such as the meaning and purpose of life and of the entire world, questions about good and evil in the world, in short, questions about wisdom itself. However, when philosophy, wishing to be *pure* knowledge, declares that it does not seek to solve *these* questions, since these are not its questions, or when someone believing that philosophy is obliged to resolve them but is convinced that in philosophy there are no right answers to these questions, then one begins to turn one's anger toward philosophy itself. It is found to be "dry and boring," and it is blamed for ignoring "our everyday" problems.

As for the charge of being "boring," what can we say about this? Philosophy studies *everything*, but by no means does it contain "everything" for everyone. There are many things that can "entertain" and "amuse" outside of philosophy. Those who want *to be* "amused" and "good," can turn to "life" and to "wisdom." Those who want to *study* "amusement" and the "good" should cease to be "amused" and should turn to psychology and history, to self-observation and to the testimony provided by those close by. Those who want to *know* how these "objects" look in the light of consciousness, the place they occupy within it, must turn away from "self-observation" and turn to philosophical reflection. To the correct question, one will receive the correct answer.

As for "our everyday" problems, the "cursed questions,"[61] philosophy examining "everything" in the proper light also has something to say about them, namely that it can depict or "describe" the corresponding attitudes or "states" of consciousness, but it cannot say, as is often demanded of it, "where evil comes from," "what is the purpose of life," and "how did the world arise." *For it*, for philosophy as knowledge, these very questions are *vacuous* ones. However, if the word "vacuous" is unclear in this instance, we can still say that they are *real* issues that must be addressed by pseudo-philosophy and wisdom. Moreover, it must be understood that in general it makes no sense to reproach philosophy for not solving, not attempting to solve and for not being in a position to solve issues that are *our own*, this so-and-so's, and not its issues. To expect philosophy to begin giving *us* answers to *our* questions, for example, what *I* should do, how *I* should live, etc., can be likened to the schoolboy who, not having learned his lessons, lays his book under his pillow and expects that

---

[61] [The expression was a common one among the Russian intelligentsia to signify the preoccupation among many in the nineteenth century. See, for example, Ovsjaniko-Kulikovskij 1908: 145.]

the next morning the necessary knowledge will be in his head. Each of us must *personally* solve *our* own problems. To expect that someone somewhere will solve them for us – whether that person be Kant, Nietzsche, Muhammad, one's parish priest, or someone else – is all the same. It is the most impudent display of one's Eastern laziness. However, speaking in general, we are too hasty in calling *our* questions and doubts *philosophical*. One must become a "philosopher" and, consequently, escape *one's* problems, to "die," in order to have the right to call one's questions *philosophical*.

# XIX

But as is clear, herein lies the entire difficulty of the question: "How does one become a philosopher?" In any case, it is not by means of the "deductions" and the "applications" that are found by other principles. The correct philosophical formulation of the question, however, is not even "How does one become a philosopher?" but "What is a philosopher?" and "What makes them a philosopher?" This is actually one of the themes of philosophy. Undoubtedly, some image of a "philosopher" hovers over our ordinary consciousness, but in the history of philosophy we find attempts to determine it and its essential traits. In Plato, along with the mentioned description of a philosopher as "in love" there is another that we would now say is a "pedagogical" description, but of course it does not contradict the former in any way, but, rather, forestalls it. The philosopher directs his thought toward what truly exists, our petty and personal concerns barely touch him; he contemplates the eternal, the logically regulated and as much as possible imitates and assimilates himself to it. Accordingly, we conceive the pedagogical significance of philosophy as arising from two moments: the moment of "cleansing" and the moment of "inspiration." As we already know, the dialectic, as such, serves, in particular, the first of these moments. It "accustoms" us to "cleansing" our expressions of prejudiced theories and "opinions," of "doxosophia" (according to the *Sophist*), of confidence in the fact that we know what we do not know. This is the constant and methodic check on our *concepts*.

We cannot do more than this, but we also do not need to do more. Cleansed of prejudices, our pure *look* stands before the truth (is "present" to it) in its originary and immediate givenness. A life in philosophy, therefore, is a constant turn to the "philosophical." Attention is directed toward it; the constant "attitude" of consciousness is toward it. Such is what creates the philosophical consciousness itself, the consciousness of the *philosopher*. This distinctive "practice" – an asceticism – in philosophical matters not only accustoms us to resolve properly philosophical questions in a freer and more direct manner, but it also distinctively molds the entire human consciousness, creating in us a *sui generis* "philosophical mindset." We begin to live in this philosophical state as "naturally" as *homo civilis* lives in his/her "mindset," and as *homo religiosus* lives in that one, etc. A person becomes a natural *homo philosophus*. This person "naturally" approaches everything "from the point of view" of the essential, of the "philosophical," *sub specie aeternitatis*. A person becomes a philosopher not only in philosophy, but also in life. Such is the only path of the philosophical "ascetic," the path from the "theoretical," "detached from life," principles *to life itself*. It does not solve our problems for us, but it transforms us. Philosophy demands personal self-renunciation, not because *it* needs us, but because truth cannot be personal. This is why there is no reason to fear that philosophy will take away our personal "concerns" and our personal "life." It is not that philosophy needs us, but that *we* need philosophy. We must devote *ourselves* to it. Only in this way can we affirm our own rights to human individuality. Philosophy returns to us what we surrendered, though now cleansed and brightened. Such a transformed person – the philosopher – is, therefore, the living connection between truth and the practical. It grasps the *one* truth, but carries out its *sole* concern.

*Herein lies the pedagogical* significance of philosophy, and not in "conclusions" and not in the fact that it can solve or "help" (!) us answer our questions about the "meaning of life" and about the sense of any nonsense. Morals and wisdom may not appeal to the philosophical "type of person," but philosophy is little offended by this fact, since its concern is only in knowing whether this or that is or is not a philosophical consciousness. And even when philosophy takes a step farther – its final step – and discovers that the very idea of a "philosopher" is only a "sign," the "sense" of which, i.e., the *rational* basis of which, lies in the idea of *humanness – humanitas* – it here only establishes and describes but does not prescribe, does not issue "commandments." It does not give sermons and does not evaluate whether this is good or bad, important or unimportant, *honorable* or dishonorable. It says only that this *is so*. It seems to me that the distinctive trait of *European* philosophy in comparison with the wisdom of the East is revealed not only in its "ontic" character, in its *first* words, its *alpha*, but especially in its *final* word, in its *omega*, viz., humanness, or, in the *verbally* rational guise of the latter, viz., in its *paganism*. This is the last word of European philosophy, because the final "rational foundation" and, consequently, the ultimate *justification* lies in it: the world must be humanized.

On the contrary, the East asks, "how is man justified before God?"[62] Wisdom, of course, is also one of the themes of philosophy, although it occupies only a modest place. However, having in mind here an exclusively pedagogical question, I will limit myself to certain pedagogical remarks alone. *Wisdom* is the experience of a moral order, and, therefore, it is a certain "virtue." It appears precisely as such sometimes in the role of a regulator, above all and essentially as a *practical* regulator and then as a criterion. As a regulator, it acquires a quasi-theoretical significance, the significance of "reason" in the popular sense of the word, i.e., always with a touch of the practical (for example, "he acts rationally," "the rational way of life," etc.). "Behold, the fear of the LORD, that is true wisdom; and to depart from evil is reason."[63] "Wisdom" is not completely identical with "common sense," only because

---

[62] Cf. Job 9: 2.

[63] Job 28: 28 [Shpet here quotes, of course, from the Russian translation of the Bible, which renders the last word as "razum" – "reason." The English King James version of the Bible renders that same word as "understanding." If the quotation were left intact as given in the latter, the unsuspecting reader just might fail to see why Shpet provides this particular passage.]

the former is a refinement of the *latter*, the quintessence of common sense. Wisdom does not understand that cognition can be had for its own sake. From the standpoint of wisdom, cognition must itself be morally justified and certainly must be put to some use in practical life. Cognition of the "first sort" is cognition of a moral duty, the distinction between good and evil, a probing into the secrets of Providence, etc. All non-practical knowledge is a distortion and is stupid. Wisdom gives commandments; it portends, warns, and encourages. "And being but one, wisdom can do all things: and remaining in herself, she maketh all things new: and in all ages entering into holy souls, she maketh them friends of God, and of the prophets. For God loveth none but him that dwelleth with wisdom. ... Wisdom reacheth from one end to another mightily: and sweetly doth she order all things. ... For she knoweth and understandeth all things, and she shall lead me soberly in my doings, and preserve me in her power."[64] Wisdom cannot be like the knowledge that is accessible to all. It is for the select: "For the wisdom of doctrine is according to her name, and she is not manifest unto many."[65] This is why wisdom resonates and is distinguished by a distinctive *practical* skepticism: "a man cannot find out the work that is done under the sun: because though a man labour to seek it out, yet he shall not find it; yea farther; though a wise man think to know it, yet shall he not be able to find it."[66] "Seeing it is hid from the eyes of all living, and kept close from the fowls of the air."[67] Nevertheless, wisdom itself judges unmistakably, and against it there are no and cannot be any objections. Truth can vacillate and change; wisdom never can. Wisdom is *gratia gratis data*: "There is One who is wise, greatly to be feared, sitting upon His throne" and "All wisdom comes from the Lord and is with Him for ever."[68] "And thy counsel who hath known, except thou give wisdom, and send thy Holy Spirit from above?"[69] Wisdom, therefore, not only is devoid of the sense of any spontaneous activity and individual initiative, it also nips in the bud any interest in investigating "what is," since it gives the answer of Jehovah himself to any question: "I am that I am."[70] In the presence of Jehovah the face of a living person is insignificant. The problem of each of us is replaced by impersonal questioning: "What is man, and what is his grace? and what is his good, or what is his evil?",[71] a questioning which in its tone already contains a ready answer: insignificantly small. Such is the *East*.

Wisdom always teaches. This is why it is organically connected not only with morals and practicality, but also with *enlightenment*. The entire history of Christianity is a history of enlightenment. Europe also has its wisdom, and the Enlightenment is most vividly and originally a result of the latter, whereas European morals are

---

[64] Cf. Wisdom of Solomon 7: 27–28; 8: 1; 9: 11.

[65] Ecclesiasticus (The Wisdom of Sirach) 6: 23.

[66] Ecclesiastes 8: 17.

[67] Job 28: 21.

[68] Ecclesiasticus (The Wisdom of Sirach) 1: 6; 1: 1.

[69] Wisdom of Solomon 9: 17.

[70] [Exodus 3: 14.]

[71] Ecclesiasticus (The Wisdom of Sirach) 18: 7.

entirely of an Eastern and Christian origin. Even government and technology are the same original fruits of purely European wisdom. Perhaps, however, the most insipid – equal in insipidness perhaps only to so-called theosophy – is the aspiration, manifested in connection with this, to subordinate life and the culture of the individual to abstract, scientific theories.

Taking into account the entire content of wisdom in the Eastern-European culture of Europe and of the whole world, we cannot help but recognize in it its exceptional and thereby quite real power. It is a wonder only that up to now it has not destroyed and has not eliminated its archenemies: pagan humanness and pure philosophical knowledge. Perhaps the basis of this lies in its *wise* solution: vanquishing one's enemies and turning them into slaves, forcing them to serve itself, having taken away even their own rightful name. In this way, "humanness" is renamed a "hypostasis" and "philosophy" becomes a "love of wisdom." The Biblical *chochma*,[72] as we see from the citations above, is actually "wisdom," but *sophia* is not "wisdom" and *sophos* does not mean a "wise person." Formally, *sophia* is the *perfectio*, which I already mentioned, and *sophos* is essentially one who understands the *sense* of what one is doing. A *sophos* can also be a carpenter and a flute player, a poet and a thinker. Here is the genuinely European idea of *sophia* – a mastery of something undertaken. It is a genuinely European virtue. Eastern laziness created wisdom, prejudging everything even personal concerns and needs. But European leisure – the *scholē* (σχολή) – spawned philosophy, even the love of mastering the resolution of personal doubts and concerns.

# XX

Thus, the Eastern influence on Europe made virtue a source of knowledge and from cognitive mastery it derives *moraline*.[73] Against this, the undistorted European instinct must be outraged. This is why it is appropriate to raise the issue of "pedagogy" in connection with "philosophy." Just as the philosophical dialectic cleanses "knowledge" of "opinions," so philosophical pedagogy has the task of "cleansing" personal paths in life of obligatory rules, commandments, authorities, of the conviction that someone who knows something can calm our unease, in short, from the *laziness that holds sway over us*. After a dialectical cleaning, philosophy as knowledge becomes a pure positive doctrine, indivisible and internally homogeneous. Pedagogy is entirely a negative doctrine. It must always again and again be worked out and must therefore reflect precisely the negative character of the "art of life" itself. It is impossible to overcome morals with morals, and therefore the sole thing that remains constant in pedagogy is bare negation. Pedagogy cannot impose on us *human beings* a different demand than the one it rejected *for itself*, for its own "purpose." All paths have already been experienced. Consequently, just as in *cognition*

---

[72] [The Hebrew word המכח meaning "wisdom."]

[73] [A reference to Nietzsche 2007: 19. Much of what follows in this section is directed against Nietzsche.]

there is tradition and the path of experience, so in the *realization* of the "human" there is freedom and free will. The human being needs no justification, since the sole justification of everything can only be "humanness." All human paths and means must realize it. The world and God need justification, i.e., personification, but not the human being.[74]

The direct path of justification of what is justifiable lies in refuting *every theory* about it insofar as it is a matter of theories concerning the origin and reality of what is justifiable. Therefore, it happens that philosophy as knowledge by its very existence and concerns refutes all morals, every cosmogony and theogony, everything Eastern, and thereby it inculcates the pagan principle of negation – the principle of humanness. This, though, is not the goal of philosophy, which neither worries nor thinks about it. Philosophy does not exist for this purpose, but it just so happens by itself that where there is pure philosophy there is pure humanness. Philosophy, as we saw, yields a kind of asceticism. One of its results is that the human being no longer needs authority, whether it take the form of an individual or abstract norms, and we are absolutely free in our choice of a way of life or an "ideal." Even in imitating, the human being preserves for oneself complete creative freedom, deeper penetration, transformation and overcoming of one's "models."

This *opinion* requires some clarification, all within the sphere of the same pedagogy. The fact is that the source of the most pedagogical aspirations of *each* of us, as a so-and-so, is the self-aversion that is naturally so inherent in each of us. A love of others, their high estimation, cannot extinguish in us our self-aversion, although these feelings give rise to the desire "to be worthy" of another, which also dictates concrete, albeit ultimately feeble ideals of perfection – the ideals of imitation. The more radical means of obtaining this ideal turns out to be a "withdrawal" either *from oneself* into "society," in the form of a service to the "social good," or *into oneself*, away from "society." However, a human being cannot withdraw completely from "society." We always carry "society" within ourselves. In seclusion or in solitude, it is impossible not to take along one's past, one's *history*. It is precisely for this reason that the human being is actually realized only in "society." The sole absolute "escape" is an escape into another world, the world of the *ideal*. Here philosophical asceticism, as we saw, can play a role in the lives of each of us. However, its sense lies in the fact that it *liberates* us humans from our "accepted" burden and having become freer – in terms of the idea, absolutely free – one will have to exert even more effort and creativity on the "art of living." Not many see this as an inducement. So that there *be* morals, others will always prefer someone else to write their *diary* for them.

The "withdrawal" mentioned above has long since been seen as a kind of "dying." There is some fascination in this, because it is a dream about the means to extinguish self-aversion. Although unreasonable, this dream is interpreted antirationalis-

---

[74] [In his "notes" to his edition of Shpet's essay, A. A. Mitjushin suggests that Shpet had in mind here a line from the Russian Symbolist poet Konstantin Bal'mont: "The entire world must be justified so that one can live in it." Mitjushin 1994: 366. See Bal'mont 1914: 76. Shpet, apparently, was quite fond of this line, for he had quoted Bal'mont's line already in his 1912 essay "Odin put' psikhologii i kuda on vedet" ("One Path in Psychology and Where It Leads"). See Shpet 2006: 262.]

tically as a "struggle with the flesh." Plotinus's shame for the body is only an image. The body is not at all shameful. This notion is only a contrivance of the East, but it is its "soul" that happens to be shameful. The "human being dissatisfied" and the "pig satisfied," the "Socrates dissatisfied" and the "fool satisfied" – as Mill classifies them[75] – are souls and not bodies. But the dying of a soul for the concrete ideal of "Man" is nonsense and not salvation. It is, rather, a crude self-deception, although necessary for many to the highest degree.

Paganism, as a faith in the creature, and not in a Creator, also knows concrete ideals. It is not the same thing to each and every one. It is not Man. There are many ideals, many are "anointed": Themistocles and Spinoza, Brutus and Giordano Bruno, Pericles and Galileo, et al., without end. There is more. It not only envelops these names with "ideal" fictions, but creates pure phantasies, and sets them up as concrete ideals. Among these, there are Prometheus, Theseus, Romulus, Achilles and Patroclus, Manfred, Hamlet, husbands, wives and children. But a faith in the creature does not recognize "dying" *with* a concrete ideal. The idea of "humanness" is the genuine instrument of suicide. Salvation lies beyond "what is given," understood not in the Eastern sense, against which the "theses" cited earlier of the Engadin suicide were aimed, but in the sense of a *negation* of the experienced, since only a completely absolute negation can lead to the absolute cleansing of our "former" ideals and to the spontaneous manifestation "on its own" of the "humanness" of humans, when "each" human does not write off one's "diary," but writes so that, contrary to St. Augustine, "Christ died in vain."[76]

In particular, I want to stress the idea that *only when one rejects all the paths experienced by others does one's "natural humanness" spring from oneself by itself, advancing one along one's own path.* No one knows how long the energy has been amassed in us and its source, but suddenly it produces an enormous outburst. We live by these outbursts. Here is the true beginning of "morals," and when what has accumulated is not expended in small fits, the "outbursts" strike our imagination. An example of this is Tolstoy's departure.[77] Intrinsically more striking than these actualized forms, however, are the forms of potential concentration as long as they still can "last." Here are the genuine "conflicts," but their actualization is often a secondary moment, a "resolution." Properly speaking, it is in this potentiality that the human being "is humanized." The actualization is often only a new "false" step, a new occasion for a "negation" by the criterion of pedagogy.

All of this is only a personal opinion that is ready to hear its own "negation" and take its place in the sphere of the "less probable," but the limitation of positive morals is intolerable and the conceit and complacency of the theistic East, particularly in its *newest* assertions, are intolerable. "Everything is fine with us" declares an

---

[75] [See Mill 1957: 14.]

[76] [See, for example, Augustine's numerous references to these words in Augustine 1992: 23, 24. The expression stems from Galatians 2: 21.]

[77] [A reference to Tolstoy's sudden departure in 1910 from his estate Yasna Polyana, leaving behind his wife with whom he had had a most quarrelsome relationship for many years. This was a media event, both nationally and internationally, at the time.]

apologist and enemy of human "passion" some nicknamed a "philosopher." Actually, paganism was *passionate* about everything. This is why it can take up philosophy only passionately. Let philosophy be "divorced from life," but not divorced from the life of the dilemma: wisdom and the East or philosophy and humanness? Jerusalem or Athens?

Moscow, January 1917.


# Bibliography to "Wisdom or Reason?"

Aristotle. 1984. *The Complete Works of Aristotle*, ed. J. Barnes. Princeton: Princeton University Press.

Augustine, St. 1992. On Nature and Grace. In *Four anti-Pelagian Writings*, 22–90. Trans. John A. Mourant and William J. Collinge. Washington, DC: Catholic University of America Press.

Baader, Franz von. 1857. *Sämmtliche Werke*, vol. 15. Leipzig: Hermann Bethmann.

Bal'mont, K. D. 1914. *Polnoe sobranie stikhov*, vol. 2. Moscow: Izd. Skorpion.

Benda, Julien. 1913. *Une Philosophie Pathétique*. Paris: Cahiers de la quinzaine.

Couturat, Louis. 1905. *Les principes des mathématiques*. Paris: Félix Alcan.

Dillon, John. 2011. The Ideas as thoughts of God. *Études platoniciennes* 8: 31–42.

Friedman, Michael. 2001. *Dynamics of Reason*. Stanford: CSLI Publications.

Husserl, Edmund. 1970. *Logical Investigations*. Trans. John Findlay. New York: Humanities Press.

Husserl, Edmund. 1994. *Briefwechsel. Band III: Die Göttinger Schule*, ed. K. Schuhmann. Dordrecht: Kluwer Academic Publishers.

Husserl, Edmund. 2002. Philosophy as Rigorous Science. Trans. Marcus Brainard. In *The New Yearbook for Phenomenology and Phenomenological Philosophy II*, 249–295. Seattle: Noesis Press.

Husserl, Edmund. 2014. *Ideas for a Pure Phenomenology and Phenomenological Philosophy*. Trans. Daniel O. Dahlstrom. Indianapolis: Hackett Publishing Company.

Lactantius. 1905. The Divine Institutes. In *The Ante-Nicene Fathers*, ed. A. Roberts and J. Donaldson, vol. VII, 9–233. New York: Charles Scribner's Sons.

Leibniz, G[ottfried] W[ilhelm]. 1996. *New Essays On Human Understanding*. Trans. and ed. Peter Remnant and Jonathan Bennett. Cambridge: Cambridge University Press.

Mill, John Stuart. 1957. *Utilitarianism*. New York: Bobbs-Merrill Company.

Mitjushin, A. A. 1994. Primechanija. In Shpet 1994. 337–371.

Natorp, Paul. 2004. *Plato's Theory of Ideas. An Introduction to Idealism*. Trans. Vasilis Politis and John Connolly. Sankt Augustin: Academia Verlag.

Nietzsche, Friedrich. 1982. *The Portable Nietzsche*. Trans. Walter Kaufmann. New York: Penguin Books.

Nietzsche, Friedrich. 2007. *Ecce Homo: How to Become What You Are*. Trans. Duncan Large. New York: Oxford University Press.

Ovsjaniko-Kulikovskij, D. M. 1908. *Istorija russkoj intelligencii*, vol. 1. Moscow: V. M. Sablin.

Plato. 1969. *The Collected Dialogues of Plato*, ed. E. Hamilton and H. Cairns. Princeton: Princeton University Press.

Robinson, John Mansley. 1968. *An Introduction to Early Greek Philosophy*. Boston: Houghton Mifflin Company.

Russell, Bertrand. 1918. *Mysticism and Logic and Other Essays*. London: Longmans, Green and Co.

Shchedrina, Tat'jana G. 2004. *"Ja pishu kak ekho drugogo…": Ocherki intellektual'noj biografii Gustava Shpeta*. Moscow: Progress-Tradicija.

Shchedrina, Tat'jana G. (ed.). 2005. *Gustav Shpet: zhizn' v pis'makh. Epistoljarnoe nasledie.* Moscow: ROSSPEN.

Shestov, L. 1917. Memento mori. (Po povodu teorii poznanija Edmunda Gusserlja). *Voprosy filosofii i psikhologii*, kn. 139: 1–68.

Shpet, Gustav. 1991. *Appearance and Sense: Phenomenology as the Fundamental Science and Its Problems.* Trans. Thomas Nemeth. Dordrecht: Kluwer Academic Publishers.

Shpet, Gustav. 1994. *Filosofskie etjudy.* Moscow: Izd. gruppa «Progress».

Shpet, Gustav. 2006. *Philosophia Natalis. Izbrannye psikhologo-pedagogicheskie trudy.* Moscow: ROSSPEN.

Shpet, Gustav. 2007. *Iskusstvo kak vid znanija. Izbrannye trudy po filosofii kul'tury,* ed. T.G. Shchedrina. Moscow: ROSSPEN.

Shpet, Gustav. 2010a. *Filosofija i nauka. Lekcionnye kursy,* ed. T.G. Shchedrina. Moscow: ROSSPEN.

Shpet, Gustav. 2010b. *Filosofskaja kritika: otzyvy, recenzii, obzory,* ed. T.G. Shchedrina. Moscow: ROSSPEN.

Spinoza, Benedictus de. 1958. *Selections.* New York: Charles Scribner's Sons.

Wolff, Christian. 1968. *Philosophia prima, sive Ontologia, methodo scientifica pertractata, Gesammelte Werke.* Hildesheim: Georg Olms.

Wolfio, Christiano. 1730. *Philosophia prima sive Ontologiia.* Frankfurt: Rengerian.

Wundt, Wilhelm. 1897. *System der Philosophie.* Leipzig: Wilhelm Engelmann.

# Appendix 3: Philosophy and History

## Editor's Introduction to Shpet's "Philosophy and History"

The following essay first appeared in the philosophy journal *Voprosy filosofii i psikhologii* in 1916.[1] It is the re-worked text of an address given by Shpet at Moscow University on 9 May 1916 before the defense of his enormous thesis *Istorija kak problema logiki* [*History as a Problem of Logic*]. Shpet begins with a theme that would also figure prominently in his 1917 article "Wisdom or Reason?". He attacks the notion that philosophy, unlike the natural sciences, has made no progress since its emergence in pre-Socratic Greece, that it is merely a set of useless opinions. But Shpet also seeks both here and in the later piece to attack the view he largely associated with the reigning neo-Kantianism, viz., that philosophy is a handmaiden to mathematical physics, which not only yields demonstrable laws but is directly applicable in the world, yielding, as a result, technology. No, philosophy, properly understood, does have a subject matter distinct from the empirical natural sciences. It studies everything, albeit everything taken ideally. That is, whereas the objects of the empirical sciences are studied in their particularity, philosophy studies everything essentially, i.e., as given in ideal intuition. The implication here is that the natural sciences, for example, employ a particular methodology, but philosophy has another "logic," another way of approaching its concerns. The object of natural science and that of philosophy are the same, but philosophy takes the object "not in its empirical givenness, but in its idea or in its ideal givenness."[2] In this respect, Shpet joins with Husserl.[3] Shpet, however, with a keener sense of history than that publicly displayed by Husserl at least at this early date, believed it possible to see this conception of philosophy as far back as Plato.

---

[1] Shpet 1916.

[2] Shpet 2002: 71.

[3] See Shpet 1991: 12; Shpet 2005: 50.

© Springer Nature Switzerland AG 2019

G. Shpet, T. Nemeth, *Hermeneutics and Its Problems*, Contributions To Phenomenology 98, https://doi.org/10.1007/978-3-319-98941-9

The other essential characteristic of philosophy, in Shpet's view – and one that Husserl overlooked, although Shpet does not say so explicitly – is its dialogic character, which can be traced back to Socrates. This dialogic character ensures philosophy's sociality. Husserl had always explicitly conceived phenomenology, properly executed, as rigorous science. However, he also conceived it to be a collaborative venture, that all of his own investigations were subject to revision and emendation by himself but, more importantly, by others as well. What he did not explicitly state – perhaps did not even fully realize – is that this ever tentative, ever collaborative character of phenomenology is an *essential* feature of philosophy itself. The dialogic nature of philosophy entails neither a lapse into psychologism nor even a sociologism, for Shpet, ever the ontological realist, emphasizes the object is always the concrete whole taken ideally. Unlike negative philosophies, which seek to "reduce" the object or phenomenon of some empirical discipline to that of another discipline, positive philosophy repudiates the very idea of such reductionism, but instead takes its object in its originary givenness. In doing so, philosophy – again properly understood – employs description. As Shpet explained in the only posthumously published second part of his *History as a Problem of Logic*, "The fundamental science has the task of studying objects as they are. They can be essentially diverse and varied, depending on the various descriptions we obtain in the fundamental science. But the general task always remains to describe what is, without inventing anything and without creating any theories in doing so."[4]

Shpet, clearly, in the following article finds the "fullest expression" of the concrete in the social. Already in his 1914 summary and commentary on Husserl's recently published (1913) *Ideen I*, Shpet faulted Husserl for not realizing this, i.e., for not realizing that in addition to experiencing intuition and ideal intuition we have a peculiar "intellectual sight" or "intelligible intuition" that allows us to disclose the entelechy of an object, and therefore its sociality.[5] Shpet, unfortunately, never devoted the kind of attention to a detailed elaboration of the means, or the "mechanism," by which we, as investigators, determine or uncover the purported sociality of an object that Husserl did to eidetic intuition.[6] Shpet, though, does not insist that he has uncovered a hitherto unknown or unrecognized third "source" of cognition standing alongside empirical intuition and our reason. He leaves the matter in the following piece unresolved.

Another complicating factor that Shpet seemingly confronted directly and that forced him to re-orient his thought toward a phenomenological philosophy of lan-

---

[4] Shpet 2002: 563. Again in the *History*, Shpet writes, "Phenomenology gives a pre-theoretical investigation of the object, and this is why it can serve as the foundation of a theoretical study of any object. In this sense, it surely is the universal fundamental science." Shpet 2002: 577.

[5] Shpet 1991: 158. Shpet's example in 1914 is that of an axe, which we "intellectually see" is for chopping even though it "naturally" is a piece of sharpened metal attached to a wooden handle.

[6] One could argue, however, that Shpet replaced this notion of "intellectual intuition," with its unfortunate metaphysical and historical overtones, with language. That is, the acquisition of a language brings along with it and conveys the sociality of that which it concerns. Shpet's turn to a phenomenological philosophy of language is evident in his 1927 work on Wilhelm von Humboldt, *Vnutrennjaja forma slova* [*The Inner Form of the Word*].

guage arose from his keen sense of history. Unlike the Husserl he knew – or at least the Husserl of the works published to that time – Shpet found the social to be, as he expressed it here, "encumbered in its entirety by the past." For Shpet, the past is displayed everywhere in the present. However, if the historical is past, our only access to it remains by way of what is present, and apparently interpretation of the latter becomes inevitable with the goal being understanding. Again, as he wrote in his *History*, "Philosophically (and psychologically) I try to approach an analysis of the originary given in social and historical phenomena by means of an analysis of understanding or *comprehension*. I see here the philosophical source of sociality."[7] Shpet already in 1914 had at least a dim awareness in writing that in hermeneutical acts we "intellectually see" the noema as a sign for the object's entelechy and that any consciousness can be hermeneutic.[8] By 1916, Shpet came to a clearer recognition of the central role of understanding, writing, "If I am correct, if in fact it is impossible to reduce comprehension to 'deductive' processes, then here lies the specific feature of the social, which fundamentally distinguishes it as an object from all other objects. ... History is essentially not a technical, but a *hermeneutical* science. Herein precisely lies its unique philosophical significance."[9]

Addressing a Russian audience in the throes of a major war with Germany, Shpet understandably invoked domestic names with which the attendees at the thesis defense would have been quite familiar in an attempt to buttress his own alleged turn to the "concrete." We can also hardly be astonished that Shpet failed to mention the name of eminent representatives of philosophy in the principal enemy country even though Husserl, for one, was largely apolitical.

In the following text, items enclosed within brackets are editorial additions not found in Shpet's original publication.

## Philosophy and History

### Gustav Shpet

There is a rather widespread conception of philosophy, which in some circles has become so popular that it is already beginning to sound as if it were the voice of common sense. This opinion has it that the study of philosophy is sterile and useless. Philosophy has existed for almost 25 centuries with a pretense to scientific knowledge, and yet it has not attained a single position shared by all. Rather, philosophy is merely a collection of "subjective" and arbitrary opinions and constructions.

The philosopher recognizes, however, that such a judgment by its proponents shows both an incorrect understanding of scientific knowledge in general as well as

---

[7] Shpet 2002: 63.

[8] Shpet 1991: 153, 157.

[9] Shpet 2002: 63.

of philosophy in particular. The idea of science taken for granted here is the singular model of mathematical natural science, which, for no reason, is construed as the universal and sole ideal of scientific knowledge. Characteristically, such knowledge establishes "laws," or mechanical formulas, which give us a "foresight." The value of such science lies in the fact that thanks to this "foresight" it serves a purpose: ultimately it provides *technology*. The idea of philosophy taken for granted here simply ignores one of the oldest features of philosophy, viz., its essentially dialectical character. The dialectic is a rigorous and precise method, but this rigor is just not that of a mathematical proof. Moreover, though, the dialectic, as Socrates defined it, is a form of *collaborative thinking*, a διάλογος, in its fullest and most genuine sense. From this follow the specific characteristics of philosophy that decisively distinguish it from other sorts of knowledge. Just as the action in a drama cannot be reduced to a monologue, so one cannot demand that philosophy be a form of knowledge with a precision similar to mathematical natural science or that its value and its meaning be determined by technical applicability! In a dialogue, in the vivid activity of *personae dramatis*, its vitality, its originality, its uniqueness lies within the sphere of knowledge. Philosophy is not a science in the sense of a set of mechanical formulas, nor is it a form of art in the sense of a technique. Understood so, it certainly is useless and understood so it certainly has no firmly established positions shared by everyone!

However, if that is the case, why then is there for every philosopher one model, one starting point and one inexhaustible source, namely, *Plato*? Why is it that even for the non-philosopher Plato is clearly the exemplar, the ideal, the philosopher καί ἐξοχήν, the *philosophus archetypus*? With the arbitrariness and subjective character of philosophical opinions, what is the basis of such consistency in our recognition of its fundamental model and approach? Like everything in the world, philosophy abides and philosophy is one – not in its empirical manifestations and "occurrences" but as an *idea*, and Plato is its embodiment!

Indeed, it is not hard to see that positive philosophy, posing, together with Plato, tasks for itself, has always moved in one direction throughout its entire history driven by one goal. Although the faces and the times, the languages and the peoples have changed, positive philosophy has remained true to its principle and forged a strong tradition. Neither in Euclid, nor in Archimedes, Ptolemy, Hippocrates, Herodotus, but only in Plato do we find clear originality and a unique character as well as the distinct impossibility of confusing philosophy with our other types and sorts of knowledge! Here is the surest criterion of positive philosophy.

Above all, philosophy differs from the other sorts of knowledge both in terms of its object and its subject matter. It has always had from the start up to our own time – and so it remains – one object, a *concrete* one. This object is concrete reality! Here is the distinctive trait of philosophical knowledge: *philosophical knowledge is always and essentially concrete, integral knowledge*. Such is the simple conception and incessant effort of all philosophy. It cannot be satisfied with the particular, the abstract and the partial. As Plato demanded, philosophy is directed toward the all, "everything," but toward everything ideally. That is, it is directed *essentially* toward the concrete and integral: ἐν καί πάν. This is why philosophy cannot be compared with specialized knowledge, which is always particular and abstract. It can only be compared with knowledge that like it is also directed toward the integral, the complete, the concrete. Whatever be the topic, even if it be something particular, philosophy immediately transforms it into one that is general and fundamental!

How did it happen, however, that there is so much that is abstract in philosophy? How did it happen that philosophy is often blamed for being abstract? And importantly, the accusation is, apparently, not without merit.

In speaking of philosophy as a single, internally connected whole, I had in mind the very idea of philosophy, the realization of which constitutes positive philosophy. However, it is impossible to ignore the voices of negative philosophy – the "villains" in this drama. For if we did, we would have to exclude Protagoras, Kant, Condillac, Spencer, and its many other empirical manifestations from the development of philosophy. However, how do we distinguish negative philosophy?

With negative philosophy, we would seek in vain for a unity and continuity of tradition. Each such philosophy begins anew with a negation of the past and of its predecessors. However, there is one *common* way to break with philosophical tradition and that is to replace what is being negated with something of *one's own*: to put the abstract in place of the concrete, a part in place of the whole. If we leave aside a consistent philosophical nihilism, which, as such, is not philosophy, the characteristic of negative philosophy is always its abstractness. Negative philosophy is abstract philosophy. It is impossible to deny the important role that negative philosophy plays in the development of philosophy on the whole. It often poses *new* problems and identifies *new* aspects. However, we should simply not pass off some particular, partial and abstract thing as complete and integral. The evil of negative philosophy lies in such counterfeiting.

Still, something else is, perhaps, more important for clarifying the sense of positive philosophy. Philosophy is not only knowledge but also a certain *type of very complex experience,* which goes far beyond the bounds of purely intellectual concerns. Its structure in this sense is determined by extraordinarily varied conditions. Not only do the scientific concepts of the time have significance, but also the prejudices, worries, anxieties, and moods, in short the entire worldview of the era. It is quite significant that these moods and outlooks very often predetermine not only the subject matter of its problems, but also the character, form, and structure of its cognitive object.

In light of these concerns, it is easy to understand how it is that with regard to the question concerning the nature of the concrete we get answers that are similar in logical form but quite dissimilar in terms of their subject matter and sense. On the whole, though, this testifies once again in favor of the essentially concrete character of philosophy and of its aspiration to resolve problems related to the integrity of life. It also explains, however, the variety of answers we get when, from the point of view of our formalistic expectations, we expect to get a single answer from a single position "shared by all."

We need only recall how Socrates and Plato philosophized in order to convince ourselves of the concrete character of *their* philosophical problems, which were taken directly from life itself and which were returned to it after careful dialectical processing. The subject matter of Plato's *Republic* is a concrete object of this philosophy! We must bear this in mind in order to understand also an entire series of distinctive methodological techniques dictated by the subject matter of such an object. Let me avail myself of merely one example. Negative philosophy has adequately accustomed us to a kind of "logical materialism" with its general methodological demand: reduce the complex to the simpler – physiology to physics and chemistry; psychology, physiology and even sociology to biology, and so forth. An attempt to analyze the subject matters under study in the reverse manner would have to appear strange and paradoxical from the viewpoint of such a fundamental simplification. For example, let us place, say, "sociology" as the foundation. This would surely mean recognizing, both logically and methodologically, not the most abstract but the most concrete as the fundamental sort of knowledge!

We could adduce here many examples and models of biological and individual psychological analogies from contemporary philosophy, but let us take an example from Plato. In the *Republic*, he defines the "just" and only then moves to the individual human being. For what has been found in an even larger whole, we can easily see, in his words, in an individual person. In our language, we would say that psychology here "is reduced" to sociology, and not sociology to psychology. However, precisely this is an explanation of the abstract through the concrete, the part from the whole!

Be that as it may, the ancient world philosophized over *its* concrete subject matter. A new era changes this subject matter but also concentrates sincerely and seriously all of its intellectual powers on the concrete, to which it gives its own designation – *Civitas Dei*.[10] It is not difficult to see how the successes of natural science again transform the subject matter of the concrete. It appears first as dead but quite palpable matter and then as a living, animated principle. The concepts of matter, spirit, soul, energy, idea, monad, *élan vital*, etc. here, one by one, figure in turn. The *Civitas Dei* passes into the *Regnum hominis*,[11] and the human being is perceived in the numerous ways along which the *Interpretatio Naturae*[12] moves.

Now, however, after so many centuries of decline, are we not returning to an understanding of the concrete, the fullest expression of which, as only our own life knows, is precisely the "social"? However, the "social" is not only an aspect, or moment, of a given intuition, but something encumbered in its entirety by the past. The present, in each of its parts and in its entirety, gravitates to the past. The present displays the past everywhere and is connected to it by myriad threads. This concrete thing in its exhaustive entirety is nothing other than the *historical*! I believe that such is actually the idea of the concrete in contemporary philosophy.

Apart from its all-encompassing entirety, the historical is still characterized by the fact that it, as concrete, is necessarily conceived as moving and active. Such a

---

[10] [Latin: City of God. Most likely a reference to St. Augustine's great work by that title.]

[11] [Latin: reign or kingdom of man. Most likely a reference to an expression in Francis Bacon's *The New Organon*: "…there will be only one entrance into the kingdom of man, which is based upon the sciences…." Bacon 2000: 56.]

[12] [Latin: interpretation of nature. The expression occurs a number of times in *The New Organon*.]

concrete thing is essentially *dynamic*. In this regard, we sometimes have to hear complaints in contemporary philosophy against ancient philosophy. It is said that ancient philosophy is static, whereas dynamism is the overcoming of Platonism. A popular philosopher today declares that modern philosophy began at the moment when Galileo rolled a ball down an inclined plane. The conclusion that could be drawn from this would demand that we recognize not just Plato, but all of Platonism – and by our definition, all positive philosophy – as non-historical philosophy!

Is this the case? Are we not forgetting to contrast the fundamental difference between the *conditions* of the worldview of antiquity and those of our own? The different conditions, however, do not exclude, the unity and the identity of the very object of philosophizing! The philosophy of ancient Greece, above all, with wide open eyes contemplated itself in its "present." It began with contemplation, and its works were free and grandiose. Its memory was not burdened; the world for it was fresh and young. On the other hand, we begin with memory, with "tales." We see our world through "the dust of time."[13] "A tale of the times of old"[14] is for us sometimes our only source but is always close by and necessary. We look as one with the ancient world, but παντα ρει has for us a new subject matter and a new sense. For us, it is a stream of things and people, of works and days, of centuries and nations. The stream that passes before *our* mental gaze, is above all, the *flow of history*.

We think that this is *our* own acquisition. In any case, we often come to hear that such a formulation of the philosophical problem is a feature peculiar to our own time. It is said that the nineteenth century seriously posed the problem of history. In order to do so, having created a dynamic worldview, it had to break with the static picture of the ancient world. It broke with rationalism, grasping the irrational; it broke with traditional logic, affirming the rights of the alogical, etc. Nevertheless, we can ask whether it is by chance that the idea of a "new science" found a brilliant exponent in the person of the *Platonist* Vico,[15] that a conscious reflection on historical methodology found its exponent in the rationalist Chladenius, that Herder was a Leibnizian, and that the Platonist Leibniz was a dynamist. Are all these and similar facts accidents? A recognition of contingency here would be an indication of the absence of historicism!

However, in characterizing the nineteenth century as the historical century *par excellence* it is true that our epoch, in fact, came to a *clear awareness* of the historical problem. In this sense, our philosophy becomes a historical philosophy *par excellence*. The more the idea of the concrete, as historical, permeates it, the more it will become a historical philosophy.

Of course, in speaking of a concrete object, we are still not saying very much. The subject matter, or "object," in its logical meaning is only an *indefinite* "bearer" with varied content connected into a single unit in some central core, which comprehends it. The object is only a certain *point*, which determines the direction of our

---

[13] [From Pushkin's play *Boris Godunov*: "And he, like I, will light his icon lamp, And, shaking from my words the dust of time...." Pushkin 2007: 19 (Scene 5).]

[14] [From Pushkin's poem *Ruslan and Lyudmila*. Pushkin 2017: 9 (First Canto).]

[15] [A reference to Vico's *The New Science*, the first edition of which appeared in 1725.]

efforts and searches. Above all, we must point out in the object's manifold content the *types* of relations that we empirically characterize as, for example, cultural, legal, and religious.

We can discern our relations toward our surroundings in the general flow of history. These relations, on the whole, are as varied as the surroundings themselves. We can point out not only our limited relations to the "real" world, such as technical, cultural, and cognitive relations, but we can also establish a specific one, for example, a relation toward the "supersensible," and accordingly speak of religious relations. Finally, we can point out that our relationships toward other human beings are primarily legal and moral. On the whole, we can see how group relationships, for example, classes, strata, and states, arise from our relationships to each other. We learn that all of these relationships are subject to a certain definite form, the *form of organization*. From this organizing and organized flow of history, we extract individual things, individual people, individual relationships and connections, and we make them the object of our reflection and of our knowledge. We are already used to resolving "things" into a complex system of relationships, but not so with "people." This is precisely why we still are inclined to see the genuine object of history to be a "person." However, that we already have experience is essential. We already have learned and can see the "object" in relationships. But a question arises here: Is this not the way it is in the historical too?

*What is historically important*: the flow of history itself, or what is carried along on its waves? Quite a lot depends on the answer to this question. We must learn to grasp this flow in its entirety. We must learn not to fish out bits and pieces from it, but be able to embrace the moving whole. We must direct our attention to the *historical* content itself.

Here, methodological tasks of historical knowledge arise with their exceptional significance and their all-encompassing interest. The old opposition of the many to the one rises here with particular acuity! If we do not forget that the philosophical solution is essentially a *concrete* solution, does the usual opposition between sensibility and the understanding, then, satisfy us? Are we satisfied with a solution by which the path from the particular to the general is through abstraction, through an impoverishment of the content of the particular? Is this not the way contemporary philosophy arrived at the paradox that the farther away we move from the real manifold, the closer we come to truth? However, then with even greater antinomic acuity, the manifold and the one in their respective concreteness stand opposed to one another! Certainly, fundamentally, in principle, we have here the old "antinomy" between experience and reason, seeing and insight.

But do we really have an antinomy here? Do we really have to choose between these two horns of the dilemma? It is highly instructive here to recall the dialectic and the history of the *concept of experience*. It arose and became the focus of philosophical interests as a very healthy reaction to verbal formulas in favor of sense and things. There were so many claims that experience was the means of cognition, that it was the instrument of thought. However, from the very start, it demanded the participation of reason. Every attempt to limit the rights and significance of reason meant at the same time a limitation and impoverishment of experience. Within limits, the minimum of reason coincides with the minimum of experience. Such is, for example, the position of sensualistic phenomenalism, which confines all of consciousness to the sensibly given with its gloomy and dull formula: the world is a complex of sensations! On the contrary, a broadening of the content of "experience," above all, beyond the bounds of confined sensibility, in the depths of empiricist philosophy itself, leads so-called radical empiricism to an enrichment of the concept such that "experience" [*opyt*] becomes simply identified with "lived experience" [*perezhivanie*]. Experience loses its restrictive forms and inevitably must recognize that there is no seeing without insight [*umozrenie*], that in a real lived experience we see not with the "eyes," but with the "mind" – our eyes being its obedient instrument. The more reason assumes its rights and obligations, the more we want to find the stable and "enduring" in a capricious and whimsical change in lived experiences. As a result, we are convinced of the quite universal significance of the theses: the eyes without reason look but do not see, the ears hear but do not listen, and all of scientific logic captures its prey in the net of its concepts but does not understand what it has caught.

Nevertheless, if in restoring the rights of reason our logic copes with all this, then will not new and even more insurmountable difficulties arise when the concept of *experience* must be expanded, as it were, far beyond the bounds of lived experience itself? When we must state that for our understanding "even the stones take on a voice," when even "the ashes of an increasingly decrepit universe"[16] are an "eloquent" ash, entering as a necessary constituent moment in our consciousness?

A question arises automatically: does not the concrete that has been our concern – the concrete, as historical – does it not need for our cognition of it a special source that is not experience in the ordinary sense? If, in general, we recognized two sources of cognition – experience and reason – are we not suggesting something quite new, a third source of cognition? And if we see in experience and in reason two consistent moments of penetration into the depths of the cognized, then again are we not faced here with a new, a third, even deeper penetration? If, to use more precise philosophical terminology, we were to distinguish reason from sense intuition, would we not have to talk then about a very special intuition, let us say, an intelligible intuition? For everyone sees that the significance of lived experiences, be it that of a "stone" or of "true tales," or from other historical sources, lies primarily in their interpretive or hermeneutic character.

Actually, in order to comprehend any "passage" in the flow of history, we need, it seems, a special "faculty" or activity of the mind (*dukha*). It simply takes, as it were, a special ability to grasp a picture of the *whole* where only a "part" is thought. We *talk* about the physical, about the living, the moral, the economic, the political, etc. All of this must be restored as a single thing before our mental gaze! But surely still more is needed. Proceeding from the outside, from the external, we need to penetrate through to reach the interior, the intimate something, for this is the path of comprehension and interpretation. We are surprised by the naturalist, who from one fossil bone is able to restore for us the appearance of a once existing but now extinct species. How much more difficult, though, is the concrete intuition with the help of

---

[16] [These two quotations are from a poem by Evgenij Baratynskij "Fragments from the poem 'Recollections'." See Baratynskij 1894: 6, 7.]

which we restore the image of a historical being from the sometimes most insignificant trace of a person.

Surely, I am not insisting that we are dealing here with a special "third" independent source of cognition. It is obvious, though, that there is some peculiarity here that the philosophical mind with its logic and methodology cannot overlook. It must pose its problems here and must seek *its* solutions for them.

As problems of the concrete, they are not completely new to philosophy. But the new subject matter of the concrete yields a new characteristic. *The tasks of contemporary philosophical knowledge are the tasks of historical philosophy.* Just as the subject matter of life and of our "worldview" changes and progresses, so also changes the subject matter of the philosophical concrete! The philosophical tradition is not passed from one generation to a generation of buried talent. It represents spiritual growth and enrichment. To demand that philosophy establish unshakable theses, as in the specialized abstract sciences, would be to demand that our philosophy merely copy precisely the experiences of our ancestors in life and not worry about its own experience! The specialized sciences are actually satisfied with their unshakable theses, impressing the particular into them and with its abstract nature. There are still such formulas. Growth in these sciences is nothing other than *accumulation*. In philosophy, growth is always an ever new begetting. Philosophy does not accumulate, but *productively expends*. This is precisely why its concern is not with the inviolability of theses, but about the unity and continuity of its creative movement.

I understand this unity in the tradition of positive philosophy. And I dare to think that I sense this tradition not as some remote, general and indirect connection, but as the closest spiritual unity, which is living and immediate. Let us take simply *our own*, nearest tradition. Who will deny that the philosophical theories of P. Jurkevich, Vl. Solov'ëv, S. Trubeckoj, L. Lopatin are part of the positive philosophical tradition, which stems, as I indicated, from Plato? We see that Jurkevich understood philosophy as *complete* and *integral* knowledge. For him, philosophy, as an integral worldview, is not the concern of a person, but of humanity. Solov'ëv begins with a critique of abstract philosophy, and already in the "Philosophical Principles of *Integral* Knowledge" he presents a veritable concrete-historical philosophy. Trubeckoj calls his view "*concrete* idealism." Lopatin's system is a "system of *concrete* spiritualism."

All of this is enough to see the unity that our positive philosophy should continue to pursue. We must concentrate our efforts in this direction, and our forces must be applied in this direction.

## Bibliography to "Philosophy and History"

Bacon, Francis. 2000. *The New Organon*, ed. L. Jardine and M. Silverthorne. Cambridge: Cambridge University Press.
Baratynskij, Evgenij A. 1894. *Polnoe sobranie sochinenij*. Kiev: Ioganson.

Pushkin, Alexander. 2007. *Boris Godunov and Other Dramatic Works*. Trans. James E. Falen. Oxford: Oxford University Press.

Pushkin, Alexander. 2017. *Ruslan and Lyudmila*. Trans. Roger Clarke. Richmond/Surrey: Alma Books.

Shpet, Gustav. 1916. Filosofija i istorija. *Voprosy filosofii i psikhologii*, kniga 134: 427–439.

Shpet, Gustav. 1991. *Appearance and Sense: Phenomenology as the Fundamental Science and Its Problems*. Trans. Thomas Nemeth. Dordrecht: Kluwer Academic Publishers.

Shpet, Gustav. 2002. *Istorija kak problema logiki. Materialy*. Moscow: Pamjatniki istoricheskoj mysli.

Shpet, Gustav. 2005. *Mysl' i Slovo: Izbrannye trudy*, ed. T.G. Shchedrina. Moscow: POSSPEN.

# Appendix 4: Skepticism and Dogmatism of Hume

## Editor's Introduction to "Skepticism and Dogmatism of Hume"

The following essay was originally published in the major Russian philosophy journal of the time, *Voprosy filosofii i psikhologii* in 1911, thus just shortly before Shpet's introduction to Husserl and phenomenology.[1] Most likely, this essay arose from Shpet's seminar on Hume at the University of Moscow in the spring semester of the 1909/10 academic year.[2] However, Shpet's interest in Hume and skepticism went back to his undergraduate days. Although not published until 1903, Shpet wrote in 1902 a highly critical review of a new Russian translation of Hume's *Enquiry Concerning Human Understanding*.[3] He prefaced his specific remarks about the translation, saying that Hume enjoyed a particularly exceptional status in the history of philosophy. His "ruthless logic, clarity of thought and presentation, the consistency of his general constructions, and his attention to detail make him attractive to anyone who turns to philosophy not only for intellectual and moral enlightenment, but also for purely aesthetic enjoyment."[4]

In his undergraduate thesis for Kiev University on the topic "The Problem of Causality in Hume and Kant," Shpet held that Kant had correctly presented Hume's point of view regarding causality, but Hume, in Kant's eyes, had concluded incorrectly that the causal connection is purely subjective, a matter of habit. Hume's

---

[1] Shpet 1911.

[2] See Tihanov 2008: 285. Of interest is the fact that Boris Pasternak attended Shpet's seminar and wrote an essay entitled "Hume's Psychological Skepticism" in connection with it.

[3] See Shpet 2010. Regarding the translation, Shpet wrote that, although it appeared at a very propitious moment, it was "imperfect" and that it "sins against all the rules of a good translation." Shpet 2010: 23. The translator, Sof'ja I. Cereteli (1871–1943), wrote to Shpet that she recognized the merits of some of his remarks, but not all. See Shpet 2010: 26. In contrast to Shpet's assessment, Nikolaj D. Vinogradov (1868–1936), who taught philosophy at the Moscow Higher Women's Courses and later published a two-volume set on Hume's philosophy, viewed the translation as "satisfactory. It, with very few exceptions, correctly conveys the original, reads easily, and gives an idea of the elegant style of the entire *Enquiry*." Vinogradov 1903: 734.

[4] Shpet 2010: 21.

© Springer Nature Switzerland AG 2019
G. Shpet, T. Nemeth, *Hermeneutics and Its Problems*, Contributions
To Phenomenology 98, https://doi.org/10.1007/978-3-319-98941-9

error, according to Kant, stemmed from having in mind things in themselves, rather than appearances. Once the correction is made, Hume's doubt in the necessity of causality vanishes.[5] However, we should keep in mind here that Shpet fundamentally rejected Kant's bifurcation of things in themselves and appearances. For Shpet, Hume never doubted the *real* necessity of the causal connection, only its *logical* necessity, i.e., the possibility of epistemologically proving such necessity. In effect, then, whereas Kant would hold that causal judgments bear an objective necessity, Hume considers the necessity to be merely subjective. Shpet adds, as if merely in passing, that it is just this subjectivism that leads Hume to skepticism; the latter doubted that the law of causality could be proved, i.e., logically proved. Whereas Kant believed it could, he was, however, unable to do so, at least for the reason – if no other – that any logical proof required first assuming its universal applicability. In this sense, Hume was correct that the law could not be "proved." But, then again, Shpet concludes, "it was not necessary to prove anything."[6]

With his firm commitment to ontological realism and a hostility to both skepticism and Kantian epistemology, Shpet's positive reception of the early Husserl, not unlike that of the latter's other Göttingen students, becomes that much more understandable. Unlike many of his fellow students, however, Shpet attempted to understand Husserl's newly published *Ideen I* (1913) not as a reversion to idealism, but as an affirmation and elaboration of a number of central tenets found in his earlier works. In his principal study of Husserl, *Appearance and Sense* (1914), Shpet saw Hume and Locke as "negative" philosophers who, nevertheless, "have rendered a real service to philosophy" by drawing attention "to new aspects and to new types" of being.[7] It was Kant who labeled Hume's empiricism a skepticism, but Hume's "skepticism" was qualified. Whereas Kant found it scandalous to both philosophy and human reason that the existence of objectivity, of things existing independently of our awareness of them, had to be accepted on faith, Hume, in Shpet's telling, found nothing "particularly scandalous" in this.[8] Certainly, Hume's reservation concerning reason's ability to resolve philosophical issues could be termed a "skeptical attitude," but it also led him to the brink of pursuing the "positive" problem concerning *how* we relate to the world, taking "world" in the most general sense possible, i.e., to use Husserl's terminology, in the "natural attitude." Unlike Kant, whose narrow understanding of "reason" led him to see nature only in terms of laws, Hume posed the problem phenomenologically.

Shpet's 1916 thesis, *History as a Problem of Logic*, dealt primarily with figures and topics other than Hume and causality. Yet arguably for that very reason Shpet's brief comment on the topic is all that more poignant. Hume's treatment of causality

---

[5] Shpet 1907: 171–74.

[6] Shpet 1907: 202.

[7] Shpet 1991: 4. Shpet began the "Introduction" to his 1916 thesis writing "The dominant philosophy at present is a negative philosophy. Negation is in it not only the final result, but belongs to the very essence of contemporary philosophy. It starts from negation, is based on negation and proceeds to negation." Shpet 2002: 41.

[8] Shpet 1991: 137.

is from a phenomenalistic standpoint and is understandable only under phenome-nalistic presuppositions. Hume's "subjectivism," then, is simply a consequence of that initial standpoint. Kant unhesitatingly followed Hume along the same path. Phenomenalism makes every theory, be it ontological or methodological, into a theory of cognition and renders impossible any theoretical study of the real world.[9]

In the course of Shpet's further career, he largely neglected traditional philo-sophical issues. Not surprisingly, there are few direct references to Hume. Nonetheless, Shpet's most extensive discussion of skepticism was a lengthy essay "The Skeptic and His Soul" from January 1919. Despite the topic and his earlier association of skepticism with Hume, the British philosopher scarcely plays a role therein, being mentioned, as it were, almost in passing. The reason for this relative omission is not hard to find. Shpet now found skepticism to be, properly speaking, not a philosophical position, but rather a "mood," "attitude," or a "state of consciousness."[10] It represents a failure in philosophy itself to grapple with its prob-lems, and, as such, "lies *outside* philosophical theory."[11] Skepticism, being a mood or a psychological fact, cannot be refuted any more than can another psychological or physical state, such as a case of bad digestion or a toothache.

Shpet, on the other hand, saw Hume as an empiricist and – contrary to most post-Kantian depictions – not as a skeptic, at least not as commonly depicted. For Shpet, empiricism is a philosophical theory, albeit a negative one. If we pursue empiricism, it will *eventually* lead to skepticism, a metaphysical skepticism, in which there is no objective knowledge and the bifurcation between things as they "really" are and things merely as they appear is firmly established. Thus, the genuine skeptic is not Hume, but Kant!

We could not possibly hope to summarize Shpet's 1919 essay here nor do we need to do so, since, as mentioned, its primary concern is not with either the skepti-cism or the dogmatism of Hume's position. Indeed, the attentive reader of Shpet's relatively "youthful" piece – he turned 32 in the year of its publication – will notice that notwithstanding the title Hume's alleged "dogmatism" is hardly addressed. Shpet remarked that Vladimir Solov'ëv saw three certainties at the start of philoso-phy: the validity of the subjective states of consciousness, the validity of logic and the validity of the philosophical intention, i.e., of the intention to know the truth in its essence. The last of these is absent in negative philosophy, which is satisfied with phenomenalism.[12] Skepticism is "obviously" close to negative philosophy, and if Solov'ëv is correct, its intention is non-philosophical. Hume's "skeptical solution" to causality refrained from veering in the direction of an extreme skepticism, of any

---

[9] Shpet 2002: 121.

[10] Almost from the outset, Shpet approvingly referred to Emerson, for whom the skeptic's place "is the vestibule of the temple." Shpet 2006: 366; Emerson 1996: 97. In his lecture "Montaigne, or the Skeptic," Emerson wrote, "Skepticism is the attitude assumed by the student in relation to the particulars which society adores, but which he sees to be reverend only in their tendency and spirit."

[11] Shpet 2006: 371f.

[12] Shpet 2006: 393–94.

contact with the real world. Unlike Kant, Hume's phenomenalism – and skepticism – is limited. His dogmatism is not a *terminus a quo*, but a *terminus ad quem*. While dogmatically rejecting the real world, in the end he dogmatically recognizes it for the sake of cognition.

As with the other essays in this collection, the items enclosed within brackets are the translator's additions. All of Shpet's references, however, are to more recent editions than those he gave when this editor deemed it to be appropriate.

## Skepticism and Dogmatism of Hume[13]

### Gustav Shpet

Let us consider the generally accepted view that skepticism is a *logically* baseless and self-defeating theory. For this reason a historian of philosophy naturally assumes a great responsibility when referring to some direction as skeptical or calling some person a skeptic. Moreover, this responsibility increases in step with the historical significance of the theory or its author. The issue becomes even more acute when the label "skeptic" is applied to a writer who asserts that with the hegemony of skepticism: "All discourse, all action would immediately cease, and men remain in a total lethargy till the necessities of nature, unsatisfied, put an end to their miserable existence."[14]

With this, serious questions inevitably arise about the legitimacy of calling Hume a skeptic. We can resolve this matter only by correctly determining what Hume doubted. With this in mind, we must ask above all: What did Hume actually doubt, and, then, what is the nature of this doubt?

Assuming that there is a good reason for every doubt, we can ask what the basis of Hume's doubt is. That is, where do we look to see the source of his doubt? The answer to this fundamental question must be based on our investigation into the philosopher's own train of thought. Let us further suppose that this doubt – like a pang of conscience – is by its psychological nature a restless state, in which a person cannot stay. The question arises: If we are dealing here not with a simple negation, how does Hume resolve his doubt? What ultimately sooths his logical conscience?

Hume's position in the *history* of philosophy is usually fixed in terms of his relationship, on the one hand, to rationalistic metaphysics – he stands in a critical relation to it – and, on the other hand, to the philosophies of Locke and Berkeley – he stands as a successor to both. *Theoretically*, Hume's position is characterized as an empiricism and a positivism. A historical and a theoretical consideration of a given philosophy represent, so to speak, two different coordinate systems that determine that philosophy's form and status. They amount to the same thing, but for the purposes of the investigation both can have a methodological advantage over the other.

---

[13] This was read by the author as a test lecture. [Shpet did not elaborate what he meant.]
[14] Hume 2004: 104.

Let us ask on what does Hume's skepticism depend. We assume that the critique of rationalism, as a source of the doubt, is out of the question. For any critique in terms of formal logic presupposes its dogma. And to answer our question from a historical point of view, we would have to show how the consistently developed philosophy of Locke and Berkeley leads to skepticism. From the theoretical point of view, the same task arises before us with respect to empiricism and positivism.

Since Kant's day a second path is usually followed in discussing Hume's philosophy. From that time on, Hume has appeared as a skeptic insofar as he is an empiricist. More precisely, Hume's skepticism is seen as the inevitable consequence of his empiricist theory of causality. At the present time, Windelband, Jodl, and others look on the matter in just this manner.[15] However, this path and such a solution cannot satisfy those who are not interested at all in this problem, but it is interesting to those individuals for whom what is important is *Humean* skepticism and not the relationship of empiricism to skepticism in general. Therefore, if our interest here is specifically in Hume, the first way, the historical way, of examining his philosophy is preferable.

Without entering into a detailed examination of the relationship of Hume to Locke and Berkeley, we need note only one point of decisive importance for our problem, namely, the starting point in the arguments of these philosophers. Having rejected the presence in us of innate ideas, Locke had to recognize perception as the sole source of knowledge. However, by means of perception we can cognize only the properties of things as they are given to our cognition, but by no means their essence. It is true that among our perceptions there are those that fully correspond to reality. These are perceptions of primary qualities. However, they show only the properties of things and nothing more. Berkeley goes a step further, but only in that he transforms primary qualities into secondary ones. To be, in general, means to be perceived. However, for Berkeley along with ideas there is yet another source of cognition, which gives us knowledge of the spirit. Hume finally takes the final step, attributing all knowledge to one source and ascribing to it a single quality. Outside perception, there is no knowledge and no being. Therefore, we come to a pure phenomenalism as the starting point of his philosophy.

Actually, adhering to the schema of the *Enquiry* we can express Hume's starting point and immediate conclusions in the following way: The entire content of our consciousness consists of *perceptions*. However, we can grasp within this content itself the essential difference between individual perceptions. Some of them are more lively, vivid and bolder, others less so. We can call the first *impressions*, and the second *ideas*. A closer examination of the content of consciousness reveals that between its individual elements, namely perceptions, there are certain constant and regular connections, which we can designate by a special term – *associations*. The products of these associations are, on the one hand, *relations* between ideas and, on the other, *matters of fact*. There is a difference between them in terms of their certainty. That is, affirmations of relations can be discovered by the activity alone of thought. This is why although neither a circle nor a triangle exists in nature, judg-

---

[15] Windelband 1895: 476; Jodl 1872: 25.

ments about them can be certain and true. It is different with matters of fact, because
their contradiction is always conceivable and possible. In any case, however, insofar
as they are given in perception or memory it is impossible to doubt them. It is
another matter when they lie "beyond the present testimony of our senses, or the
records of our memory."[16] In such a case, a basis for doubt actually emerges. A further examination of Hume's argument reveals that such a conclusion is made on the
basis of the relation between cause and effect. Therefore, it is natural that the doubt
is extended to this relation. By general consensus, Hume's skepticism begins here,
namely with the question: *wat right* do we have to conclude from what was to what
will be? This is a question that naturally demands a preliminary answer to the more
general question: Do we in general have such a right?

It is appropriate that we pause here. Regardless, for the time being, of how Hume
answers this question, it apparently can be shown that in the very formulation of the
latter question, as ascribed to Hume, we ought to make certain changes that notice-
ably give another meaning to this question. These changes illuminate it from a side
that has been, if not previously ignored, then, in any case, insufficiently stressed. In
order to be completely persuasive, we ought to stick to Hume's own train of thought.

If we reconstruct the consistency of Hume's arguments as they were originally
presented in the *Treatise*, we believe our discussion will more closely correspond to
the order of Hume's thoughts, which led him to his conclusions. However, we will,
then, be convinced that the question of causality for him is, so to speak, derivative
or secondary. Originally, another question stood before Hume, one that appeared to
him to be the initial question on the basis of which and with respect to which Hume's
skepticism properly developed. Already in his "Introduction" to the *Treatise*, Hume
formulated his task, namely, to investigate human nature from the point of view of
the scope and powers of the human mind. In it, Hume expresses a doubt in the
unbounded nature of these powers. He points out their limits. Experience and observation form the basis of all the sciences, those both of nature and of the mind.
Therefore, to penetrate into the essence of external things and of the mind is impossible. Distrust in the human cognitive powers entails a doubt in the first troublesome
task of cognizing the externally surrounding world. That our cognition is unable to
access its own basic essential principles is thought to jeopardize those natural principles which are considered to have already been discovered and to which we have
resorted until now for help. Thus, original sin and our very naivety force a suspicion
of the sin of hypocrisy. Hume wants to hide the sin of cognition under the guise of
modesty, the reverse side of which is the voice of doubt. As Hume says, whatever
may be the hypothesis that pretends to discover the ultimate original qualities of
human nature, it must be rejected in advance as presumptuous and chimerical.[17] The
substantiation of this train of thought begins with the first pages of the *Treatise*. It is
the central point of Hume's philosophy, the focus in which converge and from which
diverge all of its rays. With this in mind, we can understand and appraise all of the
conclusions of his philosophy, both the skeptical as well as the dogmatic ones.

---

[16] [Hume 2004: 14.]

[17] Hume 1968: xxi.

With this as the starting point, the entire structure and order of Hume's thoughts become understandable. All of our cognition, consequently, is confined to perceptual cognition, i.e., to the content of consciousness. This dogma, once expressed, already compels us to conduct a rigorously consistent immanent analysis and even partially predetermines the very path our analysis will follow. We can investigate our cognitive faculties solely by means of an investigation of the content of consciousness. In turning to it we immediately come upon a distinction that cannot be seen as the effect of a single faculty alone. We notice that there is an essential difference between the perceptions that form the entire content of consciousness. Perceptions differ with respect to their force, liveliness and relief. Some perceptions are more powerful and lively; others pale, weak, etc. We express these differences with the words: "ideas," "representations," and "impressions." The more forceful and lively perceptions are called "impressions" and the others "ideas." Between both there exists a great similarity in everything save the degree of force. All of our perceptions, therefore, turn out to be doubled. We can look at some as the reflection of others. This constant conjunction of similar perceptions forces us to assume that there is a powerful connection between the corresponding impressions and ideas. The existence of some has an influence upon the existence of others. Such a constant conjunction between them cannot be accidental. Considering the order of the first manifestation of perceptions, we find from constant experience that the impressions always precede the ideas. That is to say, it is not difficult to notice that impressions first arise in us and then ideas, which appear, as it were, as copies of the impressions. For this reason, we can consider impressions also as the causes of ideas. If we now turn to consider impressions, it turns out that they can be divided by their origin into two groups. On the one hand, we have impressions arising from sensations and on the other from reflection, i.e., impressions, so to say, of a second order, which are derived from ideas and, consequently, attend the latter. Anatomists and naturalists can more aptly solve the problem of what sensations are. For the philosopher, however, there is the quite important problem of how impressions arise from sensations. How do we obtain impressions? Clearly, given his fundamental assumption Hume can give only one answer, an agnostic one. Indeed, he gives it. This kind of impression "arises in the soul originally, from unknown causes."[18] Certainly, an investigation of the question stops with such an answer. The next question is how impressions arise from reflections. Since reflections, however, originate with ideas, our investigation must turn to the latter. This is precisely what Hume does.

If we now begin a study of that part of the content of consciousness we call "ideas," we will notice that all ideas can be conjoined and again separated. Along with this, we will notice that certain combinations of ideas have a uniform character and are not completely arbitrary. We must conclude, therefore, that there are certain general principles of combining and coordinating ideas. As is well-known, Hume calls these principles "associations." These principles, it is true, do not create an inseparable connection between the ideas, nor are they the sole principles of combi-

---

[18] Hume 1968: 7.

nation. Nevertheless, with their help the mind passes from one idea to another and thereby connects them. There is, as it were, a kind of attraction in the mental world analogous to attraction in the natural world. A philosophical question arises here concerning the nature and the causes of this mental attraction. In fact, does it depend on the properties of the things themselves, which are expressed by the ideas, or, on the contrary, on the activity of the mind? Denying, however, our cognition of every-thing whatever except the content of consciousness, or perceptions, how can Hume answer this question? His only possible answer is further denial, negativism and agnosticism. For now, Hume is actually consistent. He asserts: "Its effects are every where conspicuous; but as to its causes, they are mostly unknown, and must be resolv'd into *original* qualities of human nature, which I pretend not to explain."[19]

Such an associative connecting process of two ideas creates new formations, which can be called "complex ideas." These can be divided into relations, modes, and substances. The natural combination of ideas by association creates a relation. It is in this sense, at least, that this word is used in ordinary speech. However, it is impossible to ignore the fact that we often have to compare two ideas with their arbitrary combination. This is why in philosophy we can extend the meaning of the term "relation" to refer to the result of any comparison.[20] Having carefully exam-ined the qualities that admit to a comparison and consequently to the production of ideas of philosophical relations, we can group them under a small number of rubrics, namely seven, which are the source of all philosophical relations.

Hume omitted his theory of relations and the subsequent chapters on substance and abstract concepts from his *Enquiry*. Immediately after the discussion of the association of ideas, he passes to an examination of causality and begins with his "skeptical doubts." Here lies the basis for the common characterization of Hume's philosophy as a skepticism. However, this is not the path taken in the *Treatise*. In it, Hume begins with an investigation of the ideas of space and time, devoting to it the entire second part of the *Treatise*. That such an order of presentation is not acciden-tal is clear from the fact that Hume concludes this part with an investigation of the ideas of existence, stressing his fundamental and initial phenomenalistic point of view. Indeed, he views this investigation as preparatory for the subsequent third part.[21] In its conclusion, which expresses the result of the investigation, we again find an acknowledgment of the old idea, which apparently serves, as before, as the guiding idea, viz., the impossibility of cognizing objects transcendent to conscious-ness. "Now since nothing is ever present to the mind but perceptions, and since all

---

[19] Hume 1968: 13.

[20] Hume 1968: 13–14. Hume 1895: 25f.

[21] Hume 1968: 66. Hume writes: "It may not be amiss, before we leave this subject, to explain the ideas of *existence* and of *external existence*; which have their difficulties, as well as the ideas of space and time. By this means we shall be the better prepar'd for the examination of knowledge and probability, when we understand perfectly all those particular ideas, which may enter into our reasoning." The internal connection between the second and the third part of the *Treatise* with regard to the problem under consideration is clear also from the last paragraph of the second part, which ends with the words: "But of this more fully hereafter." Hume 1968: 68. [Shpet here refers to part IV, section 2 of the *Treatise*. See Hume 1968: 187–218.]

ideas are deriv'd from something antecedently present to the mind; it follows that 'tis impossible for us so much as to conceive or form an idea of any thing specifically different from ideas and impressions. Let us fix our attention out of ourselves as much as possible: Let us chase our imagination to the heavens, or to the utmost limits of the universe; we never really advance a step beyond ourselves, nor can conceive any kind of existence, but those perceptions which have appear'd in that narrow compass. This is the universe of the imagination, nor have we any idea but what is there produc'd."[22] As for the interpretation of the "real nature and operations" of objects acting on the senses, Hume simply rejects this task as impossible. "I am afraid," he writes, "that such an enterprize is beyond the reach of human understanding, and that we can never pretend to know body otherwise than by those external properties, which discover themselves to the senses."[23] In a long footnote in the "Appendix," Hume adds an explanatory note at this point again saying: "If we carry our enquiry beyond the appearances of objects to the senses, I am afraid, that most of our conclusions will be full of scepticism and uncertainty."[24]

So, up to this point the character and limits of Hume's skepticism are clear. However, a doubt, like a sin, is excessive. Is it not the case that Hume's doubt entails other doubts? Can the sequence be stopped? Can we obtain firm conclusions from a doubt?

Passing again to an examination of relations, Hume finds that there are some that "are the foundation of science."[25] They are indubitable, since they "depend entirely on the ideas, which we compare together."[26] However, there are also some that change without a change in the ideas themselves.[27] Consequently, they do not depend on the content of the ideas. That is, they are present or absent even though the ideas do not change.[28] These are the relations of identity, position in space and time, and the relation of causality. However, upon a closer investigation it turns out that, with the establishment of the relation of identity as well as that of space and time, both of the compared objects, i.e., both objects between which a relation is ascertained, happen to be present. Both are perceived, and with their help we cannot go beyond what is ascertained to be immediately perceived. In precisely the same way, we cannot discover the unperceived real existence or unperceived real relations between objects. Therefore, *there is only the relation of causality, which gives us assurance in a cognition of what is not immediately given in perception.* "Here then it appears, that of those three relations, which depend not upon the mere ideas, the only one that can be trac'd beyond our senses and informs us of existences and objects, which we do not see or feel, is *causation.*"[29] However, if we doubt the pos-

---

[22] Hume 1968: 68.

[23] Hume 1968: 64.

[24] [Hume 2004: 639.]

[25] Hume 1968: 73.

[26] Hume 1968: 69.

[27] Hume 1968: 73.

[28] Hume 1968: 69.

[29] Hume 1968: 74.

sibility of proceeding beyond perception to cognize the real world, real existence, real objects, then how can we avoid doubting the significance of the causal relation with its assurance of passing beyond the realm of consciousness? The conclusion is unavoidable. A doubt in the cognizability of real objects leads to a doubt in the cognitive value of the relation, which is the point of that relation. Hume's doubt in causality is, therefore, actually derivative. Such a doubt, however, would of necessity lead to a universal negation, before which everything stops. In fact, it leads to a doubt not only in the reality of the world that transcends consciousness, but also in the coming moment. There is doubt whether I will complete this line, whether I will finish my thought, is there not?

So, having doubted the cognizability of the real world, Hume was led in a quite consistent fashion to doubt that the phenomenal world is conditioned by causality. However, this is a doubt in the *general* significance of causality and, consequently, also a doubt in the *future* of the phenomenal world not yet given immediately to consciousness. Is it impossible, however, to save at least the future from doubt? Once the universal significance of causality is lost, then perhaps its particular, or perhaps its likely, significance can be recognized. From the preceding it should be clear that phenomenalism is faced here with a dilemma: either extreme skepticism or its own negation, its suicide. In essence, the *solution* to the problem and the *resolution* of our doubts lies simply in the latter path. Hume does not want to go down this road. On the other hand, however, he does not find the words to censure extreme skepticism. As a result, he attempts to follow a third path: to recognize that a resolution of the problem is possible while retaining a doubt. This is Hume's illustrious "skeptical solution." He tries to ground the applicability of causality for the future, appealing at a decisive moment to a recognition of the real world, to its cognizability, at least to such an extent that he does not deny its constancy and regularity.

Therefore, Hume's next task cannot be to doubt the causal relation, but, on the contrary, to substantiate it. However, such a substantiation could manage without a recognition of the real significance of this relation. Logically, this task can be formulated as: How do we include the excluded middle?


# II


As was shown, a doubt in the reality of our cognition of things leads to a doubt in the relation that solely can establish a real connection between things, namely in the relation of causality. Moreover, this doubt extends in two directions. First, it is directed at the very *emergence of things* and secondly at the *necessity* of their connection *in the future*. Hume, in this way, dissects his problem. Consequently, for him it is necessary to examine: "First, For what reason we pronounce it *necessary*, that every thing whose existence has a beginning, shou'd also have a cause?

Secondly, Why we conclude, that such particular causes must *necessarily* have such particular effects?"[30]

The first question is quite natural from the point of view of phenomenalism. Having doubted that the objective world beyond what is given to the senses can be cognized, it is impossible to affirm that the existence of what is given has a cause, and moreover a necessary one, in that world. The claim that everything that exists has a cause is essentially unproved and cannot be proved. Hume devoted Part III, Section III to the impossibility of proving this claim either intuitively or demonstratively from the phenomenalistic point of view. Properly speaking, having raised this question Hume, in order to be completely consistent, should have at once turned from solving it to rejecting it. The principle of existence is the principle of perception. The latter can give rise to an idea, but it itself would have to rise from nothing, since before the start of the perception it was not in consciousness. Therefore, it did not exist. But since Hume seeks an excluded third option, it is no surprise that he wants to explain the necessity in the appearance of objects from nothing.

In fact, Hume faced a dilemma: either we accept uniformity and regularity in nature, independent of sense perceptions, or we arrive at a complete illusionism, i.e., a doubt in the objective significance of the world.[31] In the first case, however, he would have to state the sources of our cognition of the real world. Moreover, he categorically rejected the possible sources of such cognition. Berkeley's "spirits" are dismissed. The phenomena of inner experience in general are also fundamentally only perceptions. To adopt this point of view would be an obvious violation of the immanent stance Hume has taken from the very beginning.

There remains, then, the second alternative in the dilemma. However, as we saw, we actually resolve the first problem mentioned, that of the causality starting the thing-perception relationship, in one way alone, namely, by rejecting it. The entire center of gravity must then shift to the second problem, viz., that of the causal connection between things and perceptions that already do exist or will come into existence. Consequently, the immediate task of the philosopher amounts to proving or grounding, without abandoning phenomenalism, that such and such cause must arouse a corresponding effect. Entirely eliminating the first problem, Hume, in the *Essay*, is concerned only with the second. The presentation in the *Treatise* reflects more accurately his actual train of thought. Nevertheless, through a resolution of the second problem he hopes to solve the first. "'Twill, perhaps, be found in the end, that the same answer will serve for both questions."[32]

---

[30] Hume 1968: 78.

[31] Hume could not have even Kant's way out, for it would contradict Hume's fundamental premise that all knowledge is obtained from perception. Hume's categories ("relations") are not a priori with respect to the ideas compared in them.

[32] Hume 1968: 82. It is strange to see such a hope in Hume. How can a *habitual* combination of perception and its causes arise when the respective cause cannot be given in perception? That is, the cause is just not there. However, Hume obviously confuses the problem of causality with that of the uniformity of nature.

Hume's resolution of his doubts is well-known. Having rejected the possibility of a rational grounding of causality, he establishes the fundamental characteristics of the causal connection: succession in time, precedence of the cause, and a constant connection between cause and effect. Since we know nothing about the actual relation between things and can distinguish things in the continuous succession of perceptions only by the temporal order of their appearance, causality turns out ultimately to be a simple temporal sequence. The qualitative difference in our perceptions, when there is a simple change in them, is distinct from the change that we consider causal. The former is obviously only subjective.

This distinction is only a function of the imagination based on associations and habit. "It [experience – TN] never gives us any insight into the internal structure or operating principle of objects, but only accustoms the mind to pass from one to another."[33] The idea of necessity connected with the idea of the causal relation is created only by a subjective compulsion that appears as a result of a habitual transition from one object to another. In this way, Hume, trying to be consistent, explains how the principle of causality is applied in the phenomenal world and how, as it were, this very principle obtains its significance. However, the entire approach of Hume's argument is so distorted that it can lead only to a greater doubt. Experience, from the phenomenalistic point of view, stands itself in need of justification, and as a means of explanation, is inadequate from the very start.

Hume moves helplessly in a circle: real objects are unknowable, and all of our cognition is limited to the sphere of appearances. Consequently, we cannot penetrate into the real relations between things. Causality as a relation, which underlies our cognition of facts, hangs in the air. After doubting one's own reason and understanding, there is only one thing left – to doubt the power of reason in general. Hume surely did this in essence from the very start. How can reason turn out to be powerful once it confronts limitations? "Thus not only our reason fails us in the discovery of the *ultimate connexion* of causes and effects, but even after experience has inform'd us of their *constant conjunction*, 'tis impossible for us to satisfy ourselves by our reason, why we shou'd extend that experience beyond those particular instances, which have fallen under our observation. We suppose, but are never able to prove, that there must be a resemblance betwixt those objects, of which we have had experience, and those which lie beyond the reach of our discovery."[34]

If Hume had wanted to be a skeptic to the end, nothing more would be needed of him. His journey would have been complete. He would never leave the sphere of negation and doubt: a rejection of the ontological cognizability of things, a rejection of the epistemological necessity of the principle of causality, a rejection of scientific inference of the future on the basis of this principle. As we indicated, however, Hume saw his task differently. He stopped with the first rejection and affirmed phenomenalism while rescuing cognition and substantiating, or explaining, its fundamental principle, the principle of causality. When there is, apparently, no way out Hume decides on a heroic remedy: an appeal to the same reason, but this time in the

---

[33] Hume 1968: 169.
[34] Hume 1968: 91–92.

guise of another of its functions. A complaint to reason about reason is accompanied by great sacrifices.

In fact, Hume, denying the rights of reason, ascribes that much greater a role to imagination. Certainly, causality is, in essence, based on rational activity, not on an understanding that is inclined to functional errors and mistakes, but instead on a sounder function of the imagination, as though it were subordinate to natural laws ("a kind of attraction"). The imagination is the principle or the function that rescues causality from doubt. Hume writes, "the imagination, according to my own confession, being the ultimate judge of all systems of philosophy."[35] However, we should keep in mind that the term "imagination" has two meanings in Hume. On the one hand, the imagination stands in contrast to memory, the former being "the faculty, by which we form our fainter ideas."[36] On the other hand, the imagination stands in contrast to reason, the former now being "the same faculty, excluding only our demonstrative and probable reasonings."[37] In line with this, Hume distinguishes in the imagination "the principles which are permanent, irresistible, and universal; such as the customary transition from causes to effects, and from effects to causes: And the principles, which are changeable, weak, and irregular."[38] Therefore, in resting the authority of causality on the imagination and habit Hume seeks not to undermine it, but, on the contrary, to strengthen and fortify that authority. Our procedure of drawing conclusions by invoking causality is, as he says in the *Enquiry*, so important, so "essential to the subsistence of all human creatures, it is not probable, that it could be trusted to the fallacious deductions of our reason, which is slow in its operations; appears not, in any degree, during the first years of infancy; and, at best, is in every age and period of human life extremely liable to error and mistake."[39] This distrust in reason, however, must not be taken as a doubt in the significance of the causal relation. On the one hand, our practical activity indeed opposes such a doubt – and here Hume appeals to the ethicism of academic philosophy – an argument that he shares in a certain respect with some representatives of neo-Kantian idealism and also pragmatism. Therefore, if this truly is a skeptical argument, it is so to no greater a degree than the arguments of some neo-Kantians who passionately speak out against skepticism, the Humean variety in particular. On the one hand, in order to avoid a doubt in the causal relation, Hume simply demands that, since the understanding is too weak, we subordinate it to some other principle "of equal weight and authority; and that principle will preserve its influence as long as human nature remains the same."[40] Thus, our trust in nature in general rests on a trust in human nature. We come to what Riehl characterizes as a biological theory of knowledge, merging Hume with Avenarius.

---

[35] [Hume 1968: 225.]

[36] [Hume 1968: 118f.]

[37] Hume 1968: 118f. Cf. Hume 1895: 160–1f.

[38] Hume 1968: 225.

[39] Hume 2004: 34.

[40] Hume 2004: 25.

For us, however, this "detour" raises a question: Has not Hume, therefore, betrayed his own phenomenalism? Did he not, contrary to his original intention, rescue causality at the cost of his own fundamental point of view? Undoubtedly! And the baseless nature of phenomenalism in general can be shown in this way.[41] Surely if we immediately reject the negation of a position that requires proof, we can naturally return to it in the course of the argument and simply affirm it. Whether this happens implicitly or explicitly depends on the temperament or clarity of the thinker. Hume, being lucid, recognizes this explicitly: "As nature has taught us the use of our limbs, without giving us the knowledge of the muscles and nerves, by which they are actuated; so has she implanted in us an instinct, which carries forward the thought in a corresponding course to that which she has established among external objects."[42] That Hume understands "external objects" here to be not perceptions, but real objects, things in themselves, is obvious from the following conclusion: "Here, then, is a pre-established harmony between the course of nature and the succession of our ideas; and though the powers and forces, by which the former is governed, be wholly unknown to us, yet our thoughts and conceptions have still, we find, gone on in the same train with the other works of nature."[43] Thus, Hume actually eliminates doubts at the expense of phenomenalism. A conciliatory approach is impossible. Hume could not find an excluded third path this way. Just as he dogmatically rejected at the start the world of real things, which determines the order of our perceptions, so he now dogmatically recognizes that world – and with it in the same role – as the foundation of the significance of our cognitions.

However, does it make sense to speak of Hume in general as a skeptic?

At the beginning we posed the questions: what did Hume actually doubt, and how did he resolve his doubt? Now, we can now provide an answer. Hume doubted the cognizability of the real world and resolved his doubt by affirming some knowledge of this world. Could Hume be called a skeptic just because he rejects the cognizability of the world of real things, limiting our cognition to the phenomenal world? Would it not actually be more correct to call such a position "agnosticism" or even "dogmatic negativism"?[44] In any case, Hume is a skeptic, though not to a great extent and in the same sense as is Kant. In Kant's presentation, Hume "deposited his ship on the beach (of skepticism) for safekeeping, where it could then lie and rot...."[45] However, Hume himself depicted his position differently: "Methinks I am like a man," he wrote, "who having struck on many shoals, and having narrowly escap'd ship-wreck in passing a small frith, has yet the temerity to put out to sea in the same leaky weather-beaten vessel, and even carries his ambition so far as to think of compassing the globe under these disadvantageous circumstances."[46] And

---

[41] Benno Erdmann presents a vivid example of the helplessness of phenomenalism to substantiate causal necessity. See his Erdmann 1905.

[42] Hume 2004: 35.

[43] Hume 2004: 34.

[44] Cf. Richter 1908: 316.

[45] [Kant 2002: 58.]

[46] [Hume 1968: 263–64.]

Kant hopes to "safely navigate the ship wherever seems good to him."[47] Certainly, in both cases their optimistic faith was legitimate. In fact, neither left the shallow waters of phenomenalism, always risking to run aground yet again on the shoals.

Someone might object, however, that Hume sometimes called himself a skeptic. In Rehmke's opinion, Hume definitely adopted the viewpoint of Carneades in order to avoid Pyrrhonian skepticism.[48] We can hardly agree with this. Hume called the skepticism of Carneades "mitigated," i.e., a skepticism in which unlimited doubts "are, in some measure, corrected by common sense and reflection."[49] There is, however, another sort of "mitigated" skepticism. This is the, so to speak, epistemological skepticism or negativism peculiar to Kant: "the limitation of our enquiries to such subjects as are best adapted to the narrow capacity of human understanding."[50] However, it is precisely thanks to this – in Rehmke's words, the "silently accepted presupposition of a reality outside us"[51] – that Hume deviated from the direct path that would lead to pure skepticism. It is precisely this that forces us to regard Hume's skepticism with less dogmatism than Kant did and after him those in the history of nineteenth century philosophy.

Hume's philosophy, therefore, simply once again proves that a limitation of the rights of reason does not proceed without impunity. It also shows that it is impossible to transform a theory of knowledge into a theory of ignorance and that the true path of philosophy lies in the development of the infinite creative powers of reason.


# Bibliography to "Skepticism and Dogmatism of Hume"

Emerson, Ralph Waldo. 1996. *Representative men: seven lectures.* Cambridge, MA: Harvard University Press.

Erdmann, Benno. 1905. *Über Inhalt und Geltung des Kausalgesetzes.* Halle a. d. S.: Max Niemeyer.

Hume, David. 1895. *Traktat über die menschliche Natur.* Trans. Th. Lipps. Hamburg: Verlag von Leopold Voss.

Hume, David. 1968. *A Treatise of Human Nature,* ed. L.A. Selby-Bigge. Oxford: Clarendon Press.

Hume, David. 2004. *An Enquiry Concerning Human Understanding.* Mineola: Dover Publications.

Jodl, Friedrich. 1872. *Leben und Philosophie David Humes.* Halle: C. E. M. Pfeffer.

Kant, Immanuel. 2002. *Theoretical Philosophy after 1781.* Trans. Gary Hatfield, et al. Cambridge: Cambridge University Press.

Rehmke, Johannes. 1896. *Grundriss der Geschichte der Philosophie.* Berlin: Verlag von Carl Duncker.

Richter, Raoul. 1908. *Der Skeptizismus in der Philosophie, Zweiter Band.* Leipzig: Verlag der Dürr'schen Buchhandlung.

---

[47] [Kant 2002: 58.]

[48] Rehkme 1896: 178.

[49] Hume 2004: 104.

[50] Hume 2004: 105.

[51] [Rehmke 1896: 178.]

Shpet, Gustav. 1907. Problema prichinnosti u Juma i Kanta: Otvetil li Kant na sochinenija Juma? *Kievskie universitetskie izvestija* 5: 165–203.

Shpet, Gustav. 1911. Skepticizm i dogmatizm Juma. *Voprosy filosofii i psikhologii*, kniga 106: 1–18.

Shpet, Gustav. 1991. *Appearance and Sense: Phenomenology as the Fundamental Science and Its Problems*. Trans. Thomas Nemeth. Dordrecht: Kluwer Academic Publishers.

Shpet, Gustav. 2002. *Istorija kak problema logiki*, ed. V.S. Mjasnikov. Moscow: Pamjatniki istoricheskoj mysli.

Shpet, Gustav. 2006. *Philosophia Natalis. Izbrannye psikhologo-pedagogicheskie trudy*. Moscow: ROSSPEN.

Shpet, Gustav. 2010. *Filosofskaja kritika: otzyvy, recenzii, obzory*. Moscow: ROSSPEN.

Tihanov, Galin. 2008. Multifariousness under Duress: Gustav Shpet's Scattered Lives. *Russian Literature* 63: 259–292.

Vinogradov, N. 1903. David Jum. Issledovanie chelovecheskogo razumenija [An inquiry concerning human understanding]. *Voprosy filosofskii i psikhologii* 69: 733–735.

Windelband, Wilhelm. 1895. *A History of Philosophy*. Trans. James H. Tufts. New York: Macmillan and Co.

# Appendix 5: Shpet [Self-Authored Entry in *Granat Encyclopedic Dictionary*]

## Editor's Introduction to "Shpet" [Self-Authored Entry in *Granat Encyclopedic Dictionary*]

The following short exposition of Shpet's overall philosophical viewpoint was written by Shpet himself and signed at the end of the piece simply with his initials "G. G-n." Although what follows appeared in the Soviet-era *Granat Encyclopedic Dictionary* only in 1932, a draft was presumably completed already in June 1929.[1] The ideas presented hardly need explanation, many, if not most, having been already stated in Shpet's previous writings. For example, that philosophy develops historically in three stages he proclaimed in a number of works including his 1922 *Ocherk razvitija russkoj filosofii* [*Sketch of the Development of Russian Philosophy*]: "I actually am a supporter of philosophy as knowledge, not as morality, not as preaching, and not as a worldview. I believe that philosophy as knowledge is the highest historical and dialectical stage of philosophy."[2] As such, what follows is a testament to his enduring intellectual concerns and his continuing attachment to a "hermeneutic phenomenology" fundamentally rooted in the early and middle Husserl, particularly the central notions of intentionality and the intuition of essences.[3] We find

---

[1] In Mitjushin's 1992 publication of Shpet's draft of the entry, there explicitly appears at the end in italics: "Written 19 June 1929." Shpet 1992: 52. However, a simple comparison to the 1932 text as published shows no mention of when it was written. Shpet 1932: 380. The date of composition, then, is presumably, that given on the actual document Mitjushin had at least temporarily in his possession (see note 3 below).

[2] Shpet 2008: 40.

[3] In his separate commentary accompanying the publication of the 1929 draft of Shpet's encyclopedia entry, Mitjushin explicitly contests Shpet's "alleged Husserlianism," finding such a characterization to be an "absurd delusion based on a superficial acquaintance with just one of his [Shpet's] books, the 1914 *Appearance and Sense*." Apparently to support his claim Mitjushin wrote that he had before him a copy of the "original text" in contrast to the published "editorial variant" that we find in the encyclopedia. He provided no evidence: (1) that the "original" is no more than a mere draft that Shpet himself reworked; (2) that Shpet had no hand in revising the

© Springer Nature Switzerland AG 2019
G. Shpet, T. Nemeth, *Hermeneutics and Its Problems*, Contributions
To Phenomenology 98, https://doi.org/10.1007/978-3-319-98941-9

Shpet, even in this highly abbreviated summary of his views, referring to the "reduction" as a method in the critique of consciousness, which serves as an additional testament to his continuing allegiance to a "Husserlianism," albeit one suitably modified to conform to his own understanding and concerns.

## Shpet [Self-Authored Entry in *Granat Encyclopedic Dictionary*]

### Gustav Shpet

In its inner dialectical development, philosophy passes through three stages: from wisdom through metaphysics to rigorous science. As the "fundamental science," it forms the foundation of the specific sciences. Philosophy "as rigorous knowledge" differs from "scientific philosophy," which rests on the conclusions of the particular sciences and which creates such particular directions as physicalism, naturalism, psychologism, etc. In contrast to Kant and post-Kantian philosophy, which formulated the problem of cognition in terms of a dilemma (cognition either reflects nature or prescribes laws to it), Shpet envisages a "third possibility." The post-Kantian path eventually found its culmination in Hegel's philosophy, which, however, ascribed reality to an "identical" moment that it discovered and in this way departed into metaphysics. In S[hpet]'s opinion, Husserl pointed to the correct solution to the problem through his introduction of the concept of "ideation" (*Wesenserschauung*). Accepting Brentano's concept of intentionality (the directedness of consciousness) and Husserl's thesis of the objectivity of cognition, Shpet tries to avoid here the hidden dangers of naturalism, metaphysics and transcendentalism.

---

allegedly "original text" to yield the final published text; (3) that Shpet did not fully endorse the published version as a statement of his views, and (4) why an unnamed editor would alter Shpet's original draft to make it arguably more, not less, idealistic in tone than the original. The principal difference between the two texts is that in the "original" Shpet wrote that he saw "the danger of naturalism in Husserl's assertion of an originary givenness in presentativism and a danger of transcendentalism in the assertion of a 'pure I' as the unity of consciousness." Mitjushin 1992: 54. Neither divergence from Husserl would be a "shock" to anyone familiar with Shpet's work in the 1910s, and to think that Shpet's non-egological conception of consciousness makes him a non-Husserlian would mean that the Husserl of the *Investigations* was non-Husserlian too. As to his continued commitment to the central role of the Husserlian conception of intentionality and in response to any possible charge of metaphysical "idealism" as a result, Shpet wrote to Semyon I. Kanatchikov, the editor of the journal *Literaturnaja gazeta*, on 20 January 1930: "Just as any physical action, even the simplest and most familiar, consists of a succession of moments that are distinguishable in analysis, so we can also distinguish such succession in acts of the imagination. An investigation of the latter and their regularity is necessarily dependent on the object to which the acts refer (to which they are 'directed'). This was actually one of the tasks that I posed for myself in my works. But I do not see subjective idealism or idealistic mysticism in this. ... The assertion that these acts and their regularity are entirely dependent on the subject alone is simply foreign to me." Shpet 2012: 233–234. For a discussion of eidetic intuition, see Shpet 2002: 1021.

If, with the help of reflection and the method of reduction, we can, actually, come to a philosophical analysis and critique of consciousness, taking immediate experience as our starting point, then we must take this experience in its full, concrete scope, i.e., as a socio-cultural experience, and not in the abstract form of the perception of a "physical thing." If it is correct that "I have a consciousness," it by no means follows that consciousness can belong only to an [individual] "I." Forms of a collective consciousness can also exist. A word-concept, originarily given not in the perception of a physical thing, but in the assimilation of a sign of social communication, serves as an element of the forms of a socio-cultural (collective) consciousness. A vital conception, for which a word serves as the material bearer, is captured by us not just as a concept, but also as a concrete unity of a flowing sense. The "seeing" of a sense is understanding, which is just as immediate as sense perception. This formulation is the central problem of Shpet's philosophy.

Shpet defines the inner logical forms of a word as the rules for the formation of concepts, but they serve as algorithms, not as formulas. They not only formulate the flowing sense, but also reveal the possibility of a special dialectical interpretation of reality, expressed in words. This interpretation, revealing all the possibilities in the movement of sense, leads philosophy to a philosophy of culture, as a movement of realized possibilities. Concrete reality is found in its realization, which presupposes a foundation (ratio) by virtue of which the given, and not another possibility, is realized. Each socio-cultural fact, as a sign, such as a word, is subject to a dialectical interpretation. However, at the same time, just like a word, such a fact turns out to be the expression of subjects, both personal and collective (nation, class, epoch, etc.), that objectivize themselves in it. In its expressiveness, the social sign can be the object of a psychological analysis and study (social and ethnic psychology), insofar as the psychological is taken here as the reaction of a subject, existing in its environment and milieu, to this milieu, and through it to the surrounding phenomena of nature and history. Inner poetic forms, as relations between a logically formed meaning and its cultural substrates, transfer the object of perception into a "detached" sphere, which forms the field of aesthetic analysis. Expressive forms are the expression of a personal and collective subject.

## Bibliography to "Shpet" [Entry in *Granat Encyclopedic Dictionary*]

Mitjushin, A. A. 1992. O tom, kak «delaetsja» istorija Russkoj filosofii. *Nachala*, #1: 53–54.

[Shpet], G. G-n. Shpet. 1932. *Granat: enciklopedicheskij slovar'*. Moscow and Leningrad: Granat. 50: 378–80.

Shpet, G. G. 1992. Shpet. *Nachala*, #1: 48–52.

Shpet, G. G. 2002. *Istorija kak problema logiki*, ed. V. S. Mjasnikov. Moscow: Pamjatniki istoricheskoj mysli.

Shpet, G. G. 2008. *Ocherk razvitija russkoj filosofii. I.*, ed. T.G. Shchedrina. Moscow: ROSSPEN.

Shpet, G. G. 2012. *Filosof v kul'ture. Dokumenty i pis'ma*, ed. T.G. Shchedrina. Moscow: ROSSPEN.

# Bibliography

Aquinas, Thomas. 1911–1925. *Summa theologiae*. New York: Benziger Brothers.

Aristotle. 1941. In *The Basic Works of Aristotle*, ed. Richard McKeon. New York: Random House.

———. 1984. In The complete works of Aristotle, ed. Jonathan Barnes. Princeton: Princeton University Press.

Ast, D. Friedrich. 1808. *Grundlinien der Grammatik, Hermeneutik und Kritik*. Landshut: Jos. Thomann.

Augustine, Aurelius. 1873. *On Christian Doctrine*. Edinburgh: T. & T. Clark.

———. 1938. *Concerning the Teacher and On the Immortality of the Soul*. New York: Appleton-Century Crofts.

Augustine, St. 2002. *On Genesis*, ed. John E. Rotelle. Hyde Park: New City Press.

———. 2003. *Concerning the City of God against the Pagans*. Trans. Henry Bettenson. London: Penguin Books.

———. 2006. *Confessions*. Trans. F.J. Sheed. Indianapolis: Hackett Publishing.

Baur, Ferdinand Christian. 1824–5. *Symbolik und Mythologie oder die Naturreligion des Alterthums*. Stuttgart: J. B. Metzler.

Berkeley, George. 2012. *Philosophical Writings*, ed. Desmond M. Clarke. Cambridge: Cambridge University Press.

Berngejm, Ernst. 1908. *Vvedenie v istoricheskuju nauku*, Trans. S. Sabinov. Moscow: M. N. Prokopovich.

Bernheim, Ernst. 1905. *Einleitung in die Geschichtswissenschaft*. Leipzig: G.J. Göschen.

———. 1908. *Lehrbuch der historischen Methode und der Geschichtsphilosophie*. Leipzig: Duncker & Humblot.

Birt, Theodor. 1913. *Kritik und Hermeneutik: nebst Abriss des antiken Buchwesens*. Munich: Beck.

Blass, Friedrich. 1892. *Hermeneutik und Kritik*. In Müller 1892: 147–295.

Boeckh, August. 1877. *Encyklopädie und Methodologie der philologischen Wissenschaften*, ed. Ernst Bratuscheck. Leipzig: Teubner.

Bühler, Karl. 1907. Tatsachen und Probleme zu einer Psychologie der Denkvorgänge. I. Über Gedanken. *Archiv für die gesamte Psychologie*, *Band IX*, Nr. 4: 297–365.

Campbell, George. 2008. *The Philosophy of Rhetoric*, ed. Lloyd F. Bitzer. Carbondale: Southern Illinois University Press.

Casilo, Antonio. 1629. *Introductio in Aristotelis logicum et reliquas disciplinas*. Rome: Corbelletti.

Couturat, Louis. 1901. *La logique de Leibniz*. Paris: Felix Alcan.

Dalgarno, George. 2001. *On Universal Language*, ed. David Cram and Jaap Maat. Oxford: Oxford University Press.

© Springer Nature Switzerland AG 2019

G. Shpet, T. Nemeth, *Hermeneutics and Its Problems*, Contributions
To Phenomenology 98, https://doi.org/10.1007/978-3-319-98941-9

Dante, Alighieri. 1889. *The Banquet (Il Convito)*. Trans. Katharine Hillard. London: Kegan Paul, Trench & Co.

———. 1920. *The Letters of Dante*, Trans. Paget Toynbee. Oxford: Clarendon Press.

de Condillac, Etienne Bonnet. 2012. *Essay on the Origin of Human Knowledge*, ed. Hans Aarsleff. Cambridge: Cambridge University Press.

Dilthey, Wilhelm. 1894. *Ideen über eine beschreibende und zergliedernde Psychologie*. Berlin: Verlag der Königlichen Akademie der Wissenschaften.

———. 1914a. *Das natürliche System der Geisteswissenschaften im 17. Jahrhunderte*. In *Gesammelte Schriften. II Band: Weltanschauungen und Analyse des Menschen seit Renaissance und Reformation,* 90–245. Leipzig und Berlin: B. G. Teubner.

———. 1914b. *Gesammelte Schriften. II Band: Weltanschauungen und Analyse des Menschen seit Renaissance und Reformation*. Leipzig und Berlin: B. G. Teubner.

———. 1921. *Gesammelte Schriften. II Band: Weltanschauungen und Analyse des Menschen seit Renaissance und Reformation*, Zweite Auflage. Leipzig und Berlin: B. G. Teubner.

———. 1989. In *Introduction to the Human Sciences*, ed. Rudolf A. Makkreel and Frithjof Rodi. Princeton: Princeton University Press.

———. 1996. The rise of hermeneutics. In *Hermeneutics and the study of history*, (trans. Frederic. R. Jameson and Rudolf A. Makkreel). 235–253. Princeton: Princeton University Press.

———. 2010. *Selected Works*, Volume III: *The Formation of the Historical World in the Human Sciences*, ed. Rudolf A. Makkreel and Frithjof Rodi. Princeton: Princeton University Press.

Dionysius the Great, St. 1999. Extant Fragments. In *Ante-Nicene Fathers: The Writings of the Fathers Down to A.D. 325*, ed. Alexander Roberts. Peabody: Hendrickson Publishers.

Doedes, Jacobus Isaak. 1867. *Manual of Hermeneutics for the Writings of the New Testament*, Trans. G.W. Stegmann. Edinburgh: T. & T. Clark.

Droysen, Johann Gustav. 1897. *Outline of the Principles of History*. Trans. E. Benjamin Andrews. Boston: Ginn & Company.

Droysen, Joh[ann]. Gust[av]. 1868. *Grundriss der Historik*. Leipzig: Verlag von Veit & Comp.

Durkheim, Émile. 1964. *The Rules of Sociological Method*. New York: The Free Press.

Elsenhans, Th[eodor]. 1904. *Die Aufgabe einer Psychologie der Deutung als Vorarbeit für die Geisteswissenschaften*. Giessen: A. Töpelmann.

Elsenhans, Theodor. 1906. *Fries und Kant. Ein Beitrag zur Geschichte und zur systematischen Grundlegung der Erkenntnistheorie. II. Kritisch-Systematischer Teil*. Giessen: A. Töpelmann.

———. 1912. *Lehrbuch der Psychologie*. Tübingen: J. C. B. Mohr.

Erdmann, Benno. 1912a. *Erkennen und Verstehen*. Berlin: Sitzungsberichte der Preussischen Akademie der Wissenschaften.

Erdmann, B[enno]. 1912b. *Gedächtnisrede auf Wilhelm Dilthey. Aus den Abhandlungen der Königlich Preussischen Akademie der Wissenschaften vom Jahre 1912*. Berlin: Akademie der Wissenschaften.

Ernesti, Io[annis] Augusto. 1776. *Initia doctrinae solidioris*. Leipzig: Caspari Fritsch.

Ernesti, Ioannis Augusto. 1785. *Metaphysica et logica*. Madrid: Typographia Regia.

———. 1792. *Institutio Interpretis Novi Testamenti*. Leipzig: Weidmann.

Feder, Johann Georg Heinrich. 1794. *Grundsätze der Logik und Metaphysik*. Göttingen: Johann Christian Dieterich.

Finnbogason, Gudmunder. *1911. Den sympatiske Forstaaelse*. Copenhagen: Gyldendalske boghandel.

Flacius, Matthius. 1617. *Clavis scripturae S. seu de sermone sacrarum literarum*. Basiliae [Basil]: Sebastium Henricpetri.

———. 1624. *Historiae ecclesiasticae*. Vol. 2. Basil: Ludovici Regis.

Frantze, Wolfgang. 1619. *Tractatus theologicus novus et perspicuus de interpretatione sacrarum scripturarum maxime legitima*. Wittenberg: Matthaeus Seelfisch.

Frege, Gottlob. 1980. Sense and Reference. In *Translations from the Philosophical Writings of Gottlob Frege*, ed. Peter Geach and Max Black, 56–78. Oxford: Blackwell.

Glasius, Salomo. 1623. *Philologiae sacrae, qua totius sacrosanctae veteri et novi testamenti scripturae, tum stylus et literatura, tum sensus et genuinae interpretationis ratio expenditur*. Jena: Steinmann.

Gomperz, Heinrich. 1908. *Weltanschauungslehre, Zweiter Band: Noologie*, 1. Hälfte (Semasiologie). Jena: Diederichs.

———. 1912. *Sophistik und Rhetorik*. Leipzig and Berlin: B. G. Teubner.

Grimm, Eduard. 1890. *Zur Geschichte des Erkenntnisproblems. Von Bacon zu Hume*. Leipzig: Wilhelm Friedrich.

Haardt, Alexander. 2009. Shpet's Aesthetic Fragments and Sartre's Literary Theory. *Tihanov* 2009: 169–178.

Harris, James. 1751. *Hermes: or, A Philosophical Inquiry Concerning Language and Universal Grammar*. London: H. Woodfall.

Heereboort, Adriano. 1680. *Hermeneia Logica seu synopseos logicae burgersdician*. Cambridge: Joan. Hayes.

Hegel, Georg Wilhelm Friedrich. 1977. *Phenomenology of Spirit*. Trans. A.V. Miller. Oxford: Oxford University Press.

Hermann, Conrad. 1875. *Die Sprachwissenschaft nach ihrem Zusammenhänge mit Logik, menschlicher Geistesbildung und Philosophie*. Leipzig: Treubner.

Hobbes, Thomas. 1996. *Leviathan*, ed. Richard Tuck. Cambridge: Cambridge University Press.

Hume, David. 2003. *A Treatise of Human Nature*. Mineola: Dover.

Husserl, Edmund. 1970. *Logical Investigations*, Trans. J.N. Findlay. New York: Humanities Press.

Immisch, Otto. 1909. *Wie studiert man die klassische Philologie?* Stuttgart: Verlag von Wilhelm Violet.

Kareev, Nikolaj. 1913. *Teorija istoricheskago znanija*. St. Petersburg: Stasjulevich.

Knight, William. 1900. *Lord Monboddo and Some of His Contemporaries*. London: John Murray.

Koffka, Kurt. 1912. *Zur Analyse der Vorstellungen und ihrer Gesetze*. Leipzig: Quelle & Meyer.

Kornilov, Konstantin N. 1916. Konflikt dvukh eksperimental'no-psikhologicheskikh shkol. In *Stat'i po filosofii i psikhologii. Georgiju Ivanovichu Chelpanovu ot uchastnikov ego seminariev v Kieve i Moskve*, 314–328. Moscow: Momantov.

Langlois, Charles-Victor, and Charles Seignobos. 1898. *Introduction aux études historiques*. Paris: Hachette & Cie.

Langlua, Sharl-Viktor, and Sharl Sen'obos. 1899. *Vvedenie v izuchenie istorii*. Trans. A. Serebrjakov. St. Petersburg: Popov.

Lappo-Danilevskij, A.S. 2006. *Metodologija istorii*. Moscow: Izd. dom "Territorija budushchego".

Leibnitz, M. de. 1765. *Oeuvres philosophiques latines et françoises*, ed. Rud. Eric Raspe. Amsterdam: Jean Schreuder.

Leibniz, G[ottfried] W[ilhelm]. 1996. *New Essays On Human Understanding, translated and edited by Peter Remnant and Jonathan Bennett*. Cambridge: Cambridge University Press.

Locke, John. 1997. In *An essay concerning human understanding*, ed. Roger Woolhouse. London: Penguin Group

Lotze, Hermann. 1880. *Logik*. Leipzig: S. Hirzel.

Lullii, Raymundi. 1651. *Opera ea quae ad adinventam ab ipso artem universalem*. Argentorati [Strassburg]: Lazarum Zetznerum.

Maier, Heinrich. 1896. *Die Syllogistik des Aristoteles. Teil 1: Die logische Theorie des Urteils bei Aristoteles*. Tübingen: Laupp u.a.

Marbe, K[arl]. 1901. *Experimentell-psychologische Untersuchungen über das Urteil*. Leipzig: Wilhelm Engelmann.

Martinak, Eduard. 1901. *Psychologische Untersuchungen zur Bedeutungslehre*. Leipzig: J.A. Barth.

Marty, Anton. 1908. *Untersuchungen zur Grundlegung der allgemeinen Grammatik und Sprachphilosophie*. Vol. 1. Halle: Niemeyer.

Meier, Georg Friedrich. 1755. *Metaphysik*. Erster Teil. Halle: Johann Justinus Gebauer.

———. 1757. *Versuch einer allgemeinen Auslegungskunst*. Halle: Carl Hermann Hemmerde.

———. 1762. *Vernunftlehre*. Halle: Johann Justinus Gebauer.

Meinong, Alexius. 1877. *Hume-Studien. I. Zur Geschichte und Kritik des modernen Nominalismus.* Vienna: Gerold.

Meinong, A[lexius]. 1902. *Ueber Annahmen.* Leipzig: Johann Ambrosius Barth.

———. 1910. *Ueber Annahmen.* Leipzig: Johann Ambrosius Barth.

Meinong, Alexius. 1914. *Gesammelte Abhandlungen.* Vol. 1. Leipzig: Barth.

Meister, Aloys. 1913. *Grundzüge der historischen Methode.* Leipzig: Teubner.

Melanchthon, Philipp. 1900. *Die Loci communes Philipp Melanchthons in ihrer Urgestalt.* Leipzig: Deichert.

———. 2007. *The Loci communes of Philipp Melanchthon.* Eugene: Wipf and Stock.

Messer, August Wilhelm. 1906. Experimentell-psychologische Untersuchungen über das Denken. *Archiv für die gesamte Psychologie*, Bd. VIII, Nr. 1–2: 1–224.

———. 1908. *Empfindung und Denken.* Leipzig: Quelle & Meyer.

———. 1911. Husserls Phänomenologie in ihrem Verhältnis zur Psychologie. *Archiv für die gesamte Psychologie*, Bd. XXII, Nr. 2–3: 117–129.

Michelis, Friedrich. 1886. *Aristotelis Περι ἑρμηνειας librum pro restituendo totius philosophiae fundamento interpretatus est ....* Heidelberg.

Monboddo, Lord James Burnet. 1773–1792. *Of the Origin and Progress of Language.* Edinburgh: Bell & Bradfute.

Origen. 1895. *De Principiis.* In *The Writings of Origen*, ed. Rev. Alexander Roberts and James Donaldson, 1–356. Edinburgh: T. & T. Clark.

Paul, Hermann. 1909. *Prinzipien der Sprachgeschichte.* Halle: Niemeyer.

Plato. 1969. *Collected Dialogues of Plato.* Princeton: Princeton University Press.

Popov, I.V. 1917. *Lichnost' i uchenie blazhennogo Avgustina, chast' II.* Sergiev Posad: Tip. Svjato-Troickoj.

Reid, Thomas. 1872. *The Works of Thomas Reid, D. D.* Edinburgh: Maclachlan and Stewart.

Scharfii, Johannis. 1694. *Manuale logicum.* Lipsiae [Leipzig]: Hübner.

Schleiermacher, Friedrich. 1835. Über den Begriff der Hermeneutik mit Bezug auf F. A. Wolfs Andeutungen und Asts Lehrbuch. In *Sämmtliche Werke, Band 3, Abteilung 3.* 344–386. Berlin: Reimer.

———. 1838. Hermeneutik und Kritik. In *Sämmtliche Werke, Band 7, Abteilung 1.* 5–389. Berlin: Reimer.

———. 1839. Dialectik. In *Sämmtliche Werke, Band 4, Abteilung 3, Teil 2.* Berlin: Reimer.

———. 1998. *Hermeneutics and Criticism And Other Writings.* Trans. Andrew Bowie. Cambridge: Cambridge University Press.

Seignobos, Ch. 1901. *La méthode historique appliquée aux sciences sociales.* Paris: Alcan.

Selz, Otto. 1913. *Über die Gesetze des geordneten Denkverlaufs.* Stuttgart: W. Spemann.

Semler, Christian August. 1822. *Versuch über die combinatorische Methode.* 2nd ed. Dresden: Walther.

Sen'obos Sharl. 1902. *Istoricheskij metod v primenenii k social'nym naukam*, Trans. P. Kogan. Moscow: A. I. Mamontov.

Shpet, Gustav. 1916. *Istorija kak problema logiki.* Moscow: A. I. Mamontov.

Shpet, Gustav. 1917–1918. Predmet i zadachi etnicheskoj psikhologii. *Psikhologicheskoe obozrenie* 1(1): 27–59; vol. 1, no. 2: 233–263.

Shpet, Gustav. 1991. *Appearance and Sense. Phenomenology as the Fundamental Science and Its Problems.* Trans. Thomas Nemeth. Dordrecht: Kluwer Academic Publishers.

———. 2002. *Istorija kak problema logiki. Kriticheskie i metodologicheskie issledovanija.* Moscow: Pamjatniki istoricheskoj mysli.

———. 2005. *Germenevtika i ee problemy.* In *Mysl' i Slovo. Izbrannye trudy*, 248–415. Moscow: ROSSPEN.

———. 2006. Mudrost' ili razum? In *Philosophia Natalis. Izbrannye psikhologo-pedagogicheskie trudy*, 311–365. Moscow: ROSSPEN.

Sigwart, Christoph. 1873. *Logik, Band 1.* Tübingen: Laupp.

———. 1878. *Logik, Band 2.* Tübingen: Laupp.

Simmel, Georg. 1892. *Die Probleme der Geschichtsphilosophie*. Leipzig: Duncker & Humblot.

———. 1907. *Die Probleme der Geschichtsphilosophie*. Leipzig: Duncker & Humblot.

———. 1908. *Soziologie. Untersuchungen über die Formen der Vergesellschaftung*. Leipzig: Duncker & Humblot.

Spektorskij, E. 1910. *Problema social'noj fiziki v XVII stoletii*, tom 1. Warsaw: Tip. Varshavskago Uchnago Okruga.

Špet, Gustav G. 1993. *Die Hermeneutik und ihre Probleme*, hrsg. Alexander Haardt und Roland Daube-Schackat. Aus dem Russ. übers. Erika Freiberger und Alexander Haardt. Freiburg/München: Alber.

Spranger, Eduard. 1905. *Die Grundlagen der Geschichtswissenschaft. Eine erkenntnistheoretisch-psychologische Untersuchung*. Berlin: Reuther & Reichard.

Spranger, E[duard]. 1912. *Wilhelm Dilthey. Eine Gedächtnissrede*. Berlin: W. Borngräber.

Steinthal, H[eymann]. 1855. *Grammatik, Logik und Psychologie. Ihre Principien und ihr Verhältniss zu Einander*. Dümmler: Berlin.

Steinthal, Heymann. 1863. *Geschichte der Sprachwissenschaft bei den Griechen und Römern, mit besonderer Rücksicht auf die Logik*. Berlin: Dümmler.

Steinthal, H[eymann]. 1864. *Philologie, Geschichte und Psychologie in ihren gegenseitigen Beziehungen*. Berlin: Dümmler.

Steinthal, Heymann. 1878a. Die Arten und Formen der Interpretation. In *Verhandlungen der 32. Versammlung deutscher Philologen und Schulmänner in Wiesbaden*, 25–35. Leipzig: Teubner.

———. 1878b. Aug. Böckh, Encyklopädie und Methodologie der philologischen Wissenschaften [review article]. *Zeitschrift für Völkerpsychologie und Sprachwissenschaft* X: 235–255.

———. 1880a. Darstellung und Kritik der Böckhschen Enzyklopädie und Methodologie der Philologie. Erster Artikel. *Zeitschrift für Völkerpsychologie und Sprachwissenschaft* XI: 80–96.

———. 1880b. Darstellung und Kritik der Böckhschen Enzyklopädie und Methodologie der Philologie. Zweiter Artikel. *Zeitschrift für Völkerpsychologie und Sprachwissenschaft* XI: 302–326.

Stöhr, Adolf. 1889. *Umriss einer Theorie der Namen*. Leipzig: F. Deuticke.

———. 1910. *Lehrbuch der Logik in psychologisierender Darstellung*. Leipzig: F. Deuticke.

Swoboda, Hermann. 1903. Verstehen und Begreifen: Eine psychologische Untersuchung. *Vierteljahrsschrift fur wissenschaftliche Philosophie und Soziologie*, 1903. Jahr 23, Heft 2: 131–188; 3: 241–295.

Szlagowski, Antoni. 1908. *Wstep ogólny historyczno-krytyczny do Pisma Swiętego*. Warsaw/Cracow: Nakład Księgarni Gebethnera i Wolffa.

Taylor, Clifton O. 1905. Über das Verstehen von Worten und Sätzen. *Zeitschrift für Psychologie und Physiologie der Sinnesorgane, Band 38*, Nr. 4: 225–251.

Theophilos [pseudo.]. 1870. *Luthers Philosophie*, vol. 1 *Logik*. Hannover: Carl Meyer.

Tihanov, Galin, ed. 2009. *Gustav Shpet's Contribution to Philosophy and Cultural Theory*. West Lafayette: Purdue University Press.

Usener, Hermann. 1882. *Philologie und Geschichtswissenschaft*. Bonn: Max Cohen & Sohn.

von Müller, Iwan, ed. 1892. *Handbuch der klassischen Altertums Wissenschaft in systematischer Darstellung*. Vol. 1. Munich: Beck.

von Prantl, Carl. 1855. *Geschichte der Logik im Abendlande, Band I*. Leipzig: S. Hirzel.

———. 1875. Reformgedanken zur Logik. *Sitzungsberichten der philosophisch-philologischen und historischen Classe der k. b. Akademie der Wissenschaften, Band I, Heft 1*: 159–214.

———. 1877. *Verstehen und Beurtheilen*. Munich: K. B. Akademie.

von Urlichs, Ludwig. 1892. *Grundlegung und Geschichte der klassischen Altertumswissenschaft*. In Müller 1892: 1–126.

von Wolff, Christian. 1751. *Vernünfftige Gedancken von Gott, der Welt und der Seele des Menschen*. Halle im Magdeburgischen: Rengerische Buchhandlung.

Waddington, Charles. 1855. *Ramus: sa vie, ses écrits et ses opinions*. Paris: Meyrueis.

Weissenborn, Georg. 1847. *Darstellung und Kritik der Schleiermacherschen Dialektik*. Leipzig: Weigel.

Wilkins, John. 2002. *An Essay towards a Real Character and a Philosophical Language*. London: Bloomsbury Academic.

Wolfio, Christiano. 1732. *Psychologia empirica methodo scientifica pertractata*. Frankfurt: Libraria Rengeriana.

———. 1736. *Philosophia prima, sive Ontologia*. Frankfurt: Libraria Rengeriana.

———. 1740. *Philosophia rationalis sive Logica*. Frankfurt: Libraria Rengeriana.

Wundt, Wilhelm. 1908. *Logik eine Untersuchung der prinzipien der Erkenntnis und der Methoden wissenschaftlicher Forschung. Band III: Logik der Geisteswissenschaften*. Stuttgart: Ferdinand Enke.

CPSIA information can be obtained
at www.ICGtesting.com
Printed in the USA
LVHW082310170219
607842LV00005B/60/P